Making Ireland Irish

Irish Studies
James MacKillop, *Series Editor*

Selected titles from Irish Studies

Anglo-Irish Autobiography: Class, Gender, and the Forms of Narrative
Elizabeth Grubgeld

The Gonne-Yeats Letters, 1893–1938
Anna MacBride White *and* A. Norman Jeffares, *eds.*

An Irish Literature Reader: Poetry, Prose, Drama. 2d Edition
Maureen O'Rourke Murphy *and* James MacKillop

Irish Orientalism: A Literary and Intellectual History
Joseph Lennon

Irish Women Writers Speak Out: Voices from the Field
Caitriona Moloney *and* Helen Thompson, *eds.*

John Redmond and Irish Unity, 1912–1918
Joseph P. Finnan

Joyce and Reality: The Empirical Strikes Back
John Gordon

Prodigal Father: The Life of John Butler Yeats (1839–1922)
William M. Murphy

Two Irelands: Literary Feminisms North and South
Rebecca Pelan

Twentieth-Century Irish Drama: Mirror up to Nation
Christopher Murray

Making Ireland IRISH

Tourism and National Identity since the Irish Civil War

Eric G. E. Zuelow

Syracuse University Press

Copyright © 2009 by Syracuse University Press
Syracuse, New York 13244-5290

All Rights Reserved

First Edition 2009

09 10 11 12 13 14   6 5 4 3 2 1

The following previously published material by the author was modified for this work, and its use herein is gratefully acknowledged: (1) "Enshrining Ireland's Nationalist History Inside Prison Walls: The Restoration of Kilmainham Jail," *Éire-Ireland* 39 (Fall–Winter 2004): 180–201. Copyright © 2004: Rish American Cultural Institute, 1 Lackawanna Place, Morristown, N.J. 07960; (2) "'Ingredients for Cooperation': The Role of Irish Tourism in North-South Relations, 1924–1998," *New Hibernia Review* 10, no. 1 (Spring 2006), 17–39.

∞ The paper used in this publication meets the minimum requirements of the American National Standard for Information Sciences—Permanence of Paper for Printed Library Materials, ANSI Z39.48–1992.

For a listing of books published and distributed by Syracuse University Press,
visit https://press.syr.edu.

ISBN-13: 978-0-8156-3225-2   ISBN-10: 0-8156-3225-8

Library of Congress Cataloging-in-Publication Data

Zuelow, Eric.
Making Ireland Irish : tourism and national identity since the Irish Civil War / Eric G. E. Zuelow. — 1st ed.
p. cm. — (Irish studies)
Includes bibliographical references and index.
ISBN-13: 978-0-8156-3225-2 (hardcover : alk. paper)
ISBN-10: 0-8156-3225-8 (hardcover : alk. paper)
1. Tourism—Social aspects—Ireland—History—20th century. 2. Tourism—Social aspects—Ireland—History—21st century. 3. National characteristics, Irish. 4. Nationalism—Ireland—History—20th century. 5. Nationalism—Ireland—History—21st century. 6. Ireland—History—Civil War, 1922–1923—Influence. 7. Ireland—Cultural policy. 8. Ireland—Intellectual life. 9. Ireland—Politics and government—1922– I. Title.
G155.I7Z84 2008
338.4'79417—dc22
2008043217

Manufactured in the United States of America

For my parents,
Helen and Richard

Eric G. E. Zuelow is assistant professor of European history at the University of New England. He has presented his research internationally and has published a number of articles and book chapters on both Scottish and Irish history. Zuelow is coeditor of *Nationalism in a Global Era: The Persistence of Nations* (2007). He is the editor/creator of The Nationalism Project (<http://nationalismproject.org>), a leading Web site devoted to the study of ethnicity and nationalism in global perspective.

Contents

ILLUSTRATIONS | *ix*
ACKNOWLEDGMENTS | *xi*
INTRODUCTION | *xv*

1. Introducing a National Interest, 1922–1939 | *1*
2. Developing Irish Tourism, 1939–1958 | *34*
3. Change and Continuity, 1958–1994 | *72*
4. Culture, Language, and Tourism | *101*
5. Tourism and the Past | *136*
6. Creating the Tourist Landscape | *178*
7. Tourism and the Tiger, 1994–2007 | *217*

NOTES | *245*
BIBLIOGRAPHY | *299*
INDEX | *333*

Illustrations

1. Killarney boatmen | *19*
2. Suggested ITA Signpost, *Dublin Opinion* cartoon, Sept. 1943 | *51*
3. Turf harvesting, County Donegal | *117*
4. Puck Fair, County Kerry | *121*
5. An Tóstal poster | *127*
6. The Planet | *171*
7. Guinness Hopstore | *172*
8. Guinness Storehouse | *174*
9. Gap of Dunloe, 1972 | *211*
10. Gap of Dunloe, 1996 | *211*

Acknowledgments

Just as Irish tourism and national identity grew from ongoing dialogue and discussion, so too did this book. The project started as a Ph.D. dissertation at the University of Wisconsin-Madison, and I benefited greatly from conversations with University of Wisconsin-Madison faculty and fellow graduate students. A number of faculty members were especially helpful in focusing my ideas. George L. Mosse, Rudy Koshar, Frank Solomon, Johann Sommerville, David McDonald, Stan Schultz, and Thongchai Winichakul were each influential in the framing of this project. I benefited greatly from countless discussions with Robert J. Kaiser both during and after an immensely valuable semester spent doing independent reading under his guidance; he has done much to help define my ideas about place, space, and national identity. My graduate advisor, James S. Donnelly Jr., deserves special recognition. His patience, advice, encouragement, and exceptional editing skill dramatically improved the quality of my work. His influence on my approach to history has been profound.

While I conducted my research for this project, Irene Furlong, Mike Cronin, Eunan O'Halpin, Michael Kennedy, Ruth McManus, Robert McNamara, Spurgeon Thompson, and Anne Dolan all offered advice at various points about documents to consult, possible interview subjects, and questions to consider. I am deeply indebted to Irene Furlong and her husband, Frank, for their hospitality during my initial week in Dublin; without them I might never have found a place to live, let alone commenced research. I also owe thanks to Franz and Peggy Geiselbrechtinger for their friendship and hospitality during my time in Ireland.

Rudy Koshar, Roy Foster, Shelley Baranowski, and Jim Rogers all read an early draft of this book and provided me with invaluable feedback. The anonymous peer reviewers for Syracuse University Press also provided me with useful suggestions that helped further improve the manuscript. While I am responsible for any and all errors, their suggestions made this a much better volume than it otherwise would have been.

The staffs of the National Library of Ireland, Irish National Archives, Public Records Office of Northern Ireland, National Photographic Archives of Ireland, and the University of Wisconsin Libraries were all exceptionally accommodating during my research. All documents from the National Archives of Ireland are published with the permission of the Director of the National Archives of Ireland and I would like to extend my deepest thanks for this assistance. Clive Brooks and Derek Cullen of the Bord Fáilte Photographic Archives were more helpful than they can imagine. Clare Hackett of the Guinness Ireland Archives was especially helpful in locating and scanning photographic images. Eugene Finn and Sunniva O'Flynn made my research at the National Film Center of Ireland a real pleasure. Brian McGee of the Cork Archives Institute was most helpful despite the extraordinary workload that he shouldered as the only archivist managing a massive and invaluable collection. Niamh O'Sullivan of the Kilmainham Jail Archives saved me significant time by providing me with copies of all the relevant documents available in her collection. I also received considerable assistance from the staff of Dúchas—The Heritage Service and especially from Joan Murphy, who both answered my questions and provided me access to closed files regarding the state purchase of Poulnabrone. Kevin O'Doherty, Michael Gorman, and Jan de Fouw were generous with their time and extraordinary recollections of their lives at Bord Fáilte. I would also like to thank both *Éire-Ireland* and *New Hibernia Review* for allowing me to republish material covering the restoration of Kilmainham Jail and North/South tourism relations respectively.

I have had useful conversations with many people over the course of my research, but the friendship and comments offered by Michael Chamberlain, Stephen E. Hanson, David Burrow, Brian Covey, Joel Green, Tara Keenan, Scott Moranda, Robert Kruse, and David Tenenbaum stand out. I am especially grateful for the hospitality, friendship, and extraordinary discussions that I was fortunate to have with Dr. Aoife Bhreatnach, whose thinking about Irish Travellers often sparked my own ideas about tourists and tourism. Brian

Covey's comments on the earliest draft of this book led to a judicious period of editing that dramatically helped the finished product.

I could not have successfully weathered the long passage from dissertation to book without the love and support of Katie Burns. Her good humor, kind words, editing skill, and constant encouragement not only contributed to this project but brighten all aspects of my life.

I owe an extraordinary debt of gratitude to my grandfather, the late Gerald E. Zuelow, without whose financial support the research and initial writing of this book would have been impossible.

Finally, although the ideas contained in the following pages developed from my experiences in graduate school at the University of Wisconsin-Madison and while conducting research in Ireland, this book has much deeper roots. I owe more to my parents, Helen and Richard Zuelow, than I can possibly acknowledge or express. My interest in history is the result of the trips to Great Britain they took me on during my early adolescence. I will not soon forget the thrill of exploring British castles and cathedrals, and wandering along Roman roadbeds, nor my feeling of pride when I was able to share my newfound knowledge with others. My parents added to the gift of travel by encouraging me to express my nascent knowledge and excitement through writing. I dedicate this book to them.

Introduction

On 11 November 1996, "Tourism Brand Ireland," a new marketing campaign, was launched in Dublin; its first and most visible project was a seven-minute promotional video. It is easy to get lost in the footage. As viewers, we are immediately struck by a blast of vibrant color and feel the thumping drumbeat of "Dreams" by the popular Irish rock band The Cranberries. We see blue skies, smiling faces, and pints of Guinness. A woman in romantic nineteenth-century dress rides down an apparently deserted beach on the back of a beautiful horse, only to be followed by a herd of wild horses frolicking in the surf. A girl, atop a vintage bicycle, rides in circles on the firm sand as the camera gazes through the spokes of her front wheel at the playing horses. Then we are in a small town in County Cork where a pack of dogs is racing down a pastel-painted street as onlookers cheer. One dog, evidently thinking better of the madness, breaks from the pack and disappears into a pub for a pint. We then soar over the ocean waves toward the Skellig rocks off County Kerry. Seabirds glide on the air around us as we pass over Great Skellig, the site of one of Ireland's most breathtaking and sublime collections of monastic remains; the camera pivots backward and we see the striking rocks disappearing behind us. The same camera technique later finds us zooming over a young couple lying at the edge of the four hundred-foot-high Cliffs of Moher. The woman, wearing a flat cap, turns to her partner and the pair shares a romantic look. Many more striking images pass quickly before our eyes: a brilliantly lit Glendalough round tower seen rising above picturesque gravestones, currachs (traditional Irish boats) racing, a young student sprinting into his exam hall at Trinity College, Dublin doorways and Georgian architecture in an environment apparently free of traffic, fresh seafood, dancing, red-haired colleens. As the song ends, we see two animated figures embrace, swinging around and then exchanging a shamrock with the word "Ireland" below. In the European version we read, "Ireland: Lead a Different Life," while in the American edition, where "lead a different life" might imply "find a gay lover," the viewer is told to "Awaken to a Different World."[1]

The images presented in those seven minutes are not entirely new. Guinness, blue skies, secluded beaches, romantic ruins, red-haired girls, friendly people, and the rest have long been a part of Irish tourism marketing. But if one were to look only at tourist guidebooks or advertisements, the complexity and sociocultural implications of Irish tourism would be lost and the historical context omitted.

The Tourism Brand Ireland campaign was announced eighteen months before the video was released; it was the brainchild of a group of tourism interests and the minister for tourism and sport, who felt that Ireland needed a new "brand strategy." Although Bord Fáilte's international marketing director, Noel Toolan, acted as project coordinator, Tourism Brand Ireland was a joint effort among Bord Fáilte (the Republic's official tourist body), the Northern Ireland Tourist Board (NITB), industry representatives in both countries, and overseas marketing partners: a collaborative effort from beginning to end.

The images presented, while similar to those imagined by late-Victorian visitors, showed a greatly expanded range of destinations and sites/sights that often bore little resemblance to those enjoyed by the first large influx of nineteenth-century tourists. Before the early 1950s most visitors went to Killarney, Galway, Dublin, Cork, and a handful of historic sites such as Glendalough, Newgrange, and Clonmacnois, or perhaps a seaside resort such as Bray, Tramore, or Kilkee. Following the Irish Civil War a series of programs and schemes emerged that ultimately sparked the expansion of tourist resources, the transformation of landscapes and townscapes, and the creation of new "traditions." The small street with its racing dogs, for example, would have looked drab and grey in the years before 1958, given that the pastel colors in the film were the product of a campaign started in the late 1950s to brighten Ireland's townscapes.

If only statutory tourist bodies were involved, few of the changes in Irish tourism since the early 1920s would have been possible. The government showed little concern with tourism until the end of the 1930s, and even thereafter it was often half-hearted as the role of tourism as a national interest was debated. Free State tourism development started life as a private campaign waged by a collection of patriotic businessmen. Following the formation of the first statutory tourist board, tourism officials still had to depend on the public to carry out much of the work required to make Ireland a successful destination. Buildings had to be painted, streets cleaned, behavior modified, landscapes preserved, and historic sites maintained and made accessible. Despite the fact that many of these projects originated in Dublin, people with parochial interests never failed to pursue their own agendas, and the dependence of tourism promoters on local cooperation ensured that these concerns were taken seriously. Tourism symbolized different things to different people; it was shorthand for a variety of ideas about the national interest that were routinely debated from the Civil War onwards. Tourism Brand Ireland is but one stage in a very complicated and still ongoing process of negotiation that helped shape and reshape Irish identity and that is explored at length in these pages. This book is about these negotiations and about how Irish men and women, together with outside interests, came together to make Ireland Irish.

The Development of Tourism

Although historians have yet to write a comprehensive history of preindependence Irish tourism, it is clear that Ireland has long been a tourist destination. For the most part, English groups, including railway companies and hoteliers, promoted pre-1921 Irish tourism for a largely English audience. Most Irish people lacked the financial resources to travel around Ireland, let alone to develop attractive tourist products crafted to charm outsiders.[2] While these realities did not eliminate tourism-inspired discourse, the pre- and postindependence periods exhibit significant differences. Following the Irish Civil War, the *Irish*, not the English, were, for the first time, completely responsible for developing their own tourist product and for determining how they wanted to present themselves to the world. Suddenly the opportunity to define Irishness was on the shoulders of Irish men and women.

Modern tourism, in Ireland as elsewhere, is a recent development with roots firmly planted in the "Grand Tour."[3] This eighteenth-century coming-of-age ritual involved sending England's young aristocrats and wealthy landed gentlemen to the European continent in order to learn languages, meet important political figures, and develop the skills that would allow them to become England's future statesmen. As it happened, the Grand Tour often devolved into a hedonistic excuse for Britannia's sons to frequent Mediterranean brothels and to consume vast quantities of alcohol—a sort of eighteenth-century "spring break."[4]

While the Grand Tour was at its height, a series of aesthetic changes gradually altered the popular attitude toward remote landscapes, beaches, and mountains. The eighteenth-century philosopher Edmund Burke's notion of the "sublime" helped to redefine what cultured Europeans found aesthetically pleasing.[5] Beaches were transformed from a transitory zone between the untamed sea and the tranquility of the land into a healthful space where people could visit to restore their strength and to take the waters.[6] Remote and mountainous areas were romanticized and recast as beautiful.[7] Ruins were reimaged as scenic rather than as eyesores or as a source of stone for local building projects.[8] Early Irish tourism developed as a direct result of these changes; the rugged beauty of the western seaboard attracted the first tourists to Ireland and the countless romantic ruins that dot the countryside also lured them.

It did not take long before Killarney emerged as the country's major tourist destination. By 1775 Killarney already provided visitors an established tourist routine. It was customary to spend two days exploring the area's beautiful lakes, a task accomplished by hiring local boatmen to row the tourist from island to island.[9] Most early tourists to Ireland seem to have been pleased by what they found. For example, Arthur Young, a famous English agriculturalist, visited Killarney in 1776 and declared it to be "the wildest and most romantic country I had any where seen; a region of steep rocks and mountains, which continued for nine or ten miles."[10] Jacques Louis de Bougrenet, a Breton Royalist who escaped to exile in England during the French Revolution, declared that "the soul most indifferent to beauty cannot but be charmed by this delightful spot (near Kenmare)."[11]

Many early English travelers found another striking attraction in Ireland: extreme poverty. The legacy of absentee landlordism, poor soil and unsophisticated agricultural techniques, a failure to industrialize, and regular famines assured that most Irish families were appallingly poor. Many tourists came to see Irish misery for themselves. British newspapers were filled with accounts of unrest and destitution, and the journalists who reported on Irish matters portrayed the country as if it were a disaster zone. According to literary scholar Melissa Fegan, English travelers "insisted that as the Irish were congenital liars, they had to come discover the truth" about Irish reality.[12]

The "romantic tourism" and outright curiosity that fueled early Irish tourism soon replaced the older Grand Tour and quickly led to the development of mass tourism. Where once the idea was to prepare for an aristocratic life, the new intent was to collect views.[13] Romantic tourism made tourists into "consumers of places, experiences, and souvenirs,"[14] and before long more and more people wanted to take part as the emerging middle class learned how to properly consume views.[15] Following the development of an efficient rail network, Thomas Cook capitalized on the growing desire for touring by launching a travel agency dedicated to providing affordable excursions and trips to exotic and not-so-exotic destinations. Initially Cook wanted only to transport teetotalers to a temperance meeting, but he quickly realized the extraordinary demand for inexpensive travel and soon was promoting tours to Scotland, continental Europe, Africa, the Middle East, America, and even Ireland.[16]

Mass tourism arrived in Ireland a few years later than it did in England, largely because railways developed at a slower pace. During the early nineteenth century, travelers in Ireland first depended on mail coaches and later on a network of inexpensive passenger carriages established by an Italian immigrant named Charles Bianconi. Bianconi's coach network crisscrossed most of Munster, Leinster, and Connacht, covering nearly four thousand miles daily. Travel in one of the Italian's carriages was inexpensive and relatively comfortable given the poor roadways, and the average speed was a blistering eight miles per hour. Even at this speedy clip, travel was time consuming and travelers needed to possess the resources necessary to take significant time away from work in order to enjoy leisure pursuits.[17]

Ireland's first railway was constructed between Dublin and Kingstown (Dun Laoghaire) in 1834, but further construction did not proceed rapidly. Between 1,829 and 2,050 miles of track were operational in England in 1843, compared with only 400 in Ireland seven years later. By 1870 the Irish rail lines were expanded to an impressive 2,000 miles, yet this distance still paled when compared with the nearly 10,000 miles of track that covered England in 1856.[18] Why did Irish railways develop so slowly? There are at least two answers. First, Ireland had precious little heavy industry and this lack reduced the demand for railways. Second, and closely related, Irish rail lines were built and managed by English companies, and these firms devoted the majority of their wealth to expanding and improving their lucrative English routes. Ireland had to wait until English lines were firmly established.

Thomas Cook was one of the first to capitalize on the expanding Irish rail network when he recommended short excursions to Ireland in 1852. He praised the construction of more and more track and expanded his Irish business accordingly. In 1856, for example, Cook conducted about 1,500 tourists in sixty packed railway cars to some of Ireland's beauty spots. Unfortunately, as in Scotland, the railway companies were impressed by Cook's success and soon became convinced that they could increase their profit by organizing their own excursion trains while refusing to sell inexpensive tickets to Cook. For seventeen painful years Cook was unable to conduct tours in Ireland while the railway companies monopolized the package tour business. Two years after the railways recognized that Cook's success actually contributed to their own, John Mason Cook, Cook's son and business partner, opened the company's first office in Ireland. By the 1880s Thomas Cook and Son enjoyed a lucrative business there.[19]

The most significant chapter of nineteenth-century Irish tourism started when Frederick W. Crossley arrived in the 1880s to manage the Thomas Cook and Son Dublin office. Crossley was convinced that Ireland had tremendous potential as a tourist destination and he encouraged his employer to dedicate resources to further development. When this support was not forthcoming, Crossley resigned in 1891. Three years later he started publishing a travel magazine called *Irish Tourist* and in 1895 he joined forces with a collection of hotel and railway companies to found the first Irish Tourist Association (ITA). Until the First World War, Crossley and the ITA worked tirelessly to lobby the government; to improve Irish roadways, hotels, and rail lines; and to assure continued public access to important sites such as the Giant's Causeway in County Antrim. At various times Crossley teamed up with British officials as well as key Irish leaders such as John Redmond. His lobbying efforts ultimately led to the 1909 Health Resorts and Watering-Places (Ireland) Act, which allowed local authorities to put aside money in support of tourist development—a special provision that was unique to Ireland and Blackpool (in England).

While the Anglo-Irish elite exhibited substantial support for Crossley's efforts, there were dissenting voices as well. University College Dublin archaeologist R. A. S. MacAlister, for example, worried that a steady stream of tourists would ultimately destroy Ireland's most cherished historic sites. He also rejected claims that increased tourism would lead to enhanced understanding between the English and Irish races. As historian Irene Furlong notes, "he [MacAlister] dreaded the arrival of what he viewed as an army of trippers who would encourage the emergence of pauperism in the Irish peasant by tipping the mobs of young children who would follow them."[20] Similarly, the Gaelic League, which was founded in the 1880s in order to promote the revival of the Irish language, expressed concern that tourists would "degrade the noble soul of the Irish peasant." This attitude greatly irritated Crossley and he shot back,

> Much has been said and written of an Irish Ireland. The Hooligans [sic] of the Irish gutter press having raised their inane heads from their native slush, babble re [sic] an Irish Ireland . . . (they) won't have foreigners coming to the island which had the honour of being selected for their place of birth . . . a great league is to be formed for keeping out foreign Englishmen and foreign Scotsmen from Irish Ireland . . . in the presence of such slavish twaddle, the average intelligent Irishman must feel ashamed unless he is saved by a sense of humour.[21]

The two sides of this debate did not vanish with Irish independence in 1921 and their respective voices became louder following independence. While English entrepreneurs led the Irish tourist industry before independence, and while most Irish people lacked the resources to take part in tourism development either as tourists or as tour operators, the tourism-related dialogue was muted. Then, when Irish men and women assumed the role of tourism developer, the lid was removed and tourism-related discourse became more widespread. Irish people from every part of Ireland could actually make a difference. Their opinions mattered.

When the First World War erupted in 1914, Crossley's tourism development efforts were subsumed by larger concerns; the 1916 Easter Rising and Irish War of Independence (1919–21) scarcely allowed for a resumption of the ITA's work. Following the ratification of the Anglo-Irish Treaty ("the Treaty") in 1921, the largely English-led ITA breathed its last. For his part, Crossley, a firm unionist, was disgusted by the turn of events and never again devoted any effort to tourism development.[22]

In 1922 Ireland plunged headlong into a traumatic period of civil war, the reason for which was inseparably connected to the terms of the Treaty. The Irish Free State had its own government, but Dáil (lower house of the Irish parliament) deputies had to swear an oath of allegiance to the Crown and the British continued to have a governor-general in Ireland who could summon, prorogue, and dissolve the Dáil. The governor-general had the power to approve money bills on the advice of the executive council, and he served as the direct line of communication between the British government and the Free State. Several British naval ports also remained in operation on Irish soil. From the moment that the Treaty came before Dáil Éireann for consideration it was clear that the country was fiercely divided by its terms. On 17 December 1921, Deputy Liam Mellows rejected the right of anybody to accept the Treaty, saying that "[w]e who stand by the Republic still will, I presume rebel against the new government that would be set up if this Treaty is passed."[23] This assumption proved prophetic: violence erupted in June 1922 after anti-treaty forces occupied the Four Courts in Dublin and after Michael Collins, the military leader who led Irish forces during the War of Independence and who negotiated the Treaty, attacked the building to remove them. Guerrilla conflict raged until 24 May 1923 when the IRA dumped arms to wait for another day. At times, especially following the assassination of Collins, the war was frighteningly violent. The Free State government responded to anti-treatyite activities by executing seventy-seven Irregular prisoners. Families split apart. Brothers fought against brothers. Although the conflict was not nearly as bloody as civil wars in other countries—roughly 927 people died during the Irish Civil War as compared with 25,000 in the Finnish Civil War and 300,000 in the Spanish Civil War[24]—the legacy of the conflict cast a long shadow over Irish history and, as will become clear in the following pages, had an impact on many aspects of Irish life including tourist development.

The Impact of Tourism

Modern travel has brought massive growth to many regions, inspired encounters between vastly differing cultural groups, and prompted a scholarly interest where previously there was little more than disdain for an aspect of the human experience deemed trivial.[25] Picking up on a long-standing tendency among the respectable to turn up their noses at participants in mass travel, scholars have painted tourists as little more than a "golden horde" invading less dynamic societies and turning them into a "pleasure periphery."[26] Like unthinking robots, they say, tourists travel a "beaten track"[27] and resemble the client in a massage parlor "more than it would be polite to emphasize."[28] Tourists do little more than mindlessly traipse to whatever sites are popular, they snap photographs, and then they go home. According to these scholars, tourism is an almost wholly inactive pursuit of pleasure tantamount to hedonistic excess.

Recently a growing number of academics have been more gracious to the lowly tourist. Dean MacCannell, for example, claims that tourists actually set out to find real artifacts, not just mechanical reproductions.[29] They are fully cognizant of what Walter Benjamin called the "aura" of authenticity;[30] they are not satisfied to rest at home with mere photographs but want to experience the real thing. Similarly, Rudy Koshar describes an "optics of tourism" through which tourists search for "meaning beyond the marketplace."[31] This meaning derives largely from the pursuit of difference. Tourists travel in order to enter into "contact with other ways of life. The most prestigious experiences are the ones that take people the furthest away from their everyday world. And the distance from home is not only measured in miles, but in cultural terms."[32] Tourists seek out the "other"—authentic representations of distinctive cultures.[33] It follows that host cultures must market themselves in such a way as to attract guests to the "other": Irish tourism officials must emphasize a distinctive Gaelicism, French villages must promote a distinctive folk heritage, and Scottish tourism must present misty bens, glens, and tartan-clad Highlanders.

The very fact that tourism promotes a process of "othering" raises worthwhile questions about the impact of tourism on native culture. In keeping with their disapproving treatment of tourists, scholars have until recently believed that tourism leads to the "bastardization" and "'commoditization' of previously authentic ethnic cultures for the purpose of touristic display."[34] Catherine A. Palmer, studying the Bahamas, goes even further, suggesting that tourism robs local people of the ability to define a national identity of their own and locks them into the perpetual use of images created during the colonial past.[35]

More recently, anthropological studies have suggested that the story is more complicated. According to Simon Abram, for example, "It is clearly not enough to question the effect of tourism on local people. This implies a one-way process by which tourists disempower the local 'hosts.'"[36] The older exploitation argument robs host cultures of agency by suggesting that once hosts begin mugging for the camera, they promptly forget that they are *acting*. Abram shows that while locals in small rural French towns are not above performing for tourists, they are fully capable of distinguishing touristic performance from local tradition, and they assign different meanings to each. These villagers have not mindlessly forgotten who they really are.

Likewise, after studying Foxwood, Ireland, a small town of 944 people in north Mayo, Moya Kneafsey concluded that while tourism has an influence on identity, this impact is very complicated. Relationships between tourism and place identities can be conceptualized in terms of social relations. On the one hand, changes to place identities occur as groups, institutions, and individuals act to commodify resources such as the local environment or heritage for tourism. The process of commodification is mediated through new social relations between individuals and groups within the town and farther afield.[37]

In other words, change is not brought about strictly by the tourist invasion; it is produced by decisions within the host community about self-presentation. At least when a local population is itself responsible for development, members of that population can choose how and if they will be altered by tourism. Producers have every bit as much control as do tourists. If scholars want to understand how tourism changes host cultures, they must adopt an approach that first pays attention to the social relations that exist in and between places, and second takes account of the other social processes that affect place identities. Taking this approach illustrates the ways in which different individuals and groups of people combine to resist or promote the commodification of cultural identity.[38]

Very little scholarship has yet followed Kneafsey's lead. Instead, the tendency has been to focus on one or two social groups, usually at the top of the social hierarchy, while ignoring the rest of society. Little attention is paid to the full range of individuals and organizations involved in creating tourist products. Yet if Kneafsey is correct and community relationships ultimately define how tourism will exert its impact on a society, it is fair to assume that such relationships must also determine the effectiveness of national tourism programs. To really understand tourism, it is necessary to examine the links between hosts and guests, between local and national groups, and among the government and local authorities, tourism bodies, and regional interest groups. The shape of the tourist product, to say nothing of the impact that tourism has on identity, is the result of these complex interactions. Ultimately tourism is a nexus at which different groups converge. Tourist guidebooks, for example, are a product of collaborative decisions about "what ought to be seen" that take place at the tourism nexus. Indeed, Irish guidebooks reflect a desire to spread wealth widely around the country, promote development in rural areas, and present a positive narrative about Irishness and Irish history. To appreciate the content chosen for these guides demands an understanding of the structure of Ireland's various tourist bodies, perceptions within Ireland about what it means to be Irish, government policies, and local concerns and political pressures, as well as global tourism trends. To comprehend the implications of tourism demands recognizing the role of the nexus between groups.

Working the Projectors?

Because of the history of colonialism in Ireland, scholarly willingness to disempower host communities by robbing them of agency is all too common. According to one postcolonial theorist,

> tourist representations hang like a weight around the neck of the cultural present in Ireland. They can be relied upon to remain resolutely cliché[d],

simplistic, and dogmatic in the worst possible ways. . . . Tourist representations were largely projected onto an Irish screen by English visitors. They served to rationalize colonialism for the home audience and, like a hotel training film, taught Irish people habits of silence and subservience. After 1921 the postcolonial bourgeoisie learned to work the projectors and bothered little with changing the reels.[39]

While this characterization might have been true during the colonial period, this book makes clear that it was not at all true after independence. Although it is right to stress the importance of the tourist product, the current tourist images of Ireland were chosen for presentation through an ongoing process by which images that were useful to the state and its people were adopted, while more harmful images were rejected and downplayed.

What is remarkable is how actively involved many people from across Irish society were in determining how their unique national identity would be shaped and presented. Consider what happened when an American travel magazine published an extensive article that depicted Ireland in an unfavorable light. The offending article was published by *Holiday* magazine and was written by Frank O'Connor, a major twentieth-century Irish short story writer; it dominated the December 1949 issue of the publication.[40] The feature sparked immediate anger on both sides of the Atlantic among Irish citizens and Irish-Americans alike. Among other complainers, the New Ross IRA Memorial Association protested;[41] Wexford Corporation passed a resolution calling for the immediate termination of any employment enjoyed by Frank O'Connor and requested that the minister for external affairs instruct the Irish ambassador to the United States to "deny the truth of the article in question";[42] and the Society of Friendly Sons of St. Patrick in Philadelphia asked *Holiday* magazine to apologize.[43] The Killarney Urban District Council declared the article to be a "lying tirade from beginning to end," and demanded that Frank O'Connor be investigated and his position at Radio Éireann terminated.[44] Even the Catholic press, which seldom commented on tourism-related issues, lambasted the piece as "a grave mistake."[45]

What was so awful? The article included a collection of gorgeous photographs in both color and black-and-white—the Cross of Muiredach at Monasterboice, the Book of Kells, a lovely thatched cottage, castle ruins and round towers, the Killarney lakes, and the Blarney Stone, to say nothing of women in Kinsale cloaks, manor houses, turf cutting, and smiling Dubliners going about their daily routines. It was a wonderful-*looking* article, but the text was problematic. O'Connor provided a catalogue of unpleasantness. Readers learned that "Ireland contains slums like you have not seen the like of elsewhere in Europe, with sickly looking children playing barefoot in the streets." Towns were devoid of industry and churches were in ruins. The author stressed Ireland's "sometimes dreadful poverty," while drawing attention to the "all-powerful" middle classes. O'Connor stressed the supremacy of the Catholic Church and alleged that

> infanticide in Ireland is appallingly common, though almost from the moment a girl starts walking out with a boy, she is kept under observation by the police; if she leaves the neighborhood, she is shadowed, and if she has a baby in another area, the police return and spread the news throughout her own town. Yet it never seems to have occurred to anybody that there is any other way of stopping the crime.

O'Connor even suggested that there was widespread anti-English feeling in Ireland. However true his allegations were,[46] he cast attention on aspects of life in Ireland that fell well outside of the scope of constructive "cultural propaganda." Little goodwill was to be gained from depictions of tyrannical clerics and sick and starving children.

Pressured by the tide of public outrage, the Department of External Affairs launched an investigation of the article so that the minister could determine whether it was "defamatory." The department's weekly newsletter criticized O'Connor's characterization of Ireland as "a rather moist baby," and challenged the overwhelmingly negative characterization of the country. More important, the department contrasted the piece with other articles addressing potential tourist destinations. It was easy enough to dismiss the bizarre allegations about spying on courting couples, but

> Irish readers will wonder not so much at the assertions . . . as at their context, and the general balance of the article. A tourist article on, say, France, is not likely to dwell on slum conditions in Menilmontant or lovingly recall epidemics which occurred seven years ago in Vieux Port or Marseilles, or recite statistics of abortions and alcoholism. Rather will it speak of France's attractions for the foreigner: it may say something about France's effort

of reconstruction and recovery. So why a different approach for Ireland? Carelessly, one may be inclined to answer that it is Ireland's own fault for breeding such cantankerous writers.

As it happened, the fault lay not with Ireland's "cantankerous writers," but instead with the "the creative process of an industrial age"—or so it was claimed.[47] In the wake of the outrage *Holiday* magazine supplied External Affairs with a summary description of the process used to produce the sordid article. The editors had instructed O'Connor to "steer well clear of [the] sentimental and corny approach" and demanded that he "dig into the almost hopeless economy of the country," while also exploring the "peculiar quirk of the Irish nature that has continually had them embroiled with their neighbours." To assist O'Connor, they provided him with "research" and set him loose. O'Connor duly provided a draft, but it "failed to take the expected crack at the clergy" and so required rewriting. The new draft still did not meet with the magazine's requirements, and the publisher asked for a discussion of an Irish family living in a cottage with a dirt floor and living space shared between pigs and people. O'Connor was put off by the notion of domestic pigs and refused to include them, but the editors still demanded that Irish poverty be emphasized and that priests be raised to much greater prominence in the narrative. When the great work was finished, the editors stressed, "The production of a thing like *Holiday* requires 'a lot of hard work, plus brains, plus talent.'"[48]

External Affairs was thoroughly displeased with the article, but the damage had been done. When the minister considered the situation, he decided that it was not a defamatory article, and no instructions were sent to the Irish ambassador in Washington to refute the charges.[49] One imagines that the minister recognized that to do so would only magnify the damage. Instead, the department urged *Holiday* to publish a new article about Ireland in a subsequent issue. This time the piece, written by John Horne Burns and published in 1950, was provided to the Irish ambassador for vetting. The ambassador in turn declared it to be "reasonably inoffensive," and, aside from the correction of a few factual errors, the article was returned to the magazine with the department's approval.[50] While a few cutting remarks, including the suggestion that Limerick city was not a pleasant introduction to the charms of southern Ireland, were present, there was little to condemn.

The response to the *Holiday* article does not support the view that the Irish people simply sat back and accepted older colonial views. The poverty that attracted many nineteenth-century tourists to Ireland was no longer an acceptable representation of Ireland. Indeed, what follows here is the story of a broad segment of Irish society actively working to erase either the image or the reality of Irish poverty. People from a diversity of groups and organizations wanted to present the best possible Ireland to the outside world. This book is an account of how the Irish people worked out exactly what the "best possible Ireland" actually was and the story of how Irish national identity was imagined and reimagined in the years following independence.

National Identity and Tourism

As with most studies of the impact of tourism on host cultures, the academic literature on nationalism tends to oversimplify the nationalization process. Most scholars describe nations as the result of an effort by a mysterious and undefined elite.[51] The problem with this view is that it fails to reflect the degree of horizontal dialogue hinted at by the heated response to the *Holiday* article or by the other cases described in this book. The "great man" view of nationalization does nothing to explain why the masses are willing to unquestioningly accept what they are told and in fact it robs them of any agency whatsoever. A smaller group of scholars suggests that nations are actually created from the bottom up. National communities, they say, are the product of preexisting cultural identities that are used to juxtapose indigenous identity with that of a colonial power.[52] While there is, no doubt, an element of truth in this view (as there is in the previous explanation), it is nevertheless unreasonable to assume that elites play no role at all. In the end, the bottom-up or top-down debate is little more than a straw man. Elites could not have imposed a new culture on the masses if there had not been a receptive audience. Likewise, subalterns undoubtedly adapted earlier identities to match new state-defined demands. It is simply not possible to understand the creation of nations if either group is written out of history.

If nations are a "deep, horizontal comradeship," then the history of the nation must reflect this fact by addressing society horizontally rather than vertically. Instead of being static, as suggested by Benedict Anderson's formulation of the nation as "an imagined community,"[53] nations are *perpetually reimagined communities that are maintained through a horizontal dialogue about community membership;* they are the sum total of cross-community dialogues about national membership and national interests, composed and recomposed by the very act of collectively discussing them. This dialogue can become louder or softer, more or less obvious, as conditions warrant. More often than not, nationalism is "banal" and it is hardly noticeable to observers. But other times, when a crisis occurs or other demands arise (like the need to create images for tourist consumption), the discussion can become much more noticeable.[54] Over time, competing practices and memories are woven into the fabric of national identities. Newer, more useful memories or images replace older ones, while conflicting visions of the national mythology are debated and discussed.[55] Nations are always in process, always changing.[56] To a large extent, this process is why nations persist, despite the many challenges that arise, and this is why Irish national identity was able to transform itself from a revolutionary identity to a state-building one.

Tourism is not the only nexus for national dialogue, but it is a particularly useful one for several reasons. First, tourism is often identified as a national interest because it is able to offer benefits to many different groups within the national community, while at the same time these groups often have disparate concerns in mind; the result is an immediate dialogue about exactly what the nation's priorities should be. Second, tourism, at least national tourism, requires consideration of precisely what it means to be part of the nation in question, of its defining characteristics, history, and geographic space. Consensus about the best image to present for tourist consumption is often difficult to attain, and thus tourism quite naturally prompts discussion about the nature of national identity. Finally, tourism involves the movement of people both within their own nation and between nations, and it places a premium on the interaction of people from different geographic spaces. The result of this contact is a continual exchange of ideas about mutual identities and "a dynamic between previous understanding and expectations and new observations and experiences."[57]

Introduction | xxxi

Between the end of the Irish Civil War and the present, tourism acted as both a subject of and a catalyst for debate about the Irish nation. Tourism inspired two closely related and coterminous debates. The first concerned whether tourism should be considered a national interest. On the one hand tourism advocates argued that tourism would help Ireland emerge from its history of colonial oppression and poverty to become a forward-looking and modern nation. On the other hand tourism opponents viewed dreams of modernization with suspicion while gazing backward toward a halcyon day when the Irish people spoke Gaelic and enjoyed a simple, straightforward existence doing as they had always done. Also part of the larger debate concerning tourism's place as a national interest was the question of who should manage tourism. Should local communities control tourism development in their areas or should the industry be administered from Dublin? To some extent this was another way of rephrasing the modernization debate. Traditionally the localities jealously guarded their distance and difference from Dublin. Regional rivalries, such as between Cork and Kerry, were long part of Irish life and they helped give many people a vital sense of place. Meanwhile, the modernizing forces behind tourism development viewed these local identities as a hindrance. Centralization allowed for a unified message, for more efficient and less fractious distribution of funds. The first three chapters of this book are organized chronologically and trace the "battle for tourism" as it evolved from the initial calls for tourism development through the start of the Celtic Tiger–related tourism boom of the mid-1990s, giving the reader an understanding of the historical evolution of Irish tourism and the actors involved in the process. Above all, these chapters describe how tourism was both a subject of and an inspiration for debate concerning the collective interests of newly independent Ireland.

The second major tourism-related debate involved determining the "best" Ireland to show visitors. As more people became convinced about the importance of tourism and more tourists visited Ireland, this question grew in importance. Not surprisingly, the "best" Ireland was composed of multiple components, the three most important of which were language/culture, heritage/history, and landscape. While the resultant debates often overlapped, different individuals and groups had their own pet issues; therefore, the next three chapters explore each issue separately.

Chapter 4 is divided into two sections. The first explores the dialogue between two groups: one that believed that being truly Irish involved a close link to the nation's Gaelic heritage and the Gaelic language, and another that felt Ireland should be progressive and seek to attain economic prosperity in preference to language preservation. Language enthusiasts, drawn primarily from the intelligentsia, argued vehemently that tourism would destroy the last refuges of Gaelic, and that the only way to prevent the end of the Irish language was to shield it from Anglophones. Meanwhile, the Gaelic speakers themselves saw little threat and demanded the wealth symbolized to them by tourists. The result was a protracted discussion about whether Ireland should be forward-looking or nostalgic, whether the language was better served by fencing it in and risking the emigration of its speakers or by encouraging tourism and risking death by drowning in an Anglophone sea. The second section of chapter 4 begins by noting that after independence many Irish adopted older stereotypes about Irish friendliness as a way to differentiate themselves from others. To encounter friendly and welcoming natives in Ireland represented a positive "other" to the harried people of industrial Europe and America. Once Irish character was defined, it was important to develop cultural events that would be widely acceptable. Traditional Irish fairs, for example, were often bawdy gatherings marked by drinking, fighting, and even some open sexuality. Some Irish people were left with deeply ambivalent feelings about presenting such scenes to outsiders, and therefore new festivals were invented and carefully made "authentic" by rooting them in the distant past.

As with Irish culture, the Irish past presented troubling challenges to tourism developers and to the Irish public more broadly. Irish history was defined by a long struggle with the English as well as by a more recent civil war, yet the priority of the new state was to create a unified citizenry and prosperous relations with England. The result was a strong desire to develop a historical narrative stressing Irish unity and deemphasizing past conflicts. Thus the primary concern when presenting Irish history was to show a united Irish people with a proud legacy of saints and scholars rather than a long-standing penchant for violent confrontation. Chapter 5 examines the reformation of Irish history from early efforts at the development of preservationist legislation through the creation of a new historical narrative that stressed unity rather than conflict. The chapter concludes by exploring the role of global trends in defining how Irish history was presented to host and guest alike.

The presentation of a positive image of Irishness involved more than language and festivals or an historical narrative that stressed saints and scholars more than conflict; it was also closely connected with landownership and aesthetics. Chapter 6 explores debates about who should have access to Irish landscapes and what these landscapes ought to look like. Opinions varied between those who felt that the Irish constitution guaranteed landowners total control over their holdings and those who considered Irish spaces to be the property of the Irish people, to be exploited for the benefit of all. Closely tied to this debate was another concerning aesthetics. Should the land be translated for tourists by using signs, or left as a confusing network of seemingly aimless tracks? Should Irish towns be left unpainted and grey or made bright and cheerful with pastel paints and flowerpots? Ought builders be encouraged to consider aesthetic concerns when erecting structures, or should they be left to their own devices and allowed the freedom to cater to market forces? Finally, should Irish ecosystems be altered to match tourist tastes or conserved as true examples of the Irish environment?

The final chapter examines developments between the mid-1990s and early 2007, demonstrating that the debates described throughout this book continued unabated into the first years of the twenty-first century. Tourism-related horizontal dialogue remains the norm. The chapter begins with a brief explanation of the dramatic expansion of Ireland's tourism sector during the 1990s. It moves on to discuss how the industry was restructured yet again starting in 2001. Finally, it concludes with a detailed discussion of the "Dingle Wrangle," a debate over what to call the small tourist town of Dingle, County Kerry: an incident that made clear the continuing vitality of the tourism nexus as a vital element in the perpetual remaking of Irishness.

In the end this book shows how a very large cross-section of Irish society, irrespective of rank or social class, took part in the process of making Ireland Irish. It paints a picture of a people who were very much involved not only in defining their tourist product but in defining themselves. The Irish people were not merely projectionists, nor hapless dupes condemned to live in the shadow of a colonial legacy. Instead, men and women, Dubliners and rural dwellers, tourist boards and local committees took part in an ongoing process in which they created both a public image and a sense of self. *Making Ireland Irish* is a story of success, of indigenous agency, and ultimately of the close relationship between tourism and national identity in postindependence Ireland.

Making Ireland Irish

1

Introducing a National Interest, 1922–1939

If there had been no widespread debate about tourism in the years following the Irish Civil War, it would not have been surprising. The country was deeply wounded both physically and psychologically. Roads, especially in rural areas, were badly damaged, and there were too few workers employed in fixing them.[1] Between paying for the war itself, repairing material damage, and housing captured prisoners, the Cumann na nGaedheal government strained under serious financial handicaps.[2] In addition, much of the population suffered from deep poverty. Roughly 800,000, many of them in North Dublin City, lived in overcrowded conditions, and infant mortality was still appalling.[3] As if these adversities were not bad enough, the government lacked legitimacy in the eyes of a substantial portion of the citizenry,[4] and certain state institutions, such as the criminal-justice system, were notoriously weak[5]—hardly an acceptable state of affairs when Republican forces continued to carry out military operations, including a machine-gun attack on British soldiers at Cobh in 1924,[6] and, more famously, the assassination of Kevin O'Higgins on 10 July 1927. It helped little that much of the population was ambivalent about the future and was deeply divided as well.[7] Republicans "swarmed together" and "formed little coteries based on nothing more than good fellowship, a welcoming household, shared experiences, and a commonly held republican faith,"[8] effectively ensuring that a large section of the population was unwilling to help in reconstruction efforts. To survive, the Free State government had to do nothing less than "remake the administration of the nation and, in so doing, to assert its preeminent authority throughout the land"⁹—hardly easy when novel problems merged with old suspicions of Dublin rule in rural areas.¹⁰

Despite the Cosgrave government's general disinterest, others, stirred by tourist development efforts in countries such as Spain, France, Austria, and Italy, overflowed with pro-tourism enthusiasm. From 1905, Spain had its own state tourist commission while France and Austria followed within the next five years. Tourism advocates in these places viewed the industry as a harbinger of modernity and an essential national interest. In Spain, for example, advocates insisted that "those anxious for progress and for our country to figure among the most prosperous, patriots in general" should take the initiative by furthering tourism development.¹¹ With the Continental countries as inspiration, an important section of Ireland's bourgeoisie fully believed tourism represented a primary national interest. These middle-class people argued not only that tourism should be developed, but that it should be viewed as a patriotic crusade, a harbinger of modernity and improvement. Between late 1923 and 1939 these tourism advocates, led by the Irish Tourist Association (ITA), worked tirelessly to promote their cause as much to the Irish people as to foreign tourists. To meet their goals, the association first had to establish itself as the leading tourism voice in Ireland, winning as many adherents as possible in the process; then it had to persuade the government that the industry was worth investing in.

The ITA's work was made more challenging by the fact that tourism meant different things to different groups within Ireland. For members of local authorities and many citizens, tourism symbolized improvement and development, but for others it represented a threat to cherished ways of life or simply a waste of money. On the one hand, this set of attitudes meant that the ITA could promise something to everyone, but on the other, it sometimes led to conflict with those who found the modernist thrust of tourism threatening or who simply believed that the government had no business pursuing tourist development. This chapter traces the pro-tourism campaign from the first appearance of tourism advocacy after the Civil War to the eventual passage of substantial tourism legislation in 1939; particular attention is paid to the symbolic meanings that various groups within Irish society assigned to the nascent tourist industry, and to how these meanings were addressed by pro-tourism voices.

Unity through Tourism

If Ireland's bourgeoisie lacked self-confidence at the time of independence,[12] the lack was not visible in the zeal with which many advocated tourism development. Even during the Civil War a Dublin-based group of business and tourism interests combined to create the Tourist Organisation Society of Ireland, a body composed primarily of representatives of railway and steam-packet companies as well as hoteliers and tourist agencies. The group was chaired by Senator James Moran, the grandfatherly vice chairman of the Dublin Dockyard Company, who saw tourism as one path toward addressing Ireland's myriad problems such as the housing crisis.[13] From the outset this organization justified its existence in national terms, claiming that its efforts "saved many . . . Irish resorts from ruin," and the society sought to continue this work by promoting the flow of tourists between Northern Ireland and the Free State. The only real problem was a shortage of money. Existing legislation—the Health Resorts and Watering Places (Ireland) Act of 1909—did not provide adequate resources, and local groups were unable to raise enough capital to develop an acceptable promotional scheme. Killarney, for example, managed to garner only £30 for tourism publicity, while Bundoran in Donegal scratched up a meager £17. Such fund-raising failures supported the group's contention that tourism was a national concern that should be addressed at the national level. "If success is to be obtained," its leaders cried, "the Irish cities, with their great tourist attractions, must be grouped with lesser communities, and the attractions of the country as a whole pressed upon potential visitors for the benefit of the entire community of Ireland."[14] The Tourist Organisation Society of Ireland promised to create a national tourism coalition by drawing representatives from corporations and counties across Ireland and by lobbying the government for money, the use of which would be audited by a government-appointed civil servant.

The Tourist Organisation Society of Ireland was not the only organization with national plans and a firm belief in the need for a nationwide solution to tourism development. During 1923 and 1924 similar bodies were formed, including the Ulster Tourist Development Association (UTDA), the West of Ireland Tourist Development Association, and the Irish Tourist Association. All of these organizations largely followed the Tourist Organisation

Society of Ireland model as voluntary bodies comprised of bourgeois tourism interests, and all were born in the belief that Ireland, North and South, could develop a significant and lucrative tourism industry if the Irish people would pull together and get to work. The problem was that these groups were each fighting for the same money, the same political support, and even the same membership. While the Ulster Tourist Development Association had no competition in the North (the UTDA continued to operate into the 1980s), the Irish Free State was simply too small to support three organizations with national aspirations.

By January 1925 the Irish Tourist Association emerged as the most likely prospect to lead Irish tourism into the post–Civil War period. Cork-based tourism advocates founded the ITA at the Victoria Hotel, Cork, in 1923, although the group did not incorporate until June 1924. Like the Tourist Organisation Society of Ireland, the Tourist Association hoped to promote tourist traffic in Saorstát Éireann (the Irish Free State) and to safeguard "the interests of tourists therein." Toward this end the group planned to establish advertising agents, to set up an agency for hotel, motorcar, railway, and shipping companies, and to develop tourist information bureaus in key tourist centers. In addition, the ITA intended to purchase property that might be used to enhance the organization's liquidity while also working to acquire money from the state to better promote tourism. While in hindsight these were overly aggressive goals, they suggest a genuine feeling of optimism among an important segment of the population in spite of the problems faced by the new state.

At the time of its incorporation the ITA had only twenty members, but this number quickly expanded by the end of June 1924 to ninety-five.[15] As with the Tourist Organisation Society of Ireland, most members were drawn from the business classes, and a sizeable cross-section of Munster's financial elite was represented. Signatories on the incorporation papers include hotel owners, shipping men, and company directors. For example, the ITA's first director was Dr. J. C. Foley of Cork city. During his varied career Foley worked as managing director of the firm John Daly & Co., was a member of the governing body of University College, Cork, and acted as a director of the Electricity Supply Board, the Cork Opera House, and the Victoria Hotel. In addition, he served on the Cork Harbour Commission and the Central

Savings Committee, not to mention the Cork Corporation.[16] The ITA's second president, Howard S. Harrington, was an American-born lawyer, educated at Columbia and Georgetown, who directed the prosecution against the White Star Line in the legal hearing following the Titanic disaster.[17] In 1921 Harrington retired to his ancestral homeland and purchased Dunloe Castle in Killarney, where he quickly developed an interest in Irish tourism development as a way of building up the financial resources of his adopted country.[18] Other early members of the executive included Robert W. Sinnott, the manager of a steamship company; John J. Barry, a railway manager; and Arthur C. Freeman, the manager of Cork's Imperial Hotel.[19]

Beyond those with a direct financial interest in the development of Irish tourism, almost from its formation the ITA employed a young man named J. P. (Jack) O'Brien, a curious-looking character of average height, with a substantial pointed nose, large ears, and dark hair. His bright, lively eyes were framed by thick eyebrows, and his intense nervous energy and endless ideas tended to impress those who met him.[20] O'Brien grew up in Ballyporeen, not far from the Cork-Tipperary border, where his parents owned a small business that was not substantial enough to support all of the O'Brien children. After he fought on the anti-treaty side during the Civil War, the Irish Tourist Association hired O'Brien as its secretary. Encouraged by President J. C. Foley, O'Brien developed an overwhelming interest in the holiday business. He studied tourist literature from such important destinations as France, Switzerland, and England, and then traveled to these places to observe their promotional activities firsthand. His enthusiasm knew no bounds; he took what he learned and began to reshape it into programs for Ireland. He saw the Emerald Isle as a potential mecca for sportsmen where tourists could hunt, fish, or simply relax. He dreamed about improving hotel facilities, training hotel staffs, and establishing schools that would reinvent the country as a culinary center.[21] For O'Brien tourism represented a means to raise money to support his countrymen and a way to show outsiders the wonders of Ireland. Tourism, in fact, represented a profound example of the national interest, even if O'Brien himself was no fan of the present state or of the terms of the Treaty that had created it. Tourism was a powerful vehicle for helping his countrymen to raise their status, and thus it bolstered his already strong sense of nationalism.

Even if tourism meant a great deal to many in the bourgeoisie and encouraged the nationalism of others, and despite the fact that Continental governments such as Spain and France were increasingly convinced of the economic and political importance of the industry, tourism was not a government priority in Ireland.[22] No tourist-traffic legislation was proposed during this period and there were no debates in the Dáil solely about tourism development. Yet neither could the government ignore tourism—too many important people were already involved in the various tourist-development groups, and it was also obvious that countries like Belgium were enjoying substantial benefit from tourism income.[23] While this recognition did not lead government officials to propose sweeping tourism legislation in the 1920s, they nevertheless mentioned tourism frequently when discussing road improvements, unemployment, and the infrastructure at such important Irish ports as Dun Laoghaire. Already in March 1924 some government ministers and Dáil deputies adopted the national terms used by the ITA and the Tourist Organisation Society to discuss tourism. As one minister put it, the government had saved

> Ireland from . . . the worst consequences of that challenge [civil war and revolution], we have saved her from anarchy, we have saved her from the intervention of a hostile army, and we have saved her from famine. But we have not saved her, and we could not save her, no power on earth could save her, from a great deal of want and suffering, the inevitable consequences of the reckless defiance of political and economic laws of which during the last eighteen months we were the witnesses and the victims.

To rescue the country from poverty, the Dáil must earnestly look for ways to reduce unemployment and distress, the minister insisted. Tourism was a very logical solution because it would "certainly be a great source of wealth to Ireland, with its world-scattered race, naturally interested in Irish history, topography, and social institutions."[24]

Others, however, were far less enthralled with the prospect of shaping Ireland into a tourist utopia. During debate surrounding a new local-government bill, Daniel Morrissey, the minister for industry and commerce during the late 1940s, reasoned that the government should not be "so very keen on making this country an attractive place for tourists" but should focus its efforts on "making the country a suitable place for the people to live."[25] Ultimately, he argued, it was in the nation's best interest to solve the country's social and economic problems, not to use government resources and energy to create a tourist mecca while interfering in affairs that should be left to the operation of the free market.[26]

Though tourism lacked universal government support, pressure from newspapers and the various tourist bodies soon forced action. In late 1924 Patrick McGilligan, the minister for industry and commerce, called a conference of tourism groups to develop a unified national approach to tourist development.[27] The meeting occurred on 15–16 December 1924 at government buildings in Dublin and was presided over by E. J. Riordan of the Ministry for Industry and Commerce. After some discussion the delegations from each of the main tourist organizations agreed that the groups should combine to form a single tourism-development body, with the Irish Tourist Association formally becoming Ireland's national tourism organization. After a further five hours of negotiation a temporary standing committee was appointed so that the group could "start work immediately."[28] Senator Moran, previously the chairman of the Tourist Organisation Society of Ireland and a well-known and widely respected advocate of "the gospel of progress" after nearly thirteen years as a significant public figure,[29] was quickly elected president. The vice presidents included J. C. Foley, the driving force behind the formation of the ITA in Cork; Martin MacDonagh of the West of Ireland Tourist Development Association; and Howard Harrington, who represented not only the ITA but, more important, the Killarney area. These men went on to appoint an executive committee "representing various parts of the Free State." J. P. O'Brien was given the task of establishing an ITA office in College Street, Dublin.

Finding a compromise that would absolve the Oireachtas (Irish legislature) of unpleasant financial decision making while still securing the necessary money for tourism development was probably the single greatest reason behind the amalgamation of the various tourism bodies. On the one hand, without substantial income it would be impossible for any tourist organization "to undertake any comprehensive scheme likely to induce visitors to come to our various resorts and places of scenic attraction." On the other hand, there was no money and little political support for sweeping legislation despite a very vocal collection of important pro-tourism groups and individuals—many of them high in Ireland's social, economic, and political circles—who were demanding money for tourism development. By paving the way for the creation of a single tourism body, the government was able to placate the pro-tourism groups. At the same time the addition of Amendment 89 to the 1925 Local Government Act made it possible to shift responsibility for funding the unified association to county councils. The amendment allowed local authorities to levy rates for advertising "the attractions and scenery in their localities"[30] and to provide revenue to any association approved by the minister for industry and commerce. The minister for local government and public health would audit the approved organization. Technically, any approved tourism body could receive money, but only the Irish Tourist Association met the qualifications stipulated in the legislation. Crucially, the amendment did not require councils to levy a rate; instead, the decision rested with the councils themselves, and the Irish Tourist Association was thus forced to lobby councils in order to secure its income.[31]

The other major reason for creating a single tourism body was the need to present a unified front to English railway and transatlantic shipping companies that had already voiced a willingness to cooperate with a new Irish tourism organization.[32] A single national voice would facilitate easy communication and the efficient production and distribution of tourism materials. Likewise, centralization eliminated potential competition for distribution outlets; there would be no tendency for tourist bureaus in Galway, for example, to shun publicity materials from Killarney.

The Local Dimension

While the amalgamation of the Irish Tourist Association created a national tourism-development body (though not a statutory one), the need for local assistance was inescapable. Above all, development activities required the support of local groups. There were too many places to visit in Ireland for a single national organization with a minimal budget to promote successfully, and once tourists began to arrive in numbers, it was vital that the areas where these visitors were directed be ready to receive them. In addition, each locality had its own political concerns and interest groups, all with different ideas about tourism development. The ITA would need to address the concerns of these various groups if development and publicity work were to be successful. Finally, as mentioned earlier, the Irish Tourist Association was largely dependent on voluntary contributions by local authorities for its existence. If the ITA failed to meet local needs, then the authorities might cease to allocate money to the group.

As a result, the Irish Tourist Association's first priority was to carry its message that tourism was a national interest to local communities in order to establish local branches and support. The ITA argued that local organization would ensure progress on the national development front; guarantee regional improvements in lighting, sewerage, roads, and entertainment facilities; and attract tourists and their currency. While tourism was a national campaign, it would be unsuccessful unless local committees took charge of efforts in their areas.[33]

After meeting with J. P. O'Brien and other ITA representatives, the Killarney Tourist Association was created on 26 January 1924, making it one of the first and most important of the ITA's local branches. Like the ITA as a whole, the Killarney branch included such community leaders and leading businessmen as Senator William O'Sullivan, later chairman of Cosgrave's party in the Seanad (senate); the major local landowner, Lord Kenmare; several representatives of the Killarney Urban District Council; Howard Harrington (who attained his post as president of the ITA in 1926 largely because of his association with the Killarney branch); and others associated with local tourism. Like the ITA, the Killarney Tourist Association cited the betterment of Ireland as the primary reason for developing tourism. At the group's formation, Major Ross Kinloch MacGillycuddy, another major local landowner, stressed that the "object of this admirable association" should "appeal to every patriotic Irishmen" because it would encourage "the tide of travel to flow once again to our beautiful and ancient land" and would bring with it valuable foreign currency.[34] It was a tune that tourism interests sang repeatedly over much of the next seventy years—tourism was in the country's national interest, and patriots should do whatever they could to attract and please visitors.

Killarney was at the forefront of tourist impressions of Ireland, so the ITA was entirely justified when it endeavored to establish a local branch in the lakeside village before making similar efforts elsewhere. Killarney was an area that poets and travel writers alike had enthused about for nearly two hundred years, a beauty spot that headed almost every potential tourist's list of places to see in Ireland. While the government was keen to avoid becoming too deeply involved in tourism, it did not hurt that there was a widespread consensus that Killarney was the country's most notable tourist attraction. With Killarney firmly integrated into the ITA, the new body was well placed to maintain important political clout and to secure its position as the only organization approved by the minister of industry and commerce to receive money under the 1925 Local Government Act.

In addition to this successful effort to establish a local branch at Killarney, and even before passage of the Local Government Act, J. P. O'Brien and members of the ITA executive visited many other local authorities and community groups to encourage the formation of similar branches. Besides promising local groups regional publicity materials—the ITA's main function—the body quickly began trying to address local concerns in order to underline the extraordinary power of tourism to cure the nation's ills. With the exception of a handful of places such as Killarney, Tramore, and Glengarriff, local communities were not concerned with tourism per se, but they definitely favored the infrastructure improvements that the ITA suggested tourism could inspire; better roads, sewerage, and the development of a safe water supply were all required if tourism was to prove a viable undertaking, and more immediately, these things made life better for residents.

Dingle, today one of Ireland's leading tourist destinations, was little more than a run-down fishing village and a rural backwater in the wake of the Civil War. The *Kerryman* newspaper, which represented an influential pro-tourism voice during the 1920s, noted that Dingle's "isolated situation" and the nature of its soil effectively removed it from any list of viable sites for industrial development. As a result, the paper urged the town to focus its efforts on developing tourism, fisheries, and forestry.[35] In December 1924, J. P. O'Brien wrote to local community leaders to suggest that they form a committee to address tourism issues. He argued that this need was pressing because the Great Southern and Western Railway had already expressed interest in taking over the Dingle railway—a narrow-gauge rail line famous for its rather terrifying path through the mountains toward Dingle town. The town followed O'Brien's advice and a committee, chaired by the parish priest of Dingle, Canon John McDonnell, was nominated.[36] After a handful of meetings, which stressed the lack of good roads, poor sewerage, and the shortage of hotels, the committee lapsed into nonexistence.[37] Yet the ITA, helped along by the *Kerryman,* did not give up and continued to urge Dingle residents to take tourism seriously. ITA representatives also carried the message to Dublin that Dingle needed improvements. The sewage system was "positively dangerous," a "menace to public health." Among other things, sewage from the local fever hospital flowed down one of the town's streets, resulting in "unusual recurrent cases of fever."[38] Partly because of the ITA's pressure, the government moved to repair the sewage system in 1925.

Early in 1926, McDonnell once again urged Dingle community leaders to develop a local ITA branch. He "pointed out the importance of the tourist business in the district. Dingle would get all the overflow visitors from Killarney."[39] McDonnell chided the townspeople, saying that he "was amazed at the apathy of the people." He stressed the area's great natural beauty and its historical attractions such as the Gallarus Oratory and the views at Slea Head, and then noted that the roads were in a bad state and must be improved if the area were to attract large numbers of tourists.[40]

The committee was soon reestablished with McDonnell as chairman, and this time it had more staying power, largely because it was the only representative body in Dingle and therefore provided the only way in which the town could effectively make its case to the Kerry County Council and, more important, the central government. At its second meeting in March 1926 the re-formed branch passed a "strong resolution" calling for the "the bad state of the streets of Dingle" to be brought to the attention of the relevant authorities.[41] Almost immediately, just days after the passage of the resolution by the local ITA branch, there was "a decided improvement" in Dingle's streets. The new ITA branch was heartily praised in the *Kerryman* and was urged to continue focusing "attention on other local grievances with a view to having them rectified. Public cleanliness is an all-important factor, not only from the point of view of sanitation, but also as an attraction to the tourist. Nothing is so repulsive or more calculated to create a bad impression in the minds of tourists than muddy streets."[42]

The local ITA branch did continue to address local grievances, exerting at least as much of its energy on improving the welfare of the community itself as on publicizing the area's tourist attractions. In July 1926, for example, the group concerned itself with flooding in a local river that was "the dumping ground for every tin can and old bucket within three miles' radius of the town." This constant trash disposal impeded the flow of the river and caused an overpowering stench during the summer months. During the winter the river overflowed as a result of blockages brought about by the heaps of rubbish and caused widespread flooding that damaged local businesses and private homes. The local tourism committee argued, "As the Tourist Association is the only local body functioning at present, it should receive all practical support from the public. Though it has no financial resources nor executive powers, that it has a considerable weight has already been clearly manifested."[43] The precise nature of the grievance mattered relatively little; it was only important to the townspeople that "tourism" represented an excellent argument in favor of fixing whatever problem happened to arise.

Local improvement efforts by the ITA and its affiliated branches were certainly not limited to the area immediately surrounding Killarney, nor were they restricted to the period immediately following the ITA's formation. The town of Kinsale in County Cork, site of a famous battle in 1601 and near to the famously scenic Old Head of Kinsale, represents a prime example of further ITA efforts to address local grievances over an extended period. In this case the local representative body was the Kinsale Development Association, which concerned itself with all forms of local development, including signposting, hygiene, road building, industrial development, and tourism. In this capacity the Kinsale Development Association addressed the ITA on numerous occasions beginning around 1930 and continuing into the 1940s, even after the Irish Tourist Board was established in 1939.

The first appeal by the Kinsale Development Association concerned improvements to the main road between Cork City and Kinsale. The road had suffered considerable wear and tear in the years since its original grading in 1913. By April 1930 the Kinsale group had already received a grant from the Road Board for half the cost of repairs and was beginning to lobby the Cork County Council for funds to cover the remaining costs. Kinsale Development Association leaders argued in the main that the "very bad state" of the road was "militating severely against the commercial and tourist traffic in our district."[44] In addition to a published flyer urging the council to support its scheme, the Kinsale Development Association sent an envoy, Ernest E. Wolfe, to the ITA annual meeting in Dublin to generate publicity for the road improvements.[45] Wolfe worked hard, keeping Kinsale's plight front and center on the meeting agenda and stressing the potential revenue that Kinsale might generate from the brisk tourist trade that a satisfactory road would allow.[46] The strategy worked. Combined publicity and public pressure inspired action by the County Council at its budget meeting in February 1931. The Cork-Kinsale road project was allocated as much as £30,000 versus considerably smaller grants for similar projects in other parts of the county, which, when combined, earned a meager £12,500 in assistance.[47] Two years later, the Kinsale Development Association adopted a similar strategy to encourage improvements to the Kinsale-Garrettstown Road and then again, beginning in 1938, to stimulate development of the Kinsale water scheme that was designed to modernize the town's woefully inadequate water system.[48]

For most citizens, then, in the years immediately following the Civil War (and even down to the 1970s), tourism was an avenue toward local improvement, an excuse for enhancements in rural areas that otherwise showed little promise of development. By arguing that road or sewerage improvements might bring tourist revenue, it was possible to justify expenditure and to raise local claims to a higher place on the already packed agendas of local and central government bodies. In fact, the success of these arguments set a precedent that was expanded throughout the years covered by this study, and that made "tourism" a common argument for everything from enhanced signage to an end to logging, to environmental protection in rural areas, to the way in which housing developments should be designed. Tourism represented a national solution to local problems and was increasingly defined as a "national interest" by local communities during the late 1920s and the 1930s because of this fact.

The ITA's immediate effort to connect itself to local authorities had two important ramifications. First, it ensured that the ITA was always responsive to local concerns. Because councils considered their budgets annually, the central tourist organization was under constant pressure to meet local demands—a pressure that frequently caused the ITA difficulty. For example, in late 1926 County Kerry branches of the ITA became dissatisfied with the amount of publicity they were receiving in ITA publications. The problem began when two Killarney representatives informed the Kerry County Council that the central office of the ITA "gave no value for the money they got last year. The manner in which Killarney was advertised in the guide issued by them was most unsatisfactory, and as far as advertising outside or in the liners, not a single pamphlet dealing with Killarney was seen."[49] Initially, after the landowner and ITA supporter Major MacGillycuddy advised the council that it would not be wise to desert the national body, the council decided to provide the Killarney branch of the ITA with enough funding to produce its own guide, independent of the national organization, while continuing to provide annual funds to the national body. The interim decision did not last, however, and on 1 January 1927 the County Council resolved to withhold funds "as a protest against the remissness of the Central Executive of the Irish Tourist Association."[50]

Far beyond the damage inflicted by the subtraction of the annual contribution made to the ITA by the Kerry County Council, the loss of support from this vital tourist center had wider implications. Other councils, not blessed with Killarney's international reputation as a tourist destination, were often reluctant to support the ITA in the first place. Kilkenny, for example, made no great rush to join when its support was first solicited early in 1925. In response to the Kilkenny County Council's obstinacy, the ITA wrote to inform them "Kilkenny is now practically the only centre of importance which remains completely unorganised from the tourist point of view." The association observed that although Kilkenny lacked the same attractions found at Killarney, the ITA was especially anxious to provide publicity for the "underdeveloped resorts of Ireland." Despite this plea, the Kilkenny County Council deferred any decision to a later meeting.[51] A favorable decision by Kilkenny officials to support the ITA was delayed until 1927.[52]

In these circumstances, when such historic places as Kilkenny were already on the fence, for Kerry, the very epicenter of tourism, to withhold funds could well prove disastrous for the ITA. If the ITA could not serve its biggest client, how would it assist those areas with fewer scenic attractions? To avoid wider unpleasantness, the ITA quickly began courting the Kerry County Council. To assuage the concerns of the important regional legislators, on 29 January 1927 the ITA altered its bylaws to allow local authorities that contributed more than £100 per annum to nominate a member to its board of directors. While this decision greatly increased the size of the board, it also left local authorities with the impression that they would have a much greater say in tourism policy.[53] The dispute with the Kerry County Council was resolved shortly thereafter.[54]

The second major implication of the close relationship between ITA leaders and local authorities was the organization's ability to speak for local interests—a capability that served it well even into the 1950s and early 1960s. Forced into constant contact with local power brokers, often bending over backward to meet demands such as the one described above, the ITA was made intimately aware of local concerns and could then relay them to the central government in Dublin.

Inside the Coven

While the Irish Tourist Association was increasingly effective at bringing its message of national renewal through tourism to local communities, it was certainly not universally successful. For those outside of tourism centers even the promise of infrastructural improvement rang hollow. During the 1920s and 1930s counties like Roscommon and Cavan simply did not attract tourists, so it was difficult to imagine that tourism might have any positive benefits there. It was hard to connect the dots between farmers and hoteliers—difficult to imagine that farmers received income from hotels and restaurants that catered to tourists, let alone that once foreign currency entered the pockets of Irish entrepreneurs, it eventually made its way into those of employees and then on to Irish shops and businesses. Even those with college degrees did not always make the connection. In fact, some of the staff hired by J. P. O'Brien to manage tourism from the ITA's Dublin office did not fully understand the role that successful tourism could play in a national or regional economy. For example, well-known civil servant C. S. (Todd) Andrews,[55] who worked at the ITA in the late 1920s after receiving an accounting degree from University College, Dublin (UCD), "conceived [of tourism] as . . . operating for the benefit of foreign visitors rather than for its native Irish employees. At that time tourism was very much in its infancy, and its commercial possibilities were still unexplored. I did not appreciate its value as an invisible export or its potential contribution to the national economy."[56] Perhaps as a result, Andrews did not approve of the idea "of an Ireland swarming with tourists."

As the Todd Andrews example suggests, being employed by the Irish Tourist Association did not necessarily imply a deep devotion to tourism. In fact, the ITA office staff were hired more for their political connections than for any passion for the development of tourism—a striking contrast to the ITA's membership and executive committee, whose passion for tourism knew no bounds. After being instructed to set up the ITA's first office in 1925, O'Brien immediately fell back on his republican connections and surrounded himself with "a coven of ex-IRA men who had opposed the government in arms."[57] O'Brien, like many republicans following the Civil War, was intensely loyal to his anti-treaty colleagues. Advertisements were placed, but the successful candidate was hired based on word of mouth among republicans. Andrews, for example, was determined not to emigrate after completing his degree at UCD. He ferreted around for work and eventually, in 1926, ran across an ITA advertisement for an organizer. After consulting with Seamus Moore, a friend and newly elected TD (Teachta Dála, member of the Irish parliament), Andrews was accorded a meeting with Jack O'Brien. It did not take long for the two men to discover that they knew one another from the Civil War. Andrews remembers that their first post–Civil War meeting largely involved "recalling our previous meetings, reminiscing on the Civil War, and discussing the new departure in the republican movement brought about by the formation of the Fianna Fáil party." While O'Brien did not find Andrews suitable for the advertised position, he immediately offered him a job as the ITA's accountant, even making a special request to the ITA executive in order to secure an extra £1 per week for Andrews.[58]

When Andrews started work, he found that he was by no means the only ex-IRA man on the premises. O'Brien's second-in-command was a man named David Barry who had served with the IRA in north Cork. Barry's primary role was to solicit funding from hotels, travel agencies, local authorities, and other businesses. The small staff also included Sean Fitzpatrick, a former adjutant of the Third Tipperary Brigade of the IRA, whose experience with printing qualified him to handle the ITA's publishing requirements. While no longer active members of the IRA, the entire staff were dedicated supporters of Éamon de Valera. In contrast to O'Brien's staff, the

ITA board, then headed by J. C. Foley, who was a close friend and backer of W. T. Cosgrave, was made up of "men of substance" who were "all strong supporters of the Free State regime and some were active politically."[59]

Although none of the above-mentioned staff was active in the republican movement while working for the ITA, the Free State's continued political turmoil did find its way into the ITA office when Andrews was asked to hire somebody to help increase the number of brochures and guidebooks. Andrews, perhaps unwisely, hired a young man whom he had met as part of University College Dublin's Republican Club, Frank Ryan. Ryan had little if any interest in tourism—indeed, he was actively fighting against the state that he now worked to promote to largely English visitors. This detail did not bother Andrews, who simply warned Ryan not to store IRA documents or other materials in the ITA offices. Ryan disregarded the warning, however, and it was not long before Criminal Investigations Division (CID) raided the Tourist Association offices, where they found a cache of IRA files. When asked, Andrews denied any knowledge of the documents, of Ryan's ownership of them, or even of the police raid, saying that "from time to time I lost my sight and hearing, and . . . I must have been blind and deaf during the raid and the subsequent interrogation."[60] Ryan was arrested and held overnight but then released. He quickly resigned his post at the ITA.

The Many Meanings of Tourism

Even in places like Killarney where tourism was broadly considered an important part of life, there were differences of opinion about how it should be developed. For most tourism supporters the development of tourism was directly connected to the desired development of Irish industry and to the construction of a vibrant economy in the wake of Ireland's period of armed conflict. But debate about tourism was also caught in the "confused baggage of ideas" inherited from nineteenth-century nationalists, which called for both the preservation of traditional society *and* industrialization.[61] On the one hand, some, such as many Gaelic-language enthusiasts, wanted to preserve Irish life as it had always been (at least in their imaginings). For these individuals tourists represented "a formidable influx of foreignism" and a "deadly threat" to traditional rural life.[62] Meanwhile, on the other hand, O'Brien and the ITA promised that tourism "developed on proper business lines can be made a source of untold revenue" for County Kerry and Ireland more generally,[63] and they stressed that revenue from tourism would be vital if Ireland was to be able to recover from its economic misfortunes.[64] It followed that local ITA branches, like the one at Cobh, stressed the need for "the co-operation of all residents of all classes of society."[65]

The expectation that "all classes" of society should contribute to tourism development had a dark side; the pro-tourism faithful showed little tolerance for statements or activities that might undermine their efforts. Tourism was a national duty and to question tourism development policy was considered unpatriotic behavior. Given the conflicting messages that nationalists transmitted about the desire for industrialization and the dream of maintaining a rural society, conflict was almost inevitable: the two ideas simply do not easily connect. Modernization cannot occur without altering the way of life experienced in rural areas; the need for faster production necessarily accelerates life, reduces the number of workers required to make a larger number of products, and alters attitudes toward time. Tourism, the ITA's great harbinger of modernity, was no different from other modernizing forces in its general effects.

Since at least the early 1900s the tourist experience in Killarney invariably involved a boat trip between the upper and lower lakes aboard a small boat rowed by at least two of the local "boatmen." Along the way tourists visited the "Meeting of the Waters" at Old Weir Bridge, negotiated some mild rapids, and listened to the boatmen spin their unique version of local lore. Tourists who did not have the time for the longer journey also tended to make use of the boatmen's services by traveling to the various islands of the lower lake.

With the foundation of the ITA, tourism developers imagined almost infinite growth of the industry and began looking for ways to service more and more visitors in an increasingly efficient manner. During the 1920s most Killarney tourists were English men and women who arrived aboard excursion trains run by the Great Southern and Western Railway Company. Trains left London for Holyhead, tourists traveled across the Irish Sea on a ferry, and then the railway whisked them across the Emerald Isle to Killarney. Each season thousands of visitors poured in, made the rounds of Ross Castle, the Gap of Dunloe, and Muckross Abbey, and paid a visit to the boatmen on the famous lakes. Given the tight train schedule, and the fact that the trips

1. Killarney boatmen row tourists to the famous "Meeting of the Waters." Courtesy of Bord Fáilte Éireann–Irish Tourist Board.

were marketed as efficient holidays for busy English visitors, the excursionists enjoyed only a very short stay at Killarney before their train raced them back to London. Recognizing the potential logjam that a growing flood of tourists might cause, and believing that tourists ultimately wanted an efficient and thoroughly "modern" experience, the Killarney branch of the ITA argued that it would be necessary to introduce motor launches to the Killarney lakes—a view that was violently rejected by the boatmen.

The ITA first seriously considered the motor-launch idea on 16 October 1925 after hearing comments made by representatives from the Great Western Railway, who promised to double the number of Killarney tourists in 1926 if the efficiency of the boat trip could be improved.[66] The Killarney tourist authorities were stunned by the idea of such tourist traffic and quickly agreed to add the motorboats. As far as the ITA was concerned, "Killarney must not and cannot be kept back."[67] If tourists wanted motor launches, then they should have them.

The boatmen were horrified. Even before the Great Western proposal was made, the boatmen expressed the belief that motorboats should not be allowed on any of the Killarney lakes because even if initially limited to the lower lake, they "would soon spread out their influence, putting the boatmen out of business"—a plea that had evidently brought immediate assurances from the ITA (in 1924) that no such outcome would ever be allowed.[68] Just one year later, however, the association completely reversed itself. Insult was added to injury when Howard Harrington accused the boatmen of being unpatriotic.[69] The boatmen did not appreciate having their patriotism and local pride questioned by an American interloper, and they quickly lashed out in a letter to the *Kerryman*, claiming that local hoteliers cared only for their own pocketbooks, not for the town's or country's good fortune, and that others in the association merely hoped to advance their own social and political fortunes through membership. Harrington, they complained, "is only a very short time here, but he acts already as if he found Killarney and owned it."[70] What right had a "blow-in" to question their patriotism and local pride or to undermine time-honored tradition? The boatmen represented 150 native residents of the community, and their way of life mattered enough that they were willing to fight the proposed change, hinting that physical violence was not out of the question. Although the association replied by offering the boatmen a monopoly on the motor-launch business, assuring them that the ITA had no desire to put anybody out of work, the boatmen were impervious to argument on the matter.

The conflict soon widened. The *Kerryman* attacked the boatmen and picked at each of the boatmen's arguments, demeaning them as "expressions of undiluted vulgarity . . . intended for savage sarcasm [but amounting] to nothing more than coarse buffoonery symptomatic of the low-caste mentality responsible for them."[71] As far as the *Kerryman* was concerned, "'Advance Killarney!' must be the slogan; and it cannot advance if we are satisfied to wage war on progressive methods."[72] Press attacks on the boatmen did not end at the Kerry border. The *Irish Independent*, one of Ireland's leading national newspapers, argued that Killarney's tourist development was threatened by "the short-sighted policy of the local boatmen in opposing the introduction of motorboats."[73] In turn, press coverage inspired letter writers who insisted, "Attacking men like Mr. Harrington of Dunloe will do no good. He is at any rate an Irishman who is proud of his Irish ancestry and not like some of the so-called Irish-Irelanders, who send their children to England to acquire an English accent."⁷⁴

At its heart, then, the motor-launch issue had become a nexus for discussion of precisely what it meant to be Irish. For the Irish Tourist Association and the promodernization media, motor launches were a way to increase tourist income and to make Killarney prosperous and Ireland a modern, forward-looking nation. For the boatmen the issue went deeper. Motorboats represented a direct attack on everything they knew and understood. The motorboats were an emasculating result of modernity. Worse still, the boats were suggested by an *English* company and were being pushed down the people's throats by an *American* newcomer. It was a debate about tradition versus modernity, about time-honored ways of earning a living versus a mind-numbing new world, and about insiders versus outsiders defining how life should be lived. In this instance tradition won out and the motor-launch debate retreated into unspoken memory. The available sources do not explain why the ITA dropped the issue, but the outcome probably owed more to financial considerations than to anything else. Although the local landowner, the Earl of Kenmare, approved of the use of motor launches on the lower lake, he did not offer to purchase the boats.⁷⁵ Likewise, with the boatmen obviously unwilling to purchase new launches, the onus fell on the ITA, which lacked the required funds. Killarney's lakes would have to wait until the 1950s to absorb the exhaust of motorized pleasure craft.

Investing in Tourism

Even while juggling political differences between the ITA executive and its staff, the Frank Ryan distraction, conflict over how tourism development should proceed, and the shoestring budget of roughly £10,000 per annum, the association forged ahead with its efforts to promote tourism and to publicize Irish attractions. By 1929 the ITA was producing thirty-six separate publications each year, covering places such as Killarney, Cork City, and Dublin among others—totaling some 1.5 million pieces of literature—as well as a monthly travel magazine called *Irish Travel*.⁷⁶ While most of these were local guides, the ITA also published a comprehensive *Official Guide* to Ireland starting in 1925. The *Official Guide* offered visitors information about Irish antiquities, language, and culture, and then highlighted sites and sights in all regions of the country.

The considerable cost of publishing the guides was supplemented by advertising placed by various clients. Foremost among these were hotels, railway companies, and Irish resorts. There were also ads, however, for linen manufactures, the Abbey Theatre, whiskey, cigarettes, and even portrait companies.[77] Irish businesses had a variety of motivations for supporting the Irish Tourist Association. For those directly dependent on tourist traffic, like hoteliers, ITA publications were an obvious advertising outlet and the association's success an important investment. For others, linen manufacturers for example, tourists represented a potentially valuable market sector. But corporate motives were not always obvious. Guinness, for example, has made quite a name for itself through creative advertising since at least the 1930s, yet its support of the Irish Tourist Association had little to do with a perceived advertising benefit. Instead, Guinness, perhaps the Free State's single largest private corporation, supported the ITA because the company believed that doing so was its patriotic obligation.

The Tourist Association, represented by its then president Senator Moran and by David Barry, first approached Guinness for support on 7 July 1925. They explained the aims of the association and showed Guinness officials a copy of the *Official Guide*, some ITA advertisements, and the organization's list of Irish hotels.[78] After the meeting Guinness officials noted that both an historic precedent and the reputable nature of the ITA membership supported giving a favorable response to the plea. Historically, Guinness had supported Frederick W. Crossley's late nineteenth- and early twentieth-century attempt at a tourist-development organization, also called the Irish Tourist Association, with a modest contribution of £25 in 1915.[79] In addition, the men noted that Senator Moran was "an important person in Dublin" whose interest in tourism was understandable and obvious.[80] More important, Guinness officials remarked that "the betterment of Ireland" had "become most fashionable."[81] Based on these points, the General Purposes Sub-Committee resolved to provide a £100 contribution to the association—one of the largest grants received by the ITA during this early period.[82] For Guinness, the ITA represented "one of those appeals" that required a positive response "on account of our position in Ireland." It was unlikely that the ITA would generate any real money for the brewery.[83]

"See Ireland First"

As noted previously, ITA officials encouraged cooperation with their movement, but cooperation could involve any number of activities ranging from providing money to actively assisting tourists. For most of those involved, the best way to support the tourism crusade was to "see Ireland first." According to the ITA, "a healthy option has been created in Ireland this year that the wisest, and certainly the most patriotic, thing Irish people can do is to see their own country in their holiday-time."[84] Viewing Ireland would not only acquaint Irish people with the Irish landscape and its "unique attractions," but it would assure that Ireland was not exporting its own people as tourists.[85]

The phrase "See Ireland First" paraphrased an older American tourism campaign, "See America First," and the choice of slogan is telling. In the United States, "See America First" was first used as the title for a Western tourism conference held at Salt Lake City in 1906. The words were subsequently utilized as the title of a magazine and in limited advertising campaigns conducted by the See America First League. It was only after American railway companies adopted the phrase that it truly ignited a mass movement, however. "See America First" was about making money, but it was also an expression of patriotism and of the desire to unify the American people. For the railway companies, tourism not only promised to help turn a profit, it represented an important component of nation building. The campaign worked. Tourist traffic aboard America's railways increased dramatically. The new national parks grew ever more popular. In fact, the program was so successful that there was even an unsuccessful attempt to copyright the phrase "see America first" so that it might remain associated with Glacier National Park.[86] In the same spirit, for the ITA the phrase "See Ireland First" represented both potential economic advantage and, just as important, the same nation-building mission behind its American inspiration.

The ITA's "See Ireland First" program involved posters, brochures, statements in the press, and tourist maps, but it also found its way more directly into every Irish home through the post office. The story is instructive of different views within government departments concerning tourism during the early days of the Free State. In May 1925 the Irish Tourist Association wrote to the Department of Posts and Telegraphs, requesting that post office mechanical stamping machines be fitted with die hubs bearing the words "See Ireland First" between May and September each year. J. Booth, a civil servant in the Department of Posts and Telegraphs, noted that fitting out the machines would cost the association £221, not including a fee for advertising. The department was concerned, however, because the advertisement did not relate directly to any government or official administrative project. Ordinarily this request might have been straightforward enough because the government would simply have charged the advertiser for use of the space, but in this case "the attraction of tourists by the Irish Tourist Association is likely to benefit the country materially, and the Minister for Posts and Telegraphs considers that the privilege of the advertisement should be free of charge."[87] H. P. Boland, then serving in the Department of Finance, did not see the matter in the same terms, however. He threw cold water on the scheme: "We [the Department of Finance] incline to the view that this means of advertising should be regarded primarily as available for governmental purposes, such as the Post Office Savings Bank, savings certificates, etc.," and should only be available to other interests, regardless of the potential national benefit, when the government could not find any product to advertise. As a compromise, the Department of Posts and Telegraphs decided to charge the ITA a nominal advertising fee of £20.[88] The terms were subsequently agreed, and the association continued to utilize this outlet into the 1930s.

The Need for Government Action

While the ITA was successful in establishing local branches, in obtaining support from local authorities, and in encouraging a growing number of people to contribute to the tourism campaign, tourism was not a political issue during either of the general elections held in 1927. Major candidates, whether from the ruling Cumann na nGaedheal party, the Labour party, or de Valera's newly formed Fianna Fáil, focused on agriculture and industrial development—as well as on attacking the other parties—rather than on tourism. Even Eugene O'Sullivan, an independent from County Kerry who was chairman of the Killarney branch of the ITA and ran in the first election of 1927,⁸⁹ seldom mentioned tourism as a campaign issue, instead focusing on the more politically salient issues of agriculture and fisheries.⁹⁰ Most of the voting public did not understand the significance of tourism, and even in County Kerry most voters displayed little interest.

As in 1924–25, the lack of public political interest during the late 1920s and early 1930s did not mean that the government completely ignored tourism. Cumann na nGaedheal was warmly supported by most of the ITA executive, and the party could not completely dismiss tourism as a result. The government was well aware that the 1925 Local Government Act created two closely related problems for the successful development of the tourist industry. First, the act did not *require* local authorities to contribute to the ITA. Second, local authorities determined their annual budgets on a yearly basis and so were able to regularly reconsider their contributions to the ITA, making it impossible for the association to engage in long-term planning.⁹¹ As much as the government believed that the current legislation provided an efficient and economical approach to tourism development, they had to admit that the association's annual income of just over £10,000 in 1930 was inadequate for the job at hand.⁹²

In May 1931 the government proposed legislation designed to push local authorities to give money to "one recognised [tourist] association," unless special permission was acquired from the minister for industry and commerce to forego payment. Under the new proposal local authorities would provide this funding over a multiyear contract, not in one-year installments, allowing the approved tourist-development organization to plan ahead.

Although the proposal was far from revolutionary, during the course of the Seanad and Dáil debates surrounding the bill, a variety of objections were raised that illustrate the poor understanding, even among Irish leaders, of tourism's economic role, the problems facing Irish tourism development, and the ideological divide between the two main political parties. Ministerial misunderstanding of tourism's economic role is primarily visible in concern over the concept of levying rates to support tourist development. Senator Thomas Linehan voiced a concern that was echoed by several others: "It seems very strange that the cost of developing that traffic, which will benefit the entire country and every class in the country alike, should be placed altogether on the ratepayers." In particular, farmers faced a significant burden under the legislation, and Linehan remarked, "The benefits derived from a development of tourist traffic are of interest to the farmers in a very small way only." Given these facts, the senator believed that, in the interest of fairness the necessary money should be provided out of the Central Fund in the form of government aid, not further taxation.

There were also justifiable concerns about whether Ireland could handle substantial tourist traffic. Fianna Fáil Senator Seán E. MacEllin, for example, noted, "I know that in the western districts of Ireland it can hardly be said that the tourist areas are ready for foreigners. The roads are almost impassable, and the sanitary accommodation is on the poor side. There are very few, if any, water supply schemes."[93] Indeed, these problems were very real. Even in the 1950s few hotels were available in most tourist centers. In Dublin during the early 1950s there were just twelve rooms with a bath, and far fewer rooms without baths than were needed;[94] the situation was undoubtedly far worse in the 1930s. Evidently it was unclear to MacEllin, and to others who agreed with him, that tourist-development legislation might help eliminate the shortage.

Lastly, there were a series of complaints that stemmed from the ideological divide and bitterness between the two major parties. Cumann na nGaedheal believed in tourism development as long as it did not cost the government anything. Meanwhile, Fianna Fáil was primarily concerned with the development of self-sufficiency, the creation of native industries,[95] and the use of tariffs to support Irish businesses[96]—hardly policies that coexisted easily with the ITA's close ties to English rail companies or with the industry's dependence on English tourists. Seán Lemass, later one of the greatest government advocates for tourism, expressed his party's objections to the legislation in an extensive Dáil debate. First, Lemass argued that devoting significant resources to tourism development was foolish because "we have not in this country either the climate or the facilities" to compete with continental destinations. In view of this situation Lemass asked why the country should spend time, energy, and money on external visitors when Irish tourism interests could direct their efforts toward attracting Irish visitors who would not only be interested in Ireland, but who would ensure Ireland's self-sufficiency by avoiding the export of Irish tourists to foreign destinations. Apparently Lemass had not yet absorbed the realities of tourism development since 1924, or, for that matter, looked at his mail, which had been stamped with "See Ireland First" for several years.

One by one, Cumann na nGaedheal ministers pointed out that the ITA *was* attracting many foreign visitors—most of them from Britain—despite having to compete with more sunny destinations. These visitors came to see beautiful scenery and to enjoy outdoor sporting activities such as fishing and hunting—the same activities that had attracted English visitors since Victoria and Albert popularized such pursuits in the 1840s during their frequent visits to Balmoral Castle in Scotland, as well as during their visit to Ireland in August 1849. One deputy pointed out:

> These results [the economic advantages of tourism] are not fully appreciated because the advantages in money spent are very often hidden. We have tourists coming into this country who do not merely spend money in travel and in living here for [a] time, but by acquiring objects which are made in the country, and these things are not always taken into consideration. A great deal of the business which is done with the tourists is not shown at all in the results given by the Tourist Association.[97]

Patrick Hogan, a deputy from County Clare, suggested that Lemass was not well informed about the activities of the ITA, and that the association was actually working to attract "every likely type of tourist." Another deputy added that the ITA had already been conducting a campaign "urging our people to patronize the many beautiful watering places we have in the country during the holiday season."

This defense of the association did not impress Lemass given that his party enjoyed little support from the powerful ITA executive. Lemass wanted to ensure that the ITA's existence was not cast in legislative stone, and he replied by asking whether the minister for industry and commerce would be willing to support another tourist organization, or whether the legislation would enshrine the ITA into Irish law as *the* national tourist body. Patrick McGilligan, the minister for industry and commerce, replied by saying that in the unlikely event that another tourist association emerged, the ITA's certificate could be revoked. This reply was enough for Fianna Fáil. As long as it was legally possible to withdraw the ITA's sanction without further legislation, Fianna Fáil had the option to support a new tourism organization that lacked the ITA's unfavorable political leanings. The Tourist Traffic Act subsequently passed on 27 May 1931.

A New Expression of Nationalism

Fianna Fáil won over 45 percent of the vote in the 1932 general election, taking seventy-two seats to Cumann na nGaedheal's fifty-seven, thus moving Ireland into a new chapter of its political history.[98] If the Irish people had voted for change, they certainly got it. De Valera's new government quickly moved to stop paying annuities to the United Kingdom as mandated by the Anglo-Irish Treaty. This move precipitated a spiraling exchange of tariffs and countertariffs.[99] The so-called "Economic War" was under way—a conflict that had a much greater impact on agriculture than it ever did on tourism. Despite the crisis over tariffs and countertariffs, the tourist business grew steadily throughout the 1930s, and the number of British tourists increased from just over 245,000 in 1932 to nearly 318,000 by 1936.[100]

Beyond failing to honor distasteful aspects of the Anglo-Irish Treaty, the new government pursued Fianna Fáil's long-term goal of creating indigenous industry in the hope of creating a self-sufficient Ireland. In the present context the most important Fianna Fáil efforts involved the creation of semistate companies. These included the Industrial Credit Company, Bórd na Móna (the Turf Board), the Irish Life Assurance Board, Industrial Alcohol Factories Limited, Aer Lingus, and the Irish Tourist Board.[101] As far as tourism is concerned, the last two of these were exceptionally important as well as intimately connected. Aer Lingus developed largely as a result of Seán Lemass's long-term fascination with aviation that began when, as a young man, he spent his free time watching airplanes taking off at Leopardstown racecourse.[102] Lemass believed that a national airline could prove a significant asset by ensuring national control of its external communications and by providing a second line of defense in case of emergency.[103] In addition, the existence of a national airline would protect the country's vital interests in trade and tourism if foreign airlines should choose not to serve Ireland.[104] But the airline's supporters had larger goals than defense or control of communications in mind, and they hoped, among other things, to make Ireland the international junction for air traffic between North America and Europe and to connect the Free State directly to other "principal countries."[105] It was an ambitious program, given that at the time Aer Lingus was operating only two aircraft, on two routes, using a temporary military airfield as its base of operations.

According to Michael Kevin O'Doherty, who served as private secretary to Lemass from 1944 to 1946 before moving to the Irish Tourist Board (where he worked in various capacities until the late 1960s), Lemass's interest in tourism developed directly from his passion for aviation.[106] For Aer Lingus to be successful it would need to carry as many people in and out of Ireland as possible, making tourists essential. Even so, it is equally important to stress Lemass's relationship with J. P. O'Brien, which stretched back to the Civil War when the two men had fought together. Lemass was intensely loyal, and O'Brien was a staunch believer in the central role of tourism in Ireland's national revival. There is every reason to believe that O'Brien used his important government contact to continue the ITA's tourism crusade.

Although Lemass had made certain that the ITA could be eliminated under the 1931 Tourist Traffic Act, when he became minister for industry and commerce he soon realized that such an action was virtually impossible because the ITA had firmly established itself as *the* national tourism body. Those who were interested in tourism were already ITA members and could not be called upon to create a new voluntary body. Perhaps more important, the ITA's long-standing policy of getting as close as possible to the local authorities made the ITA all but untouchable. Any attempt to undermine the ITA could be perceived as an attack by Dublin on local autonomy.

Any hope of extricating the tourism crusade from the hands of the Irish Tourist Association lay in creating a semistate body to handle tourism development. Several newly created semistate bodies, which Lemass preferred to call "state-sponsored,"[107] were already relatively successful; they made it possible to "substitute state enterprise when private initiative was lacking,"[108] while still maintaining a certain amount of state control even as the government was able to distance itself from day-to-day management concerns.

John Leydon, a very competent civil servant whose close working relationship with Lemass proved invaluable to the successful realization of many of the minister's plans, circulated Lemass's solution to the tourism question as an open letter to government departments on 18 May. Leydon stressed the minister's newfound belief in the importance of tourism "as a factor in the national economy and, more particularly, from the point of view of its effect on the balance of international payments." For Lemass it was no longer acceptable to follow the state's previous "passive" tourism policy. Leydon and Lemass argued that the ITA's inadequate budget, combined with the costly need to improve the poor condition and small number of Irish hotels, made it impossible for the ITA to continue to serve as the primary national tourism-advocacy body. Above all,

> the holiday habit has grown enormously in recent years and has received a new impetus from recent legislation giving workers holidays with pay. There can be no doubt that in future there will be almost unlimited scope for the development of tourist traffic in view of the fact that so many workers are now enjoying holidays with pay who never before enjoyed the privilege of a holiday. These people will require information as to how and where to spend a holiday and what the approximate cost will be, and naturally more accommodation will be necessary to receive them, and more attractions to secure their patronage.

The solution was to create "more effective machinery" that could better carry out tourism development: a statutory tourist body was needed.[109]

None of this meant that the Irish Tourist Association should be abandoned. On the surface Lemass and Leydon argued that to focus the ITA's efforts on advertising was justified because the proposed tourism company would be empowered to own and operate hotels—a potential conflict of interest if it were also creating publicity materials. There were two unstated reasons, however. First, to dissolve the ITA would risk alienating local authorities and important regional ITA branches, not to mention important business interests who were directly involved with the association, while to preserve the association might make it possible to make use of these connections to the benefit of the new tourist authority. Furthermore, the Irish Tourist Association had created the crusade to persuade people of the importance of tourism, and by so doing, it was symbolically connected to national perceptions of tourism. The new tourist legislation was designed to create greater government control over tourism development, and the legitimacy of this activity required channeling the ITA's symbolic monopoly to government advantage.

While well conceived politically, economically, and symbolically from Lemass's perspective, the proposal elicited immediate objections from within the Department of Finance, the Department of External Affairs, and even the Land Commission. These objections were based on differing ideas about the role of government, not on any opposition to tourism development as carried out by the ITA. As far as the Land Commission was concerned, no semistate body should have rights to the compulsory acquisition of land for hotels, guest houses, game, and so forth, because this right would directly conflict with the commission's powers to acquire land for the purpose of assisting the so-called congested districts. Likewise, the commission feared that any such acquisition of land might easily inspire corruption by allowing the Tourist Board to blatantly cater to specific interests.[110] On another front a civil servant within the Department of External Affairs pointed out that companies should create revenue for their shareholders—something that no "state company" was designed to accomplish. State-sponsored companies were "dressed up with capital, powers, objects, and articles, but with nowhere to go."[111] Meanwhile, civil servants in the Department of Finance argued that private enterprise should be counted on to develop tourism; government handouts were not the answer. If such enterprise had been lacking, it was because potential developers recognized that Irish resort tourism was not different enough from English destinations to warrant more substantial investment. If anything, the government should devote itself to improving local water and sewerage services and then offer grants to assist private interests, not create a new organization devoted to carrying out development on its own at great expense.[112] Likewise, a civil servant in the Department of External Affairs suggested increasing the rates allotted to the ITA in order to provide loans to local authorities for tourism and hotel development, to support cooperation with the association on training hotel workers, and to provide the association with the power to prosecute hoteliers who failed to live up to agreed hotel standards.[113] Despite these objections, no department nor any civil servant opposed the need to develop tourism. As far as most officials were concerned, it made sense to increase the advertising budget currently allotted to the Irish Tourist Association, even if a semistate development body were not created.[114]

Birth of a Tourist Board

Despite the opposition within government departments, Seán Lemass used the annual ITA meeting in Dublin on 25 October 1938 to announce that he would soon introduce substantial tourism legislation. The existing system was inadequate and the existing policy framework had to be abandoned in favor of something dramatic. He promised a budget of at least half a million pounds for the new organization and stressed that there were simply not adequate facilities in Ireland to handle any large influx of tourists. While the new tourist board would not "normally interfere with private enterprise," it would be empowered to build and operate hotels and to provide or assist in providing "services, amenities, amusements, or other attractions" for tourists. Beyond these tasks, the new tourist board would carry out publicity programs and would train tourism, restaurant, and hotel employees. Further, the Irish Tourist Board (ITB) was also to work with prospective tourist guides, assuring that visitors encountered the very best narration of Irish life. Should new tourism agencies be required, the new tourism body was empowered to create them. Finally, the ITB would administer a voluntary system of registration whereby boarding houses, restaurants, hotels, and cafes would sign on with the tourist authority so that tourists could be assured of a quality experience. Meanwhile, the Irish Tourist Association would continue to function with financial support from the Irish Tourist Board added to its previous income sources, but it would confine itself "to non-commercial activities, as it is not a body equipped for commercial enterprise."[115]

After Lemass's presentation the Irish Tourist Association remained confident in its position and was generally positive about the proposal. The only major concern was that the legislation might ultimately infringe on private enterprise by creating a government-supported tourism monopoly, but this objection was quickly set aside. Had not Lemass specifically said that there would be no such conflict? The new legislation represented no threat to tourism interests or to the ITA, while it would provide greater resources to the industry as a whole.[116]

The Tourist Traffic Act of 1939 created the Irish Tourist Board. This body had the power to acquire lands and the ability to inspect hotels and to prosecute proprietors whose premises were defined as "hotel," "guest house," "holiday camp," or "youth hostel" and who failed to meet the ITB's standards for each respective type of accommodation. The board could establish special tourism areas, operate hotel training programs, provide funds to local authorities for development projects, and operate its own hotels, not to mention engage in publicity activities such as the publication of guidebooks. If there was a catch, it was that the board was expected to do all of this on a budget of £45,000 per year, with access to only £600,000 in repayable loans.[117]

The tourist industry generally welcomed the act because it "puts our country ahead of all others in the matter of comprehensive legislative measures calculated to ensure at once the scientific development of our wonderful tourist resources and the elimination of sources of complaint and annoyance to tourists."[118] For tourism leaders this was legislation to be proud of, a powerful statement that Ireland was moving in the right direction—the direction of modernity—and was far outstripping other countries by creating a tourism body concerned with more than just publicity. Ireland was acting like a mature state that could be proud of its ability to deal with the big issues.

When J. P. O'Brien assumed his post as the newly appointed chairman of the Irish Tourist Board and began taking steps toward beginning operations, it seemed that the Irish Tourist Association had been widely successful in convincing much of the country that tourism was an important national interest; the government had finally committed itself to investing in tourism development, and the road ahead seemed clear. Of course, there were still differing opinions about the symbolic meanings of tourism, but the ITA's view of tourism now appeared to dominate. The future seemed bright for Irish tourism until Germany invaded Poland, and then nothing was certain anymore.

2
Developing Irish Tourism, 1939–1958

The newly created Irish Tourist Board barely had time to set up its offices in Dublin before tourism was once again the topic of widespread debate. The reality of war imposed new priorities on the Irish state that did not include tourism. Above all, de Valera's government wanted to remain nonaligned.[1] Neutrality was widely seen as the best way of symbolically asserting Irish independence from Britain, and many viewed it as the "acid test" for Ireland's freedom.[2] In addition, the state was not immediately under threat, and there was little to justify suffering through the horrors of war.[3] Ireland was still recovering from the struggle for independence and subsequent civil war, it faced widespread unemployment, it lacked an adequate industrial base to develop a munitions industry,[4] and it could not afford the spending required to support a war-ready military.[5]

To preserve its neutrality while maintaining domestic stability, the government implemented a widespread censorship program in the hope of keeping "'the temperature down,' both internally and between Ireland and the belligerents." Politicians hoped that the program would maintain the unity of the population by suppressing potentially divisive comments or threats to public order.[6] In order to further ensure stability, the government paid particular attention to managing the country's scarce provisions. The demand for consumables simply was not met by the supply. Gas, coal, clothes, tea and sugar, bread, and coffee were all rationed.[7] The rationing program was such a high priority that it led to the first major cabinet changes since 1932.[8] Seán Lemass became minister of the newly created Department of Supplies, Seán MacEntee was the new minister for industry and commerce, and Seán T. O'Kelly assumed control of the Department of Finance.[9] With few jobs, high emigration, and an endless string of difficult decisions to be made,[10] to say nothing of the fact that for much of the war tourists could not get to Ireland owing to grounded flights and dangerous seas, tourism was once again a low priority. This chapter traces the effort by tourist groups to convince the government and the public—both during the war and afterward, when a political crisis erupted over tourism policy—that ongoing development of tourism continued to be in the national interest. It was not until 1952 that tourism was once again widely considered an important national priority at government level, and the industry began to achieve increased public support only after an extended pro-tourism educational campaign. To reestablish tourist development as a national interest was an uphill battle, but it was one that ultimately set the basic policy framework for Irish tourism efforts through the late 1950s, and it shaped the appearance of Irish tourism throughout the rest of the twentieth century.

Tourism During Wartime

On 4 September 1939, one day after Britain declared war on Germany, J. P. O'Brien learned of the probable suspension of the Tourist Traffic Act "for as long as the Emergency Powers Act, 1939, continues in force."[11] The tourism chief wasted no time before writing to the minister for industry and commerce to argue that suspending the act would create unemployment and further disturb the country's economic situation. He claimed that sustaining the Irish Tourist Board would send a vital symbolic message to the Irish people by showing them that "carrying on" was important despite present difficulties. O'Brien did not deny that changes would need to be made. Given the likely drop in tourist receipts, the government had little reason to invest in large-scale publicity, but it *was* fair to expect a dramatic increase in tourism following the war, and the country would benefit greatly by using the lull in tourist traffic to prepare for a predictable postwar boom. The best course forward, argued O'Brien, was to continue supporting both the ITA and the Tourist Board so that these bodies might study existing amenities and possible future development, launch a hotel-grading scheme, dispense loans for resort and hotel improvements, and even initiate especially important development programs. O'Brien admitted that the continuation of his salary might create a "source of embarrassment to the government," but he offered to take on additional government-related work to fill administrative gaps when needed while still ensuring that vital tourism development continued. He concluded by pointing out that the remaining members of the ITB would be occupied in assisting the Irish Tourist Association with a survey of Irish holiday facilities.[12]

O'Brien's letter did not inspire an immediate recommendation from the Department of Industry and Commerce on the suspension issue. Instead, the minister simply circulated a memo exploring the pros and cons of each possible course of action. In favor of suspension the minister noted that the public, "who will be called upon to bear greatly increased burdens due to war conditions, will expect all possible economies to be effected, and particularly the elimination of expenditure on nonessential services like tourist traffic development, and that in any event the amount of useful work which could be done during the war conditions is very small."[13] Still, said the minister, O'Brien's argument in favor of extending the board had merit and should be afforded serious consideration. Given his close contacts with government officials, and especially with Seán Lemass, O'Brien undoubtedly knew that MacEntee's memorandum failed to present a strong case in favor of continuing tourist development during the war years, and in November he followed up his earlier letter with a detailed memorandum explaining why the Tourist Board should continue to operate and precisely what it would accomplish if allowed to function. According to O'Brien, tourism already comprised a considerable segment of the economy, bringing wealth "to all parts of the country and all classes of our people," while directly supporting some twenty thousand Irish citizens. In particular, seaside towns and many Gaeltacht (Irish-speaking) areas depended on tourism. If the ITA and ITB ceased operations, numerous Irish people would be unrepresented, unemployed, and deprived of income. O'Brien added that state support of tourism "is almost essential to counties like Kerry, Donegal, and Galway, as is the guaranteeing of minimum prices for wheat and beet in many inland counties." The tourism chief did not ignore the obvious fact that tourist economies depend on tourists, but tourists need not come from outside of Ireland, and it was in fact perhaps better if they did not. Government promotion of domestic tourism would contribute to the health and welfare of the Irish people by educating them "to save up during the year for holidays which would give them a change of environment amidst opportunities for healthy recreation," as well as teaching them about their own national territory through the continuation of the ITA's "See Ireland First" campaign. There could be no better time to promote Ireland for native tourists than a period when the Irish "people cannot go abroad." In other words, to continue the Tourist Traffic Act would avoid crippling the Irish tourist industry and avoid reducing it "to the unorganised and comparatively impoverished position of the industry in 1925," while simultaneously creating more responsible and educated Irish citizens. O'Brien insisted that the impressive benefits of tourist development could be attained using few resources and little government expenditure. Above all, the Tourist Board would execute an extensive planning program designed to make postwar development at Ireland's holiday resorts possible. More immediately, nearly all Irish resorts required substantial enhancement of health and sanitation facilities as well as road safety provisions—all improvements that could be supported under wartime unemployment relief schemes. The ITB's planning program would thus identify both long-term development projects and labor-intensive schemes that might provide Irishmen with work during the Emergency. O'Brien argued that it would be important to establish local committees to direct development projects. These would not only provide a local presence but would also encourage greater investment by local authorities: an essential component of any development project, whether in wartime or peacetime.

Beyond these recommendations, O'Brien suggested that the Tourist Board could implement the hotel-grading scheme specified in the Tourist Traffic Act, identifying facilities requiring improvements *before* the predicted postwar boom in tourism. By doing this during a period of relatively low tourist traffic, hotels would be able to raise their standards to match board requirements before the expected rush of postwar visitors. The wartime period would also give the board time to move ahead with a hotel-training scheme and the improvement of transport arrangements throughout Ireland. Publicity, Gaeltacht holidays, and inland-fishery development also required immediate attention. Indeed, the only major component of the 1939 tourist legislation that the board did not plan to address was the designation of "special areas" of the country well suited to tourism development and protection. Instead of making the designations, the board would study the potential impact of such action, carefully examining the implications for local economic and social development whenever the designations were made.

In short, the Irish Tourist Board would function as a tourism think tank, putting into effect limited development schemes only if and when they could contribute to the overall employment situation during the wartime crisis. The plan was designed to be successful despite tight finances and would cost the government a mere £9,000 per year in operating costs and £75,000 in repayable advances for development projects versus the £45,000 annually and £600,000 in loans assigned in the 1939 act.[14] From O'Brien's perspective tourism development still represented the national interest, and he went out of his way to offer a plan that would create employment in the near term while ensuring the country's ability to attract and cater to a flood of future tourists.

Despite O'Brien's aggressive efforts, the government had not made a decision at the end of January 1940, though Seán MacEntee was now firmly in favor of continuing the ITB's efforts. The minister offered three arguments in favor of leaving the board in place, all based on O'Brien's memorandum. First, the industry was increasingly important to the Irish economy and should be safeguarded. Second, the board enjoyed widespread popular support among "all sections of the community" because it filled "a long-felt want." And third, MacEntee did not believe it worthwhile to endanger the survival of the Irish Tourist Association by inadvertently encouraging local authorities to reduce or abolish their contributions to the group.[15] In short, tourism remained a national interest, and therefore continued development was the only logical course of action.

While the Department of Industry and Commerce now firmly supported the pro-tourism line, the Department of Finance and the Department of Local Government had more conservative and indeed backward-looking ideas about the national interest. The Department of Local Government and Public Health, which had statutory control over funding provided to the ITA through the 1925 Local Government Act and the 1931 Tourist Traffic Act, objected primarily to the argument that the ITA would somehow cease to function if the ITB were suspended until after the war. According to this department, any actions taken by the government vis-à-vis the Tourist Board would "not have an appreciable influence on local authorities." If financial problems arising from the Emergency caused the local authorities to cut their expenditures on tourist publicity, they would cease to fund the ITA, whether the ITB continued to operate or not.[16]

Meanwhile, as far as Finance was concerned, the Emergency was not the time to begin preparing for the postwar world. According to Finance officials, the Tourist Traffic Act was predicated on an assumption of peacetime conditions, and now that the world situation was anything but peaceful, the act was no longer viable. The minister for finance maintained that the Emergency

> has caused serious unemployment, entailed substantial additional expenditure without countervailing savings, and has reduced revenue, thereby rendering necessary a supplementary budget under which heavy additional taxation has been imposed. Further, it has been found necessary to float a loan of £7,000,000 to provide for the liquidation of short-term debt incurred, and to meet capital commitments, some of which, e.g., defense expenditure, are non-productive.

It was necessary to assume that the war would not end quickly, important to anticipate "further sacrifices on the part of the community, if services of an absolutely essential kind are to be maintained." To continue to finance the Tourist Traffic Act "would be not unlikely to create the impression in the country that economy was considered by the government to be neither necessary nor desirable." Besides, if the government adopted a policy of intelligent spending designed to help people weather the crisis, Irish citizens would continue to take holidays, and the Irish tourist industry would be more than supported by its virtual monopoly on home traffic during the Emergency. To postpone planning and development until after the war would not unduly handicap the Irish tourist industry because other states would be equally debilitated as a result of hostilities. Lastly, the resources required to undertake even small development projects were not available given the realities of rationing.[17]

That Finance immediately positioned itself against the ITB is not surprising because this key governmental body in 1939–40 was little different from the Department of Finance in 1922. As historian Ronan Fanning has pointed out, "the single outstanding characteristic of the first thirty-five years of the department's history is the absence of change, a remarkable continuity reflected both in the department's organisation and personnel."[18] Not only was J. J. McElligott the department's most important civil servant throughout these years, but there was also a general unwillingness to explore new ideas, and "early Finance men may have felt that they had little enough to learn from outsiders."[19] Established orthodoxy governed the department's response to new ideas, and its officials acted in accordance with conventions handed down from generation to generation. Finance's very recruiting system ensured such continuity by the fact that new blood was brought into the department at the tender age of eighteen, immediately after leaving secondary school and before any untoward influences, such as higher education, might creep in.[20] Beyond all else, McElligott and his longtime colleagues sought stability. McElligott's first understanding of how the national economy and government fiscal policy should function developed "after two years of chaos and disorder . . . [had] threatened to tear the infant state apart."[21] In his mind the best way to ensure stability was to continue along tried and true tracks, deviating little from known quantities. For Finance, just as for the Killarney boatmen, rapid tourism development represented a source of change and risk—a fact that led to a consistent anti-tourism stance throughout the 1930s, 1940s, and 1950s (before the *Economic Development Plan* of 1958). The Department of Finance frequently made efforts to limit state funding for tourism, yet, just as Finance lost the fight in 1938 to limit state funding for the proposed tourist board, it repeatedly proved unable to suspend the Tourist Traffic Act during the war years or to tamp down funding requests in the early 1950s. On 28 February 1940 the government agreed with the Department of Industry and Commerce concerning the desirability of renewing the board's remit for another year.[22] Then, on 15 July 1941, the government again extended the board's life until 31 March 1944 in spite of continued pleas by the Department of Finance.[23]

Why did Industry and Commerce consistently win the tourism battle throughout the war years? Part of the answer certainly lies in the decreasing power experienced by the Department of Finance following its "years of ascendancy" between 1924 and 1932.[24] After 1932 a series of new economic policies, "anathema to Finance orthodoxies," were put in place, resulting in a marked increase in the number of civil servants and giving "big spending departments, such as Industry and Commerce and Agriculture," increased power.[25] But there were other reasons as well, and the influence of the Irish Tourist Association was significant. The association had no qualms about lobbying the government in order to attain its goals, and it was very adept at speaking to government concerns. In the case of extending the Tourist Traffic Act, the ITA argued that tourism would help alleviate unemployment. Immediately preceding the 1941 debate that ultimately extended the board's life until 1944, the association argued that carrying out "certain resort improvements . . . would provide productive employment for a large number of workers"—such as the provision of footpaths, roads, promenades at seaside resorts, water and sewerage improvement schemes, the construction of swimming pools, the building of recreation halls, road improvements, enterprises aimed at limiting coastal erosion, and the clearance of unwanted vegetation near bathing beaches. While acknowledging the difficulties that led the government to scale back Tourist Board activities, ITA directors unanimously urged that "certain improvement works at resorts, particularly schemes which afford large-scale employment for unskilled workers, should be included in any emergency unemployment schemes to be approved by the government." The choice of these schemes should

> keep specially in mind those areas in the country which are situated on the seaboard, and which for natural reasons are the least prosperous. The population of such areas find it difficult, even in normal times, to earn a livelihood; they were largely dependent on holiday traffic in past years to supplement their frugal resources and are now suffering from the cutting off of this source of income. In addition, it is important to note that, in the main, these areas do not benefit from the special measures adopted in recent years for the assistance to agriculture. Not having suitable land, they could not engage in the production of such commodities as wheat and beet with the advantage of guaranteed sale prices. On the other hand, for the purchase of essentials such as bread, flour, and sugar, they have had to contribute substantially to the guaranteeing of the minimum prices above mentioned.

Gaeltacht areas faced similar concerns.[26]

In effect, the Irish Tourist Association, just as it had done in the 1920s when it lobbied for improvements to isolated towns like Dingle and Kinsale, functioned as a voice for outlying areas. This position carried with it a considerable amount of political muscle that could not safely be trifled with, especially when political stability was foremost on the government's priority list. Furthermore, the Tourist Board and ITA argument about employment schemes was difficult to ignore. When massive unemployment forced thousands to emigrate, it was not politically expedient to disregard potentially viable work-creation projects, especially ones that would aid economically challenged regions of the country. And finally, any policy decision that allowed the Irish Tourist Association to disappear would alienate important members of the community while also frustrating key areas of the country like Cork and Kerry. These were ties to the localities that, especially in a time of crisis, the national government could ill afford to break.

Consideration of the national interest and of the vital role that tourism could play in Irish affairs was foremost in the minds of tourist authorities, especially the leaders of the ITA, who continued to believe that tourism development was a powerful way to display nationalist pride. More than ever, they enthused, tourism "was of vital importance" to ensuring "the livelihood of thousands of their people, particularly in poor coastal districts" dependent on tourist traffic. After agriculture, tourism was the country's largest employer, and any failure to support it would prove disastrous.[27]

Holiday Savings Clubs

In spite of wartime conditions, local authorities provided funds to the Tourist Association throughout the early 1940s. While grants were noticeably diminished in 1940–41 (just under £14,000 versus the roughly £18,000 per year received before the war),[28] revenue from local authorities never dropped below £13,500 during the course of the Emergency.[29]

Armed with this slightly diminished budget, the Tourist Association focused its efforts on developing a holiday savings-club program that was designed to educate workers about how best to use their limited financial resources while also teaching them about their national territory. The scheme was based on similar nineteenth-century programs that helped mill workers from England's industrial centers enjoy an annual seaside holiday at resorts such as Blackpool.[30] While the association could only dream of the success enjoyed by these early English savings programs, they nevertheless believed the clubs to be an excellent way to promote native resorts, and the ITA began contacting labor unions, business executives, and workers in 1940.[31] By paying money into a large pool, workers were able to earn interest and to lower the rates at Irish resorts, ensuring themselves of affordable holidays in areas to which they might not otherwise be able to go. The scheme was designed to educate workers about the benefits of saving money for more substantial getaways rather than confining themselves to short evening trips to Howth or Bray. According to the lord mayor of Cork city, the scheme also functioned to "make people appreciate the beauties of our own country."[32] During the first year of its efforts the ITA gave presentations to the Irish Transport and General Workers' Union, employees of the Dublin Flour Mills, the Irish Brewers' Association, and the Civil Service Clerical Association, among others.[33] In 1941 alone 22 clubs were formed, and by 1945, 178 clubs, representing 45,000 workers, had been created.[34] In the immediate postwar years the program continued to grow, ultimately reaching 205 clubs by 1948 and including 47,000 workers.[35]

Exploration and Development

While the Irish Tourist Association tried to retrain Irish workers, J. P. O'Brien and the Irish Tourist Board attempted to move ahead with their planning and development efforts only to face almost immediate criticism. Hotel grading was the first planned program to be abandoned. While the grading scheme would have required the expensive training of inspectors, the primary problem was pressure on the government from the Irish Tourist Association and the Irish Hotels Federation, a collection of hoteliers who banded together during the 1920s to push their interests both within the ITA and at government level. These groups argued that any grading program that might require extensive alterations or adaptations of existing premises, especially on short notice, would be an undue hardship.[36]

At the same time that it encountered opposition to hotel grading, the ITB could not move ahead with its development and planning efforts fast enough to satisfy the ITA and local authorities. As early as November 1941 the Tourist Association expressed concern that ITB-directed development projects were not progressing as expected. The limited progress resulted in insignificant unemployment relief and did little to forward the tourist industry.[37]

The only visible development project began at Tramore in 1942. The scheme made use of local labor and a detachment of the Construction Corps for (among other things) an aggressive program of site leveling, drainage, and reclamation of land.[38] Invoking its powers of compulsory acquisition for the first time, the board also purchased several properties in the area.[39] By 1944 the scheme employed some two hundred members from the Construction Corps, and work was expected to last for at least two more years at a total cost of £40,000.[40] By 1945 the development was "practically completed," allowing the board to begin working on further plans "for commercial development of the property" at Tramore.[41]

At the same time that the Tramore scheme was being undertaken, the board suggested further development programs at other resort towns, including Portmarnock, Bundoran, and Lisdoonvarna—all of which promised to provide high employment and a long-term financial return through the construction of bathing, recreation, and amusement facilities. Like Tramore, each of these places was already a notable tourist attraction.[42] For Tramore, the program was undoubtedly considered a success, and there is no reason to believe that the ITA was displeased with the ITB scheme there, once undertaken. Other observers, especially in areas like Kilkenny where tourism had not yet caught on as a promising new industry, were far less pleased. Ultimately the development schemes helped to spark the single most damaging controversy in the history of Irish tourism. This battle derailed the board's development program, brought about a complete revamping of the ITB, and, sadly, began to destroy the effectiveness of the single most notable voice in tourism development to this point—J. P. O'Brien.

The Crisis

Despite the success of efforts to retain government support for wartime tourism development, the entire pro-tourism project nearly collapsed in the late 1940s. The crisis in Irish tourism had its roots in three areas: personal animosity toward J. P. O'Brien and the Tourist Board among members of the Irish media; the extension of the ITB's development policy to include the purchase and management of hotels immediately following the war; and the acquisition and subsequent grounding of a number of Constellation aircraft bought by Aer Rianta (then leased by Aer Lingus) to fly between Shannon and New York.

Since entering the tourist industry in 1924, J. P. O'Brien was one of Ireland's most important tourism figures, and with the establishment of the Tourist Board he became the industry's most visible leader. While tourism was a nexus for a variety of voices and interests from local groups to private interests to the central government, O'Brien was the face of tourism policy and the creative force behind much of the industry's early growth and later expansion.[43] Given his prominence, it is not surprising that O'Brien became a minor celebrity—a ubiquitous figure in nearly all newspaper articles relating to tourism. While this renown was undoubtedly flattering to the Corkman, his friend Todd Andrews later recalled that it led O'Brien to acquire "what William James called 'the moral flabbiness born of the exclusive worship of the bitch goddess success.'" O'Brien made powerful friends whom he tended to meet in the lounge bars of Dublin hotels, and he "developed a way of life which was alien to his upbringing and real sentiments." Unfortunately, these "friends" were often more interested in O'Brien because of his connections: powerful businessmen made use of an inadequately compensated public official to secure political access. At the same time he made enemies, several of whom were important media figures like R. M. Smyllie, editor of the *Irish Times*, and, most visibly, a man named E. T. Keane, who owned and edited a provincial paper called the *Kilkenny People*.[44]

Keane was born in Listowel on 16 July 1867 and began his journalism career with the *Munster News* at an early age. He developed a keen interest in politics that he exercised as a founding member of the Kilkenny branch of Sinn Féin. By 1917 Keane was friends with W. T. Cosgrave, and after supporting the nationalist politician in the election of December 1918 had his newspaper suppressed. After the Anglo-Irish Treaty was signed in December 1921, Keane took his stand with the pro-treaty forces.[45] The journalist was not above using his newspaper as a political organ, and his willingness to do so made him "'a living legend in his own lifetime' and 'arguably the outstanding provincial editor of this century.'" Keane distinguished himself as "an irreconcilable political opponent" of Fianna Fáil. During the Emergency the government found him impossible to deal with. He refused to follow directions and persistently published "censorable matter," but he was tolerated because of his now advanced age and long record as a distinguished newsman. Among other things, Keane published an anti-Axis editorial after German bombs fell on Dublin and Belfast—an action that was clearly in violation of the government's neutral position. When the censors demanded that he supply them with copies of all leading articles in advance of publication, Keane replied by not publishing any leading article at all, while including an editorial entitled "The Liberty of the Press" that was subsequently suppressed.[46]

Among his strong opinions Keane displayed an antipathy for tourism, and he was especially upset that the Tourist Board continued to function during the war while providing what Keane considered an excessive salary to J. P. O'Brien. Beginning in 1942, Keane launched his own personal anti-tourism crusade, using the pages of his paper to lambaste the tourism industry, the Irish Tourist Board, and O'Brien. The attack began in March with an editorial entitled "Where Jobs Accumulate and Men Decay." The piece attacked Fianna Fáil for allowing civil servants to draw excessive wages, using de Valera's comment that no civil servant should ever earn more than £1,000 per year as an example of party hypocrisy. Keane's primary example was O'Brien, whom he declared to be "overpaid and overemployed."[47] By 18 April, Keane's commentary on O'Brien became more personal, and he began referring to him as "Mr. J. P. O'Brien, B.A. (pass)." While Lemass had told the people that they would need to tighten their belts, the Tourist Board had been allowed to continue its spending. As far as Keane was concerned, the Irish Tourist Board was "one of the greatest fakes ever thrust upon this unfortunate country," led, "as everyone expected," by O'Brien with a shocking salary of £1,500 per year plus travel and expense allowances. Keane declared that the Tourist Board had "flopped," and he neglected to acknowledge that O'Brien had voluntarily reduced his own salary in keeping with the troubles of the day. Keane observed snidely that J. P. O'Brien's "is the only name in the telephone directory that has his letters 'B.A.' after it, but he forgot to add the word 'pass.' Man, in his time, plays many parts, but few men so many parts as this luminary." The newsman concluded that it was a "gross injustice" that people's tax dollars should be used to support the "up-keep of a useless and expensive contraption like this Tourist Board and for the payment of salaries to the holders of sinecures."[48]

Keane was in no way finished. Over the coming years—indeed, until his death in 1945—the editor attacked O'Brien and the board in at least twelve different articles. He called the leaders of the Irish Tourist Association the "Playboys of the Western World" because they enjoyed a well-catered annual meeting in Dublin in 1943,[49] and he declared the Irish Tourist Board to be little more than "a sanctuary for Fianna Fáil politicians."[50] O'Brien was compared to Hamlet,[51] he was ridiculed as the "high priest" of the board,[52] and the addition of the word "pass" with every reference to him assured that the head of the Tourist Board suffered attacks on his intelligence at every turn. Between the insults, Keane did manage to make a collection of thoughtful comments about board policy. He criticized the board's hotel evaluation program when it was finally announced in 1944;[53] he challenged the amount of alcohol consumed at ITA and Tourist Board functions;[54] he pointed out the government's lack of attention to the TB epidemic in favor of tourism development;[55] and he suggested that the board's development scheme at Tramore was marked more by the laying of concrete than by the improvement of the area's sublime and beautiful assets.[56] However valid these criticisms were, and while Keane may well have been an extraordinary figure in the provincial press of Ireland before this controversy, his conduct in this case was juvenile, cruel, and destructive.

On a personal level the attacks dramatically affected O'Brien. While initially they "only raised smiles," as the articles and years came and went, the cruel words eventually "succeeded in wrecking O'Brien's self-confidence by making him the subject of national ridicule."[57] Early in 1946 O'Brien sought legal advice from the eminent Dublin attorney Arthur Cox about how to stop the *Kilkenny People* articles. (Although Keane died in 1945, the paper remained unfriendly to tourism until the early 1950s.) O'Brien was told that in any libel action taken in Ireland the "plaintiff invariably became the defendant," and he was advised not to take any action against the paper.[58] With easy access to drink through his many meetings in hotel bars, to say nothing of the large quantity of alcohol that was ubiquitous at tourism-development functions, O'Brien gradually began to seek escape in drink and was increasingly absent from meetings. Tragically, J. P. O'Brien, the most prominent single voice in early Irish tourism development, was descending into the grip of alcoholism.[59]

The ITB's development program continued despite the unfavorable press. The purchase of property at Tramore was followed by still more acquisitions including land at Ardmore, Arklow, Ballynahinch and Recess, Bundoran, Courtown, Dollymount, Garryvoe, Glengarriff, Kilkee, Killarney, Lisdoonvarna, Newtown, Termonfeckin, Portmarnock, Rosses Point, Salthill, Skerries, and Youghal.[60] In the immediate postwar years, the Tourist Board believed that "the provision of additional accommodation is . . . considered the most urgent requirement. In normal circumstances the board could rely on private enterprise to meet increased demands, but in this case experience has shown that special measures involving the board's direct intervention are necessary." The proposed intervention involved the "conversion and enlargement" of properties that had been acquired at some of the previously mentioned sites. To the board's credit, it did not envision running these properties itself because to do so would represent a clear conflict of interest. Instead, it was proposed that an interim company be incorporated to run the newly created hotels. As quickly as possible, the board would move to sell the hotels to private interests, divesting itself of all properties and eventually rendering the interim company obsolete. From the ITB's perspective the scheme was designed to "encourage private enterprise in the provision of adequate and suitable accommodation."[61] In May 1946 the proposed company, Fáilte Téoranta, was incorporated in order "to convert and operate for hotel purposes five houses situated on properties that had been purchased by the board." The hotels were open for business throughout the 1946 tourist season, and the board looked forward to expanding them further.[62]

As noted in chapter 1, one of the most prevalent concerns about the formation of the Irish Tourist Board in 1938–39 was the board's potential threat to private enterprise; some feared that the new authority might eventually acquire a monopoly of the tourist facilities in Ireland by establishing a stranglehold on the hotel business.[63] The development of the "Fáilte hotels," on the heels of three years of constant criticism of board policy by several Irish newspapers, sparked a powerful backlash. The *Irish Times* attacked board statements about the need for "luxury hotels." Smyllie, the paper's editor, insisted that the notion of "luxury" hotels in Ireland was ridiculous, and accused O'Brien of "suffering from *folie de grandeur* or some such aberration."[64] Unsurprisingly, the *Kilkenny People* also attacked the hotel scheme. The paper responded to reports about the board's plan with a withering condemnation: "It should also be a matter of deep concern to the public generally because the proposal, if it is to take effect, will establish a most pernicious principle. Why should a state subsidized but useless body be permitted to enter into competition with people who, through taxation, are obliged to pay a not inconsiderable proportion of the annual expenditure of the Irish Tourist Board?"

The paper proceeded to rail against the recent start of board inspections of existing hotel premises, claiming that the "horde of inspectors" had been "let loose" to "harass many hotel proprietors and even wipe out of business others on the flimsiest of pretexts"—destroying family businesses that had existed for generations—all in the name of catering to the "imaginary influx of mythical foreign tourists."[65] It was not bad enough that a state-funded body was going to compete with private hotels; the ITB was putting the competition out of business by using unjust inspections. And even more damning still, the tax dollars that were paying for these hotels were not being used to help either Ireland's war-torn European neighbors or the Irish people themselves.[66] The paper pointed out that while Ireland needed 60,000 new homes to meet workers' needs,

> there has been a great falling off in the number of new houses built during the last few years, but in spite of this, it has been found possible to provide large sums for the erection or reconstruction of high-class luxury hotels to cater for wealthy tourists who pay flying visits to this country. If it can be found possible to provide building materials for the erection or reconstruction of hotels for wealthy foreigners, many of whom are as mythical as their wealth, it ought to be possible to provide some materials for the more urgent need of housing our own people.[67]

The *Irish Independent*, the daily newspaper with the largest circulation in Ireland, adopted a similar view of the hotel scheme, noting the lack of adequate facilities to house the Irish themselves. Instead of feeding and housing tourists, "the Irish people should have first claim on the food and board in this country."[68] Just where were the government's priorities? How could anybody argue that the national interest rested with foreigners and not desperately poor *Irish* workers?

As indicated in the *Irish Independent*, many were skeptical about the desirability of attracting tourists in the first place—a concern made considerably more threatening by the fact that between 1946 and 1949 Ireland enjoyed a massive influx of tourists. The *Irish Press* declared, "A fortuitous chain of circumstances in 1946, over which we had no control, established us a highly lucrative tourist trade." The English "were hungry, had plenty of loose cash, and were tired of standing in queues for anything from a pin to a tin of pineapple."[69] As a result, in 1946 "visitor receipts"—the total income from tourist traffic—reached £18 million, or 4.5 times larger than the highest prewar figure. In 1947 tourist income climbed to £28 million and then peaked in 1948 at £33 million,[70] before falling back to £28 million in 1949.[71] Regrettably, accurate visitor numbers were not recorded until the mid-1950s, making it impossible to say precisely how many tourists were involved in expending these amounts. But the perception was that Ireland was under invasion by Britons and Europeans desperate to find steaks, dairy products, and countryside and cityscapes not marred by total war. The *Irish Times* reported that as a result of a publicity campaign conducted by the Tourist Board and the ITA, "the adverse conditions in other tourist resorts, and of continued 'austerity' in Great Britain, this country now is faced by imminent threats of tourist invasions on such a scale as may seriously overtax its powers of digestion."

This "invasion" would increase inflation dramatically and thus raise the cost of living. The paper explained that when British tourists brought their currency into Ireland it was promptly converted into Irish pounds. Thus for every £100,000 brought into Ireland "another £100,000 is added to Éire's already inflated currency—£100,000 that would not have been required if those 10,000 tourists had spent their money at home or in some other country!"[72]

Although the paper did not discourage tourist development (in fact, the editors encouraged it by saying that short-term losses would mean long-term gains), the threat of rising costs in a country still feeling the effects of wartime deprivations was hardly a prediction welcomed by the Tourist Board; the specter of inflation was not the best way to sell an expensive hotel development scheme. Indeed, the *Kilkenny People* had no qualms about attacking the very notion of tourism development under the present circumstances, alleging that thousands of pounds were being squandered by the "so-called tourist industry" and calling for restraint: "We have no objections to the

SUGGESTED I.T.A. SIGNPOST FOR O'CONNELL STREET.

2. Suggested ITA Signpost, *Dublin Opinion* cartoon, Sept. 1943.

development of the tourist industry when circumstances are more favorable, but at the present time we, perhaps very selfishly, feel we have little enough for ourselves and cannot give visitors to this country the *Céad Míle Fáilte* which would be extended to them in normal days in Éire."[73]

Even in Killarney, where tourism was always a priority, the hotel scheme generated little goodwill. This time the concern was not the board's potential threat to private enterprise; it was the fact that little had been done in Killarney itself. It was true that the Tourist Board had purchased property at Killarney (Muckross House no less), and that it had offered "numerous proposals for tourist development," but "practically all the Killarney proposals had been turned down by the board because . . . they would have required either partial or total subsidy by the state."[74] As a result, Killarney tourist authorities resolved that something needed to be done to "shake up" the Tourist Board; the buying of land at Killarney was not enough—the board needed to follow through with actual development.[75] As a result, the Killarney Urban District Council filed a formal condemnation of the board and demanded that immediate proposals be submitted for development at

Killarney.[76] The ITB responded immediately to these concerns by sending a photographer to the tourist center—in itself not a strange activity as the board made sure that a photographer visited every year in order to demonstrate the ITB's interest in the area. These photographs varied little from year to year, meaning that from five to twenty new plates nearly identical to the previous Killarney shots were added to the photo library each year. The 1948 trip was different. The photographer took over three hundred photographs that were, once again, more or less identical to all previous shots dating back to (at least) 1939. Perhaps the Tourist Board could not act on its development hopes for its property at Muckross House, but at least its photographer could spend several days and shoot numerous rolls of film in Killarney and the immediate area, demonstrating a good show of concern in the process.[77]

Beyond public view the board was also harshly criticized. Badly infected by the development bug, and inspired by a trip to Germany to study the Nazi's Kraft durch Freude program several years earlier,[78] the board presented a memo urging the adoption of an Irish recreational policy that would undermine "the natural tendency, particularly with more hard-working elements of the community . . . , to use free time for mere idleness." "Preventative measures" would ensure the "physical well-being" and "mental development" of the Irish people. In pursuit of this aim the Tourist Board detailed the lack of recreation facilities in rural Ireland and looked to numerous foreign examples to show what other countries were doing to promote recreation, defined by the board as "the *beneficial* use of leisure-time."[79] Efforts to define the way in which people spent their time when not working had been around since the Victorian period, when the middle classes created museums, codified field sports, and advocated an educational approach to seaside visits (studying tide pools, for example).[80] Nor was there anything strange about the concept of state-sponsored leisure during the 1930s and 1940s. Other countries had similar programs (a detailed list was included with the Tourist Board proposal). The Nazis, for example, used their leisure organization, Kraft durch Freude, to teach the German people both how to be better Germans and what to believe politically.[81] Nevertheless, the board's proposal stands out as one of the more curious artifacts of the Emergency period in Ireland because it went so much further than anything else proposed by tourist authorities before or since. Not surprisingly, it was a document that won the board few friends.

When the minister for local government and public health was asked to offer his comments on the matter, his verdict was far from muted. The minister demanded to know "why the Irish Tourist Board considered itself free to turn from those statutory functions which should be its sole preoccupation in order to address itself to a subject with which at best it cannot be more than remotely concerned" especially because "its labours so far have been conspicuous only by lack of any practical achievement." Rather than "amusing itself in drafting absurd totalitarian schemes," the Tourist Board should strive to enhance Ireland's tourist potential. Renaming the Irish Tourist Board document "Towards an Irish Totalitarian State," the minister demanded to know if the board felt that the Creator should have spent the seventh day doing something other than resting—a clear display of "mere idleness." While the members of the board might have delusions of competency, they had no right to compel the Irish people to play during their time off.[82]

J. P. O'Brien and the Irish Tourist Board simply could not catch a break. They were criticized for not attracting enough tourists and for attracting too many of them. They were attacked for threatening private enterprise and for not developing hotels fast enough or in the right places. And they were viewed as stepping beyond their statutory responsibilities in an effort to turn Ireland into a totalitarian state. Under the circumstances it is little wonder that O'Brien began to crack, a victim of his own "success" and notoriety.

It was not only the Tourist Board that was under attack. Aer Rianta and Aer Lingus also faced controversy that spilled over into tourism—partly because of the obvious link between the airlines and tourism development and partly because J. P. O'Brien served as a director on the Aer Rianta board from 1946.[83] Following V-E Day, Aer Lingus rapidly acquired a collection of new aircraft, and in 1947 and 1948 it expanded its routes to include Dublin-Manchester-Amsterdam, Dublin-Brussels, Dublin-Belfast-Glasgow, London-Shannon, Shannon-Paris, Dublin-Belfast-Liverpool, and even Dublin-Rome.[84] These routes alone (especially Dublin-Rome, which lacked any substantial clientele during the winter months) represented an expansion that was too rapid and too costly. Yet Aer Rianta still planned to launch a new transatlantic service between Shannon and New York for which they purchased several Constellation aircraft. From their inception the two airlines had never made a profit, and the purchase of new aircraft and the costs of expanding the number of routes had a profoundly negative impact on the airlines' accounts. In 1946–47, Aer Lingus suffered a net loss of almost £75,000, or just over 20 percent of total revenue. The following year losses increased to a mind-boggling £891,000.[85]

From the perspective of the opposition parties, the purchase of the Constellation aircraft was unrealistic and irresponsible in the same way that Fianna Fáil's tourism-development policies had been during the Emergency. While more suited to the Rome route, the Constellations were ultimately leased by Aer Lingus and used to fly between Dublin and London. Given their size and relative inefficiency over short distances, they were a poor choice.[86] The airline's marketing campaign emphasized the luxurious comfort of the huge planes but did little to attract enough passengers to make them profitable.[87] Horrified by massive losses, the new interparty government quickly cancelled the proposed North American route on the eve of its maiden flight—the night before St. Patrick's Day in 1948.[88] The Constellation aircraft were sold shortly thereafter amid a considerable controversy that was linked all too easily in the minds of many with the "Fáilte hotel" controversy.[89]

Given all of this dissension, it is hardly surprising that when Fianna Fáil lost the general election in 1948 and was replaced by an interparty government, O'Brien was quickly fired and a new pro–Fine Gael Tourist Board director named W. F. Quinlan was appointed. The widespread distaste for tourism following the crisis surrounding the industry made tourism politically unpopular and dramatically undermined the effort to emphasize the national importance of the industry. During the next four years the Tourist Board was presented with the task of liquidating its properties. Just two years after its formation, Fáilte Téoranta reported that it had made a profit of £6,000 on its five Tourist Board hotels. Although the company itself hoped to continue, in October 1949 the government decided that it should be "wound up."[90] While the ITA and members of the ITB maintained that tourism was a vital national concern, neither group was in a position to successfully argue the point; an outside voice, unsullied by the tourism crisis, was needed to convince the Irish people and their government that tourism should remain a crucial concern for the nation.

America and the Irish National Interest

Even as the Tourist Board lay crippled by the postwar tourism crisis, a growing constituency recognized that tourism represented Ireland's "best hope of improving dollar earnings"[91] following British action to avoid a breakdown in trade between sterling and dollar countries.[92] In Ireland tourism represented the second most important dollar source behind emigrants' remittances and legacies. Whereas remittances totaled £3.5 million in 1947, tourism earned an impressive £1.8 million—considerably more than any other dollar income source. Better still, tourism revenues exploded following the war and had climbed to £2.7 million by 1948, whereas remittances declined to £3.1 million.

It was difficult to ignore the potential for tourism growth given that Ireland was "only receiving a mere trickle of the potentially enormous flow of Irish-American tourists and their dollars." But there remained two major problems: inadequate transportation to bring tourists to Ireland and a lack of entertainment facilities to occupy them upon their arrival.[93] Worse, the tourism crisis had left tourism development politically untenable for the Fine Gael–led government, and it is questionable whether any major changes would have taken place in the structure of tourism administration had not the American government strongly pressed Irish officials to improve the Irish tourist industry.

Ireland began receiving American aid through the European Recovery Program, or Marshall Plan, in July 1947.[94] Although Ireland did not receive substantial Marshall Plan money for tourism development, the Economic Cooperation Administration viewed tourism as an important component of the effort to rebuild countries such as France,[95] and Colonel T. J. Pozzi, the chief of the Travel Development Section of the Economic Cooperation Administration (ECA), believed that Ireland possessed similarly attractive tourist potential. With this idea in mind, he visited Ireland to survey the industry in 1949.[96] Following a tour arranged by the Irish Tourist Board,[97] Pozzi encouraged the ITB to launch a publicity campaign in America,[98] and he offered numerous suggestions for persuading tourists passing through

Shannon airport to stay in Ireland, including the installation of a movie theatre at Shannon, the dramatic expansion of shopping facilities at the airport, and the provision of far more duty-free items for purchase. In addition, he informed Irish officials that the most important task facing the industry was "to raise the quality of the hotel accommodation . . . to the level that will be acceptable to the ordinary United States tourist, and then to construct enough additional accommodation to take a further expansion in numbers."[99]

When his suggestions were not efficiently implemented, Pozzi lost patience with the Irish authorities and pointed angrily at the government's inaction and at the inefficiency of the Tourist Board itself. The ECA official doubted the ability of the board's members and expressed grave concern about the qualifications of Quinlan to handle the challenges ahead.[100] By 1950 there had still been little action and Pozzi's frustration continued to grow. Finally, in a meeting with the minister of external affairs, Pozzi "gave what he called a very private but at the same time a very definite warning that the amount of Marshall aid in 1950–51 would depend on the action which would be taken by the government." Although ECA administrators were generally friendly toward Ireland, "their patience had been exhausted," and Pozzi demanded that "effective government action in this field by way of reconstruction of the Tourist Board and otherwise was essential to avoid a complete deterioration" of relations with Washington: "If Ireland did not show some real interest in increasing her dollar earnings in the line which seemed most feasible, the ECA could hardly be expected to continue their aid at the forecast level."[101] In effect, Pozzi and the ECA were telling the Irish government that tourist growth was in Ireland's national interest, in terms of both improving dollar earnings and ensuring the continued receipt of Marshall Plan aid. Whether the task was politically popular or not, the government had to take immediate steps to restructure the ITB, hire more qualified staff, and mount an aggressive tourist-development campaign.

Tourism as Foreign Policy

At the same time that foreign pressure was brought to bear on the Irish government to develop tourism, a growing number within the Department of External Affairs believed that tourism might prove a useful foreign policy tool. The concept of mixing the activities of tourist authorities and those of the Department of External Affairs was first put forward during Dáil debates concerning the 1931 Tourist Traffic Act. At that time P. Hogan, a TD from County Clare, suggested that Irish representatives in England, America, Germany, and France could be called upon to hit "the people in those countries in the eye, so to speak, with the fact that we have a country worth seeing." From Hogan's perspective it was not that Irish consular officials should go out of their way to deliver leaflets, but rather that they should be in a position to distribute materials when relevant—to use existing resources to extend the reach of tourist advertising. Hogan's view was not universal, however, and others dismissed the idea. While Irish consulates abroad would certainly lend whatever aid was required to the Tourist Association, it was not the duty of Irish ambassadors to offer such assistance.[102]

At the end of World War II the Department of External Affairs suggested that tourism could be used to promote Irish political objectives through what it called "cultural propaganda." External Affairs noted that the new strategy "covers a wide range of activities—book, art, photographic, and film exhibitions; exchanges of students and lectureships; lecture tours; the preparation and distribution of books and publicity material to public and university libraries; and so on." These products would "make the country better known and understood" by informing outsiders about "every aspect of the country's national life and activity." The approach had a number of advantages: it was "not 'suspect' as obviously political propaganda tends to be"; there were no diplomatic limitations to be observed, and no complicated political questions to work through. Cultural propaganda would help make foreign intelligentsias "generally friendly and sympathetic." The department observed, "Our experience during the war showed how important it is to us to have—at least in the more important countries—a nucleus of public opinion which knows something about this country and has some understanding of, and sympathy with, our national aims and points of view. The influence of such a group can be of even [more] decisive importance in times of difficulty."[103]

This policy was all the more desirable because various governments, urging the development of closer cultural relations, had already contacted the department. External Affairs successfully advocated the establishment of a

Cultural Relations Committee, and although sources are spotty concerning the early activities of the committee, it is clear that relations were forged between External Affairs, the Irish Tourist Association, and, later, Bord Fáilte (the Irish Tourist Board). As it became more established during the 1950s, the Cultural Relations Committee included members of Aer Lingus, Bord Fáilte, the Department of External Affairs, Irish Rail (Córas Iompair Éireann or CIÉ), the Export Board (CTT), and later Radio Telefís Éireann (RTÉ), and it carried out joint operations intended to improve the image of Ireland abroad.[104]

Effective Action?

Thus, by the first months of 1950 it was very clear that something had to be done about tourism, whether the necessary actions would be politically unpopular or not. Government statistics made clear that tourism was now Ireland's second most important industry behind agriculture and was the country's leading export[105]—facts that could not be ignored because the economy was quickly plunging into a "huge" trade deficit.[106] Furthermore, Pozzi and the ECA continued to argue that the government was ignoring a primary national interest and a guaranteed source of valuable dollar income.

In February the minister for industry and commerce finally took tentative action by requesting a proposal from the Irish Tourist Board outlining its vision for the future. The subsequent report advocated a new five-tier structure for the board, including divisions concerned with hotels and catering, publicity, transportation, general promotion, and finance, along with substantial pay increases in order to secure the best talent available, and an expanded advertising campaign.[107] While the minister for industry and commerce, Dan Morrissey, agreed broadly with the proposed structure and the need for increased spending, he was largely ambivalent about the proposal.

Morrissey's colleagues at the Department of Finance were anything but ambivalent and charged that the scheme was little more than an excuse for increases in pay and personnel which "only incidentally . . . suggest[ed] how the board might approach the problem of maintaining and expanding the tourist industry." As far as Finance was concerned, nothing in the plan justified the requested £3 million. As an alternative, the minister suggested that substantial improvements could be attained simply by revamping the existing hotel-grading scheme, developing hotel-training programs, and providing easy credit for private organizations interested in improving existing tourist facilities. Finally, he argued that an expanded publicity campaign in the United States might also be implemented by using repayable advances rather than a substantial budgetary increase. The minister justified these suggestions by arguing that "it would be unwise to spend large sums on advertising the attractions of this country abroad before positive improvements had been effected in standards of accommodation, etc. Such a policy would lead to speedy disillusionment of visitors and would undermine the prospects of developing an assured dollar income from tourism."[108]

Following the inability of either the Tourist Board or the government to offer a coherent direction, three other groups were formed to provide their opinions. The first was sponsored by the European Travel Commission (which Ireland joined at its foundation in 1948) under the aegis of the Marshall Plan and involved a three-month trip to America by Irish tourism officials, including Kevin O'Doherty of the Tourist Board, to visit a number of hotels. Although O'Doherty was impressed by the high standards of American accommodations, he soon concluded that it would be far more helpful if a group from the Irish Hotels Commission made a similar tour. Such a trip might open the hoteliers' eyes to the sort of improvements necessary if Ireland were going to compete for American dollars. A group from the Irish Hotels Commission was established in March to visit both Irish and American hotels under the auspices of the Organization for European Economic Cooperation and the ECA.[109]

The Hotels Commission's report was given to the Department of Industry and Commerce at the end of September 1950. Although the commission's report offered a series of suggestions, including the production of more tourism films and the publication of more professional publicity materials that featured both historical and scenic information, its major concern was directed at the atrocious state of Irish accommodations. "Almost all" lacked central heating, 80 percent were without a private bath/toilet, Cobh was more akin to a Third World port than a suitable place to greet wealthy American travelers, Irish hotels were manned by untrained staffs (which the commission blamed on emigration), and the Tourist Board was attempting to improve the situation by using a faulty inspection policy implemented by guileless inspectors. The Hotels Commission suggested four principal solutions. First, the statutory tourist authority should contain at least three members of the hotel and catering industry who would be equipped to develop an effective grading scheme. Second, the tourist authority should be able to levy taxes in order to guarantee an adequate budget. Third, the tourist authority should execute its own publicity activities, ensuring continuity across the industry by eliminating the need for communication between a public body (ITB) and a private one (ITA). And finally, the tourist authority should provide grants for the reconstruction, improvement, and development of hotels.[110]

The third and most important of the three fact-finding bodies consisted of a group of American hoteliers led by Robert K. Christenberry, president of the Astor Hotel in New York, and the group's report represents an extraordinary example of an outside voice effectively interjecting itself into the debate about Ireland's national interest. The "Christenberry report" was submitted to the Irish government in July and August 1950 and has been widely recognized as an important contribution to the tourism debate during the early 1950s.[111] Although few of the committee's suggestions had been adopted three years after the release of the report, the document nevertheless provided government officials with a well-argued and extensive, if often less than complimentary, commentary on the state of the tourism industry in Ireland from an outside perspective. Above all, Christenberry believed that Ireland had all of the raw materials necessary to create an excellent tourist destination, and that such an undertaking would have dramatic benefits for the country, but there was much work to be done. While still in the United States, prospective American visitors found it nearly impossible to find "authentic information concerning the country." What information was available came in the form of "a flood of confusing brochures describing every section of Ireland, but very little of it containing the essential information" that the tourist would need.[112] Once in Ireland, American visitors faced "the trip by tender to the pier at Cobh, the customs inspection in the bleak and windy shed, the lack of even the most primitive sanitary facilities, [and] the currency inspection under the leaky roof of a dismal crowded room." Upon leaving Cobh by rail, the tourist found advertisements for Norway, Austria, and Britain, but not Ireland. "Never before have we found competitive advertising so strategically placed," the committee noted sardonically. Once beyond these early horrors, the tourist would experience more frustrations staying in substandard hotels, riding on filthy trains, dining on dull food, and vainly seeking evening entertainment.

The Christenberry report offered a variety of very specific suggestions for improving the structure of Irish tourist development and for enhancing the country's ability to attract American dollars. Above all, the Christenberry committee urged the complete restructuring of tourism administration by November 1950. To begin with, there should be one tourism organization in Ireland, and it was advisable to merge the ITB and ITA into a single body. In a break with the past, appointments should be based on professional qualifications, and candidates drawn from business, advertising, and the hotel and hospitality industry. Above all, appointees should be "completely divorced from politics." No longer could the industry afford to have longtime republicans like O'Brien or anti-treaty stalwarts like Quinlan. At the same time it was considered important that the new chairman be Irish.[113] Christenberry's argument in favor of instituting an ethnic hiring criterion is completely understandable given Ireland's rapidly declining economic situation at the beginning of the 1950s. To have placed a foreigner in such a prominent position would have undermined the entire tourism project.[114] Indeed, Christenberry fully acknowledged the political difficulties inherent in any major tourism initiative, and for this reason the *new* tourist agency should be renamed in order to avoid any association attached to the old Irish Tourist Board.

In order to ensure success, Christenberry argued, the new board should take full advantage of ECA technical assistance over a period of six months, making use of the international expertise available in order to bring the body up to high standards quickly. It was also important that the new tourism organization receive adequate funds. Penny-pinching was ill-advised and would do little more than cripple the new body before it could take its first steps. Clearly, the increased staff and higher salaries required "a far larger budget and a more realistic method of raising funds. It means that the government will have to get completely in the swim of tourism instead of merely wetting its feet." While Britain and Bermuda devoted $350,000 and $200,000 respectively to promoting their tourist products in the American market alone, Ireland spent a meager £30,000 in all markets in an effort to attract visitors.

Furthermore, Christenberry pointed out that authorities had made no real effort to sell tourism to the Irish people since the war: "Despite the importance of this one industry in the nation's economy, the average Irishman knows practically nothing about its value," in stark contrast to Switzerland, where "every citizen is aware of tourist spending and what it means to him personally." In Christenberry's mind the success of tourism required that the "Irish people themselves" have sympathy for tourist development. The battle for tourism was now centered in the halls of power, but it really needed to be fought in the country as a whole. If Irish men and women themselves did not recognize tourism as a national interest, if they did not understand "the dollar economy involved," then they would not play their part in developing tourist facilities and welcoming visitors.[115]

In sum, the Christenberry report provided the government with a clear blueprint for a new tourist authority and offered concrete suggestions about the work that was required. Yet few of Christenberry's suggestions were adopted. Tourism remained "political" until the late 1950s, and the Irish Tourist Association continued its activities until 1964. Although the budget for tourism was increased dramatically, it fell far short of what was really required, and instead of centralizing tourist development with one board, Ireland ended up with *three* tourist boards. Even the suggested cooperation between the ECA and Irish tourism bodies failed to materialize—a victim of the board's "non-cooperation."[116] Even so, over the coming months the document was seldom absent from discussion. The committee of American hoteliers did push government officials to further acknowledge what Pozzi and the ECA had been already arguing fiercely, namely, that tourism development should be taken more seriously. In the wake of all of the scandal and a general perception that the board had made few gains, few Irish citizens really believed that spending money on a tourist board was worth the investment; Christenberry made a strong counterargument.

Behaving "Like Ostriches"

In the immediate aftermath of the Christenberry report the government created a cabinet committee to address the tourism issue, consisting of the

Taoiseach, the Tanaiste, the minister for external affairs, the minister for defense, and the parliamentary secretary to the minister for industry and commerce. The committee advocated immediate steps to publicize Ireland as a stopping place for Americans making the Holy Year pilgrimage to Rome, efforts to promote Ireland through Irish-American organizations, the provision of improved souvenirs, enhanced cooperation between the ITA and Tourist Board, and the appointment of a new ITB chairman. Nevertheless, few if any members of the committee seriously discussed substantial revision of tourist-development policies or organization.[117] Above all, the committee flatly rejected the idea that the ITA should be disbanded because

(a) both organisations [ITB and ITA] have separate sources of income;
(b) the association has an established tradition with a record of achievement;
(c) tourism is a sphere of activity well suited to co-operative effort and to organisation by persons whose purpose is not profit but community service; [and]
(d) there is public interest in the association of a proprietary or representative nature.[118]

The ITA's political significance is clearly visible from this list. With its important local connections and influential membership, the organization was almost untouchable, its preservation almost a national interest in itself. Far from disbanding the ITA, the Taoiseach believed that it should "be strengthened financially."[119]

The Department of Industry and Commerce enthusiastically greeted Christenberry's notion that the Tourist Board should launch a widespread campaign to educate the Irish people about the importance of tourism, because "it is necessary to explain the value of tourism and how tourist earnings benefit the country and the individual. In the schools, on farms, and in workshops and offices, propaganda for tourism must be set in motion."[120] Yet the department was reticent about restructuring the board, apparently believing that throwing money at the Tourist Board would solve the problem, with no restructuring required. Selling tourism to the public would eventually assuage the problem created by the tourism crisis, but in the meantime radical change was out of the question.

Meanwhile, outside of government circles frustration was increasing. Within the Tourist Board, Roger Greene, whom Colonel Pozzi had suggested as the ECA's choice for a board chairman in 1949,[121] resigned in disgust in June 1950. Greene told the *Irish Times* that his resignation was the result of "dissatisfaction with the government's attitude" and had nothing to do with the common feeling that the Quinlan-led board was notable for its "incompetency and neglect" of its duties. Greene claimed that he and the board had presented numerous reports to the government, only to have them ignored, and his resignation certainly illustrates growing frustration within the ITB.[122] The ITA was similarly irritated. Speaking at the association's annual general meeting, J. P. O'Brien, who was in the midst of an ill-fated attempt to start his own travel agency, Irish Express,[123] blamed the various government departments and stressed that the "government should do much more than the merely advisory part towards increasing hotel accommodation in the country."[124]

The media, and particularly the *Irish Press*, were also increasingly critical of government inaction. The *Press* blamed a decline in tourist traffic during 1950 on the "lack of leadership and organisation" from the "archvillain," the Irish Tourist Board.[125] The paper reasoned that anyone with a "sense of responsibility" should recognize the need for prompt and efficient improvement in tourist-development policy because "no country, particularly a small and poor one like ours, can afford to throw away a huge source of revenue such as poured into Ireland in 1946, 1947, and 1948." It was no longer acceptable to "behave like ostriches" by ignoring competition for tourists from other countries like Great Britain, while failing to do everything possible to ensure a continuation of the impressive tourist receipts of the late 1940s.[126]

In addition, the ECA continued to be greatly dissatisfied with the rate of progress. Throughout January, February, and March 1951, Marshall Plan representatives attempted to work with the Tourist Board on various development projects, primarily the distribution of grants, but they found it "impossible to get the ITB representatives to take any effective part in the discussion."[127] By 1 February the Department of External Affairs realized that Ireland was in danger of forfeiting "the goodwill" of the ECA mission because of the failure to make headway on tourism development.[128] By 7

February the mission began to threaten to withdraw a £100,000 grant for tourism development, as well as various agricultural grants totaling almost £1 million altogether.[129] When External Affairs was finally able to push the board into a meeting in mid-March, the tourist authority, which was tied up in efforts to promote government acceptance of its restructuring ideas, was unprepared to offer adequate feedback to the ECA, and consequently, the Marshall Plan money for tourist development, as well as the mission's willingness to provide advice, were placed in further doubt.[130]

When the government finally introduced legislation early in 1951, the proposals of the Christenberry report were little more than a distant memory for Fine Gael and its government partners. The new legislation included a dramatic increase in spending, provision for a *larger* board—not the lean and mean board suggested by Christenberry—and small changes to the ITB's hotel-registration scheme.[131]

The Lemass Solution

Consideration of the Fine Gael tourism bill was terminated in June 1951 by the dissolution of the Dáil for elections that produced a Fianna Fáil victory, and Seán Lemass, again minister for industry and commerce, did not present his bill until early 1952. During the period between Fianna Fáil's return to power and the introduction of a dramatically revised Tourist Traffic Act, Lemass "undertook a very careful and thorough review of policy in relation to tourist development," even inviting Christenberry to return to Ireland to brief him on the now famous report.[132] Above all, Lemass wanted to reach a decision about the fate of the ITA, the structure of the ITB, and what new roles, if any, should be given to tourist authorities.

Lemass had another consideration in mind as well—how to help his ailing friend and former Civil War comrade J. P. O'Brien.[133] Since losing his job in 1948, O'Brien had made an unsuccessful effort to establish his own travel agency. When this effort failed, he was faced with the problem of supporting a wife and children in decent comfort, not to mention his worsening alcoholism. Lemass quickly decided to establish a tourism publicity board, in addition to the existing Tourist Board, for his friend O'Brien to manage.

Lemass justified the need for a separate publicity board by noting that local authorities were able, under the 1939 Tourist Traffic Act, to establish their own associations and to seek approval from the minister to divert publicity payments to the local group. While this had never been an issue before, in 1950 a local publicity association was established in Sligo and had been subsequently authorized by the former minister for industry and commerce, Dr. Thomas F. O'Higgins. Given this precedent, it seemed likely that other local authorities might do the same, resulting in a dramatic decrease in Tourist Association income that would cripple the ITA and Ireland's tourist publicity effort as well. Adding further support to this argument, O'Higgins had also decided to end Tourist Board contributions to the ITA, further robbing the voluntary organization of valuable income. The new publicity board would circumvent the threat of ITA dissolution while providing the Dáil with statutory control over publicity. The proactive approach begged the question: Why not wrap up the association immediately? Lemass explained the step not only by citing the risk "of controversy and agitation," but also by asserting that the ITA represented something "of real value" by virtue of its long history. It was better to arrange for the association's "continued participation in tourist publicity work in conjunction with the Tourist Board" by ensuring the ITA a place on the board of directors for the statutory development and publicity boards.[134]

Lemass's embrace of the multiboard structure did not inspire universal approval, to say the least. One official even declared it "evidence of political cowardice on the part of the minister."[135] T. K. Whitaker, a high-ranking member of the Department of Finance, agreed and argued that instead of two boards, the publicity functions could be carried out within the larger vehicle of a single tourist board made up of "separate committees," with O'Brien as deputy chairman. Likewise, McElligott, also of Finance, insisted that the publicity board should be a subsidiary of the tourist board and should not have a separate staff.[136] The minister of finance was "horrified" at the extent of expenditure planned in the new legislation,[137] and his department worked to limit grants-in-aid to the proposed boards—an effort that Lemass was "not prepared to accept."[138] Ultimately Lemass secured the budget of £250,000 and £3,000,000 in loan guarantees that he had requested.[139]

Far more damning in the longer term than Department of Finance rejection, however, was that the Tourist Board itself responded with anger over the proposed separation of publicity activities from the main ITB structure.

Lemass was unsympathetic and quickly replied that he had never given any consideration to granting the board power over the new publicity body, which in his view would need to be able to "run its own ship."[140] The board's opposition to the separate publicity body should have sparked some concern at Industry and Commerce, yet no anxiety was visible.

The new tourism development structure became a reality even before legislation was presented to the Dáil. By October 1951 the publicity body was already functioning, leaving only its name to be seriously debated.[141] After an extensive discussion about possible names that included considerable bickering about the nuanced meanings of various Irish words, it was decided to call the publicity board "Fógra Fáilte" and the tourist-development board "An Bord Fáilte."[142] These names were not especially popular, and a number of TDs expressed reservations about the need for a Gaelic name in the first place; former minister for industry and commerce Dr. O'Higgins sneered that "it cannot be suggested that the change to an Irish name assists the saving of the language . . . I take it that we are not going to endeavour to teach tourists the Irish language."[143] He followed up this jibe by predicting that the name might confuse tourists from England and elsewhere, fatally undermining the tourist-development effort. Although teaching tourists the Irish language was not Lemass's reason for using an Irish name, he appears to have felt that it was important for the government to stress the country's unique Gaelic past and present, pointing at every turn to Ireland's rich heritage, especially at a time when the nation's fortunes were in decline. To use Gaelic names sparked memories of a proud past, deflecting attention from the failed Irish Tourist Board and the failing Irish economy.

Back to Business

With the passage of the Tourist Traffic Act of 1952, the two statutory tourist bodies quickly got to work developing tourism products and trying to educate the Irish people about the industry's national importance. The national education program took two forms. Most dramatically, the tourist authorities inaugurated a new Irish homecoming festival called "An Tóstal," which was held annually between 1953 and 1958.[144] Although An Tóstal was most obviously intended to increase dollar earnings and to extend the tourist season by drawing a sizeable portion of the nation's twenty million "exiles" back to Ireland, the event was supposed to increase internal awareness of tourism while educating Irish people about the importance of the industry, the country's proud cultural heritage, and the way in which Irish landscapes should look. An Bord Fáilte boasted that the "pre-eminent" position of tourism would be "clearly recognised by all" as a result of Tóstal festivities.[145] In newspaper articles and advertisements the Irish were encouraged to plant flowers, paint their homes, clip hedgerows, and generally tidy their surroundings. As Taoiseach John A. Costello said when opening the 1955 Tóstal,

> its secondary but closely related object is to provide opportunities for national spring cleaning, whereby to promote individual, local, and national conceit in, and responsibility for, the neatness, attractiveness, and order of our cities, towns and villages, of our houses, gardens, and public buildings, and to stimulate our own interest in, and appreciation of, our culture, shrines, and holy places and the beauties of our own land.[146]

Ireland's national festival was intended as an important component of a national retraining scheme in which tourism was strongly positioned as a national interest and its development regarded as a patriotic duty. According to tourist authorities, "the success of An Tóstal depends on the individual citizen" and represented "a first-class business proposition for the nation." If successful, the festival would create "a better Ireland for generations to come."[147]

The second reeducation program (launched at the same time that An Tóstal was being planned) consisted primarily of a booklet entitled *What Does Tourism Mean to You?*, which featured the slogan "Tourism is everybody's business—the tourist is everybody's guest." The publication lectured the reader: "Tourism is a living, dynamic activity which touches many aspects of our national life," but which could "flourish only when there is a general public appreciation of its value." The booklet attempted to define tourists and to describe the role of the industry in the economy by graphically suggesting that it was the country's largest single export in 1949,[148] listing Ireland's main tourist attractions, stating the significance of domestic tourism, and drawing attention to the fundamental importance of the general public in the industry's success. According to the publishers, "Every one of us can help the visitor feel at home in Ireland by extending to him that extra courtesy and consideration to which every guest is entitled"—a task made easy because "it is a natural instinct with the Irish people."[149]

The campaign to teach Irish citizens about the importance of tourism did not end with the demise of An Tóstal. In fact, the message that "Tourism is Everybody's Business" remained a staple component of Bord Fáilte Éireann's (BFÉ) activities into the late 1970s, when BFÉ created a short film that again emphasized the financial significance of tourism to the Irish economy—by then responsible for one in every ten jobs and worth £230 million per annum—and suggesting annual spring-cleaning, the development of local festivals, and the friendly treatment of tourists. Ultimately, the board claimed, tourism "enriches our own lives" by sparking the creation of improved roads, parks, a healthier environment, and "pride in our way of life, history, and scenery."[150] Much as in the 1920s, so too in the 1950s, tourism still constituted a harbinger of local improvements and a conduit to a better life.

Bord Fáilte Éireann

In spite of the launch of numerous new programs, the two-board structure collapsed in 1954 as a result of J. P. O'Brien's declining health and an almost total lack of communication between O'Brien and the director of An Bord Fáilte, J. A. Nugent.[151] As previously noted, Nugent and his team already resented Fógra Fáilte before the passage of the 1952 Tourist Traffic Act, and it certainly did not help that Nugent and O'Brien refused to speak to one another from the outset. Nugent was a Fine Gael appointee who had started with the Irish Tourist Board in 1950, while O'Brien was a longtime member of Fianna Fáil—politics and the legacy of the Civil War remained a significant and damaging component of tourist administration.[152]

In August 1954, two months after Fine Gael returned to power at the head of another interparty government, the two statutory tourist organizations jointly agreed to request legislation to dissolve Fógra Fáilte in favor of a single statutory tourist body. When presenting the requested legislation in February 1955, the new minister of industry and commerce, William Norton, argued that "the existence of these two bodies results in unnecessary duplication of staffs and lack of central direction. This must give rise to overlapping and must weaken the effective control and direction of staff and of functions. Such a situation can only give rise to unhealthy rivalry between the two bodies and perhaps clashes of personality."[153]

The desire for a single statutory body did little to diminish the power of the Irish Tourist Association. As always, the ITA engaged in its usual heavy lobbying efforts to guarantee its continued position in Irish tourism development. This time the association asked for official recognition in the new legislation, a "position of dignity" that "granted more power and a definite status" to the ITA.[154] Toward this end ITA leaders successfully persuaded the County Council Chambers to pass a resolution demanding specific reference to the Irish Tourist Association in the new bill.[155] Norton provided this recognition by noting "the special position of the Irish Tourist Association in connection with tourism," and he proposed "to give the association suitable representation on the new board" as long as local authorities continued to provide the ITA with significant funds.[156] The association remained politically untouchable.

After passage of the 1955 Tourist Traffic Act, An Bord Fáilte and Fógra Fáilte were merged into a single statutory tourist body called Bord Fáilte Éireann; there would be no further significant legal changes in the shape of the statutory Irish tourist organization until the late 1990s. Unlike the previous statutory bodies, the new tourist board was less driven by a single top-level figure and instead drew much greater attention from its board of directors, who now began to take a more direct interest in various policy options, leaving the chairman to address questions of day-to-day administration.[157] Even more important, the days of political appointments also quickly came to an end. Whereas O'Brien, Quinlin, Nugent, and an interim director named J. F. Dempsey were all political appointees, Timothy J. (T. J.) O'Driscoll, who took office in 1956, was not. Instead, O'Driscoll was a tough-minded man from Cork who had little patience for politics of the ordinary kind. Before his long career as director-general of Bord Fáilte Éireann, O'Driscoll had been a star athlete; later, as a civil servant, he had been involved in the establishment of CIÉ under the tutelage of John Leydon. After getting involved in an insider-trading scandal, the Corkman was transferred from his post at Industry and Commerce to another department based in the Phoenix Park, a position that did not satisfy the ambitious O'Driscoll. Rather than await reassignment, the future Bord Fáilte leader cycled back to the offices of Industry and Commerce, discovered that his desk was still vacant, and simply transferred himself back to his old job. According to Kevin O'Doherty, who worked extensively with O'Driscoll, the Corkman was a "very dominant character," a "real go-getter," and "he could get things done." O'Driscoll was precisely the man that Bord Fáilte needed. Whereas the accepted approach to securing employment during this period was to know somebody, O'Driscoll refused to see anybody who presented references before establishing his or her qualifications. He simply wanted the best people he could find and did not care about their politics.[158]

With tourism now separated from its once clear links to the major political parties, tourist revenue increasing (by 1958 revenue had reached £34.6 million, the highest on record), and a host of development and promotional projects being aggressively pursued by the Tourist Board, the tourism industry seemed ready to take off. Adding further fuel to the fire, the *White Paper on Economic Expansion* of 1958 afforded the industry a prominent place in government economic priorities and pledged £1 million in grants to assist in tourism development through 1968.[159] In turn, the *Second Programme for Economic Expansion* called for a doubling of tourism revenue between 1960 and 1970.[160]

In many ways it was a new era for tourism development in Ireland—a period of setting goals and expecting to achieve them. The more objectives that were set, the more tourists were needed to meet them, and the more attentive policy makers had to be to industry demands. While the government had previously debated the status of tourism as a national interest, the industry was now assured of a place in government thinking; tourism was again considered an important national priority.

3
Change and Continuity, 1958–1994

Between 1958 and the early 1990s Ireland underwent massive social and economic change. Society became increasingly urbanized as traditional rural industry collapsed and workers left agriculture,[1] tuberculosis was eradicated, and infant mortality was reduced.[2] Even Irish Catholicism, once widely considered a defining characteristic of Irishness, changed dramatically as church influence declined and mass attendance dropped precipitously in the late 1980s and the 1990s.[3] During the second half of the century as a whole, the Irish economy dipped and climbed like a vicious rollercoaster. The 1950s were marked by a lackluster economy and dizzying emigration.[4] The 1960s featured a dramatic economic improvement and a virtual end to the mass exodus of the previous decade. The brief prosperity did not last. After the shock of the first world oil crisis of 1973, joblessness climbed once more and did not drop below 13 percent again until 1994.[5] Despite this painful problem, there was reason to hope for a brighter future, even if it did not seem likely at the time. In 1973 Ireland joined the European Economic Community (EEC), opening the door to vital economic assistance. The eventual implications would be significant (see chapter 7).

As Ireland slowly moved from widespread poverty and underdevelopment to become a somewhat awkward modern country on the cusp of a great transformation during the 1990s, tourism became an increasingly important component of the Irish economy and an ever more obvious national interest.[6] New tourism enterprises and growth targets after the first *Programme for Economic Expansion* in 1958 reflected this growing recognition. At the same time, the government voted larger and larger budgets to the Tourist Board and so showed its deepening belief in the value of tourism.[7] Naturally, expanding government interest and increasingly aggressive goals meant that tourism administration grew more complicated. From the 1960s tourism plans had to balance the elements of development, the environment, and carefully targeted ad spending. Marketing programs needed to cater to the tastes of a widening number of audiences; advertising had to be tailored to match a dizzying array of visitor gazes. At the same time Irish tourism had to compete with countries such as Spain, whose tourism growth outpaced all others in Western Europe during the 1950s.[8] These new pressures forced Bord Fáilte Éireann (BFÉ) to expand its market research efforts and to become increasingly savvy in its approach to promoting the country.

Even as tourism budgets and planning pressures increased, Irish tourism retained many of the concerns that had existed since 1923. The industry remained a nexus for discussion about the national interest and identity. Although there was now considerable consensus about the importance of the industry in economic terms, there were still diverse local and regional interests, still divisions over precisely how Ireland should be presented to the world, still shortages of accommodation, an infrastructure needing constant improvement, and the problem that Irish tourism remained a highly seasonal product. Just as in the two earlier periods of post–Civil War tourism development, the years after 1958 saw a diverse collection of individuals and groups using tourism as an excuse to push local grievances at central government level. At the same time the government's newfound dedication to tourism development meant that it was no longer willing to leave local tourism administration to a body outside its control. In 1964 the ITA was finally disbanded and replaced by Regional Tourism Organisations with direct administrative links to Dublin. Finally, just as Marshall Plan administrators had earlier tried to coerce the Irish government into further tourist development, so too the European Union pushed tourism in Ireland as a path toward economic development and self-sufficiency in the 1980s and 1990s. Outside pressures, just as much as inside voices, continued to define tourism as a national interest.

During the years between 1924 and roughly 1955 the national tourism debate had centered on whether tourism was desirable and for what reasons, unfolding in a more or less linear manner. By 1958 there were few who doubted the importance of tourism, yet there remained divisions about how to shape the industry and about precisely why tourism was important to the nation. At the same time, more and more people were concerned about how Ireland should be represented to the world at large. Tourism officials gradually became more adept at dealing with the challenges posed by the new dialogue. They improved their ability to collect information, made an effort to improve national control of local development efforts, launched more and more spectacular marketing initiatives, and actively used tourism as a means of defining and expanding the national community—all as the diverse voices present during the pre-1958 period continued to make themselves heard.

A "True Patriot"

By 1962 tourism revenue reached nearly £47 million and was climbing rapidly every year. Not surprisingly, local groups desperately wanted to secure as much of this meaty pie as possible and continued to exert considerable influence over tourism development. For some, tourism represented a potential source of great wealth, but for many others it presented a solution to the pressing problems of poverty, underdevelopment, and massive emigration—all shockingly obvious on the western seaboard.

Father John J. Scanlon arrived in the rural parish of Tuosist in 1961, and his interest in tourism can stand for that of many small rural communities along the western seaboard. Situated on the Kerry side of the Cork-Kerry border in the Caha Mountains, Tuosist is rugged, rural, and stunningly beautiful. It sits in a rocky and heather-strewn landscape, dotted with forested areas, more welcoming to midges than men. While most tourists know the Healy Pass and the Coast Road, they seldom stop for more than a few moments to snap photographs and take in the view of Hungry Hill, Glanmore Lake, the Cascade waterfall, and the other quickly accessible scenic attractions of the area.

Scanlon had no sooner arrived at his cottage, devoid of modern sanitation or electricity, than he realized that his parish faced a crisis; the community was "dying . . . , or more correctly, almost dead."[9] In 1841 the area had been home to 7,485 people. By 1926 the population had fallen to 1,800, and by 1963 it had dropped still further to just 860. Worse still, the emigration that was destroying the community showed no sign of stopping. There were 150 bachelors in the parish and just 25 marriageable young women.

Upon reaching eighteen, young women immediately left for England, leaving behind aging parents who generally followed their children as soon as the young people had established themselves in a new life abroad. In 1963 as many as sixty houses lay vacant, collapsing quickly as moisture seeped into the support structure. Beyond the specter of constant emigration Scanlon perceived another major problem: mounting foreign ownership. While Irish industrialists and tourist authorities expressed little interest in the parish, he feared that German and English developers were actively purchasing large tracks of land, and predicted that Tuosist would soon be most notable for proliferating "Trespassers will be prosecuted" signs.[10]

At first Scanlon thought that the solution was to find a matchmaker who would arrange marriages that might help to prop up the dwindling population. Scanlon wanted to find a diplomat and an authority on Tuosist family history. The successful candidate was expected to smoke a pipe—to "lend authority to his statements"—as well as to "know the parishioners of Tuosist like the back of his hand." Impossible job qualifications, to be sure, and it did not take Scanlon long to recognize that a matchmaker was not going to solve the rural crisis anyway. Something more proactive was required.

In Scanlon's mind tourism became the most viable solution. Tuosist has little arable farmland, and without electricity or running water, to say nothing of better road access, industrial development was out of the question. Even so, the parish did have scenic beauty in spades. Writing to Bord Fáilte, to the Department of the Taoiseach, and to Erskine Childers, the minister for transport and power, Scanlon argued that the famous Healy Pass, Glanmore Lake, Glenbeg Lough (famous for trout fishing), the groves of Dineen, the mountains, the seas—all give variety for the tourist; no wonder then that tourists who pass through are amazed by its beautiful scenery and disgusted with the tourist bodies who even have left the very name of Tuosist off the maps.

Scanlon wondered why Bord Fáilte was "doing big things elsewhere in places such as Killarney and Ballybunion" while ignoring Tuosist, robbing the parish of vital revenue by encouraging tourists to pass from Glengarriff to Kenmare or Killarney without stopping to spend a few days in this scenic Shangri-La. He suggested that the government could improve the situation dramatically by bringing electricity and improved sanitation to area homes, thus allowing the rapid development of tourist accommodation and enhancing the attraction of the area to visitors.[11] It was a heartfelt plea, not at all unlike those from Kinsale and Dingle during the 1920s, 1930s, and 1940s.

The plight of Tuosist caught the attention of Listowel-based playwright John B. Keane,[12] who interviewed Scanlon and published an extended article on Tuosist in the *Sunday Press*. For Keane the plight of Tuosist was one of national importance, and the fight to save the parish was every bit as nationalist in its inspiration as Easter Week had been. Keane held that

> [a] patriot is not a man who boasts about the Irish heritage, Irish culture, the Irish language as such. Idealist, yes, but not patriot. A patriot is a man who contributes in a practical way to the development of his own country. A man who stays at home and marries at home in spite of the overwhelming difficulties is a true patriot.
>
> He is a patriot who fights with his heart and mind for the countryside which gave him birth. He is a patriot who helps communities less fortunate than his own. Men of consequence and substance who take an interest in places like Tuosist are the real practical patriots.

Keane was writing to the government, to wealthy investors, to men of influence, in the hope that he could make them see Scanlon's plight and feel a desire to help, if not for Tuosist, then for Ireland. "Money and incoming people will bring the natives back," he insisted. "If a man is drowning, won't you give him priority?" Tourism would surely "make all the difference" by supplementing farm income, sparking marriages, ensuring the development of "a well-appointed guesthouse," and allowing Scanlon to return to his spiritual tasks of conducting christenings and marriages and saying Sunday mass.[13]

The government took Scanlon's comments seriously, applauding his efforts to install signposts along key parish roadways and assuring the priest of "the great importance that the government attaches to the development of tourism, not only in the national interest, but as a means of promoting the economic welfare of rural areas." Scanlon was told that the position of Tuosist would be systematically considered.[14]

After its referral from the Department of the Taoiseach's office, Scanlon's plea found a willing audience in the members of the Kerry Development

Team. After considering his proposals (which also included a handful of agricultural suggestions), the team determined that tourism was the region's most promising prospect and that the erection of holiday chalets should be encouraged. The chalets would be ideal for financially pinched families from Great Britain, Europe, and America, while requiring little staff and increasing the "spending population" of Tuosist.[15]

If the British and American markets were seriously to be considered, the erection of saleable chalets first demanded electrification. After receiving direction from the minister of transport and power, the Electricity Supply Board (ESB) quickly began to consider electrifying at least that part of Tuosist parish near Lauragh and its immediate vicinity.[16] In the meantime Scanlon continued writing letters, explaining that "the poor mouth excuse of lack of money carries no weight, as the tourists in many ways will pour it back again into the national purse."[17] The rural priest was difficult to ignore, and by February 1964 the ESB confirmed that its staff would be able to extend power to thirty households in the parish.[18] It was a significant victory, but certainly did not guarantee Scanlon's ultimate success.

The next major challenge was to win approval from Bord Fáilte for the chalet scheme. Such support would have seemed likely because Tourist Board development policy was now based on the provision of loans and grants, and special monies were available for development in the western counties, where tourism was increasingly seen as the most promising harbinger of economic relief. On 19 June 1962 a general program was approved under which money was to be provided to develop farmhouses to serve as bed-and-breakfasts, while further schemes were planned to develop chalets in Gaeltacht areas.[19]

Unfortunately, Tuosist was a small and relatively isolated parish without a significant preexisting service industry, nor was it a Gaeltacht district. Thirty electrified homes near the Kenmare River hardly represented a sound investment. Tourist authorities wanted to support larger projects, such as communities of holiday homes, rather than isolated groups of two or three, along with promotional policies designed to attract substantial numbers of visitors. Yet the logic was more than just economic. By the early 1960s, Bord Fáilte was fully aware of the importance of scenic beauty and was beginning to view itself as an environmental watchdog organization. In particular, the success of the Tidy Towns program, inaugurated in 1958 (see chapter 6), demonstrated to the board that building and planning controls were beneficial to the tourism industry; the board believed that "a rash of isolated building could be injurious to the scenic amenities of the area."[20] Given the circumstances, Tuosist was not a viable site for substantial board investment.

Scanlon did not give up. While little money was forthcoming to develop holiday cottages, the priest was eventually able to secure Bord Fáilte assistance in creating a brochure advertising the attractions of Tuosist. The brochure featured photographs of area scenery and families seated around gas lamps recounting ancestral stories or perhaps remembering the beautiful sites/sights witnessed during the day's adventures. The text attempted to sell the area as "a holiday with a difference," desirable precisely because it was not modern in any way. Prospective visitors were informed, "You will find the people in Tuosist living the same kind of life as they have lived for decades past." The very fact that electricity was still not widely available in 1971 ensured that "the ancient art of story-telling has not been displaced by the impact of radio and television—the local people have it at their fingertips, and it is fascinating to hear the stories take shape from the lips of a seanechaidh." This was an area where poetry was as obvious as the staggeringly beautiful scenery, and boating and pony-trekking also beckoned the visitor.[21]

Scanlon's efforts were not a complete failure. He did, after all, bring electricity to a small area of his parish, prompt the development of two small hotels, and successfully publish a tourism brochure. Given that Scanlon was essentially a single voice calling out from the Kerry wilderness, these were no small achievements. The guidebook and limited tourist accommodation did not end the exodus from Tuosist, and Scanlon's dream of large-scale tourism development was never realized, but his voice had been taken seriously, echoing through the halls of government and prompting inquiries by Bord Fáilte, the Department of Transport and Power, the ESB, and the Kerry County Council. Even when local pleas were unsuccessful, they demanded the government's ear and inevitably drew the attention of tourist authorities.

Not all local interests were represented by single individuals. Local authorities, development companies like the Shannon Free Airport Development Company, bodies like the Kilmainham Restoration Society, and other tourism-related groups and organizations all exercised a significant influence on tourist authorities and/or the government. Negotiations with Belfast during the 1960s, for example, were partly influenced by local interests in the border counties who demanded assistance with canal-development programs, the foundation of the Enniskillen airfield, and increased ease of movement for anglers interested in fishing the numerous lakes in the "Lakelands" area.[22]

Local pressure often prompted swift action by tourist authorities, as in 1972 when hoteliers in Clare became upset with a Bord Fáilte booklet entitled *Where to Eat in Ireland: Traveler's Guide to 100 Selected Restaurants*. After the initial complaints it did not take long for the Irish Hotels' Federation to call on the Tourist Board to cease distributing the guide. Despite the protests, BFÉ insisted that *Where to Eat* was little more than an indicator of top restaurants. Even so, within days of the federation's demand, Bord Fáilte suspended distribution of twenty thousand copies of the booklet.[23] It was more beneficial for the statutory Tourist Board to placate the federation and the Clare hoteliers than it was to risk alienating either group further. Local demands were certainly not limited to the distribution (or not) of guidebooks; they ranged from County Clare's insistence that BFÉ work to develop angling tourism because it would be the "savior of Clare tourism,"[24] to complaints by others about the omission of their region from a Bord Fáilte slideshow.[25] Just as in earlier days, tourism authorities were constantly reminded that tourism development concerned more than a handful of Tourist Board officials.

"Eight Little Monsters"

Given the continued importance of local interests, the rapidly expanding size of the industry, and the growing government investment, it was only a matter of time before government interest in tourism clashed with the now old-fashioned and inefficient Irish Tourist Association. From the government's perspective it was now important to directly control local tourism efforts as well as those at the national level.

The conflict finally erupted when in early 1963 the local tourism promoters in west Cork, headed by Michael R. Boland, contacted Bord Fáilte about establishing a tourism-development association for that region under the terms of the 1931 Tourism Traffic Act. Because the request fit neatly into a growing government and Tourist Board desire to create local associations as a means of bypassing the ITA, a meeting was quickly arranged between Tourist Board chief T. J. O'Driscoll and Cork County Manager Michael Conlon to discuss the proposal.[26] The meeting was intensely productive and quickly resulted in a plan to establish the West Cork Tourist Development Company, a plan that was subsequently expanded to cover the county as a whole. On 1 March, Conlon invited interested parties to an emergency meeting of the Cork County Council to discuss an immediate realization of the plan. The ITA was not amused. By the time the emergency County Council meeting took place, the ITA, still comprising powerful figures from Irish political and social life, had intensely lobbied all members of the Cork County Council to reject the proposed organization, fiercely arguing against any county contributions to the new body. Boland was furious that the proposal had been torpedoed, and he complained bitterly to the Taoiseach himself.[27]

The association's response to the west Cork proposal was not surprising. Although the ITA had settled easily into running tourism bureaus in both North and South following the 1952 Tourist Traffic Act, its leaders guarded their diminished role with an iron fist. Unless it showed constant vigilance, the ITA feared that grants from local authorities would dry up, bringing about the demise of the organization. Any attempt to establish alternative local organizations was thus greeted with outright hostility.

The ITA's survival strategy could not have clashed more sharply with the policy of Bord Fáilte and the Department of Transport and Power in encouraging local associations through development grants—grants that guaranteed a local voice and also ensured that the new associations were dependent on the central tourism organization rather than on local authorities. This new government policy had been announced in October 1961; in addition to endorsing local tourism organizations, the policy document also advocated a merger of the two national tourism bodies, or at the very least, a complete retooling of the ITA "in light of current conditions." More than any minister before him, Erskine Childers wanted to see the abolition of the ITA, and in February 1963 he ordered his department to investigate the means available for dispensing with the association.[28] The minister believed that it was "essential to have a central organisation coordinating this growing local effort, eliminating overlap and breaking new ground."[29] While the ITA lobbied intensively to attain statutory responsibility for local coordination,[30] Childers did not think that its leaders were "suited to this task as regards staffing, constitution, or methods of administration." In addition, he was appalled by the Cork story and could not imagine entrusting "a task of leadership" to the association. In the minister's eyes the ITA was little more than an excuse for lavish annual gatherings in Dublin and had not contributed substantially to tourism development for many years.

The very reasons that had enabled the Irish Tourist Association to survive since 1924 made disbanding it difficult. O'Driscoll, for example, expressed a desire to avoid conflict with the ITA, while Childers recognized that "it is clearly a delicate business in view of the previous contribution of the ITA to tourist development and the prestige which still attaches to the director's position. A number of them are our people." The minister wondered whether the ITA could be reshaped into some kind of "advisory National Tourist Association, with appointed officers to exchange information and represent the combined forces of tourism," and he hypothesized that the time was right for a change given that longtime ITA director J. Fitzpatrick was nearly ready to retire.[31] Lemass agreed to the idea, assuming that it could be "applied harmoniously," and suggested that Childers should move ahead.[32]

On 11 April 1963 the minister met with a deputation from the ITA and outlined his thoughts concerning the future of local and regional tourism promotion, including his views on the future of the association. Childers called the current two-body structure "a misapplication of effort to have all this background and knowledge—and in particular, the invaluable local connections through the local authority representatives—devoted to what I feel are rather limited functions." A single statutory body would also avoid confusing the public and local associations, and it would improve communication, especially given the growing number of local tourist organizations. Childers proposed the creation of six or seven regional bodies representing homogenous geographical areas "that would constitute a viable unit in terms of promotion as a holiday area." The new regional tourism bodies "would have a good measure of discretion in regard to the servicing and generation of traffic within their own areas." They would operate information services, improve local tourism amenities, publish regional brochures, and run regional publicity campaigns. Most important, each regional body would be composed of men with "experience, energy, and representative quality." Although each of the regional tourism organizations would have "a degree of autonomy," Childers firmly intended that Bord Fáilte would oversee the various groups and provide a degree of centralized control.[33]

Of course, from the ITA's perspective the new plan offered little to love and was not greeted warmly. As far as the old tourist body was concerned, the ITA continued to symbolize the national importance of the tourist movement, and this symbolism was worth fighting for. One member immediately leaked the minister's new plan to the press despite the very clear "confidential" stamp on the cover letter that Childers supplied to the deputation. It is not clear whether the leak was motivated by a well-considered desire to humiliate the minister and rally support for the old standard bearer of Irish tourism, or whether it was simply an emotional outburst, but it did have the effect of embarrassing Childers, who quickly notified the Taoiseach of the ITA president's formal apology for the leak.[34]

Meanwhile, the press quickly jumped on the leak and began reporting the impending death of the Irish Tourist Association, not with merry glee but with a hint of nostalgia. Even the *Irish Press,* which was founded by Éamon de Valera in 1931 to ensure positive coverage of Fianna Fáil and its policies,[35] was not overwhelmingly positive about the death of the old voluntary organization once hated by the party. Instead, the paper noted the unpromising prognosis for the ITA and stressed that the association had "earned much good-will, not alone by the establishment of its bureaux, but also among county councils, many of which have annually contributed funds to the organisation."[36] There was no immediate welcome for the minister's proposal and no formal government statement, just the slightly premature publication of an obituary for the forty-year-old parent body of post–Civil War Irish tourism—a body that had not quite yet uttered its audible death rattle.

Undaunted by the unfortunate ITA leak, the Department of Transport and Power officially announced the new regional plan on 15 October.[37] Unlike the initial proposal made to the ITA deputation, the plan called for the creation of eight Regional Tourism Organisations (RTOs): Dublin Regional

Tourism (Dublin city); Eastern Regional Tourism (Dublin, Kildare, Louth, Meath, and Wicklow); South-Eastern Regional Tourism (Carlow, Kilkenny, Tipperary South, Waterford, and Wexford); Southern Regional Tourism (Cork and Kerry); Mid-Western Regional Tourism (Clare, Limerick, and Tipperary North); Western Regional Tourism (Galway and Mayo); North-Western Regional Tourism (Donegal, Leitrim, and Sligo); and Midland Regional Tourism (Cavan, Laois, Longford, Offaly, Monaghan, Roscommon, and Westmeath). Childers stressed that the plan would seek to tap the interest, goodwill, energy, and experience of "tourism-conscious people" in the service of their respective regions. Each RTO would be incorporated as a company under the 1931 Tourist Traffic Act and would be supported by the relevant county council. Local authorities, local development associations, and other tourism concerns would receive membership, as would business people and private citizens if they so desired, all under the guidance of Bord Fáilte. The bodies would deal with regional publicity and provide local contacts, foster interest in tourism by local authorities, and educate the people about the benefits of tourism; they would also organize local amenities and work to improve facilities, encourage coordination among all local groups, and run special campaigns to attract tourists and encourage constructive county planning.[38]

Not long after the announcement, Kevin O'Doherty, then Regional Development and Travel Facilities manager, was assigned the task of establishing the new Regional Tourism Organisations. O'Doherty, a tall, physically powerful, and intensely hard-working man who started his professional life with the tourist board after a stint as Seán Lemass's private secretary, had an encyclopedic knowledge of regional politics and the personalities involved in tourism. He found a situation in which meetings had already been held and disputes and deepening rivalries were beginning to emerge. Counties that historically disliked one another—Wexford versus Carlow and Cork versus Kerry, for example—found the prospect of working together difficult enough, but when the specter of disproportionate representation within the new RTOs was introduced into the equation, they became positively hostile.

O'Doherty decided to tackle the most challenging rivalry first: Cork and Kerry. To successfully bridge the gap, the longtime Bord Fáilte man needed a director acceptable to both counties. He wanted to find someone who was outside the usual collection of tourism-development suspects, who was thoughtful and energetic, and who recognized the difficulties. As luck would have it, O'Doherty found his man during an early meeting at the Imperial Hotel in Cork when Liam Devlin, a graduate of University College Cork, a member of the Harbour Board, and a successful small businessman, spoke from the back of the room. Devlin's questions were intelligent and well articulated, and he quickly caught O'Doherty's eye—especially because Devlin immediately recognized that the RTOs could easily become "eight little monsters" if not carefully constituted, eight little monsters all with their own individual interests and concerns, no more the subordinates of Bord Fáilte than the ITA had been. Devlin proved an inspired choice, and he "took to it like a bird," cleverly circumventing the problem of giving either Cork or Kerry top billing by naming the RTO "Ivernia." With the most difficult counties out of the way, O'Doherty easily moved on to establish the other seven companies, finishing with Dublin on 2 March 1964. Despite the many potential snares, all eight Regional Tourism Organisations were incorporated in less than eighteen months.[39]

As efficient as the establishment of the RTOs was, problems remained in relation to both the operation of the eight organizations and the fact that some members of the Irish Tourist Association remained hostile to the new structure. Even before all eight companies were established, there was "some misunderstanding as to the nature and scope of the regional organisations."[40] As far as Bord Fáilte was concerned, each regional body existed primarily to pursue development activities, leaving the bulk of the marketing to emerge from the Baggot Street Bridge offices of the national Tourist Board. In the rush to establish the RTOs, however, Galway-Mayo and Wexford-Waterford were not adequately briefed about the extent of their authority, and both immediately began working to attract as much attention to their own regions as possible, effectively usurping central control over publicity in these areas. Naturally other regions soon followed suit, quickly establishing a de facto promotional role for the local bodies. In effect, the RTOs were in fact emerging as the feared "eight little monsters," running their own operations to a degree not envisaged by Bord Fáilte or Erskine Childers.[41]

Adding to the headaches, the Irish Tourist Association refused to die quietly, even as several of the top jobs in the new RTOs went to longtime ITA members in order to facilitate a smooth transition. Many of the directors were "befogged by the suddenness of the demise of the ITA" and believed that the organization should continue, if only in an advisory capacity. The selection of RTO directors was especially troubling to some members of the ITA. As previously noted, Bord Fáilte made the initial selection of RTO directors. "If a region consisted of two counties, the aim was to have 7 or 8 people and to spread the representation over the counties concerned—to get people generally, commercial and tourist interests, people who were prepared to serve, people who attended the formation meetings of the regional organisations," and, of course, people who were popular enough with the Tourist Board to be invited to serve. This heavily top-down composition at the start, even if elections were planned to occur just two years later, struck some in the ITA as "a kind of qualified democracy" carried out by a board that had little understanding of voluntary organizations and by appointees who in many cases lacked any comprehension of such groups. It was suggested that many of those who had been appointed were involved in for-profit tourism businesses (travel agencies, for example), rather than people "who are putting something into it without hope of reward."[42] For ITA members tourism was a national interest, tourism promotion a nationalist act, and these new RTOs seemed to be motivated more by personal profit than by patriotic duty.

In spite of an agreement that the ITA would voluntarily wrap itself up, no such decision was taken at the extraordinary meeting called on 6 May 1964. Instead, nine of the fifteen directors present voted to continue the ITA until the annual meeting in the fall, when the final terminating vote would be rendered. The final months of the association were filled with acrimony and were notable only for remarks such as one made by Eamon Quinn, an ITA board member, who angrily declared that "Bord Fáilte are not a fit and proper body to administer the tourist industry."[43] The ITA had been in existence for over forty years, despite numerous challenges, and its members believed deeply in the patriotic purposes of the group. In the end, however, the ITA's success in shaping popular consensus about the national importance of tourism was paradoxically the cause of the association's demise. The group had become little more than a relic of the past, while tourism was the road to the future.

The Growth of Government Interest

When the Irish Tourist Association finally succumbed, the industry was growing more rapidly and had a larger impact on the economy than at any previous time in Irish history. Beyond the creation of the RTOs, the government showed a slowly growing faith in the tourist industry. In 1958 the industry received a significant stamp of approval with its inclusion in the *White Paper on Economic Expansion* and was allocated at least £1 million in grants "to help the development of major resorts"[44]—support that continued to grow stronger when tourism income reached £42.4 million in 1960 (up by £4.6 million over the previous year),[45] £46.9 million in 1961,[46] and £49.5 million in 1963.[47]

Encouraged by these increases, the government included tourism in the *Second Programme for Economic Expansion*. This time the plan called for a doubling of tourism revenue between 1960 and 1970. Faced with such a big challenge, tourism interests—including Bord Fáilte, various hoteliers, RTO representatives, trade union officials, and travel agencies—passed a resolution calling for complete cooperation, effective communication, and the full devotion of resources to attaining the government's objective.[48] Partly as a result of this newfound solidarity—combined with greatly expanded marketing efforts in Europe and North America,[49] a growing list of tourist sites (see chapters 4–6), expanding tourist accommodation, and more rapid transatlantic travel—during the period covered by the *Second Programme,* tourism revenue increased from £39 million to £97 million—growth of more than 5 percent per annum.[50] Just as exciting, growth came not only in the British market, always Ireland's most important single source of tourism revenue, but also from the United States. In 1962, some 85,000 Americans traveled to Ireland.[51] By 1967 this number grew to 140,000 and by 1970 it had reached 230,000—a clear indication that tourism development efforts were increasingly effective.[52]

From the perspective of the Department of Transport and Power this increase was dramatic and important, especially because it both assisted the balance of payments and provided a significant economic stimulus. Irish markets expanded, vital revenue flowed to the rural west, and development companies benefited through the constant construction of new hotel and resort facilities.[53] While the government had been aware of the far-reaching benefits of tourism for many years, the age of planning inaugurated in 1958 now painted these bonuses in much brighter colors, and the *Third Programme* showed even more government confidence in tourism development by setting £112 million as the revenue target for 1972.[54]

In spite of the apparent growth in government confidence, industry observers remained concerned that the government had yet to show a firm dedication to supporting tourism through even larger grants, and they feared that officials might just as easily withdraw funding, especially if there were a change in administration. In late 1965 and early 1966 reports from within the government suggested that there was to be no major increase in tourism spending in the new budget. This news left insiders surprised and upset. *Irish Travel Trade News*, the major industry journal, expressed shock. It declared that the government's projected tightfistedness was "nothing more than a piece of monumental cheeseparing," and noted that the Tourist Board would be forced to carefully reconsider all of its financial allocations, scaling back publicity spending and resort development—areas that Ireland could ill afford to shortchange.[55] Ultimately the 1966 Tourist Traffic Act did provide the industry with a financial boost. Nonrefundable grants for development schemes were increased to £3.25 million, and a £5 million ceiling on the board's overall budget was removed.[56]

Even with the spending increases the government was still not providing funds fully commensurate with the importance of tourism. In 1966 the Organisation for Economic Cooperation and Development (OECD) released a report urging member countries, including Ireland, to increase tourism spending. The report noted that tourism was "among the fastest growing economic activities" in many of the twenty-one member nations. Ireland received 18 percent of its export earnings from tourism, placing it in third place behind Spain (42 percent) and Austria (24 percent). The OECD argued that increased spending would not only boost the number of tourists but also have significant benefits "from the social, educational, and cultural point of view," while generally contributing "to a better understanding among nations." Flexible and well-funded tourism development was essential.[57]

Some members of the industry hailed the international body's comments and also argued loudly for increased spending. The Eastern Regional Tourism Organisation was one of the most prominent critical voices and attacked the Department of Finance in the press, declaring that the minister's "actions appear to be aimed at keeping tourists away from our shores." Picking up on a point that the OECD had made in its report, Eastern Regional chairman J. A. Corr argued that improved research and development were essential to future success in this industry. Corr fumed that "the state allocation for the industry is completely unrealistic in relation to its real value," and he demanded that the government "come to their senses and provide the necessary funds for the industry." More than simply failing to spend enough, Corr insisted that the government had managed to increase costs in Ireland, making Irish holidays more expensive, while also failing to provide adequate resources to allow the industry to prepare for the coming of jumbo jets to Dublin airport in 1970. The government, in short, was undermining the national interest. He concluded, "If government attitudes are not quickly revised on these matters, then Ireland will find itself in a high price bracket, competing in one of the world's most competitive industries—the consequences could prove irretrievable."[58]

While the government did offer a small £500,000 increase to the board's development grants in 1968,[59] this action did little to silence criticism about low tourism spending. In 1970 P. J. Breen, chairman of the South-Eastern Regional Tourism Organisation, declared that "tourism in Ireland is being starved to death by a lack of financial support," with spending defined by short-term considerations. Development was "artificially retarded," opportunities were "not being converted into business," and vital growth-promoting projects were "being axed or shelved for indefinite periods"—all results of the "grossly inadequate" resources allocated to Bord Fáilte. Even T. J. O'Driscoll, who ordinarily made his financial complaints behind closed doors, had publicly protested about the situation, said Breen. The South-Eastern regional manager concluded "the blunt situation is that unless there is a sizable increase in the amount of monies being made available to tourist development bodies, their future must be called seriously into question. . . . Crisis point has been reached."[60]

The government was not deaf to the complaints, and in 1972 the amount allocated for resort development was increased by £750,000, and an additional £2 million was provided for the expansion of accommodation.[61] Three years later, another £750,000 was injected into the fund for development grants, together with £3 million more for the creation of more lodgings.[62] Government spending increased even more dramatically in 1983, when £30 million (from £16 million) was allocated for accommodation, while development funds were raised to £14 million (from £4.75 million).[63] In 1987 another £10 million was added.[64]

But it was in 1988 that the government truly put its money on the table when its *Programme for National Recovery* "set about creating an environment which would encourage investment in tourism." The plan featured tax incentives, grants, and EU support, and it led to an increase in tourism investment from £25 million in 1987 to £200 million in 1992. Investment expanded even more rapidly thereafter. By 1993 some £770 million had been pumped into the industry over five years, £380 million of which came from the state purse; this was more than had been invested during the previous twenty years combined. Spending did not slow thereafter, and a further £707 million was spent between 1994 and 1999.[65] Indeed, during the course of the 1990s, the government showed an astounding willingness to spend money on tourism marketing. For example, the Irish government invested some £30 million in the Tourism Brand Ireland campaign,[66] and then created a £14.5 million fund devoted exclusively to marketing in 1999.[67] Now that tourism was a £2.5 billion industry, the government no longer appeared to have any qualms about investing aggressively.[68]

Government decisions to spend such huge amounts of money on tourism were not entirely precipitated by industry pressure, however. As during the late 1940s and 1950s, outside factors also contributed to government decision making. This time the primary outside factor was the European Union. When Ireland joined in 1973, European powers had yet to establish a unified continent-wide policy on tourism, and the EU paid little notice to the industry until a commissioner was finally given responsibility for it in 1980. It was only in 1990 that the EU began to pay serious attention to tourism, allotting 5 million ECUs to support its "European Tourism Year" program. Spending was subsequently increased to 5.64 million ECUs in 1992 and then to 7 million in 1993.

Much of the early tourism-development support that Ireland received from the EU was provided in the form of European Regional Development Funds—monies given to "contribute to the correction of the principal regional imbalances within the community by participating in the development of structural adjustment of regions whose development is lagging behind and in the conversion of declining industrial regions." Of these funds, slightly less than 2 percent was devoted to tourism, most of this going to the United Kingdom and Italy. Ireland received European Regional Development Funds beginning in 1983, though only 0.9 percent was allotted specifically to tourism. Most of this money was devoted to the improvement of Irish ports and the development of cultural and heritage sites.

Beginning in 1987 the EU revamped its structural-funds program, a reorganization that coincided with renewed Irish government interest in tourist development (other than publicity) resulting from growing unemployment throughout the 1980s. From 1989 to 1993 the government invested some £450 million in the improvement of Irish tourist facilities, much of which (£380 million, or 53 percent) came directly from the EU.[69] The result of this influx of cash was a veritable explosion in the number and quality of tourist sites available to visitors. Tourist routes were improved, existing facilities expanded, and new tourism centers constructed.

Although dramatic infrastructural advances had taken place before 1989, with the expansion of EU tourism-development monies at the outset of the 1990s, projects were undertaken that would have been unimaginable earlier. Starting in 1989, for example, groups that included local residents and the Dublin city branch of An Taisce (National Trust for Ireland) began to take an interest in developing the Temple Bar area of Dublin. A proposal was circulated advocating the redevelopment and renovation of Dublin's "Old City," the cornerstone of the plan being the proposed reinvention of the "Temple Bar" area that had been owned by Córas Iompair Éireann (Irish rail) from 1966 and was slated for development as a transportation hub. By the mid-1980s, however, it was home to a significant community of citizens, nearly all of whom wanted to see the area turned into a cultural center rather than a bus or train station.[70] As a result, a new proposal was hatched through which the area would become a kind of Parisian "Left Bank," including cobbled streets, cultural venues, and artsy shops and restaurants, as well as a mix of housing.[71] In 1991 the interested parties successfully convinced the government and Dublin city to allow development of the area and a company called Temple Bar Properties was established under a government act to administer an urban pilot project and organize a development programme for the area.[72] Bord Fáilte soon moved the Temple Bar project to the very top of its list of investments (much of this money was drawn from European Union development funds), and it spent some £2 million in 1993 alone on the enterprise. Temple Bar was by far the largest development undertaking funded by the Tourist Board during this period, well ahead of the second highest funded site, a heritage project in Cobh that received about £450,000.[73] By the late 1990s the Temple Bar area had become one of Europe's leading short-term tourist attractions, plagued only by its success as a center for "hen and stag parties."[74] Partly as a result of this success, as well as because of the renewal of Grafton Street (whose renovation began somewhat earlier when it was permanently pedestrianized in 1985),[75] Dublin has become the third most successful city in Europe (following London and Paris) in terms of the number of tourist "bednights."[76]

While increased spending is one indication of official views about the importance of tourism, another is the way in which the cabinet addressed tourism. The Department of Industry and Commerce handled tourism until October 1961; at that point responsibility was transferred to the Department of Transport and Power.[77] Because a dedicated minister did not have responsibility for tourism, industry officials believed that their enterprise was not truly important to the government. In 1973 the National Tourism Council, essentially a pro-tourism lobby, suggested that tourism should be serviced by its own parliamentary secretary. It argued that tourism "did not appear to be fully recognised as a major industry either in the extent of government assistance or in the tax concessions which would be appropriate. . . . The ratio of official assistance, when related to the generation of foreign earnings by tourism—this country's second largest overseas revenue earner—is negligible." Furthermore, the existing ministerial structure meant that issues like landing rights and airfares were not adequately addressed by the government. As far as the National Tourism Council was concerned, tourism legislation was outdated, the preservation of Irish culture was neglected, the environment was spoiled, and other tourism issues were generally ignored. In order to ensure that these issues were addressed in the interests of tourism and, for that matter, Ireland, the industry should receive its own minister, as in the case of agriculture.[78] A year later, the president of the Irish Hotels Federation expressed a similar concern, declaring that tourism was "at the bottom of the cabinet list of priorities."[79] In response to these demands and as a reflection of genuine official interest, the government finally acknowledged the industry fully by forming a new Department of Tourism and Transport in 1977, abandoning its original plans to give tourism responsibilities to the newly created Department of the Environment.[80] Since 1977 responsibility for tourism has been moved two more times. First, between 1997 and 2002 tourism was assigned to the Department of Tourism, Sport, and Recreation.[81] This department was disbanded in 2002, however, and responsibility for tourism was then given to the Department of Arts, Sport, and Tourism, where it remains at the time of this writing, a symbol of the government's strong continuing concern about tourism.[82]

Pursuing New Markets and Growing Professionalism

Whether tourism funding was adequate or not, higher spending demanded greater results. More than ever before, tourism administrators needed to develop strategies that would attract ever-increasing tourist numbers. This requirement had two effects. First, it assured that tourism developers had to become increasingly professional in their activities, always striving to expand existing markets and to develop new ones. Second, it fueled increased debate about the shape of the Irish tourism product—the topic of the next three chapters.

While it has been claimed that the Irish decided "to sell out Irish culture to a predominantly English audience,"[83] the truth is far more complicated. It is certainly true that the English market has long dominated Irish tourism planning. The Irish Sea did not impose any language barrier, London was less than one day distant by train, and the British railway companies were more than willing to invest their own resources in developing the lucrative route between London and Killarney. As early as 1925 the Irish Tourist Association spoke of "new and stronger ties of friendship" between Ireland

and England, thus already pushing the recent conflict out of mind.[84] Even as British servicemen were murdered in an ambush at Cobh,[85] British railway companies sent representatives to meet with the Irish Tourist Association.[86] Promises of 1,000–1,500 excursionists each weekend and of 1,500–2,000 longer-term visitors to Killarney were hugely attractive to the young Tourist Association, and the group bent over backwards to assist the railway companies as a result.[87]

Despite the eagerness to attract as many English tourists as possible, the political relationship between Ireland and its former colonizer was sometimes difficult. On occasion, the influx of English tourists sparked minor conflicts. In 1939 the IRA painted anti-English slogans near tourist facilities in Killarney, including these three examples: "England, damn your concessions, we want our country," "Down with England," and "We want no uninvited guests." The Irish government refused to act, not wanting to "fire the first shot in a new war with the IRA," and some British travel agencies responded by pulling Irish Tourist Association advertising from their shelves, a move that prompted tourism interests in Killarney to demand an end to these IRA activities.[88] Similarly, in 1963, when a comparable incident brought about the cancellation of a trip by some young English servicemen to Achill Island, it inspired horror both at the local and the national levels. An anxious Taoiseach, Seán Lemass, wrote to Erskine Childers that in future, "whenever arrangements contemplated by them [Bord Fáilte] appear likely to involve political consideration[s], they should consult with you [as the responsible government minister] in advance."[89]

From time to time, conflict arose over the incursion of British financial interests into the Irish marketplace. In 1925 Killarney hoteliers complained when a collection of English journalists visited Killarney, only to have their attention monopolized by the English railway companies, which not only operated the train routes but also owned the largest hotel in town, prompting local businessmen to cry foul because they "did not get a look in." Likewise, local hotel owners complained that they could not realistically compete with the railway's practice of offering combined rail and hotel rates, which had the effect of underbidding Killarney-based hoteliers and thus completely excluding local competitors.[90] While the *Kerryman* agreed with the local businessmen and urged the ITA to take the issue up with railway officials, the situation did little to deflect cooperative efforts or the ITA's strong desire to cash in on a growing stream of English tourists.

In another representative incident in 1951, the English publisher Edward J. Burrow and Company offered to publish a guidebook for Kilkenny at no expense to the local authority, a proposal that prompted criticism from the Irish Tourist Association and Irish Tourist Board. One concerned individual declared "it a terrible thing that an English firm could produce a guide book and that the Irish Tourist Board, to the upkeep of which the Kilkenny County Council contributed a share . . . , had done nothing."[91] The *Kilkenny People,* long critical of Irish tourist authorities, chided both the ITA and Irish Tourist Board for their lack of action and commended the County Council for demanding board action.[92] Ultimately the publication went forward, prompting R. Burke of the County Council to say in disgust, "After a quarter of a century's freedom it is a sad thing that such guides cannot be produced in Ireland."[93] One year later, when the first preparations for An Tóstal were being made, several "show cards" and a full-color poster were also printed in England as a result of the inadequate printing facilities in Ireland combined with an Irish printers' strike. This created a minor furor within the Department of Industry and Commerce as civil servants demanded to know why An Bord Fáilte and Fógra Fáilte were not working together to pursue all possible avenues for printing their publicity materials in Ireland.[94] Jan de Fouw, the graphic designer responsible for much of Fógra Fáilte's and subsequently Bord Fáilte's graphic output, recalls that the English print run was horrifying to many because it meant that "the national identity was reproduced on foreign paper."[95] In keeping with this concern, de Fouw, Guus Melai (who designed the logo for An Tóstal; see chapter 4), and their Dutch colleagues, who had come to Ireland in search of work and an opportunity to make their mark in graphic design, were asked to leave their names off the various design projects they undertook in Ireland because doing so "was only stirring up feelings and waves which we could do without."[96] When Fógra Fáilte began publishing *Ireland of the Welcomes,* officials insisted that the entire publication be produced in Ireland—a requirement that severely limited the use of color and the design complexity of the publication for a number of years—and without de Fouw's name in the credits.[97]

Despite the occasional conflict, early ITA support for developing the English market was far more characteristic of relations between the two states in this area than the handful of incidents like those mentioned above. It was generally agreed that tourists from Britain and Northern Ireland would always form Ireland's largest market segment, and that efforts should be made to ensure that Britannia continued to send its tourists across the Irish Sea and the border.[98] Britain and Ireland showed an exceptional willingness to work together, actively seeking greater cooperation between their respective tourist bodies throughout the 1950s and beyond.[99]

From the very beginning of tourism development after the Civil War, the tourist authorities also dreamed of attracting visitors from the lucrative American and continental European markets. Guidebooks were translated into German and French, and some companies even wrote guides specifically to cater to foreign tastes rather than producing translations. In 1932, for example, Guinness published a Francophone guidebook that focused on the types of Guinness, the adaptation of stout to fit French tastes, and the proper way to serve the tasty black liquid, as well as the correct color, taste, and pouring technique necessary to serve the ultimate pint of stout.[100] English-language guides, meanwhile, addressed the brewery's history and spent far less time on the aesthetics of the beverage produced there.[101] No stranger to marketing, Guinness hoped to exploit the French love for good food and drink by appealing to their supposed aesthetic and gastronomic sensibilities.

Even so, expanding promotional efforts to the continent or to the United States was a daunting and expensive challenge. While Europe was not far away, it was culturally and linguistically diverse. Meanwhile, America was thousands of miles distant—a serious problem when transatlantic transport was limited to slow-moving steamships—and the United States both geographically huge and culturally varied. As Michael Gorman realized soon after beginning work at Fógra Fáilte, the marketing of Ireland in the United States was like tackling all of Europe at once.[102] Given small budgets, the authorities had to monitor their efforts, gradually expanding their marketing campaigns as transportation improved, financial support increased, and experience was acquired.

The Irish Tourist Association began to pursue the American market as early as February 1924. At the monthly ITA meeting in Cork, George Harris, a passenger agent from the White Star Line in Cobh and one of the original members of the ITA executive, stressed that it was both "desirable and urgent" to launch a major marketing effort in America.[103] Over the next three years several ITA members, including Howard Harrington, the association's president and himself an American, journeyed to the United States to meet with travel agents and others of importance.[104] In 1927 the Tourist Association opened a bureau in New York City when the Great Western Railway Company offered space in its offices. The association hoped that its new offices would allow for a more efficient distribution of literature and other publicity in the States.[105] The thought was right, but with an annual budget of only about £15,000, and with the reality that American tourists would need to commit to at least two weeks of steamship travel in order to make the journey, very little was actually accomplished.

Following World War II, Marshall Plan officials and the Christenberry committee urged the Irish authorities to move into the American market.[106] An Tóstal was partly an effort to attract Irish-Americans back to Ireland as tourists. As tourist-development efforts grew throughout the 1950s, Bord Fáilte continued to explore ways to expand its promotional efforts in America. In 1956 the board's director-general traveled to the United States to explore the possibilities for expansion, and he urged the addition of a Chicago-area office.[107]

The Irish tourist authorities were similarly interested in continental markets, and as early as 1938–39, when the first major Tourism Traffic Act made its way through the Oireachtas, senators expressed their hope that the new Tourist Board would pursue the continental market. Citing Ireland's long isolation from continental culture, senators suggested that tourism might draw Ireland back into Europe.[108] After Bord Fáilte received larger financial grants from the government during the 1960s, its leaders were able to increase efforts to attract continental tourists. Whereas materials had once been distributed either through the Department of External Affairs (see below) or Aer Lingus in places other than Britain and the United States, Bord Fáilte now opened offices in Italy, Austria, and France. When the Bord Fáilte office was opened in Paris during the late 1960s, the board spared no expense. Careful attention was paid to geographic location, and the new office was sited adjacent to the Paris Opera in order to ensure substantial foot traffic. Next, the board hired a leading French advertising and marketing company to publicize the event. They placed full-page ads in *Paris Match* featuring the slogan "Ireland is not on the Mediterranean, thank God!": an indication that a trip to Ireland set the tourist apart from the growing hordes on Spanish beaches. The board leased a chateau, complete with lakes in both the front and the back, near Paris, and they threw a massive party—the invitation to which included a box of smoked Irish salmon. In front of the estate visitors were directed by a member of the Irish police, a tricolor flew on the flagpole, an Irish army piper played as visitors entered, descendants of the old Irish Brigade in period uniform greeted guests, Owen Dillion of the Shelbourne Hotel prepared traditional Irish cuisine, contemporary poets recited the works of Yeats and other Irish writers, fly fishermen demonstrated the art of fly-casting on one of the lakes, and a professional Irish golfer offered lessons in a nearby field. While contemporary marketing organizations might use many of these tactics today, in the 1960s the program was revolutionary. The Tourist Board was willing to do "anything to make it [the Irish tourism product] stick out," remembers Michael Gorman, Bord Fáilte's European publicity manager at the time.[109]

Beyond opening new travel bureaus, Bord Fáilte launched major marketing campaigns in the Benelux countries in 1968,[110] increased its foreign-language publications with a particular emphasis on German-language materials,[111] and held travel workshops in major European markets (like Germany) that were intended to educate travel agents about the attractions of an Irish holiday.[112] Bord Fáilte also improved the market research efforts that it had begun in the early 1950s; it clearly wished to enhance its understanding of the likes and dislikes of potential customers in foreign markets. The first survey was conducted in 1955 and included 3,000 travelers, allegedly representing the views of some 7,500 people. When asked what pleased them most about their Irish adventures, most replied, "The Irish people themselves."[113] This fact set Ireland apart from popular destinations such as Paris where few tourists encountered actual French people.[114] Officials learned that 10 percent of Americans came to Ireland to visit relatives, and that Belleek china, Waterford crystal, and Limerick lace were among the most popular

Irish souvenirs.[115] In subsequent years additional questions were added about visitor nationality, purpose of visit, length of stay, why Ireland was chosen over other potential holiday destinations, how visitors used their time in Ireland, and how they allocated their expenses.[116] The surveys revealed that word of mouth was by far the biggest motivation for coming to the Emerald Isle, that Americans made more use of travel agents than Britons, and that Dublin and County Kerry were by far the most popular destinations.[117] The board eventually established a research department and adopted increasingly scientific approaches to its survey work. In 1973, for example, Bord Fáilte conducted an extensive survey of *Attitudes of American and English Tourists Towards Shopping in Ireland and Irish Merchandise.* Unlike the first surveys, which were conducted by schoolgirls in airport-based interviews, this one was done through small random samples of British and American tourists divided into groups of six respondents. The board then used "non-directive" interviews to gauge participant opinions, striving for self-directed discussions in order to avoid influencing results. Interviewers typically began by asking basic questions about country of origin, occupation, length of stay, reason for travel, and the type of holiday desired. Shopping was almost inevitably listed as one of the activities included in an Irish holiday, and this answer allowed discussion to shift to perceptions of Irish shops, impressions about Irish products, window displays, mythology about specific crafts, brand recognition, women's attitudes to Irish clothes, and, finally, the motivation for purchase.

The results of the souvenir survey revealed numerous differences between British and American travelers that allowed the authorities to further differentiate their products by market. For example, it became clear very quickly that American travelers were drawn primarily from one social group, were defined by social class rather than ethnic background, and had a series of interests in common. They anticipated a romantic and relaxing holiday rather than one that was intellectually stimulating or purposeful, showed surprise at the amount of history to be found in Ireland, and looked forward to beautiful scenery, tranquility, and friendly people. In contrast, English tourists came from two distinct groups. The first of these was the upper-middle and upper class; members of this group came to Ireland with a substantial level of interest and knowledge about Irish culture. The second group, drawn from among the middle and lower-middle class, was inclined to be economical and chose Ireland primarily as a suitable destination to take their children. Even so, both groups of English visitors looked forward to beautiful scenery, tranquility, and escape—to say nothing of a "more 'natural' life rhythm." Although both Americans and Britons agreed in anticipating beautiful scenery, the British found little that was exotic or exciting about travel in Ireland. Decisions were made at the last minute and trips were shorter. The feeling that Ireland was not exotic spilled over into British attitudes toward shopping. While Americans actively sought out Aran sweaters, for example, English visitors thought them "bulky and unfashionable," and experienced little of the rustic charm cited by American visitors. British visitors spent little money on Irish products while in the country, and they were far more apt to criticize souvenir shops that they found "cheap, trashy, [and] filled with foreign (Japanese) goods."[118]

In the 1990s Bord Fáilte took another step forward in its study of foreign markets. By this time annual reports contained detailed information about visitor statistics for North America, Britain, Northern Ireland, and all of the major continental markets, including Spain, Italy, Germany, France, the Benelux countries, and Switzerland. These data were supplemented by a series of publications entitled *Know Your Market*; each book painstakingly explored the activities popular with each nationality. For example, Italians spent most of their time in Dublin, but by the mid-1990s they were increasingly interested in car rentals and were moving beyond the city in larger numbers. Italians were far more interested in hiking or walking than in other activities and enjoyed visiting historical sites.[119] In contrast, the French favored the southwest and showed less interest in historic sites, though they too enjoyed hiking and walking. French visitors were disproportionately interested in the Irish way of life.[120] Meanwhile, the main interest of Americans was in sightseeing and in finding distant ancestors. They expected a friendly welcome and an opportunity to view Ireland's historic places and scenic sites.[121] Armed with such visitor information, tourist officials could target specific social and national groups with a precision not previously imagined.

Conclusion

The Irish government was never completely disinterested in tourism, but the status of the industry as a primary national interest only developed over time.[122] From the 1920s onward officials recognized that tourism might bring valuable revenue into Ireland, but there were fundamental divisions about what role the government should take in promoting tourism. As tourism revenue increased, pressure was brought to bear by various sectors of Irish society, and as foreign bodies from the Marshall Plan administration to the OECD and the European Union stressed the importance of tourism, government officials increasingly recognized the vital place of the industry in Irish economic and social life. But one other point must also be made. Throughout the period between the Civil War and the start of the Celtic Tiger, Ireland was a very poor country. Regardless of the potential financial gain offered by tourism, officials had finite resources to invest in tourism expansion, especially before 1960. With numerous challenges facing the nation, tourism was not always the most apparent or easily understood concern of government officials, for whom the national interest seemed more obviously aligned with addressing agricultural productivity, manufacturing growth, emigration, the Northern question, and a number of other major issues. As a result, the entire period between 1924 and 1994 was often marked by debate about the relative importance of tourism as well as about the precise results to be sought through tourism development.

Although it was only quite recently that tourism rose to the top of government spending priorities, the gradual increase in expenditure that followed passage of the 1952 Tourist Traffic Act sparked a significant increase in the exchange of ideas about the precise "product" that tourist developers would present to outsiders, about the very nature of Irishness. This increased interchange focused attention on the definition of Irish culture, history, and landscape and it involved a wide cross-section of society that was, if anything, even more extensive than that which participated in the national interest debate. It is to this dialogue that we must now turn.

4
Culture, Language, and Tourism

Introduction

Language and culture are two of the most obvious components of national identity.[1] Nearly all nations feature their own festivals, traditions, costumes, dances, sporting events, and any number of other defining characteristics, while language both reflects these cultural artifacts and allows them to be perpetuated through ongoing education. The trend in nationalism studies, to say nothing of nationalist discourse itself, is to stress national consensus and homogeneity in cultural and linguistic concerns. Scholars have fiercely debated when common culture developed, seeing it variously as almost timeless[2] or modern and invented,[3] but they are less prone to examining the contested nature of culture *within* a specific national group. Language is generally presented as integral to either the perpetuation of timeless traditions or the invention of new ones,[4] and the tendency is to focus on transnational conflicts over language or to describe specific nationalist movements without addressing the diversity of opinion within a single nation.[5] In Ireland, for example, considerable attention has been paid to the importance of the Gaelic League[6] and the Gaelic Athletic Association,[7] but less attention has been given to the fact that these movements were not universally important across Irish society.[8] Despite the attention paid to the language revival in the story of the Irish nationalist movement, for example, the success of the revival effort was limited, and the story of the Gaelic League is very much that of a minority of the population. While in 1986 the number of Gaelic speakers in Ireland had climbed to 1,043,000 from 541,000 in 1926, the former figure still represented only about 31 percent of the population—up from 19 percent sixty years earlier.[9] In other words, since the 1920s, if we believe these census figures,[10] the percentage of Irish speakers in the Republic of Ireland has never risen above about one third of the population, leaving one to wonder why the vast majority of the Irish people exercised little interest in a language that conventional wisdom holds rests at the center of Irish identity. In one sense the numbers were a success story, of course. The number of Gaelic speakers *had* increased, and the language continued to play a significant role in a substantial number of lives. Yet if Gaelic was as central to Irish identity as the language revivalists believed, why is the entire Republic not a Gaeltacht?

While it is true that both language and culture have played tremendously important roles in various nationalist movements—the Catalan, Quebecois, Welsh, Cornish, and Flemish nationalist movements are five relevant examples—the Irish case demonstrates that ambivalence and debate has been as common as homogeneity and consensus. The first three chapters demonstrated that Irish perceptions of their common interests changed over time according to economic and political circumstances, and they also made clear that definitions of these interests varied among different groups and individuals; the same was true of ideas about both language and culture. While revivalists wanted to protect the Gaeltachts from the threat of modernization, the native speakers themselves were more interested in employment and economic improvement. Likewise, "traditional" Irish culture inspired more ambivalence than consensus. It was one thing to hold gatherings such as Puck Fair in Killorglin, Co. Kerry, for Irish people, another thing to present the filth, drinking, and brawling endemic at the event to outsiders.

As noted in the introduction, although there was certainly considerable debate about the specifics of how Ireland should be promoted, there was consensus that the country should always be presented in the best possible light, and anger was widespread when the presentation of Ireland fell short of the ideal. This chapter examines the role played by tourism in debates about Irish language and culture. At every turn those involved in promoting the country as a tourist product wanted to present the "best" that Ireland had to offer, but in doing so, they were forced to balance differing ideas about what the "best" of Ireland was, as well as to display widely diverging ideas about how to protect authentic Irishness from unwanted change. The dialogue detailed here unfolded in two phases corresponding to the debate about tourism as a national interest. During the first phase, which corresponded with the debate detailed in chapters 1 and 2, the question of selling Irishness centered on the tourist threat to the language revival. While tourism interests saw Gaelic as a tourist attraction, and the influx of tourists as potentially beneficial to the Gaeltachts, language enthusiasts feared that an influx of "foreignism" might undermine efforts to save the Irish language by introducing Anglophone tourists into Gaelic-speaking areas and encouraging the use of English rather than Irish. The second phase, which began in earnest during the 1950s, corresponded to the growing consensus that tourism development was a national interest and featured a push to present Ireland as in accord with widely internalized stereotypes of friendliness, warmth, a relaxed attitude toward life, and the innate ability to tell a great story—an objective that sometimes clashed uneasily with the realities of Irish life.

Phase I: The Tourism Threat

From the very first efforts of the Irish Tourist Association to develop the tourist industry in the Cork and Kerry region, tourism was presented as a potential savior of the Gaeltachts. During 1925–26, when the ITA strove to establish a Dingle branch of the association, the Dingle Peninsula was portrayed as a likely tourist hotspot. It was an area with majestic coastal scenery and unequalled "archaeological wealth," and it was "one of the few [areas] in which the true Gaelic atmosphere can be found in its original purity."[11] The region promised to be especially enticing to language enthusiasts interested in visiting historic sites while studying the Irish language in quiet surroundings. The ITA believed that visitors did not want to see Irish people imitating the "Anglo-Saxons"; they wanted to see authentically Irish people, and the association's view was supported by advice from American tourists that the Irish should "never forget . . . to keep alive the glorious Gaelic traditions of Ireland."[12]

Of course the ITA was also subject to local pressure, and it was clear from early on that many people in the Kerry Gaeltacht were anxious to see tourism developed quickly. From the initial establishment of the Dingle branch of the ITA, its members urged the creation of a special advertising campaign that would inform visitors of the Gaelic "purity" to be found on the peninsula. Not only were these Dingle residents excited about the idea of language tourism in their backyard, but they were also actively upset that the ITA had not done more to provide them with legions of Gaelic-seeking tourists.[13]

Reflecting the association's belief in the marketability of the Irish language and the pressure exerted on that body by those in Gaelic-speaking areas, the 1929 ITA guidebook stressed the deep roots of the Gaelic language and informed tourists that "the Irish people maintained their language, customs, and literature down to modern times," thus preserving a continuity with the past. The guide presented a positive appraisal of the Gaelic revival: "Today the Irish language is the official language of the country and is taught in all the schools. Already the revival movement has given [the country] a talented group of novelists, poets, and dramatists, whose works are an augury of its continued success."[14] Gaelic was something to be heard and enjoyed by tourists, a clear sign of unchanging Irishness as well as of the success enjoyed by nationalists in keeping this past alive.

Not only did the ITA mention the Gaeltacht in its guidebooks for Ireland as a whole, and Kerry in particular, but the association also published a special guide encouraging tourists to visit the Gaeltacht and endeavored to circulate it to government offices in the hope of attracting civil servants to visit Connemara, Kerry, and other Irish-speaking areas.[15] The guide stressed the attractions of the regions for sportsmen, drew attention to bathing opportunities, and focused on the astonishing scenery. While these attractions did exist, there was also a considerable amount of outright fiction in the booklet. The ITA's enthusiasm led its leaders to claim that Gaeltacht roads "are now beyond reproach by the motorist," and that "accommodation is available to satisfy the most fastidious and the plainest tastes—from modern, excellently appointed and managed hotels to farmhouses in which clean and comfortable accommodation can frequently be had."[16] These promises represented a vast exaggeration of the truth.

Archie Bell, a travel writer from Ohio, took a particular interest in Gaelic during his 1928 trip to Ireland, noting with pleasure when he met a waitress who "spoke Irish as fluently as she did English." Bell was excited because he had noticed that relatively few Irish adults were able to speak the native tongue. He explained how matters stood:

> As with Mussolini at Rome, the hope of the Irish government lies with the future generations. The children are learning Irish in the schools. Teachers are attending special sessions all over the country to polish up. Political speeches are frequently delivered in the native tongue. Street signs are printed in both English and in Irish. Some of the newspapers have at least one editorial each day in Irish. Young people who speak and read it are supposed to get better jobs in official offices. But the fact remains that while interest in the language is increasing every day, the majority of the adults cannot speak it.[17]

For Bell the experience of meeting a Gaelic speaker was unique and authentic, but it was more than that. Throughout his narrative Bell wrote about the revitalization of Ireland without ever mentioning English rule or the fight for independence, let alone the Civil War. For Bell history ended in the late Middle Ages; Ireland was defined by pretty scenery and amusing myths and stories, not by poverty and disease, emigration, political conflict, and a legacy of violence. The Irish language connected the present with a distant mythical past. The language movement and the prospect that more and more Irish people would be directly connected to this ancient soft-focus Celtic arcadia was a very positive thing; it would recreate Ireland in the green-tinted pastels of ancient history.

A "Deadly Threat"

In contrast to the ITA's faith in the value of marketing Gaelic, or the desire for development commonly voiced in the Gaeltachts themselves, by the 1930s a growing number of revivalists found tourists threatening because the visitors did not speak Gaelic. As early as 1934, Seán MacEntee, then minister for finance, produced an extensive memorandum responding to a proposal for development of the Gaeltacht as a tourist centre. He believed that the industry "must be regarded as the largest source of potential wealth for these areas," but he also stressed that even in this light the government's primary responsibility was to ensure the preservation of the Irish language.[18] MacEntee did not speak Irish himself, but Gaelic preservation was very important to him. His family spent holidays at Dunquin, Co. Kerry, the children were raised to be Irish speakers, and his wife, Kate Browne, taught Gaelic at various schools including University College Dublin.[19] As minister for finance, the challenge was to balance economic reality with this dedication to the revival. In his memo, MacEntee explained that any successful policy should harmonize "the economic and language interests" of the nation. The problem was that previous experience suggested that it was necessary to isolate the Gaeltacht in order to guarantee linguistic security. The language survived in the Gaeltachts precisely because they were remote and isolated. In order to maintain this isolation it was necessary to develop schemes calculated to attract only *the right kind of tourists:* Irish-speaking tourists. MacEntee was skeptical about the idea of developing Gaelic communities as holiday centers where Anglophones might come to hear and learn Irish. If Anglophone families were to arrive en masse in the Gaeltachts, even given their heartfelt desire to learn the language, they would soon lapse into English. The visitors would tend to interact with one another, not with the local families. As a result, "the presence of such [English-speaking] families in the heart of the Gaeltacht would only endanger the hold the language has at present as a vernacular in the Gaeltacht." MacEntee suggested that a more radical approach was required in which extensive development of special holiday villages would be undertaken in Dingle, Connemara, and Donegal. The program would constitute "a drastic reorganisation of the whole area." Tourists would stay in these new developments among Irish speakers employed to converse in the native tongue with the visitors, and no English speaking would be tolerated. The idea was modeled on a "successful" program adopted by Father Lawrence Murray in Rannafast, Co. Donegal, who maintained a watchful eye over visitors to his village, ensuring that no English-speaking tourists were allowed into the homes of Irish speakers. MacEntee's plan would keep damaging Anglophones at bay by using the authority of government departments and local disciplinarians like Father Murray. Such a program would be expensive, but MacEntee felt strongly that "the holiday industry in the Gaeltacht should not be approached from the aspect of profit-making"; instead, what was needed was a state program that would guarantee the success of the language revival while also bringing money into poor areas.[20]

The 1939 Tourist Traffic Act threatened to create an unprecedented influx of Anglophone tourists, and the perceived risk sparked a positively xenophobic response among many observers. One letter-writer protested emphatically against the proposed scheme of tourist development and the expenditure of public moneys thereon, while no effective steps are being taken to protect the Gaeltacht from *such a formidable influx of foreignism. For it is a deadly threat to the Gaeltacht, if not to the whole Gaelic revival movement.* Of the huge increase in visitors expected, 99 per cent will be English-speakers from Great Britain, America, Australia, and New Zealand. Add their influence to the predominance of English already in our midst and the position of Gaelicism will be pitiful.[21]

Others agreed, prophesizing that "an enormous influx of British and American tourists is bound to be a great Anglicising agent in what is left of the Gaedhealtacht." This was a problem for the language, but it sparked another concern as well because it made certain that the money and energy needed to make tourism one of the state's main industries would be used not to build "a prosperous Irish nation" but to arrange "Ireland to suit the tastes of British and American tourists. Not tourists of the thoughtful, discriminating type—but tourists of the average, unthinking sort, whose wants are luxurious hotels, fishing, and jazz dancing, who leave every "beauty spot" defiled with rubbish, and whose idea of Ireland is a place where ridiculous peasants will amuse them."[22] The development of tourism, at least for those who spoke out about the Tourist Traffic Act, represented a betrayal of all that was fundamentally Irish. The danger to the language movement was just one of many negative outcomes, and some defense of those things most Irish was sorely needed. While it might not be necessary to "close the frontiers of the Gaeltacht, as Hitler might do," it was certainly the case that the government, "pledged and elected to restore the language, should hesitate before financing a scheme that, if launched before any measures are taken to strengthen the Gaeltacht, will almost certainly destroy the language in its native territory."[23]

Of course the Irish Tourist Association saw things much differently. As far as the association, and specifically the Killarney branch, were concerned, increased tourist traffic would mean "increased employment in the Gaeltacht, thereby helping to stop emigration of Irish speakers and [to] preserve the language," not to mention increasing the amount of farm produce consumed, much of it grown by Gaelic-speaking farmers. The xenophobic response was itself anathema to true Irishness. As Fred Crowley, a TD and director of the ITA, put it, "The Celtic race had a reputation for being capable of absorbing rather than being absorbed."[24] If Cu Uladh, the most prolific of the antitourism language enthusiasts, would come to Kerry, he would see "districts where the language, to a great extent, was a living force, and the people there were very anxious to have visitors and tourists, and the visitors and tourists were delighted to hear the Irish language spoken." The Gaels had played a part "in the national struggle in every shape and form for the past 500 years," and nobody should feel any "apprehension that [an] increased number of tourists will injure" the Irish people. Indeed, the further development of Irish customs would attract more tourists while making Ireland still more Irish.[25]

The conflict between the ITA and the "Gaelic Leaguers"[26] made its way into the Oireachtas during the late stage of the debate concerning the Tourist Traffic Act; the tone, however, was almost entirely favorable to tourist development. Senator Donnchadh Ó hEaluighthe, for example, stressed that his experience in Gaeltacht areas suggested that tourism brought valuable revenue and employment to Irish speakers and that the proposed legislation would help the congested districts, not harm them. Seán Lemass echoed this view, saying that the legislation would be "wholly beneficial" to the Gaeltacht areas.[27] Yet, as positive as most of the discussion within the government was, even here there were voices of concern. C. S. Almond, a civil servant in the Department of Finance, echoed the fears voiced by the Gaelic Leaguers. Almond warned that tourist development would have "serious repercussions" for the language movement, and argued that the language "is finding difficulty in combating the strong forces of cinema, the dance-hall, jazz, etc." Faced with an influx of tourists and a "programme of development which must have as its foundation the encouragement of all the forces which militate against the Irish language," the result could only be the extinction of Gaelic.[28]

Developing Language Tourism

Following passage of the act, the Irish Tourist Board and the ITA were faced with developing tourism in Gaeltacht areas while addressing the Gaelic Leaguers' concerns. As far as the Tourist Association was concerned, tourism remained "the only industry whose development could be made to supplement the income of large numbers of uneconomic holders in Gaeltacht areas."[29] As a result of this view, the association continued to push visitors toward the Gaeltacht regions, and its publications changed little from past efforts, continuing to draw attention to the many visitors who "annually flock to learn from them [Gaelic speakers in the Dingle area] the pure, musical Gaelic which they speak."[30]

The Tourist Board, on the other hand, was pushed toward considering potential schemes as part of its program of planning and development during the Emergency. The board began investigating Gaeltacht tourism after de Valera encouraged its leaders to explore the possibilities available. The request came following the taoiseach's receipt of a memorandum from An Fear Mór, a six-foot, six-inch-tall Gaelic enthusiast who had previously established the Ring Irish College and published several popular Irish-language textbooks.[31] An Fear Mór was particularly interested in Bunbeg, Co. Donegal, as a likely development site, and the Tourist Board was encouraged by the taoiseach to survey the area. The board was less than excited about the task, apparently doubting its qualifications to adopt the project, and the ITB urged the creation of a public company, similar to Aer Lingus or the Turf Board, to administer it—a view that was angrily denounced by the Department of Finance, which insistently recalled, "It was always contemplated that the improvement of holiday facilities in the Gaeltacht would be one of the main tasks of the board."[32]

In November 1944, J. P. O'Brien submitted the board's proposal to de Valera and expressed the opinion that "the district is in every way suitable for a first experiment in the provision of improved and enlarged accommodation for Irish summer courses." Using the Ring Irish College as a model, the board argued that it would be necessary to develop a set of buildings to provide classrooms, dining facilities, and accommodation for at least a hundred adults. In order to ensure that the plan would earn a profit and therefore be covered by the requirements attached to their wartime operating agreement, tourist authorities visualized using the buildings as a fosterage school during the academic year. There were also to be facilities for a vocational-education program to teach "domestic economy" to local housewives, who would be called upon to cater for visitors.[33] As it stood, the board's survey discloses shortcomings at all centres in the matter of accommodation, catering, public health services, and recreation amenities. Generally speaking, they have not kept pace with the times, and their survival depends on a substantial program of improvement in respect of the matters above mentioned. The system of control operating in practically every case is such that no improvement can be expected without some impetus and encouragement from some government source.[34]

Three years after receipt of the board's proposal, the minister of industry and commerce appointed a four-man committee comprising civil servants in the Departments of Finance, Lands, Industry and Commerce, and Education to assess the report. The group's assessment was overwhelmingly negative. While the Irish Tourist Board suggested that the entire Bunbeg development could be accomplished for £30,000, the committee expected the project to cost more than £100,000. Furthermore, the board's claim that the project could be profitable within a short period of its completion was sharply challenged, and the interdepartmental committee concluded that it would take at least *thirty years* before the necessary loans would be paid off. Indeed, the Bunbeg college would probably operate at a yearly deficit of at least £6,200. Given the cost, as well as serious doubts about the ability of the program to attract an adequate number of students, the interdepartmental committee recommended that the Tourist Board's plan be dismissed.

Development through Grants

In assessing the Tourist Board's proposal, the interdepartmental committee surveyed all of Ireland's Gaeltacht areas, paying particular attention to the amenities available. The committee found areas with flawless scenery and attractive recreational facilities, but also other districts that lacked running water, adequate sanitation, and lighting. Most visitors were accommodated in private homes, and overcrowding, unsuitable toilet facilities, and poor catering were endemic. Worse still, very few families were in any financial position to meet the economic challenge that would have to be overcome if they were to improve their homes in order to accommodate visitors—Irish or otherwise. The committee therefore advocated the provision of grants and loans to homeowners in Gaeltacht areas so that they could improve their homes. These loans would cover improved sanitation, enhanced water supplies, and the addition of guest rooms. The government should also step up efforts to provide a piped water supply and sewerage systems to Gaeltacht villages. It would be desirable to extend rural electrification schemes to as many Irish-speaking areas as possible. In addition, strong efforts should be made to provide "housewives who keep visitors"—women with "some training in domestic economy, with special regard to general cleanliness, the maintenance of the house and surroundings, the provision of a variety in food and its cooking, and [knowledge about] the importance of the economics of the guest-house, of the proper rearing of fowl, and the production of an adequate supply of eggs and milk." The committee also advocated the destruction of "dilapidated structures, neglected outhouses, sheds, unsightly waste materials, etc." Buildings should be painted, and trees and shrubs planted. Local committees needed to be encouraged to take control of their surroundings so that the natural beauty of Gaeltacht areas was not marred by the presence of eyesores—all concepts that were adopted several years later during An Tóstal and ultimately during the Tidy Towns and Villages Competition. Finally, the interdepartmental committee stressed that roadways in Gaeltacht areas were generally "unsatisfactory." The government should improve roads as well as improve access to beaches, boat launches, and swimming facilities.[35] In effect, the accommodations, people, and landscape of the Gaeltacht areas needed to be improved for the benefit of tourists: if Irish speakers, those "virtuous countrymen,"[36] were to be acceptably Irish, they needed to be properly trained and their lands suitably groomed.

Throughout the 1950s and beyond, it was the interdepartmental committee's suggestion for the provision of grants and loans that was adopted to develop the Gaeltacht. In October 1952 the minister for local government approved a program to improve "roads of tourist value in the Gaeltacht and the congested districts." The program was supposed to last for eight years, and expenditure in any given year was not to exceed £400,000.[37] Similarly, in 1959 the government passed a Housing (Gaeltacht) Amendment Bill "to give a new kind of financial assistance to families in the Gaeltacht areas" and to "provide accommodation for visitors to these areas, particularly students of the Irish language."[38] In 1965 Irish-speaking regions were once again under study to determine how to "foster the growth of farmhouse holiday accommodation." Far from frowning on the idea as too expensive or expansive, the Department of Finance responded to a somewhat truncated Bord Fáilte proposal by arguing that it should be extended to as many western districts as possible. The old concern about Anglophone tourists undermining the Irish language was completely surpassed by a feeling that the Gaeltacht might be particularly appealing to foreign visitors.[39] Nobody publicly challenged the proposal.

From the 1950s to the 1990s and beyond, the government promoted rural development, not language preservation. From the perspective of the state there were more pressing concerns than the language movement, and development monies were increasingly designed to assist the congested districts because they were economically challenged, not because of the desire to protect the language per se. This policy of firm support for economic development over language preservation was fully in keeping with the government's larger failure to make compulsory Irish seem important.[40] For those who genuinely cared about the language movement, it was a painful pill to swallow. The government was allowing the language to die "by stealth,"[41] and while occasional antitourism comments were made as late as the 1950s about allowing Anglophones into the Gaeltachts, such comments were notable more for their anachronistic presence in an ever-more-modern Ireland than for their widespread public acceptance.[42]

Phase II: Representing the Best of Irishness

As fear about the negative cultural implications of tourism waned, three simultaneous developments occurred that focused attention on Ireland's image: the number of tourists to Ireland rose, the government's interest in tourism increased, and the Tourist Board's development activities expanded. From the central government level, where cultural propaganda was an important component of Ireland's foreign policy, to average Irish men and women, there was a real desire to ensure that the world's impression of Ireland did not mimic the *Holiday* magazine article mentioned in the introduction. Not only would such an image undermine the tourist industry; it would also reflect badly on the Irish people themselves.

Many historians and literary critics frequently cite the widespread use of negative stereotypes to describe the Irish. At various points these scholars note that the Irish were often seen as rustic, simian, plebeian, and drunken.[43]

When not presented as potentially violent and threatening, the Irish were often seen as clowns, rogues, comic heroes, or "stage Irishmen."[44] Many perceived the Irish as inferior to the English, a fact made intuitively obvious by their "inferior" brogue.[45] Just as in the Raj, these stereotypes helped to justify colonial rule because the Irish were considered to be little more than "hapless dupes, hapless petitioners, and victims of discrimination" who required England's paternalistic assistance.[46] Yet this emphasis on the negative fails to acknowledge the variability of opinion. For example, Roy Foster demonstrates that Irish stereotypes were always rife with contradiction and negative characterizations were usually based more on class than upon race. "Marginal men" who were dissatisfied with their lives at home in England—men such as Thackeray, Shelley, Trollope, Lord Randolph Churchill, and even Frederick Engels—often saw Ireland as a realization of the dreams and fantasies that left them uncomfortable at home. Yet, just as these men were prone to viewing Ireland through romantic green-colored glasses, so they were equally disturbed when the Irish nationalist movement threatened the status quo. Trollope, for example, viewed the Irish as his kinsmen, yet he was violently opposed to Home Rule and defended the British government's actions during the Famine. He even tried to dismiss the "Irishness" of his character Phineas Finn when Irishness increasingly symbolized something to him that was more disturbing and divisive than he had previously imagined. "The qualities of perception which make Trollope the best 'Irish' novelist of the mid-century had by old age been thrown into reverse," states Foster.[47] Stereotypes, in other words, could be used as a matter of convenience, providing an "other," whether positive *or* negative, as circumstances warranted.

The ability to pick and choose stereotypes was not limited to "marginal men" (or to "Micks on the make" for that matter). Following the Irish Civil War, the Irish rejected unappealing characterizations of Ireland and Irishness and adopted more positive ones to serve new purposes. Most Irish people opted for a harmonious vision of Ireland that was rooted in older stereotypes, including Irish warmth and friendliness, a relaxed attitude toward life, and the innate ability to tell a great story—the same things that had often been appealing to Foster's "marginal men." Images were chosen because they matched tourist perceptions, offered visitors something different from what the tourists were used to, *and,* perhaps more important, because many Irish people believed in the images. During the 1920s the ITA used the welcoming and friendly image of Irishness to contrast with the horrors of recent war and expressed confidence that, despite Ireland's recent civil strife, tourists would "meet with a hearty 'Céad Míle Fáilte'" upon entering the country.[48] The threat of violence surrounding the general elections in 1927 was similarly dismissed because "the Irish people maintain their proud traditions for hospitality and kindness to their visitors."[49] Such reassuring words were not limited to tourist publications; they were frequently repeated in newspaper articles and speeches. Seán Lemass, for example, informed the Irish Tourist Association, "We are the heirs of a great tradition of courtesy and hospitality which has survived throughout all the centuries of our history, and the observing of that tradition today should be the keynote of those engaged in the tourist movement."[50] This same confidence was expressed by Taoiseach Jack Lynch in 1968, when he argued that for the Irish "hospitality to strangers is almost a way of life," a tradition "summed up in the Irish welcome 'Céad Míle Fáilte'—a hundred thousand welcomes. It means much more than the provision of food and drink and accommodation for the tourist. There is a genuine friendly interest to make the stranger feel at home."[51] None of these comments was made directly for the benefit of tourists, but rather they were offered by one Irishman to another.

Ultimately the Irish welcome, Irish hospitality, and the friendliness of the Irish people made Ireland a unique and desirable place, bolstering the Irish self-image. Many experienced a feeling of pride when the American humorist Will Rogers, for example, commented glowingly about the extraordinary welcome that Americans received in Ireland during 1926: "I have been in twenty countries, and the only one where American tourists are welcomed wholeheartedly by everybody is in Ireland . . . ; they don't owe us and they don't hate us." Finally, he quipped, "This endorsement is on the level and calls for no appointment from Tammany Hall whatever."[52] Comments like this one raised Ireland above other European destinations, displaced more unpleasant stereotypes, and fueled the patriotic zeal of tourism officials.

Post–Civil War travel writing also reflected these refurbished images. For example, Bell, the travel writer from Ohio, reminisced about the "lurid tales" presented by an engaging jarvey (hackney coach driver) "with the skill of a veteran novelist."[53] Years later, British comedian Tony Hawks told of his adventures hitchhiking around Ireland with a refrigerator to fulfill a drunken bet, claiming that such an undertaking would only be possible in the Emerald Isle. "In some parts of the world," he writes, "a stranger pulling a fridge on a trolley into a bar on a Friday night might be a recipe for a good kicking, but here I felt it more likely [that] if set upon, I would be held down and sung to."[54] In virtually all cases travel writers found the Irish eccentric, engaging, and endearing.

Kitsch and the Rural Image

From the vantage point of early twenty-first-century America, it might seem perfectly logical to assume that Irish tourism officials would adopt images of leprechauns, people dressed in green, rainbows, and pots of gold. The lexicon of American images of Ireland includes an inventory of green beer, Lucky Charms cereal, horror movies about demented leprechauns, and bath soap that promises to make the user smell as fresh as a soft morning in Ireland (never mind that a soft morning in rural Ireland is more likely to smell of livestock than soap). Indeed, Ireland's tourist shops are packed with kitsch, but tourism authorities have seldom made use of these products in any official capacity. Before the Irish Tourist Board was formed in 1939, Killarney was often described as a "fairyland"[55] and Irish scenery as "fairy-like," but the ITA made no effort to play up leprechaun-based "Paddywhackery." Likewise, the ITB, Fógra Fáilte, and Bord Fáilte have similarly avoided mindless kitsch. In fact, when Bord Fáilte did publish a folder that emphasized Irish folklore and the important role of the "little people" in Irish storytelling, it presented an essay by W. B. Yeats that described Ireland's fairy mythology in literary terms, and the booklet did not reflect the frivolity of the cereal-hawking little people in popular culture.[56] Low-class kitsch was avoided because tourism officials believed strongly that the "lazy leprechaun" idea of Ireland should be avoided. It was acceptable to exploit "native charm and character" as well as legends, antiquities, the native language, and traditional dress, but these should never be allowed to overshadow "a modern progressive outlook on life." Any projection of Ireland should show "the sophisticated side of Irish life" and break with "sentiment in a deliberate way."[57]

In 1950 the government formed a subcommittee to assess Ireland's tourist industry, and after looking into the matter, the committee immediately complained that the souvenirs offered at Irish shops were unsatisfactory. In particular, "the bog-oak pipe, the shillelagh, and the Birmingham broach should be driven from shops and shop windows." These items reflected an undesirable stereotype of Irishness, not an "appropriate and tasteful design in harmony with Irish culture and history." Likewise, the "caubeen and pipe type of advertisement" was to be avoided in favor of campaigns focusing attention on the many places of natural beauty in Ireland.[58] Rather than catering to the lowest common denominator, the authorities exhibited a sense of national pride in their perception of the mementos that should be made available. Moreover, some officials believed strongly that souvenirs should be manufactured in Ireland—providing employment to Irish people and establishing a reputation for the quality of Irish crafts. During the late 1950s, Bord Fáilte undertook a special initiative to increase the number of suitable souvenirs available; it oversaw an increase from 30 to 120 product lines by 1957, as well as substantial growth in the number of shops stocking these gifts.[59]

The fact that tourist authorities avoided leprechauns certainly does not mean that they rejected presentations of the Irish people as culturally distinct and different. In particular, Irish people have been portrayed as rural and agriculturally centered. The "Pre-1960s Types" collection in Bord Fáilte's photographic archive offers a striking illustration of the images of Irish people that were most often presented to tourists. The photographs include Irish men and women gathering and stacking turf, harvesting various crops, making hay, collecting and stacking kelp, driving horse-drawn carts, weaving, participating in livestock fairs, dressed as Mummers or Wren Boys, managing sheep, working on currachs (traditional boats), fishing, plowing, and so forth. The traditional "Kinsale cloak" worn by many women in west Cork through the 1940s was also a popular photograph and found its way into numerous guidebooks and travel narratives as well. Ultimately Irish people were presented in striking contrast not only to their industrial neighbors in Britain or on the continent but to the denizens of Dublin and Cork city as well. In many of these images work, and hard work at that, is clearly being done, but the tasks, clothing, and traditions reflect, or seek to project, a timeless Irishness.

It would be wrong to interpret these images purely as a desire to capture a past age or a reflection of foreign perceptions of Irishness—donkey carts,

3. A farm family harvesting turf near Downing, County Donegal. Courtesy of Bord Fáilte Éireann–Irish Tourist Board.

currachs, and turf cutting remain very much a part of the lexicon of Irish tourism, as is clear in the Tourism Brand Ireland campaign (see introduction). Instead the images represent a vision of what the tourism developers of the 1920s to the 1950s imagined Ireland to be. Of course, Ireland really *was* rural during this period. When Jan de Fouw, the Dutch graphic designer who was largely responsible for defining the look and content of *Ireland of the Welcomes* from 1952 into the 1990s, made home movies of his travels around Ireland, he captured people wearing shoes made of rawhide, donning handwoven trousers, and working their land in a manner that had been current since the years immediately following the Great Famine.[60] In some ways the tourist images used into the 1960s showed Ireland as it was and had been for decades. On the other hand and more important, this imagery illustrated Ireland as the nationalist imagination wanted it to be portrayed: Irish *poverty* was reformatted to symbolize Irish *purity*.

Shortly after the Civil War the Irish Coinage Committee recommended the issue of coins bearing images of Irish animals and wildlife, clearly showing the symbolic significance of rural settings.⁶¹ Not everybody agreed with the choice. Reflecting the long-standing debate surrounding modernization, some urged the use of industrial symbols. Coinage Committee chairman W. B. Yeats dismissed this suggestion by musing, "we have so few industries & doubt the decorative value of a porter bottle." Others feared that the coins suggested "paganism," "Freemasonry," and Ireland as a "land of devil-worshippers." Still others, including Maud Gonne, denounced the designs because an English artist, Percy Metcalfe, created them. Despite the objections, the coins were generally approved of.⁶² Allegations of devil-worship aside, the salience of rural Ireland was real and did not diminish with the change of government in 1932. In what is perhaps his most quoted policy statement, Éamon de Valera declared to radio listeners on Easter Sunday 1943,

> That Ireland which we dreamed of would be the home of a people who valued material wealth only as a basis of right living, of a people who were satisfied with frugal comfort and devoted their leisure to things of the spirit; a land whose countryside would be bright with cosy homesteads, whose fields and villages would be joyous with sounds of industry, the romping of sturdy children, the contests of athletic youths, the laughter of comely maidens; whose firesides would be the forums of the wisdom of serene old age.⁶³

De Valera was dreaming about precisely the same things that were depicted in tourist guidebooks. To show a rural Ireland in which the people diligently worked the land and appeared forever content was not just a message for tourists and foreign governments; it was a message to the Irish people themselves—a way of bolstering the native self-image during a time of economic hardship.

There was one additional reason for depicting an overwhelmingly rural and traditional Ireland: tourism had the potential to bring untold riches into underdeveloped areas that could no longer hope to support themselves on agriculture or fishing. As I have stressed in earlier chapters, by pushing tourists into small western-seaboard communities, and especially the Gaeltachts, the authorities hoped to stem the tide of emigration. Today, far outstripping any desire to stress symbolic links to the land, the focus on rural images grows directly from the need to pump money into rustic communities. The development of "agri-tourism" is only the most recent movement to assist underdeveloped areas. During the 1980s the government was faced with extremely high out-migration from such places. Between 1981 and 1986 alone rural population growth was cut in half, and rural unemployment climbed steeply during this period. Seventy-five percent of the agricultural products that were produced were in excess supply in the European Union, driving farm prices down and continuing to exacerbate the emigration problem.[64] The future for rural Ireland seemed desperately bleak. Only 35 percent of the rural population could find agricultural employment; part-time farming did not provide an adequate way of life because there were no jobs to supplement the meager income produced. Service-sector work was also limited; even in areas where tourism was important, the work created was seasonal.[65]

In the 1980s ACOT (the socioeconomic section of the Agricultural Advisory Service) began to promote the concept of more diversified tourism in rural areas.[66] In particular, this body advanced the idea of developing agri-tourism that involved attracting tourists to working farms in order to experience rural life. The program was to be locally run, but it experienced early problems. Few efforts were made to develop acceptable medium-range planning objectives, and community members failed to combine their resources to mount adequate marketing campaigns.[67] Still, by 1988, Bord Fáilte became convinced that agri-tourism might be viable if adequately administered. The Tourist Board's 1994–99 sustainable-development plan expressed a desire to create "rural tourism areas" that "generally lie outside the tourism centres and cater for a market segment that is seeking a quiet holiday where tourists can get to know a local area intimately, immersed in the traditions of rural Ireland."[68] Rural tourism has the added advantage that it keeps tourists in a specific area for longer periods, ensuring that their funds flow directly into the local community for an extended time. Just as tourism developers in the 1940s hoped to use language tourism as a means of promoting economic development in Gaeltacht areas while also encouraging the language, so too contemporary tourism interests hope to advance economic growth in sparsely populated rural districts.

Festivals and Irish Tourism

Markets and fairs have been a part of Irish life for many hundreds of years and initially emerged as "a response to a local need to exchange surplus produce." More than simply places of business, fairs brought people from different social backgrounds and geographic locations together, helping to shape Irish society in new ways: "town met country; farmer met trader; and the influences of the wider world were introduced into the local culture."[69] Later, the larger fairs attracted not only people from around Ireland but also from Britain and even the continent.[70] By the late nineteenth century the number of markets and fairs held throughout Ireland began to decline.[71] This downturn sped up during the twentieth century as fairs covered larger market areas, trains ceased running to many old parochial centers (especially after 1960), respectability gained an ever stronger hold on society (demanding an end to the drunken revelries that held sway during earlier times), and traditional sites of economic activity were replaced by multipurpose stores.

Today those fairs and festivals that remain—"like the 'Auld Lammas Fair' of Ballycastle in County Antrim or Puck Fair in Killorglin in County Kerry—do so as much for social or touristic as for commercial purposes."[72] In fact, beginning in the early 1950s with the first mounting of An Tóstal, fairs and festivals emerged throughout Ireland in order to attract tourists rather than cattle or horse traders. Organizers developed new traditions that allegedly represented time-honored examples of Irish culture. Whereas traditional fairs were often bawdy gatherings, filled with drink, thinly veiled bestial sexuality, violence, and the presence of marginal groups like Irish Travellers, tourist festivals presented a happier side of Irish culture, celebrating food, theatre, music, and friendliness. The official desire to present Ireland as a land of welcoming people and joyous, time-honored customs combined with the economic need to draw an ever-increasing number of visitors and with the tourists' dream of experiencing a little piece of authenticity.

Puck Fair and the Problem with Traditional Entertainment

Puck Fair was originally a cattle fair held every August in Killorglin: a little town at the head of Dingle Bay in County Kerry. In some ways Puck Fair was a relic of an earlier age when many fairs adopted animals as symbols of the festival and the commercial spirit of the event.[73] On the first day of the fair, Gathering Day, a wild goat, captured in the mountains above Killarney, is crowned king and hoisted onto a tall tower to preside over the fair. The second day is primarily given over to cattle trading, and the third, Scattering

4. Fair authorities place King Puck on his platform at the start of the 1955 Puck Fair. Courtesy of Bord Fáilte Éireann–Irish Tourist Board.

Day, sees the dethroning of the king and his release back into the Kerry mountains. The actual act of crowning the goat is undertaken by a small girl, the "Green Queen," who reigns with Puck (though not on the tower). The sexual overtones of a young girl and a well-endowed goat are not explicitly pointed out in the ceremony, but they are carefully emphasized in Muriel Rukeyser's account of the event.[74] In practice, the three-day fair was marked by incessant drinking and dancing,[75] to say nothing of the distressing accumulation of muck that one might expect from a large number of livestock.[76] Traditionally Puck Fair was also the site of frequent fighting—often attributed to the presence of Irish Travellers sparring with rival Travelling families as well as with unfriendly locals. Despite the ethnic or cultural ill-will between the Travelling community and landed locals, the fair was reportedly made a "real Irish fair" only by the "Tinkers"—whose presence brought two culturally diverse components of Irish society into close contact.[77]

Many Irish people were ambivalent about mixing "traditional" fairs and tourism. In her account of a 1958 trip to Puck Fair,[78] Rukeyser recounts numerous comments by Irish people, most of them from Kerry itself, arguing that Americans should not visit Puck Fair because "it's so materialistic. It's all about drinking."[79] Another local observer went further, describing the three-day festival as "all hatred and dreariness" marked by "long, slow, slugging fighting, breaking everything it passes through."[80] One Killorglin resident even predicted that the author "won't be able to stand it. She's American, after all."[81] Even as Rukeyser prepared to leave following the final day of the fair, she was asked by one of her Kerry friends to "go easy on Puck."[82] Although Rukeyser would not necessarily have been aware of it, attitudes toward Irish Travellers were also undergoing a dramatic change in the years following World War II. No longer viewed as free spirits as they were before the early 1950s, the Travelling people were increasingly seen as dirty, dangerous, and repulsive—outsiders from mainstream Irish society, despised people to be hidden away, not celebrated.[83] Puck Fair's intimate association with Irish "Tinkers" certainly added to the widespread ambivalence about presenting the fair to tourists.[84] For many locals Puck Fair was simply too dirty, too violent, too bestial, too primordial for any outsider to understand.

Despite local concerns, the fair was included in tourist guidebooks and in much travel writing. During the 1920s and 1930s the Irish Tourist Association made a point of drawing attention to the fair, including it in their *Official Guide to the Kingdom of Kerry*.[85] During the immediate postwar period the Puck Fair Committee made a point of publishing a souvenir guide for the event, including photographs of King Puck and a debate about the origin of the fair.[86] Travel writers like Sean O'Faolain also maintained an interest in the curious tradition of crowning a goat. O'Faolain made a point of mentioning the fair in his *Irish Journey*, and the Irish-born travel writer Leslie Daiken demonstrated an interest in the fair through numerous articles and a BBC radio broadcast.[87]

As the number of tourists in Ireland began to increase, the authorities became somewhat less enthusiastic about promoting Puck. In Fógra Fáilte's

Ireland Guide, published in about 1953, Puck Fair received an extensive description.[88] In 1958, when Rukeyser visited the fair, Bord Fáilte's annual calendar of events not only listed Puck Fair, it provided readers with a description of the event and the various groups known to participate.[89] This complete listing continued into the 1960s,[90] but by 1973 it was scaled back to a mere name-and-date listing. It was not that the format of the calendar of events had changed to exclude descriptions—the Dublin Horse Show, for example, retained a detailed caption; rather, the authorities appear to have become increasingly tentative about recommending that tourists "do" Puck.[91] Indeed, the Tourist Board's *Ireland: 1980* guide, which offered visitors descriptions and photographs of the country's attractions, did not suggest Puck as a suitable August activity.[92] Although Puck continued to be included in Bord Fáilte's *Ireland Guide* as part of descriptions of Killorglin, it was no longer prominently placed in "what's on" schedules—despite the fact that by this time it bore little resemblance to its earlier incarnation after having been reinvented as a tourist fair, albeit with the same sexual overtones and mass drunkenness of thirty years before.[93] But the fair was treated as a curiosity taking place over "three days in August"—three *undefined* days. What had happened?

It seems likely that Puck Fair began to fall from favor because it did not offer an altogether acceptable picture of Ireland or Irishness. Tourist authorities could not have legions of American tourists realizing, as Rukeyser did in 1958, that they were going "to an orgy."[94] Leslie Daiken did not see Puck Fair as offensive. He recognized that Puck was a "bucolic fiesta which must be the last survival in these Islands of a pagan orgy of hard drinking—tempered with dancing, singing, and those occasional faction-fights which invest the balmy, midnight air with yells of priapine frenzy."[95] But Daiken saw something else that he believed to be more important, a relic of the romance of ancient Ireland. His gaze focused on the timeless tradition involved, and he worked, through his travel articles and a BBC radio presentation entitled "Where Puck Is King," to share the fair's "character and particular atmosphere." Puck Fair was, he insisted, uniquely Irish, "the only ritualistic congregation of men and women of goodwill in all north-west Europe where a wild goat is tamed for kingship."[96] He romanticized the event as something that "every poet in Ireland" comes to see "because every native of Kerry is at heart a poet." Although the fun was often "fast and free," in Daiken's mind it was "never a riot or bacchanal, but nimble as a Kerryman's tongue with spontaneous jollity; friendly as a big family party; honestly countrified like any true fair-day ought to be."[97]

Tourist authorities were less convinced. In fact, when Daiken contacted Michael Gorman, then editor of *Ireland of the Welcomes,* about publishing an article on Puck Fair, the editor responded with interest but with the caveat that Daiken should "keep the *Ireland of the Welcomes* readership in mind and only stress those aspects of Puck Fair which are universally acceptable as attractions."[98] This was *not* the Ireland to which Bord Fáilte wanted to direct tourists, *not* the Ireland that it wanted to feature in the glossy pages of its travel magazine, and *not* the Ireland that it wanted to emphasize in its calendar of events. Puck Fair could not be eliminated from official guides because it was still something of interest to many tourists. More important, it was Killorglin's only claim to fame—beyond the town's geographic location at the beginning of the "Ring of Kerry" scenic motoring tour—and the Tourist Board's mission was to promote tourism and related employment throughout Ireland. Puck was also, until the launch of An Tóstal and the ancillary festivals that sprang, Athena-like, from it, one of Ireland's few remaining fairs. Once more fairs and festivals became available, Puck was easily downplayed in favor of more respectable entertainment like the Cork Film Festival or Galway Oyster Festival. New "traditions" were required to replace their more dated and much less respectable antecedents.

Inspiration

An Tóstal: Ireland at Home was the single largest tourist development project undertaken during the 1950s and it stands as an excellent example of how Irish identity was influenced both from within and without Ireland. While actual events were planned in Ireland, the idea and inspiration for An Tóstal came from abroad. Juan Trippe, the president of Pan-American Airlines, first suggested the concept for a new tourist festival in 1951,[99] the same year that Britain held its Festival of Britain. Trippe's idea fell on receptive ears partly because just one year before the Cabinet Sub-Committee on Tourism had argued that Ireland should promote "an event of international significance which would appeal to our own people at home and abroad" and that would be "somewhat on the lines of the proposed Festival of Britain."[100] Holding an Irish version of the Festival of Britain allowed the Irish to demonstrate themselves to be on par with their neighbors across the Irish Sea. At the same time, the festival idea allowed the Irish to create events that reflected a more widely acceptable Irish culture while also addressing issues raised during the tourism crisis of 1948–51.

Although the Irish were certainly inspired by the Festival of Britain, the two events were fundamentally different. An Tóstal was far more focused on tourism earnings than the British festival, which was primarily a "pat on the back" to reward the British people for winning the war while also providing a "tonic for the nation" during a period of economic and political difficulty."[101] In contrast, the success of Tóstal hinged on "an emotional desire on the part of people of Irish descent to visit Erin" and events were designed accordingly.[102] The Irish tourist festival was intended to lengthen the tourist season (hence the fact that it was planned for the early spring) and to attract people of Irish ancestry back to the Emerald Isle from America, England, and the various Commonwealth countries. In a strict sense, then, any failure to immediately attract legions of tourists would mean that An Tóstal had failed (despite subsequent rationalizations of government and tourism officials).

History was a central theme of both the British and Irish festivals, yet here too important variations were prominent. Festival of Britain organizers planned an event that offered an "autobiography" of the nation. A carefully chosen history was offered and the people were presented as quiet, unassuming, and tough—rather like the hobbits in J. R. R. Tolkien's *Lord of the Rings* trilogy, first published three years later in 1954–55. History was defined in terms of timeless traditions that would carry the people forward toward a bright future; indeed, modernity and progress were stressed above all. There were conflicts, of course, and local festivals in Cornwall, Wales, and Scotland gave primacy to local distinctiveness rather than the narrative designed by central planners in London, but the more centralized administration of British events assured that a picture of timeless traditions and "unity through diversity" predominated. Even where divergent historical narratives were notable, few questioned the desirability of modernity.[103] History mattered, but only insofar as it contributed to the glories of the present and the promise of the future.

Meanwhile, An Tóstal, though first proposed in 1951, was presented as a vestige of Irish history—a surviving exemplar of a long and ancient tradition of Irish festivals. An Tóstal was a descendant of "great festivals of long ago—Tara, Tailteann, Carmain, Uisneach, and all the rest." The new tourist festival was designed to revive this long tradition.[104] Of course, in reality, Tailteann, a sort of medieval Olympic Games, had not been held since 1169 (with the exception of a short-lived revival in the 1920s), Tara was more associated with medieval governance than hedonistic enjoyment, and the other two events were pagan religious holidays and bore virtually no similarity to the very modern and mostly secular An Tóstal.[105] None of this mattered. Indeed, when explaining the choice of the name An Tóstal, organizers said that they hoped it would inspire memories of "Ireland's earliest national assemblages."[106] Of course the term, which translates as "a gathering," had probably never been used in antiquity. It was chosen after representatives of Bord Fáilte argued that a Gaelic title should be given to the festival and a five-pound note was offered to the government's translation office for suggestions.[107] Several days later "An Tóstal" emerged as the leading recommendation and was soon presented as a clear link with the ancient past. As a way of making Tóstal's lineage graphically obvious, organizers commissioned the design of an emblem that was to symbolize "ancient Irish festivals and gatherings." That Guss Melai, a Dutch designer, developed the logo was carefully kept under wraps.[108] The insignia included a "traditional Irish harp," the fore pillar and head of which included ornamentation drawn from the Book of Kells—ornamentation "inspired by the Celtic decoration engraved on the old Irish harps."[109] The An Tóstal logo not only graphically linked this very modern tourist gathering to the distant past, it also linked modern Ireland symbolically to the musical and artistic outpourings of a previous age. Whereas the Festival of Britain was intended to point British attentions toward a bright future,[110] An Tóstal pointed festival-goers backward toward an unobjectionable past. "Ireland at Home" was offered to visitors as being just as traditional as Puck Fair, if not more so; yet there were no aspects of Tóstal that needed to be downplayed in order to stress "only those aspects [of Irishness] which are universally acceptable." An Tóstal was inherently suitable for all audiences.

An Tóstal drew attention to the national community and celebrated the achievements of the *Volk* in a manner that was much different than in Britain.

5. Publicity poster for the 1954 An Tóstal, featuring Guss Melai's famous Tóstal harp. Courtesy of Bord Fáilte Éireann–Irish Tourist Board.

Both festivals put the national "cultural attractions . . . on display,"[111] but in Ireland local communities created these attractions, not a centralized committee as in Britain.[112] From the moment that the Irish government accepted the Tóstal idea, the two statutory tourist bodies launched an aggressive campaign to hire an organizer, publish spectacular publicity materials, and plan a series of monumental parades and other events around Dublin, but it was local "Tóstal Councils" that actually developed the majority of the events. An Tóstal lacked the traveling exhibits and regional displays that were a core component of the Festival of Britain and the Tóstal's organizational structure assured that the festival reflected a truly grassroots sense of Irish identity.

New Traditions for a Modern Age

What cultural attractions did the committees include? Tóstal Councils developed a wide variety of events that included sporting events, parades, musical concerts, plays, pageants, exhibits, and so forth. The 1953 Tóstal opened during Easter Week with a special mass at the Pro-Cathedral in Dublin, presided over by Archbishop John Charles McQuaid.[113] This mass was followed by a massive military parade down Dublin's abnormally clean streets—"one of the biggest reviews in Ireland's history," including members from all three of the Irish armed services, and an inspection of the troops by Irish President Seán T. O'Kelly. This was followed by the raising of the Tóstal flag, a tribute by Taoiseach Éamon de Valera at the 1916 memorial, the release of carrier pigeons instructed to bring goodwill to the country, and the lighting of candles throughout Dublin. Similar displays occurred simultaneously in Cork city, and a torchlight procession took place at the Hill of Slane, where a massive bonfire was lit to symbolize Saint Patrick's introduction of Christianity to the Irish people.[114]

When selecting events, "the strongest possible emphasis" was placed "on Gaelic life, history, language, and culture." Both the Gaelic Athletic Association and the Gaelic League were called upon to provide "complete cooperation." Promoters, both regional and national, were invited to develop events under the headings "nationality," "culture," and "constitutional and civic life," with national traditions, language, music, art, drama, folklore, recreation, and leisure all given special attention.[115]

Pageants were an important component of Tóstal schedules, allowing organizers to send a dramatic message to visitors about Irish life and history. During the first year a special "Tóstal Show" was presented at the Theatre Royal in Dublin that dramatized important phases of Irish history defined by the theme "four green fields," symbolizing the four provinces of Ireland. County Waterford went one better, providing two historical pageants, including one that dealt with the Danish invasion and another featuring that of the Normans.[116] In the following year national organizers planned a more elaborate event and presented a monumental "Pageant of Saint Patrick" that spanned two days and four locations, including Drogheda, Navan, Slane, and Tara. At each site an aspect of the Saint Patrick story was presented, ranging from the saint's arrival in Ireland, to his arrest at Slane, to his eventual peaceful conversion of the Brehons and Druids at Tara.[117] Organizers used 500 costumes for the choir alone and employed the services of 1,300 volunteers to carry the event off. In addition, 1,000 pigeons, 24 wolfhounds, and 30 horses, as well as deer and other game, were integrated into the event.[118] As it happened, the occasion attracted fifty thousand largely Irish spectators to Tara alone, despite bitterly cold March weather.[119] The spectacle impressed government officials, who suggested that a similar pageant might be included in subsequent Tóstals, but only at five-year intervals, as it was too expensive a proposition for annual repetition.[120]

Despite the heavy costs, organizers opted to include the pageant in the 1955 schedule, though it was staged at Croke Park rather than across the broad canvas of the Boyne Valley. This time the pageant functioned as the Tóstal opener and told of Patrick's meeting with the high-king of the Druids in the Court of Tara and of "his over-throwing of the forces of paganism." Saint Patrick was played by leading Dublin actor Anew McMaster, and the pageant was written and produced by Micheál MacLiammóir, and directed by Hilton Edwards of Dublin's Gate Theatre, assuring that the luminaries of Dublin's theatre world were all involved.[121] The 1956 pageant was also presented at Croke Park, but organizers broke with previous practice in telling the story of Cuchulainn, the great Irish warrior so feared by his adversaries that even after his death, when his body was propped up facing the enemy, Cuchulainn's foes dared not approach until they saw crows pecking at the dead warrior's corpse. A thousand actors presented six performances of the epic play under the floodlights at Dublin's great Gaelic sports ground.[122]

Sporting matches were among the most commonly promoted Tóstal events. As the official souvenir guidebook stressed, "Every tourist knows that Ireland is a sporting country," and it drew particular attention to the fact that "Ireland is home to one of the world's greatest amateur sporting organisations." From the perspective of festival promoters Gaelic sport was important because "they are the games of the people"—as popular in Ireland as baseball in America or Australian Rules football in Australia. Of Ireland's four million inhabitants, some three million, it was said, "are either present or past members or else consistent supporters" of the Gaelic Athletic Association (GAA). To know the Irish people was to know Gaelic sports and especially hurling. In spite of the fact that the geographical centers of hurling strength are traditionally found only in a handful of mostly southern counties (especially Kilkenny, Tipperary, Cork, and Clare), the sport nevertheless was "in the blood and bone of the Irish breed," and, even at the elite level it was allegedly played purely "for the love of the game and for the honour of the county, parish, or little white-walled village, as the case may be." Just as important, the focusing of visitor attention on Gaelic games offered another instrument allowing tourist authorities to point toward Ireland's ancient cultural traditions. "Men were hurling [in Ireland] when the gods of Greece were young," boasted the guidebook. Hurling was "immortal," and even restrictive colonial policies could not suppress it.[123]

Of course, Fógra Fáilte made it abundantly clear in their souvenir handbook that Gaelic sports were not the only game in town. Equestrian sports, angling, motor sports, hunting, running, sailing, hiking, and a wealth of other activities were also present in abundance, making it impossible to "give a comprehensive view of sport in Ireland in the course of a few pages."[124] Fundamentally, the message was that Ireland offered something for everybody—whether in sporting interests or in serious cultural activity. Indeed, the Tóstal guidebook drew attention to a number of aspects of Irish life, including its people, landscape, work habits, and cultural achievements. Visitors were to be made to understand Ireland not only through the games its people played, but also by the success of Irish industry since independence and the long list of literary, visual, and musical accomplishments of its people. The guidebook did not attempt to present Irishness as a simple combination of friendliness and good humor, but instead claimed that the Irish "character tends to be a baffling one," marked by dramatic changes in mood from gaiety to somber melancholy. Only a long stay in Ireland would reveal the complex national personality of its people.[125]

Before this discussion returns to specific Tóstal events, it should be noted that while Irish sport was a prominent feature of festival events, organizers also placed a substantial emphasis on the Irish work ethic. The world of labor was not only considered important to understanding the Irish people, it was also viewed as essential to understanding the achievements of independent Ireland. Having outlined the prevalence of agriculture, the Tóstal guide noted that although "there was no systematic establishment of manufacturing industries until the independent Irish state was founded," since that time "substantial advances have been made towards effecting a satisfactory economic balance between agricultural and manufacturing enterprise."[126] For tourism organizers it was a matter of substantial pride that "considerable progress has . . . been made in a comparatively short time towards increasing the industrialisation of Ireland."[127] This satisfaction was not limited to the tourist guidebooks. For example, Kilkenny launched a substantial "industrial exhibition" as part of its 1953 Tóstal effort,[128] even including a special pageant devoted to the county's industrial success.[129] In both 1953 and 1954 the Cork Tóstal Council combined forces with the Cork Chamber of Commerce and the Cork Regional Group of the Federation of Irish Manufacturers to host a "Cork Makes It" exhibition featuring products manufactured in Cork city and its environs.[130] Limerick presented an annual parade celebrating Irish industry.[131] Far from the workplace being absent, as Barbara O'Connor mistakenly suggests in an article about Irish tourist representations,[132] "Ireland at Home" showed visitors a nation of men (and to a much lesser extent women) who worked hard but knew well how to enjoy a bit of *"craic"* when not building a vibrant and successful nation.

An Tóstal was primarily about showing the nation's guests a good time. Ireland was nowhere more successful than in its extraordinary output of music, literature, and theatre. Both Irish music and Irish literature and theatre personified the message of ancient cultural achievement advanced by Tóstal organizers. Gaelic-language writing was traced to an epic, pre-Homeric literary tradition.[133] Anglo-Irish writing, although more recent, grew from "certain racial or national qualities," and traits such as "Irish humor" were the result of "several perceptibly indigenous strains" that combined to create something uniquely Irish.[134]

Perhaps most important of all, Irish music was clearly a major element of ancient Irish life. The Muireadach high cross at Monasterboice, for example, included a thousand-year-old carving of harp and pipe players seated around Christ. When such representations were taken "in conjunction with the numerous references in early mediaeval manuscripts, they make it clear that music entered largely into the life of the ancient Irish."[135] The corpus of folk music that resulted from this almost timeless tradition formed "an integral part" of Irish heritage and, not surprisingly, played a substantial role in Tóstal events. When announcing Tóstal in *Ireland of the Welcomes,* Fógra Fáilte made a point of including photographs of pipers, a choir, and a symphony, as well as of featuring a harp and a young dancer done in spot color to draw attention to them.[136] De Valera's opening speech delivered in Cork city drew attention to Ireland's musical tradition and addressed the numerous musical events planned to occur there, including an opera, a *cailidh,* sacred music performances, recitals, and so on.[137] Indeed, Cork was one of the first areas to create a special competition in the form of a choral contest that ultimately continued to be held after the demise of An Tóstal in the late 1950s.[138] Eventually other localities added music and theatre festivals to their Tóstal schedules as well, including Dublin's Festival of Grand Opera, the Wexford Music Festival, Dublin's International Festival of Music and the Arts, the Cork Film Festival, and the Dublin Theatre Festival.[139]

In spite of the wide variety of events offered to potential Tóstal tourists, very few made the trip and the festival was far from the success of its British cousin. Between 1953 and 1958 both the government and the Tourist Board saw one visitor target after another hopelessly missed. Instead of massive crowds of excited tourists, more often than not the scene was of "flags and bunting bedraggled, bands playing bravely, no sign of tourists, and ministers of state standing under umbrellas saying their piece."[140] As early as 1954 there was debate about the early spring timing of the event, but it was pointed out that the "point was to extend the tourist season," and no changes were made.[141] In planning for the 1956 Tóstal, Bord Fáilte argued that it should be staged from 6 to 21 May, and the event was moved one month forward.[142] It proved no more successful, however, in attracting tourists. Despite the poor showings, the minister for industry and commerce announced in 1955 that the event would run through at least 1958, thus putting off any serious discussion of dissolving An Tóstal.[143]

In July 1958 a committee was convened to discuss the future of "Ireland at Home." After much deliberation the group concluded that Tóstal had not been successful in extending the tourist season and therefore did not justify the considerable expense. Rather than abandon the festival idea outright, however, the committee suggested that the Tóstal period be *extended* to run all the way from June through September. It was argued that this approach would attract visitors to the country while retaining the growth of civic pride and the successful local events that had developed under the rubric of An Tóstal. Furthermore, seaside resorts would be able to create special events in July and August rather than in the dreary spring months when few tourists ventured to the seaside, while urban centers could launch indoor events such as film festivals either earlier or later in the season as desired.[144] Now Bord Fáilte's message was that Ireland was a land of festivals.[145]

The story of Ireland's tourism festivals does not end with the emergence of the "Ireland of the Festivals" idea. Almost immediately, virtually all the local events began to lose money, requiring Bord Fáilte to step in to provide financial support. The Tourist Board's first grants were given in 1962, and it promised to continue funding the events for three years. Initially, the board offered £26,000, spread among eight festivals, including major celebrations in Dublin, Cork, Wexford, and Waterford, as well as several angling events and the Yeats Summer School in Sligo. In the following year £28,000 was given to the same festivals. By 1964 the number of events securing aid had increased to eleven, with total grants now estimated at £30,000 and with the larger festivals receiving in the range of £4,000 each. During the first two years of the program Bord Fáilte estimated that the festivals benefiting from its aid took in some £100,000 in tourism earnings. The larger events were more bullish still. The Dublin Theatre Festival estimated an annual income of £100,000 on its own, earned from 2,700 foreign tourists in attendance at its events. Likewise the Cork Film Festival cited £21,000 in earnings over eight days. The Cork Choral Festival was far less successful, however, running a deficit of some £900. Bord Fáilte hoped that its grant program would inspire corporate sponsorship, allowing the board to eventually end the scheme. Guinness, for example, already supported the Festival of Kerry, the Wexford Festival, the Dundalk G & G Festival, the West Cork Festival at Clonakilty, Bundoran's Lobster Festival, the Kilkenny Beer Festival, the Sligo Festival, and many others. If similar corporate interest could be generated, perhaps through tax incentives, the Tourist Board predicted a bright future.[146]

As it happened, the 1965 review of festival policy found it impossible for the Tourist Board to cease financial subventions, and it was decided to continue the program through 1970. Tourist Board chief T. J. O'Driscoll stressed that decisions about aid would be based increasingly on the level of local support—financial and otherwise. Only those communities strongly behind their tourism festivals could realistically expect substantial assistance from the Tourist Board. Meanwhile, even as its director-general noted that board finances were being stretched more thinly each year, he encouraged the expansion of Ireland's festivals by local groups in order to "offer scope for the generation of tourist traffic in volume" and for giving "special attention" to "festivals which are distinctively Irish in character." Each festival should establish a local company and a tighter administrative structure to ensure financial solvency.[147]

Bord Fáilte never escaped the need for the provision of festival grants, but the number and the professionalism of the events do seem to have increased. By 1970 the Dublin Tourism RTO decided to begin developing a weeklong St. Patrick's Day celebration, modeled largely on U.S. ideas about "Ireland's national holiday."[148] After a brief decline in the mid-1990s,[149] the event has steadily gained momentum since that time, and in 2002, Dublin visitors were treated to four days of fireworks, parades, dancing, and music.[150] Likewise, outstanding events like Wexford's Opera Festival and Kerry's "Rose of Tralee" contest have also persisted.[151] Today hundreds of festivals, large and small, enliven the Irish countryside every year, designed to attract tourists without any of the unsavory aspects of Ireland's ancient markets and fairs.

Conclusions

While there has long been kitsch available for purchase in Ireland's souvenir shops, the stuffed shamrocks, pots of gold, and wee ceramic leprechauns are only one small piece of the tourism puzzle. The conscious desire to present the "best" of Ireland was far more prevalent. Tourism developers, whether at the local or national level, all hoped to present a positive image of the Irish people and to stave off economic malaise, yet beyond this consensus, different opinions about how best to define "Ireland" for tourists were obvious. Was it a Gaelic-speaking country or an Anglophone one? Were the Irish a modern nation with family-friendly values or a traditional country in which man and beast were intimately linked?

The story of the cultural presentation of Irishness for tourists suggests two main conclusions. First, as with the debate surrounding tourism as a national interest, the presentation of Irish culture was a collective process. Language enthusiasts were every bit as vocal as tourism advocates, even if their view ultimately failed to win the day. Those who enjoyed traditional fairs added their voices to the debate just as did those who favored more modern and respectable tourist festivals. Outsiders such as tourists, Pan-American Airlines, Dutch graphic designers, and Festival of Britain planners all had an influence on events in Ireland just as did those who had lived in Ireland all their lives; tourism product development was a collective process. Second, cultural images were not unchanging artifacts of the colonial past. While older images were maintained when they met contemporary needs, it was just as possible to abandon older ideas when demands changed. Just as the conception of Ireland's "national interest" evolved with time, so too did ideas about the cultural appearance of the nation itself. In short, tourist images were hardly a "weight" around Irish necks. Instead these images were a canvas upon which the Irish (including tourist authorities and local communities) could paint their own vision of themselves: a vision of friendly, welcoming, industrious, and independent people.

5
Tourism and the Past

Like language and culture, history plays a significant role in imagining the nation. National groups find their "ultimate moorings in history."[1] A shared past provides the nation with legitimacy, allowing nationalists to catalog the numerous challenges successfully faced by their ancestors, to recount the countless glorious deeds carried out over time, and to lay claim to territory that has been (or should have been) in the possession of the nation since the beginning of time.[2] The past creates a structure for "the world as a product of the interplay of various communities, each possessing a unique character and history, and each the result of specific origins and developments."[3] Nationalists need only remind their compatriots of the past to inspire a desire to relive old glories, thus revitalizing the nation for a new age.[4]

Just as genuine Irish culture provided a challenge to the positive stereotypes of Irishness, so too the realities of Irish political history posed a formidable barrier to the portrayal of Irish welcoming friendliness to all visitors. On the one hand, Ireland's modern history was largely defined by nationalist struggle against English rule, while on the other, English tourists represented the single largest source of tourism earnings in Ireland: some £24.3 million per annum in 1962.[5] At the same time, memory of Ireland's Civil War was still rife during the 1950s and even the 1960s. Thus, while in theory nationalists need only point to a few specific historical events in order to energize their countrymen and countrywomen, the Irish case suggests that matters can be significantly more complicated. While it is one thing to agree that a nation has a common past, it is another thing altogether to agree on precisely what that past was. Which stories are most important? Who are the heroes and who the villains? In a country like Ireland where civil war has blighted the national memory, which faction should take precedence? Yet the challenge of presenting Irish history to tourists was not limited to problems with historic memory. Access to the Irish landscape, and to historic sites, was contested. Limited funds, or at least a failure by government officials to provide adequate funds, and the necessity of linking site-development efforts to international trends also played a role in shaping the Irish heritage product.

This chapter examines the presentation of Irish history to tourists from 1923 to the end of the century. The initial development of historic sites for tourist consumption mirrors closely the larger debate about the position of tourism as a national interest. The first portion of this chapter traces the efforts by preservationists and antiquarians to obtain legislation to protect Ireland's historic places. The chapter then recounts the early efforts of the statutory tourist authorities to develop and present historic sites to visitors, paying particular attention to both the choice of sites and the narratives chosen to accompany them. Careful notice is paid to the strong desire to avoid all controversy, while also exploring, as a focal example, the development of Kilmainham Jail as a museum—a project that at first seems to fly in the face of the usual conservative approach to developing historic sites. It is argued that the Kilmainham development was possible only because the story of the prison was manipulated to reduce controversy while presenting Irish history as a unified struggle for liberty and freedom. The final section examines how larger trends in the presentation of "heritage" have helped to define the character of Ireland's heritage tourism products.

The Past as Irish Tourist Attraction

Although the heritage industry is relatively recent,[6] the use of historic sites as a tourist attraction is not. In the ancient world, Egyptian and Greek ruins fascinated Roman tourists.[7] Much more recently, "modern" tourists from across Europe were fascinated by ancient ruins from at least the early nineteenth century and found these places both mysterious and romantic. In Ireland, Victorian visitors were attracted to places like Glendalough, Newgrange, Clonmacnois, and Monasterboice, drawn by aesthetics, not historical narrative. From the very beginning of the tourist movement after the Civil War, the Irish Tourist Association recognized the potential attractiveness of historic sites and made a conscious effort to present places like the Gallarus Oratory on the Dingle Peninsula and the various ruined castles and monasteries near the Killarney lakes to interested tourists. The first editions of *Ireland: Official Publication* made a point of addressing, in words and pictures, Ireland's impressive collection of historic sites. The guide informed visitors that "Ireland is of special interest to the antiquary, the number of ancient monuments of many kinds being extraordinarily great."[8] Throughout the 132-page guidebook the ITA included images of churches, high crosses, round towers, Neolithic sites, the Gallarus Oratory, the Rock of Cashel, and other notable ancient sites.

Early visitors displayed interest in the past, though for most tourists this interest appears to have been limited to the scenic attributes of ruined buildings—continuing the Victorian love affair with "romantic" ruins—and the legends and stories attached to many of the sites; more contemporary events were seldom mentioned.[9] Archie Bell, the travel writer from Ohio, thrilled at his driver's exciting tales of the origins of castles and of the various Killarney-area ruins, not to mention the ruins of Brian Boru's castle, various ancient burial places, and the stunning detail in the Book of Kells.[10] Likewise, "Kuklos," an English travel writer, expressed awe at the sight of the Gallarus Oratory and drew attention to the local legends about fairies guarding the beehive huts at Dunquin near Slea Head, Co. Kerry.[11] Little attention was paid, either by tourists or the Tourist Association, to the actual history of the sites/sights in question.

Government officials were conscious at a very early stage of the importance of preserving historic sites, although the fact that tourism had not yet achieved widespread recognition as a national interest meant that tourism was seldom, if ever, used as a justification for preserving ancient ruins. As early as 1925, academics began to call for the Irish Free State to "take its place among the other nations of Europe" by passing an act that would preserve ancient sites. Officials argued,

> It is hardly necessary for us to dwell here upon the importance of the preservation of ancient monuments; that is admitted by the common consent of the civilised world. In Ireland such preservation is doubly necessary: first, because education in the past has not been such as to develop in the people at large an understanding of the value of ancient monuments; and secondly, because of the great importance of Irish antiquities for an understanding of the early civilisation not merely of Ireland but also of Europe.

If anything, the Civil War made Irish antiquities even more valuable "as survivors from the wreck."[12]

The desire to put Irish preservation into a European context is telling and it demonstrates that the symbols of national identity are not created in isolation. The preservation movement was European in scope and was almost always tied in one way or another to a nationalist impulse. Although Pope Pius II passed the first preservationist edicts during the fifteenth century,[13] most European countries generated either nationalist preservation groups or state-sponsored monuments acts beginning in the middle of the nineteenth century. France, for example, passed its hugely influential Historic Monuments Act in 1887 following a growing nationalist preservation movement with roots in the French Revolution.[14] In Germany, Göethe expressed preservationist ideas as early as the 1770s, but the first widespread interest in saving ancient structures emerged only after German unification and during a period of pronounced German nationalist feeling. State-sponsored monuments acts followed later.[15] In virtually every case, preservationists insisted on the national importance of preserving the past. Victor Hugo, for example, declared that "long histories make great peoples," indicating that physical markers of the past serve to remind people of their glorious history.[16] Likewise, Bismarck reportedly insisted that it was "of greatest harm to a nation when it allows the living consciousness of its connection to its heritage and history to fade."[17] Built structures represented, insisted German preservationists, a corporeal link to the past. Thus University College Dublin archaeologist R. A. S. MacAlister,[18] one of the primary architects of early Irish preservation, echoed the larger discourse when he stressed that preservation and archaeological study represented "a truer patriotism."

The introduction of monuments legislation shortly after the Civil War was both a means of expressing the modern state's connection to the glorious Irish past *and* a way of putting the new state into the same orbit as the major European powers. Failure to establish monuments legislation would have represented not just the rejection of the anguished pleas of a few hypereducated intellectuals but also the rejection of the widely accepted discourse of modern European nationalisms. Ireland would have been alone in Europe—hardly a viable strategy at a time when the new Irish government hoped to introduce Ireland into the pantheon of nation-states.

While there had been isolated calls for the protection of Irish monuments before 1921, all responsibility for such efforts rested with the British government.[19] Whereas English legislation was careful not to diminish the rights of landholders by depending on goodwill rather than enforced restrictions, legislation addressing Ireland placed more control in the hands of the Office of Public Works than it did landowners.[20] The first Irish preservation act, the Irish Church Act, was passed in 1869. England had to wait thirteen years for a similar statute. This legislation placed many Irish churches under the protection of the government. The Ancient Monuments Protection Act of 1882 assured the preservation of further sites and a special Irish monuments act was passed in 1892 in order to add still more relics. By 1904, 189 Irish monuments were protected and £1,000 per year was provided for the upkeep of important ancient and monastic sites.[21]

Perhaps as a result of the long struggle over Irish property, from the very beginning of debate regarding a Free State monuments act concerns were raised that any protection of ancient monuments would interfere with property rights, a contention that preservation advocates took immediate exception to. As far as preservationists were concerned, "a man is regarded rather as a steward of his property than as absolute owner." These sites were of national importance, and it was not acceptable that any landowner should deprive future generations of the ability to enjoy these places.[22]

During the 1920s, perhaps even more than access, the biggest danger to Ireland's ancient sites was from individuals who freely removed inscribed stones or other monuments either for sale or for their own enjoyment. In an impassioned letter to the Irish president, MacAlister stressed that legislation was required immediately to guarantee the preservation of Ireland's ancient sites, in spite of the country's difficult financial and tenuous political situation. He made particular reference to inscribed stones, which he considered "especially valuable national heritage" because "every specimen is unique; and every specimen lost or destroyed is a definite national loss." MacAlister cited his recent visit to Loughcrew megalithic cemetery, where he discovered that one sculptured slab had been removed: "What has become of it is impossible to say; but everyone who could hire a donkey could easily have removed it and sold it."[23] Many other sites were threatened by farmers who raided the ruins for construction supplies or who plowed through ancient earthworks while trying to improve tillage land.

Protecting Irish Heritage

The major challenge in drafting legislation was to develop language that would provide the required protection while not being offensive to or undermining the rights of landowners. The solution to this problem rested largely with the development of an acceptable definition of the type of monuments to be protected. In the context of the time, it was a fairly easy decision. Although the English Georgian Society began advocating for the protection of eighteenth-century structures beginning in 1933, before the 1940s and 1950s most European preservationists focused on buildings constructed before 1700.[24] The Irish were no exception. Whether in Ireland or elsewhere, older buildings tended to inspire less political or aesthetic controversy while at the same time drawing attention to a long heroic past. Thus Irish legislators assumed a very specific and chronologically limited definition of "ancient monuments"; monuments were

> held to comprise all remains bearing upon the racial characteristics or the social, political, artistic, or religious history of the Irish people. It shall include religious history of the Irish people. It shall include religious and secular buildings of all kinds, whether still in use or not, and ruins thereof; fortifications and other structures of stone or earth; lake-dwellings; burial mounds or other sepulchral monuments of all kinds and their contents, including the bodies or bones of the dead; inscribed and sculptured stones; dolmens, stone circles, and all other megalithic monuments; written records in any language, on paper, parchment, or other writing materials; and all portable weapons, garments, implements, utensils, and ornaments whatsoever, in stone, pottery, metal, bone, wood, or other materials, as well as human bones, shells, and animal bones, the contents of ancient midden heaps and cave deposits. The year 1800 A.D. shall be deemed "ancient," except in the case of manuscripts in the Irish language, when the limit shall be 1850 A.D.[25]

While it was not widely discussed, this definition conveniently eliminated consideration of most sites tied to the long struggle for Irish independence, minimizing potential conflict with the British and ensuring that painful political differences and social divisions within Irish society would remain absent from discussion.

Although initially proposed in 1925, appropriate legislation languished behind other priorities until it was finally passed in 1930. The new act made it illegal to damage protected historic sites or to export valuable items of historic significance, and, most important, it outlined the government's ability to claim guardianship over major sites.[26] According to the act, the commissioners of public works could, with approval from the Department of Finance, acquire important sites, either by using legal force or by being entrusted with care of the site by deed. Local authorities could also be entrusted with the care of major sites, though supervisory responsibility was always vested in the Office of Public Works. Guardianship did not necessarily ensure that a given site would be made accessible to the public unless the government owned the monument, although the bill did provide the commissioners with access rights. Finally, in cases where the commissioners believed that a national monument faced imminent damage or destruction, they could file a preservation order, imposing an immediate halt to harmful activity and forcing the landowner to allow access to the Office of Public Works in order to repair any damage.[27]

Role of the Tourist Board

In spite of the importance assigned to historic sites in ITA guidebooks, tourism authorities spent precious little energy on the improvement or development of such sites before 1952. For this situation there were three reasons. First, the 1939 Tourist Traffic Act was primarily designed to promote the improvement and construction of hotels and tourist resorts, not historic sites. Second, the Office of Public Works had statutory authority over Ireland's national monuments, and Public Works was concerned with restoration and preservation, not the promotion of tourism; in fact, it was standard policy to erect signs warning people to stay away from historic sites; little or no effort was made to provide interpretative signage.[28] Finally, government officials gave scant attention to the fact that historic sites were of particular interest to tourists. The prevailing wisdom was simply that tourists wanted to enjoy natural scenery and take pleasure from the Irish coastal resorts, not visit ancient piles.

Despite official ambivalence, the Irish Tourist Association, with some assistance from the Irish Tourist Board, used the war years to develop a catalogue of potential postwar tourist attractions throughout Ireland. Thirty-three surveyors carried out the project. These men conducted "a thorough exploration of every parish [through] contact[s] with local authorities, development committees, sporting, archaeological, cultural, and other organisations, with clergy, teachers, Gardaí, and various other individuals";[29] their efforts marked an even more ambitious undertaking than the association had tackled in 1926 when the ITA attempted to complete a photographic survey of the country.[30] As far as the association was concerned, the facilities survey represented "one of the most important activities undertaken by the ITA since its inception." The project took four years and was finally completed in September 1945.[31]

Even after the ITA survey, government thinking remained static during the 1940s, and it was not until the release of the reports of the Christenberry and Hotels Commission that official attitudes about the relationship between historic and cultural sites and tourism began to shift. In his report Christenberry explained that most Irish-Americans came from poor agricultural areas and lacked any real knowledge of Ireland's historic and religious shrines. It followed that Irish castles would have a "positive appeal" for Americans, while the country's cathedrals, churches, and shrines would attract Irish-American Catholics.[32] At the same time the Irish Hotels Commission stressed that religious and historical sites were of particular interest to American tourists and urged that "a complete survey of our guide-book literature should be undertaken with the least possible delay, and that historical and archaeological societies should be invited to co-operate in the preparation of new issues."[33]

Whether as a result of these reports or not, when Seán Lemass began to consider comprehensive tourism legislation following Fianna Fáil's 1951 election victory, he made it clear that "the proposal for the exploitation of national monuments and shrines" was an especially important part of his tourism-development plans. As a result, Lemass provided powers of compulsory acquisition to An Bord Fáilte in the 1952 Tourist Traffic Act, and he also directed the Tourist Board to erect signage, enhance access to historic sites, and improve the quality of tourism literature. In spite of considerable debate and outright opposition from the Office of Public Works, which considered the provision of such powers to the Tourist Board to be "fundamentally unsound,"[34] the new powers were included with the rest of the new tourism legislation.

Even before passage of the 1952 tourism act, An Bord Fáilte had undertaken an assortment of development projects. Initially, board activities were limited to the erection of signposts to "some of our most important tourist attractions and many of our finest archaeological sites." It was hoped that the program would increase interest in historic places in almost every county in Ireland. At the same time men such as the Rev. Denis Ó Floinn, a professor of Irish at Maynooth College, urged An Bord Fáilte to put up signs intended to provide tourists with "a coherent idea" of the "glorious history" at the country's various historic sites. An Bord Fáilte soon followed this advice and approached the local authorities in Kerry, Donegal, and Wicklow to encourage them to assist in the campaign by erecting signs provided by the Tourist Board.[35]

In order to carry out the signage project, the Tourist Development Board hired Patrick Hartnett, an archeologist employed by the National Museum who was best known for his excavation of the Fourknocks passage tomb in County Meath, to compose straightforward informational signs, including data about when, by whom, and why a given structure was created.[36] Narratives that might have proven in any way contentious were stripped from the information presented to tourists. Even so, by contextualizing a site like Mellifont Abbey, with its famous Cistercian ruins, the board redefined the monuments there to say something about medieval Irish Christianity, showing continuity between Catholicism in that distant era and the faithfulness of contemporary Ireland.[37]

Early Efforts

Little was done to improve historic sites, beyond the erection of signs, until July 1953. An Bord Fáilte recognized that both the Office of Public Works and, to a lesser extent, the local authorities were opposed to having the Tourist Board undertake any activities related to the preservation of historic sites. Before commencing any major projects and in an effort to address conflicting opinions, An Bord Fáilte held a series of meetings with advisory committees in Cavan, Donegal, Galway, Louth, Offaly, Roscommon, Sligo, Tipperary, Waterford, Wicklow, Cork, Dublin, Kildare, Limerick, and Meath; the purpose of these meetings was "to explain in detail how An Bord Fáilte might be of assistance in problems concerning monuments in their district and to inspect with the members as many sites as possible."[38] During the course of these and subsequent meetings, the tourist authorities took note of sites that might warrant publicity as well as locations that would require development work in order to prepare them to accommodate increased tourist traffic. Tourism officials paid special attention to determining the identity of the relevant landowners at each site, because "unrestricted access to the sites" would come only as a result of "goodwill." Board officials were very much aware that "we must clear the ground by securing the goodwill of the local people, otherwise nothing can be done. With all the powers of the National Monuments Act . . . , we cannot appropriate private property."[39] Although this was not strictly true, given that compulsory acquisition of national monuments was permitted under both the 1930 Monuments Act and the 1952 Tourist Traffic Act,[40] the reality was (and is) that a clear line was drawn between public and private land—a line that the government has been loath to cross, regardless of the archeological, scenic, or historic importance of the sites involved. While the government was willing to forcefully acquire land for low-income housing and even industrial development, it was not willing to exercise the same authority in the name of historic or scenic sites (see chapter 6).[41]

Once the goodwill of local landowners was obtained, the Tourist Board undertook an assortment of limited projects from 1954 to the early 1960s and provided development grants after that. At different times the Tourist Board provided lighting for the Lusitania Memorial at Cobh,[42] improved parking facilities at various sites, developed the approach to the cloisters at Mellifont Abbey,[43] cleaned up graveyards and cleared vegetation,[44] built a small shelter and toilet facilities at Newgrange,[45] and carried out other related projects. The ITB seldom (if ever) overlapped in its operations with those of the Office of Public Works as Public Works had feared, and the board did not become directly involved in large-scale restoration work.

The conservative nature of Tourist Board (and Office of Public Works) activities from the 1950s through the 1970s was defined primarily by budgetary constraints. Not only did the board lack adequate funding for development projects, but Public Works was similarly strapped for cash. Kevin O'Doherty, responsible for the Tourist Board's development efforts during the 1950s, recalls that the National Monuments Division of the Office of Public Works had an annual budget of just £4,000 during the early 1950s—an amount easily spent on one minor project.

More aggressive development, like the reconstruction of Bunratty Castle or the restoration of Kilmainham Jail, had to be accomplished through private initiative. At Bunratty Castle, one of Ireland's most famous and popular tourist attractions since it opened in 1960, restoration and development was made possible by the energy of the site's owner, Lord Gort, by archeologist John Hunt, and the by Shannon Free Airport Development Company. Although the project had to be approved by the Office of Public Works (Public Works approval was reluctantly given) and received development grants from Bord Fáilte, it was certainly not a government project; this was also true of the other Shannon-area castle developments at Knappogue, Dunguaire, and Craggaunowen. The idea, first put forward in 1962, to create an historic park and to hold medieval banquets at Bunratty was also the product of private initiative by the group noted above.[46]

Choosing Sites and Narratives

It was relatively easy for the Office of Public Works and Department of Finance to focus their preservation efforts because they were primarily concerned with sites brought to their attention as needing immediate protective action. Likewise Bord Fáilte was limited by significant budget constraints and was thus forced to restrict its activities to access development, occasional minor restoration (as at Mellifont Abbey), and the installation of signage. Even so, other considerations often had to be taken into account. Were sites long-standing stops on the tourist trail, as were Glendalough or Clonmacnois? Were there larger political or memory questions to be considered? Just how expensive would any restoration be? A site's status as one that was particularly important in the story of the Irish nation did not necessarily equate to government recognition that restoration was in the "national interest." The authorities were more than willing to ignore restoration requests when the history involved might prove contentious.

While sites were chosen for development on a case-by-case basis, and while no documents survive that lay out a clear selection process, sites designated for development were overwhelmingly ancient or medieval in nature. Taken as a whole, these sites reflect larger European preservation trends while also suggesting a vision of Ireland that is at once timeless and pious, a land of saints and scholars, heroic chieftains, and ancient mysteries. It was equally important to the tourist authorities that sites be easily understandable to visitors. For example, early consideration was given to tourist development at the Hill of Tara, but it was determined that it would be too costly to make the collection of grass-covered mounds understandable to tourists; at the very least, a full-time guide would be needed at the site.[47] It also appears that the board consciously decided *against* developing some sites, such as the passage tombs at Loughcrew, in order to "save them for ourselves."[48]

Even if there was a reluctance to develop a few choice sites, others virtually demanded attention. The monastic "city" at Glendalough, Co. Wicklow, was one such place. During the height of Victorian tourism this site, with its beautiful round tower, its curious oratory named for the site's founder St. Kevin, and the stunning mountainous panorama surrounding the ruins, was always a favorite of visitors from England.[49] Post–Civil War tourist organizations showed a similar level of interest, and Bord Fáilte accumulated a disproportionate number of Glendalough photographs in its photographic archive—not because of political pressure, as at Killarney, but because the site simply lent itself to the gaze of tourist and camera alike.[50] In 1951 Córas Iompair Éireann led tours to the monastic city, and most visitors reportedly found it to be a high point of their trip.[51]

Even popularity did not guarantee prompt and thorough restoration. Although Glendalough was among the seven hundred sites under Office of Public Works protection in 1949,[52] it remained largely neglected and uncared for. In 1951 Peadar S. Doyle, TD, submitted a question to the Office of the Taoiseach and then to the minister of finance that noted that Glendalough was "losing its natural beauty due to the absence of a responsible authority for preserving the surroundings." Doyle wondered if An Taisce, the Irish National Trust, would take action, or whether the relevant government department would step in to ensure the proper level of maintenance and preservation.[53] Doyle was not the only critic. The Rev. Denis Ó Floinn referred to the government's "shameful disregard for our holy places" and argued that if located in continental Europe, Glendalough would be beautifully presented to visitors, who would find a "coherent idea" of the site's history.[54] Public Works contended that its officials had no "executive functions or funds," and argued that the local authorities should take responsibility for sites like Glendalough. For academics like Michael J. O'Kelly of University College Cork, it was not a question of finger-pointing but of preserving this "irrevocable" link "with the country's whole cultural inheritance, ecclesiastical and secular." It was not possible to excuse allowing sites like Glendalough to "crumble to dust or become overwhelmed in a jungle of overgrowths."[55]

After the passage of the 1952 Tourist Traffic Act, Bord Fáilte went some distance toward correcting the problem at Glendalough by constructing a new parking area and making other access improvements, while also developing ground plans to assist in the exhibition of the site. The plans showed "the original layout and existing remains," noting "the various periods to which these remains belong and [assisting] visitors in their examinations of the buildings by indicating clearly the various sections—cloister, nave, etc."[56] It was a substantial step forward but still failed to meet the complete satisfaction of Erskine Childers, the future president of the Republic, who was so filled with development ideas that he had a habit of jotting them down on a notepad that he kept for the purpose by his bedside.[57] Among his ideas Childers proposed a development at Muckross House (see below) and another at Glendalough. Monastic history fascinated Childers, and he wrote to the taoiseach in 1962 that a museum featuring Irish missionary work from the fourth to the eighth centuries should be built behind the Royal Hotel at Glendalough. The displays would stress Ireland's proud history as a home for saints and scholars as well as its heritage of bringing spiritual knowledge to the heathens beyond its shores. Such a museum would address the conversion of England and the foundation of English cathedrals by the Irish, the scientific studies carried out by Irish monks during the time of Charlemagne, and the efforts of Irish saints such as St. Dunstan, St. Fiacra, and St. Columbanus (Columcille) to convert heathens on the continent and in Britain. Childers enthusiastically noted that much of the material, including photographs, translations, dioramas, maps, and "modern devices for dramatising journeys and fields of activity," including "a film or two . . .

[and] tape recordings, etc," would have to be constructed.⁵⁸ It was certainly a creative proposal, perhaps even before its time, but it was not greeted with enthusiasm. Lemass did "look into" the scheme, perhaps out of friendship or loyalty, but he ultimately dismissed it because the topic was too controversial. According to the taoiseach, historians believed the scanty source material to be "unreliable":

> For example, historians may feel that statements about the conversion of England to Christianity by us may need some qualification if a true impression is to be given to the public; there are conflicting opinions, in fact, about the conversion of Ireland to Christianity (one is that the mission to Armagh was distinct from the mission to Tara—that it was significantly earlier and undertaken by a different missionary). In the present controversial state of this matter it may be felt premature for the Office of Public Works to formulate an official state version of this very important part of our history.⁵⁹

While it is now difficult to imagine holding back the development of a museum because of inconclusive evidence (such a thing certainly seems unlikely in the present age of mushrooming heritage centers), at the time the state's unwillingness to take a firm stand on an official state history was fully in keeping with its lack of interest in providing state funding for the restoration of Kilmainham Jail or for other modern-history sites. The development of historical sites had to meet a series of criteria that included low cost, willing landowners, and a complete lack of controversy.

While the absence of development of more recent sites of historical significance is striking, it must be made clear that the revolutionary struggle was not forgotten. During the period from the foundation of a statutory tourist authority through the 1960s, the struggle with England was very much a part of public culture in the form of a campaign by the Dublin Brigade of the Old IRA to establish a Garden of Remembrance near the Rotunda Hospital,⁶⁰ calls for the restoration of Kilmainham Jail, and a massive commemoration of the Easter Rising in 1966. In each case the major focus was on the role that memory work would have for domestic consumption, though tourism did have an important place in the Kilmainham Jail Restoration Society's original proposal.

The tendency to avoid modern history in the development of tourist sites can be explained by three likely causes. First, in the wake of the Civil War there was a desire to relegate unpleasant divisions into the dark recesses of the unspoken past. As late as the 1950s Ireland's political leaders continued to be divided by memories of the Civil War. Living together peacefully required pushing this bleak chapter of the nation's history into the background. It was not that the past was forgotten, only that "silence was better than hypocrisy," and it was easier than feeling disgust at having done to fellow Irishmen what the British had done so recently to them.[61] Second, after 1959, when state finances began to improve, the commemoration of Ireland's revolutionary struggle had immediate policy implications for the country's relationship with Northern Ireland. With the ascension of Lemass to the taoiseach's office in 1959, Irish policy toward Northern Ireland changed to one of advocating cooperation. This change, combined with the primacy of tourism as a point of common effort, made it important for the Republic to carefully consider the implications of tourism activities in light of the government's desire to create a smooth working relationship with the North. Finally, and perhaps most obviously, the overwhelming majority of tourists in Ireland have always been from mainland Britain. Given this dependence on tourists from across the Irish Sea, it is hardly surprising that Irish tourist promoters have not gone out of their way to emphasize conflict with Britain.

Nevertheless, occasional development proposals were made and private initiatives were free to move ahead. In 1938, Arthur R. Vincent and his wealthy American in-laws, who had purchased Muckross House for Vincent and his wife as a wedding present, gave the house in Killarney to the state. The estate was expansive, covering ten thousand acres of scenic land around the Killarney lakes, and Vincent believed that it would provide a valuable park for the Irish people and thus serve as a fitting memorial to his late wife.[62] Faced with possession of the new lands, the state was immediately plunged into uncertainty about what to do with the property. At various points the space was considered for commercial development, a hostel (Vincent's preference), a religious retreat, a biological research station, a dairy instruction center, a country residence for the president of Ireland, a hotel, a convalescent home, a civil-service training facility, and a folk museum.[63] It is the folk museum proposal that will concern us here.

Like the missionary museum at Glendalough, the folk-museum concept was born during one of Erskine Childers's late-night epiphanies in 1962. Initially he suggested a "museum of the Irish heritage from the sixteenth century to the present day," including American presidents of Irish heritage; the inventor of the torpedo, turbine, and submarine; the first steel worker in the Ruhr valley; famous Irish actors and playwrights; and so on.[64] In the following year Childers expanded dramatically on his idea for both the house and its grounds. He suggested that the grounds be developed to include extensive footpaths so that tourists could enjoy beautiful views of the Killarney lakes, and that the gardens be expanded and embellished. Careful study was to be done to ensure a balance between motor access and the traditional jaunting-car route to and from the house. Picnic facilities were to be developed and located in such a way as to limit their impact on the surroundings. Muckross House itself would be turned into a museum featuring rotating exhibits from various state museums, including Irish silver, lace, furniture, tweeds, and couture, as well as traditional cottage implements, domestic ware, etc. Waterford glass and Waterford chandeliers would receive prominent placement, as would Irish ceramics, art, and historic portraits. Photographic exhibits would display Celtic crosses and Irish abbeys, while "first-class" Irish souvenirs would be available. More striking still, Childers suggested that a room be set aside to display material from the "1916 Rising or the general struggle for independence," and that another room be devoted to "national progress." Beyond merely displaying artifacts of Irish history and culture, Childers dreamed of developing Muckross as a first-class museum, and he therefore suggested that scholars be brought in to advise, local experts be consulted, lectures on Irish history be offered, conferences be run, garden tours be given, and Irish dancing, song, and orchestral music be performed.[65] The plan was nothing if not ambitious, and Childers immediately began working to develop support, enlisting the backing of Arthur Vincent, who expressed disgust at the other leading suggestion—that Muckross House be used as a training facility for civil servants.[66] An Taisce also favored the folk-museum proposal, dreaming that the Muckross estate might cater to American visitors captivated by the museum and to artists who would be inspired by the outdoor scenery and the beautiful objects within.[67] Similarly, at least one visiting Irish emigrant wrote to the *Irish Independent* to express his hope that the estate would be developed as a park rather than used for some other, less public purpose.[68] Local tourism interests also supported the museum plan.[69]

In spite of Childers's enthusiasm, the Vincent endorsement, and the other public support for the museum, the Department of Finance was outspoken in its opposition. As far as Finance was concerned, the museums in Dublin, Bunratty Castle, and the proposed folk museum at the Royal Hospital, Kilmainham,[70] were more than enough to satisfy the demands of visitors, while the proposed training facility might also serve as a hotel during the summer months, providing an enhanced return on the government's investment. At Killarney, Finance officials said, scenery should take precedence, not museum exhibits.[71]

In the end, however, Childers won the day. Widespread public support for a parklike facility at the Muckross estate trumped the Department of Finance. After opening to the public in June 1964, the "Bourne Vincent Memorial Park" attracted twenty thousand people to the house during the first year of public access.[72] In spite of a brief conflict in 1968 with local jarveys,[73] the museum and grounds have continued to be a popular addition to the tourist trail. Bord Fáilte cited the facility as a "successful experiment in interpretation and historical representation" in its 1981–85 tourism plan, hinting that others interested in developing heritage sites would do well to follow the Muckross model.[74] In 1989 the verdict was similarly positive, with *Irish Travel Trade News*, the industry journal, noting that the house, by then the headquarters for the Kerry Folklife Association and displayed in the "great house tradition," with some rooms devoted to interpretive displays, could be expanded to become even more attractive. Farm outbuildings could be turned into craft workshops, museums of folk life, displays of farm machinery, theatres for traditional entertainment, and even barn space for preserving "distinctive Kerry cattle."[75] Although the 1916 Rising and independence-struggle display was apparently never introduced, probably because it would have been too controversial, the Childers proposal proved attractive to tourists and a beneficial addition to the Killarney-area product mix, thus demonstrating that public pressure, well-organized political effort, and an unthreatening rural message could overcome opposition and achieve success.

Representations

When the past was to be presented to outsiders—in guidebooks, for example—every effort was made to assure that the representation that was offered was the *right one:* one that would not offend outsiders while also assuring equanimity within Ireland itself. The group best positioned to oversee such concerns was the Cultural Relations Committee that was established following World War II to undertake Ireland's "cultural propaganda" program (see chapter 2). Ireland faced a significant problem: it was largely unknown abroad. Even American St. Patrick's Day celebrations featured French and Scottish beverages over Irish ones. There were then no major Irish rock-and-roll bands, no offshore Irish pubs, and no Irish dancers thumping out their Celtic rhythms on the world's stages as would be the case during the tourism boom of the 1990s (see chapter 7). "We wanted to get Irish things known. Create an image of Ireland. It was something that was in everybody's interest, including [that of] the Department of External Affairs," recalls Michael Gorman, who was a member of the Cultural Relations Committee in 1958. From the beginning each member of the committee was on an equal footing—the government did not attempt to dominate the agenda—though tourism was a focal point for discussion because it was important to the Tourist Board, Aer Lingus, and CIÉ, while simultaneously creating a wider audience for Irish exports.[76] Though the Department of External Affairs originally proposed the creation of the Cultural Relations Committee, the semistate bodies, not External Affairs, soon dictated the group's agenda and scope. In 1960, for example, the department received five proposals about ways to expand publicity activities abroad. In considering the various suggestions, government officials were surprised to find that "our own proposals are by comparison [to those of the Tourist Board, etc.] extremely modest, palliatives rather than cures."[77] Tourism interests were literally shaping the government's approach to cultural propaganda and molding its effort to present Ireland in a favorable light internationally.

In keeping with the tourism industry's leading role in framing cultural policy, the Department of External Affairs did not usually intervene in the content of tourist publications. Instead, the department focused its efforts on ensuring that Irish consulates around the world were well stocked with tourist materials. In 1953, for example, the committee made certain that Fógra Fáilte's *Ireland of the Welcomes* magazine was distributed to cities in the United States, Canada, Brazil, Australia, Italy, Spain, the Netherlands, Sweden, England, France, and Belgium—a list that was maintained and expanded throughout the 1950s and 1960s.[78] Likewise, the Cultural Relations Committee made certain that guidebooks, tourist maps, and brochures were also widely available abroad.[79] Foreign consulates frequently requested additional materials, and a number of ambassadors took a special interest in distributing pamphlets and flyers to receptive parties.

The Department of External Affairs showed a strong interest in how Ireland was portrayed in guidebooks, magazine articles, and other publications, however: part of the reason that the department was so responsive to public pressure concerning the *Holiday* magazine feature (see introduction). Interest in the content of tourist publications was not limited exclusively to public scandals. On a day-to-day basis External Affairs commented on a variety of publications and in so doing they showed a desire to balance the need to avoid controversy with the need to maintain goodwill among the still politically divided population of the Republic. For example, Conor Cruise O'Brien, who served in the cultural wing of the Department of External Affairs during the early 1950s, was asked to comment about a guidebook called *Ireland for Everyman,* published by J. M. Dent and Sons of London. O'Brien replied that the "guide sections are good" but that the "brief outline of Irish history would be better omitted if it could not be improved." He argued that the period from the Act of Union forward was "seriously lacking" in balance, "and sections of it use language which would be quite in place in, say, a history of the French Resistance Movement by a German journalist." O'Brien complained that Emmet's rising was referred to as "'a mere street riot'—a reference which will certainly be regarded here as gratuitously offensive to Irish feeling." Likewise, the Great Famine was treated as little more than an economic catastrophe, with no indication of the Irish view that it was both economic and political and that the British deserved much of the blame. O'Brien took issue with a description of the 1867 Fenian Rising as "an outrage," saying that "if the Fenian risings were outrages, then all rebellions and revolutions against legally constituted authorities are outrages, and all governments now existing, based as they are on some series of outrages in the past, are really illegal conspiracies."[80] Four days after O'Brien submitted his comments, the J. M. Dent and Sons managing editor apologized and promised that the history section would be either dramatically revised or omitted from all future editions of the guide.[81]

Saving the "Bastille of Ireland"

Although the Irish government showed little interest in developing controversial sites of any kind, from the mid-1930s there *were* calls for the construction of sites commemorating recent revolutionary history. The most prominent of these requests was made by the Dublin Brigade of the Old IRA, which also called for the creation of a Garden of Remembrance at the Rotunda Gardens near Parnell Square in Dublin.[82] While it took thirty-one years for the idea to be realized, the government ultimately did create the garden with relatively little public controversy.[83]

Kilmainham Jail was potentially much more problematic. It was first opened in 1796 and functioned as an active prison until 1924. The jail was a product of the late-eighteenth-century prison-reform movement that placed an emphasis on punishing the mind (rather than taking revenge on the body), while also improving hygiene and thus humanitarian acceptability. The vast majority of convicts who passed through the prison were confined there for assault, burglary, shoplifting, rape, highway robbery, murder, bigamy, cattle stealing, and other such "common" crimes. During the Great Famine, for example, many afflicted people actively courted arrest in order to obtain relief, and the prison soon became vastly overcrowded. While life in the prison was unpleasant, at least there was food to eat. Even so, it is the political prisoners incarcerated there from the first day of prison operation who are placed front and center in the museum's narrative. The list of famous inmates includes Henry Joy McCracken, the Sheares brothers, Lord Edward Fitzgerald, Robert Emmet and Anne Devlin, Charles Stewart Parnell, members of the Young Irelanders, Fenians, and Invincibles, T. M. Healy, Michael Davitt, the 1916 leaders, Éamon de Valera, members of the IRA during the War of Independence, and numerous "Irregulars" during the Civil War.[84] Indeed, the first four Free State executions (November 1922) of anti-Treaty prisoners took place in the prison yard on the opposite side of a wall from the site used by British troops to kill the 1916 leaders.[85]

Given the prison's long history as an unwelcome home for Ireland's various nationalist heroes, the site was doubly challenging as regards tourist development. First, it raised troubling memories of the long conflict with England, and more damning still, the execution of Irregulars in the prison yard strongly associated Kilmainham with the still festering psychological wounds of bloody civil conflict. Given the desire to avoid these memories, it is hardly surprising that, when the prison was decommissioned in 1924, nobody called for its preservation. For most people Kilmainham Jail was a site of suffering more synonymous with oppression than heroism, better ignored or, at the very least, used for purposes other than official memory. At various points Kilmainham was utilized as a storage facility for materials being used in the Shannon Electricity Scheme,[86] was suggested for conversion to office space,[87] and avoided outright demolition only because the government was unwilling to foot the bill.[88] Nobody considered it important to preserve the prison.

By the late 1930s various groups showed increasing interest in Kilmainham. The most important development was a formal proposal by the National Graves Association, a republican organization devoted to the preservation of nationalist gravesites throughout Ireland, to develop the site as a memorial and museum to house artifacts related to the 1916 Rising.[89] The plan proposed the installation of a plaque at the site where members of the Irish National Invincibles were hanged in 1883 for the Phoenix Park murders.[90] At the site of the 1916 executions, a few hundred feet away, there was to be an eighteen-inch wall surmounted by grave-railings along with a fountain. A plaque was to proclaim, "On this hallowed spot the executed leaders of the Rising fell [followed by their names]."[91] The proposal made no mention of the Civil War executions that occurred roughly forty feet to the south, nor did it draw attention to the site where James Connolly had been shot, located on the opposite end of the stone-breakers' yard from the rest of the 1916 killings. The latter omission may have been the result of poor research by the Graves Association or of Connolly's Marxism, which was periodically raised as an issue during this period of intense anticommunism. Perhaps a different plan was simply judged undesirable from an architectural or political standpoint: better that the leaders be commemorated *together* in order to spatially demonstrate Irish unity in the fight for freedom. As will be noted below, just such a concern later provided the motivation behind the Kilmainham Jail Restoration Society's unwillingness to allow a separate Connolly memorial.

The commissioners of public works had no immediate objection to the Graves Association proposal, even suggesting to the Department of Education that a museum be developed at the site. Public Works officials estimated that the scheme would cost £600 to implement. In order to stock the museum with artifacts it was suggested that the "National Risings Collection" be relocated from the National Museum in Kildare Street to a new jail museum. The Department of Education rejected the proposal, however, on the grounds that the collection was a popular attraction at its present location, where it could be adequately cared for, whereas if moved to Kilmainham, the collection would likely deteriorate in the increasingly run-down prison buildings. Instead, Education officials suggested that the site could be maintained in its current condition, and paintings of revolutionary leaders mounted in their corresponding cells in order "to recall the history of the liberation movement," while the great hall of the jail could be fitted up to display the automobile collection then housed at Kildare Street. This was intended as a constructive suggestion, but it was quickly tabled at the onset of the Emergency in 1939.

Consideration of Kilmainham's restoration did not reemerge until the immediate aftermath of the war when the Office of Public Works commissioned an architectural inspection of the buildings. The results were distressing. Though the inspectors found that the walls were in no immediate danger of collapse, they alarmingly observed that "there is constant danger from falling slates, glass, and plaster, and . . . timber floors and roofs are far from safe." Under the circumstances the commissioners suggested that it would be extremely costly to repair and maintain the buildings: "Any considerable expenditure merely for the purpose of removing their present dangerous condition would not be worthwhile." Because the Department of Education was still unwilling to consider establishing a museum at the site, and given that the Office of Public Works believed that the building would not make acceptable office space, the commissioners recommended a limited preservation program. Their plan would have preserved those cellblocks having historical significance, as well as the yard where the 1916 executions had occurred, while the rest would have been disposed of for building purposes.[92]

This suggestion did not demand dramatic expense, but it functioned to pay lip-service to remembering Ireland's revolutionary history—a concern of at least a minority of the population during the immediate postwar years. Again, however, little happened.

By 1953, while the prison was rapidly descending into ruin, commemoration plans resurfaced. This time the Department of the Taoiseach initiated discussion of a prison-restoration and museum-development project—not because de Valera wanted to relive his days as a prisoner at Kilmainham, but as an employment scheme.[93] Unemployment in Ireland was reaching crisis levels and emigration was now a national disease. The restoration of Kilmainham Jail could provide jobs while meeting the republican desire to remember Ireland's proud fighting past. The planning committee adopted the old National Graves Association proposal, but once again little happened and the condition of the site continued to deteriorate with alarming rapidity. By 1955 the commissioners of public works warned that the public should no longer be allowed any access to the site. Slates were blowing off the roof, glass and plaster were falling, and ceilings were caving in. The situation had now reached a crisis. Kilmainham Jail was collapsing and would not last for many more years if the government persisted in its disinclination to act. If there was to be a solution, somebody or some organization outside the government would have to provide it.

The Restoration Society

The Kilmainham Jail Restoration Society began to gestate in the mind of a young North Dubliner named Lorcan C. G. Leonard in 1952. Leonard had become interested in the prison while waiting for a bus ten years earlier; he perceived a "friendliness" at the site that was almost certainly absent for most visitors, both past and present. Ten years later, Leonard and his friend Tommy O'Brien jointly agreed that the Invincibles had been unfairly exiled from Irish history and that something should be done about it. "Even radical republican thought . . . maintained an ignorance of them. Evidently, the efforts of the Invincibles were too 'earthy' for even their refined palates." The men's answer to this historical quandary was to plan a documentary film about the Invincibles and to use the proceeds to install a memorial at the jail. Among other potential collaborators Leonard contacted "Cre" O'Farrell,

Sean Dowling, and Paddy Stephenson. These men told Leonard that he was "dealing with a dangerous subject which is best left alone." Dowling eventually agreed to take part as long as his name was never formally associated with the project. The next step was to film key locations inside the prison itself—a task made impossible by the unwillingness of the Office of Public Works to provide access. The film project immediately foundered, but Leonard's interest in the prison did not.

Not long after the death of the movie idea, Leonard received word that the Office of Public Works was accepting bids from demolition companies to tear down the prison. Leonard was horrified: "This was indeed the last act of the philistines, who had already provided a rash of 'Mother Éire's' and Celtic crosses from one end of the country to the other to prove, I suppose, the respectable and Catholic character of the 'four glorious' years." Leonard quickly approached a friend and fellow member of the Old Dublin Society, Paddy Stephenson, who agreed to participate in any "mass action" to preserve the penitentiary.[94] Discussing the matter further, they hatched a plan to restore the site by using volunteer labor and donated materials in order to establish a museum, and communicated this intention to Sean Dowling, later chairman of the restoration campaign. They asked for help "in an effort to save Kilmainham Jail from the ravishes [*sic*] of time and the indifference of politicians," for "what was once [a] monument to heroic endeavour is now the silent mocking cavern to the indifference of our times." Good Irish men and women simply could not allow "the most holy spot in Ireland" to vanish into thin air.[95]

In September 1958, Leonard brought a small group together at Jury's Hotel in Dublin to discuss restoration plans. There was skepticism about the viability of a volunteer effort, but the participants kept talking. It did not take long for the group to agree that "in order to preserve unity of purpose, nothing relating to events after 1921 would be introduced into any activity, publicity, or statements in connection with Kilmainham." With a common understanding of the road ahead taking shape, Leonard began recruiting workers—primarily from among known republicans. Leonard and his colleagues believed that members of the Old IRA would furnish the bulk of volunteers because these men "needed no instruction on Kilmainham or its unique position" as a building of major significance in the republican history of Ireland.

Support began to mount. The Congress of Irish Trade Unions informed the fledgling society that the TUC would not frown on voluntary efforts to restore the jail, though it was unwilling to offer an official endorsement. Likewise, the Building Trades Council agreed to back a voluntary restoration effort. The Old IRA was also willing to aid the plan, but only on condition that "nothing of or relating to the period after 1921 would be identified with the Kilmainham project."[96] Dublin Corporation had already shown an interest in preserving the building and probably also supported the proposed idea, although Leonard does not specify whether he or his colleagues had contacted city councilors.[97] With all of the essential groups lined up in support of the plan, or at least not in opposition, the time had arrived to submit a proposal to the government.

While Leonard was pushing forward with his voluntary restoration scheme, the National Graves Association was also petitioning the government on behalf of the jail. As in 1938, it advocated plaques, a fountain, and grave-railings, but it now added the new elements of a pathway to the site of the graves of the Invincibles and a museum in the nineteenth-century great hall that would house "national relics, mementos, documents, guns, and other articles associated with our fight for freedom." Seán Fitzpatrick, the secretary of the association, told the press, "There is no place more intimately and dramatically associated with our fight for independence than Kilmainham, and no matter what else may be done in the way of memorials to our past, we all want Kilmainham restored and preserved. It is really the focal point of our centuries-long struggle."[98]

Likewise, the Old IRA Literary and Debating Society also lobbied the government to act on the restoration. Writing to de Valera, leaders of the Old IRA argued that the matter should be "treated as urgent," for the decaying jail should not be allowed to disappear:

> There is a craving for knowledge of local and national history waiting to be satisfied, and where better in a properly organised museum than in Kilmainham; make it the capitol's showplace for our people and a tourist attraction. Make that stone-breaking yard where our leaders died a Garden of Remembrance. We look forward to the day when that gaunt pile will be converted into a place of national pilgrimage, where the story of Ireland's long fight for freedom could be told better than [in] any history books.[99]

When Leonard's proposal appeared late in 1958, it must have been a welcome sight for Department of Finance officials. With pressure from the Graves Association and the Old IRA on the one hand and a lack of any real interest in spending money on an ever-more-expensive restoration program on the other, the new voluntary proposal appeared to be the best of all possible worlds.[100] The plan offered "a major step forward in civilian initiative" and promised returns "of immeasurable value to future generations, not to mention the immediate asset of a tourist attraction." The plan was also financially bold. Its authors estimated that the restoration could be accomplished in five years at a cost of £60,000 to £70,000 using entirely volunteer labor.[101] The plan left little room for government objection, and it was formally approved by the Department of Finance in February 1960.[102]

Above all, the Restoration Society viewed the jail as a national shrine, but they also believed that it would become a successful tourist site as well and they placed tourism at the forefront of their proposal. By 1958 many displayed a growing awareness of the important role that tourism could play in stimulating the lagging economy, especially following the publication of the *Programme for Economic Expansion*. Stressing tourism made it possible for the Society to both delineate a potential revenue stream and to hold the restoration up as an important element of national renewal. Thus restoring Kilmainham was to be a nationalist activity on multiple levels: it meant reclaiming and commemorating the nationalist past while at the same time striking a symbolic blow at the economic malaise of the 1950s. Thanks to the Society's proposal, tourism and Kilmainham were now closely joined, thus ensuring that the prison would become more than a site for domestic cultural consumption.

A Unifying Symbol

There was very little public conflict concerning the reconstruction—with one exception. Although the Civil War issue had been erased early in the process, the treatment to be accorded to the Marxist leader of the Citizen Army, James Connolly, remained a stumbling block. In September 1966 the Labour party proposed the erection of a special Connolly memorial in the yard where he had been executed—on the wall opposite from where the other executed 1916 leaders had fallen. Such a memorial was absent from the

Graves Association proposal, and it was similarly excluded from the Restoration Society's plans. According to Sean Dowling, chairman of the Restoration Society, the unwillingness to provide a separate memorial *on that spot* was not politically motivated in any way. Dowling argued, "James Connolly belonged to the whole Irish people and not to any political party, not even to the one he founded." As a result, the society "decided . . . that no separate plaque to any leader would be permitted in the execution yard, but that the Labour party might erect a plaque to the memory of Connolly anywhere else in the jail." For the Labour party this solution was unacceptable. Its leaders charged in their reply that the Restoration Society was clearly "subservient" to Fianna Fáil and alleged that "the republican party" was using the prison for its own ends—accusations that were strenuously denied by Dowling.[103] Perhaps as a measure of the popularity of the restoration project, the public in general sided with the society. One Labour supporter argued, "A separation [of the 1916 leaders] would diminish both Connolly and the other signatories [of the proclamation of the republic]."[104] Another letter writer, who did not specify his political affiliation, "fully agree[d] with the committee's decision to keep the execution yard a sacred place, free from all references to present-day political parties."[105] By now Kilmainham Jail was not just the project of a few republicans anxious to remember 1916 rebels, the Invincibles, or activists in the War of Independence; it was instead a commemoration of Irish national identity, a symbol not only of the nation's past but also of its present.

What made the site so powerful in cultural terms was that its restoration was almost entirely a grassroots effort—just as had been proposed. During the reconstruction of the prison the Kilmainham Jail Restoration Society received only small contributions from the Irish government. In 1966, Seán Lemass wrote to Dowling to inform him that monies collected from the pool at the newly opened Garden of Remembrance near Parnell Square would be donated to the society—a grand sum of some £50.[106] In addition, the government did provide £1,000 per year through the Office of Public Works to cover insurance for the workers,[107] and furnished roughly a hundred glass display cases for the museum.[108] Government officials, however, were far less forthcoming when the society requested roof slates valued at £1,500.[109] Overwhelmingly the costs of restoration were met through voluntary contributions from individuals, businesses, and other organizations willing to support the project—a significant indication of how popular the restoration eventually became. Not only did the voluntary nature of the project allow the society to work around unpleasant memories, but it also reshaped the central memory of the prison into that of a site representing the *whole* of Ireland. The project would not have been possible without government approval, but the lack of government funding or other major official involvement kept tourist authorities well clear of the enterprise. This made it possible to evade the fact that the conflict commemorated had been with the British—Ireland's single largest tourism market, valued at some £24.3 million annually in 1962.[110] In addition, the Civil War was removed from the table as a subject of contention, and only positive memories of Irish nationalist activity were specifically invoked. Most important of all, it was the voluntary effort of disparate nationalist groups that made the reconstruction possible—men from both sides of the Civil War conflict and from all age and social groups.

From the beginning the Restoration Society drew careful attention to the workers. In their first newsletter the leaders of the group boasted that the number of workers now included "over two hundred tradesmen and skilled workers giving of their spare time, working hard night after night and on Saturday afternoons. Praise is silenced. Let what must be said of this magnificent effort be said afterwards—now is the time for work and effort." Of course, these sentiments did not stop them from pointing out that the workers were of "all ages and walks of life," that "lads of 15 and 17 years" were present along with 80-year-old veterans, Dublin dock workers, and even an ex-British army sergeant.[111] When Lemass visited the site in 1964 to survey progress, he was lavish in his tribute: "The work of restoration to the buildings was of national importance. The work already carried out by voluntary labour was . . . truly remarkable."[112] He was echoing a sentiment that the media had stressed as early as 1962. The *Dublin Evening Mail*, for example, featured a story that consisted of short biographical sketches of the workers, and not, as might have been expected, of the numerous illustrious prisoners who had served time in the jail. Among the commonplace figures mentioned was Jim Bruce, who had worked on the prison since September 1960, focusing his attention on the roof; Damien and Raymond Cassidey, who had "devoted their evenings to rebuilding the jail since reconstruction began"; and Joe Magill, a bricklayer "who has found more bricks than enough to lay in his hours after work."[113] For a time at least, heroism was about giving something back to Ireland through the rebuilding of an historic site. Another paper went so far as to boast, "Who said idealism is dead in Ireland? Go to Kilmainham Jail any evening, even with snow on the ground, and you will find a living proof that the idealism of 40 years ago is still very much alive."[114] Even in 2003, the Dúchas guide to the prison recalled the restoration as "an epic feat of voluntary effort and enthusiasm achieved without the support of government grants."[115]

Through comments such as these, the voluntary labor to reconstruct the jail was itself integrated into the mythology of the prison, in effect adding to the register of heroes associated with the site. These workers may not have fired on an enemy, but they had taken aim at the economic and spiritual malaise that gripped Ireland in the 1950s, and they stood as flesh-and-blood reminders of the improving fortunes of the early 1960s. During the 1950s industrial output fell, the country's GNP dropped, unemployment climbed at an alarming pace, and between 1951 and 1956 the population fell 2.1 percent.[116] When "remarkable" growth replaced distressing decline in the early 1960s, the workers were already in place to symbolize the reversal.[117] Their labors were born of a need to draw people into a national rebuilding program, and their progress physically illustrated the success of those efforts at a time when the *Programme for Economic Expansion* was beginning to turn around the economy. The restoration project held up the spectacle of everyday Irish people physically demonstrating their national pride through distinctly corporal memory work. In striking contrast to the tens of thousands who emigrated during the 1950s, these ordinary Irish people were not only staying put but also constructing Kilmainham as a totem of the national struggle while they themselves became symbols of that struggle. The enemy was different, but the nationalist zeal was still very much alive.

Paul Connerton has argued that collective memory is engendered through physical participation in the memory process.[118] This is nowhere more true than in connection with Kilmainham Jail, where the whole process of voluntary restoration created memories of a collective past devoted to nation-building in both violent and peaceful forms. By participating in this protracted process, volunteers created a new history of the jail, with their own actions of swinging hammers and clearing rubble not only permitting the prison to persist as a site of memory, but also making the restorative action itself part of the memory continuum. Kilmainham was originally built by the British to imprison Irishmen. By reconstructing it, the Irish built a site that could enshrine their past as one of unified struggle against imperial oppression and of the improvement of Irish lives.

The preservationists intended to create Kilmainham as a memorial to Irish revolutionaries and as a tourist attraction, but for this goal to be achieved, the enterprise had to be undertaken by Irish citizens themselves because only a grassroots voluntary effort could circumvent the challenges facing the construction of any tourist site devoted to modern Irish nationalist memory—not the least of which was government unwillingness to pay for any large restoration project. By removing the Civil War as a source of contention immediately, by linking revolutionaries of diverse political views together in one group, and by not allowing any single nationalist figure to be appropriated for contemporary political ends, the restorers of the prison developed a uniquely "national" site, dedicated to Ireland as a whole. Finally, the fact that Kilmainham was reconstructed through voluntary effort ensured that Irish tourist authorities remained distanced from memories of earlier historical struggles, unencumbered by the past as they tried to entice the old enemy into taking relaxing Irish holidays. Indeed, Bord Fáilte maintained this distance by not mentioning Kilmainham or any related revolutionary sites or events in the pages of its tourist magazine until the 1980s.[119]

Since its restoration Kilmainham Jail has evolved to meet modern tourist tastes by incorporating more elements of Irish history, including attitudes to crime and prison reform, the Great Famine, and even the Irish Civil War. Yet even with these new additions, the jail remains Ireland's primary tourist site devoted to revolutionary history. Kilmainham not only projects its history as a prison for Irish nationalists since the late eighteenth century but also stands as a symbol of continuing Irish nationalism even after the end of armed struggle—a shrine to Irish nationalist feeling both before and after the revolution.

Packing in the Flash

Particularly in the last ten or fifteen years, it has ceased to be enough to develop historic sites because an idea came easily in the night or because a committee of volunteers felt a desire to commemorate the past. Today sites must be designed to match the tastes of tourists raised on Disney-like heritage centers featuring flashy multimedia presentations, holograms, and interactive displays. While a small visitor center, access improvements, and electric lighting were enough to make Newgrange acceptable for tourists in the 1950s,[120] today sheer visitor numbers and tourist tastes have led Dúchas to develop an impressive visitor center, complete with a full-sized replica of the passage tomb, multimedia presentations, diorama displays, and a building designed to resemble the great megalithic tombs. It is as much like going to Disneyland as it is visiting an historic site. Similarly, the Céide Fields and Corlea Trackway feature buildings designed to communicate meaning, with the Trackway housed in a massive Celtic cross and Céide Fields combining "physical grandeur, antiquity, and death" in a "single, simple, and very ancient architectural image" that springs like the pyramids at Giza from the Irish countryside.[121] Further demonstrating contemporary tastes, the 1798 Center at Enniscorthy features a less than dignified debate between the holographic heads of Edmund Burke and Thomas Paine, disembodied voices, and marching drummers complete with interactive TV screens in their instruments.

The need to develop these more "contemporary" attractions was brought home to Bord Fáilte following a scathing report by the Ventures Consultancy during the late 1980s. The report found that Ireland's

> existing product is tired and unprofessional. . . . Many of your new proposals are 'copy-cats' of existing attractions. . . . Ireland's history is complex, and many facets are being overlooked. . . . Your interpretation and interpretive planning is unimaginative and lacks originality and variety. . . . Projections of visitor numbers are unrealistic, marketing planning is poor, and market research is almost non-existent.[122]

As a result, the Tourist Board adopted a framework of "themes and subsidiary storylines" that could be developed. These included *Living Landscapes, Religion and Ritual, War and Conquest, Earning a Living,* and *The Spirit of Ireland.* Existing attractions and proposed new ones were worked into this framework, consultants were hired to assist in development, and a heritage-marketing consortium company was established. The result was a dramatic increase in the number of tourist attractions charging an admission fee (from 85 in 1983 to 219 in 1993), a doubling in the number of admissions to such sites (from 3.4 million to 6.9 million), and a dramatic increase in visitor spending.[123] Among other emphases, the board drew renewed attention to the Gaelic language (including the marking of additional Gaeltacht holidays), monuments, music, and literature and song, and to traditional activities like fishing, the development of agriculture, and leisure activities. Just as important, the tourist authorities began considering new ways in which to present heritage, including the use of interactive media systems to "enhance interest and understanding."[124] In order to meet government targets for the doubling of tourism revenue, Bord Fáilte focused its attention on modernizing, diversifying, and expanding its heritage product.

A large part of the task of producing heritage extends beyond determining the products and narratives to be presented to the interpretation of those stories. The Glendalough proposal was problematic, not because stories were unavailable but because the government was unwilling to decide on a fixed narrative that would interpret the evidence available. Likewise, the restoration of Kilmainham Jail was made possible because all parties agreed at the outset that the site would present an unambiguous story of Irish *unity* in the fight against oppression. Heritage requires "more than preservation: its significance should be conveyed to the visitor, leading to an enriched understanding of the context of the present."[125] In order to be successful, interpreters must translate the past into a modern language, linking the present to the past with common symbols. This goal is accomplished by using "a range of methods, media, materials, and management" that work together as "'culture brokers' or mediators between tradition and modernity.[126] As popular culture changes, the brokers used for accomplishing translation evolve to meet new tastes—an evolution that has been tremendously obvious in the development of the tourism product offered by the Guinness Brewing Company.

Lovely Day for a Guinness

For Guinness, tourism represents a successful form of advertising. Since opening in December 2000, the Guinness Storehouse became (perhaps)

Ireland's leading tourist site, building on the sound reputation of the company's previous tourist facility, the Hopstore.[127] The Storehouse is nothing if not modern, making use of so many "culture brokers" as to leave the visitor exhausted by the time he reaches the rooftop tasting room, high atop a giant pint-glass-shaped atrium. The facility is a virtual assault on the senses, with running water, loud noises, multimedia presentations, interactive displays, music, artifacts, and no less than three bars. This facility did not develop in a vacuum and actually represents the most recent in a series of Guinness tourism attractions.

The company initially recognized the potential value of advertising after the launch of its first campaign in Scotland in April 1928. Under the guidance of S. H. Benson, the campaign materials featured the now-famous slogan "Guinness is good for you" and displayed "a picture of a large glass of stout with a typical Guinness head." A poster was circularized to all doctors in the advertising area along with "free samples for 'medical use.'"[128] This campaign was followed up with parodies of *Alice in Wonderland,* with rugby sponsorships, and later with Gilroy's famous "Guinness for Strength" and "Lovely Day for a Guinness" posters, with their toucans, lions, and other animals thirsting for stout.[129] The result was a 7.3 percent increase in Scottish sales, even as sales in Britain as a whole dropped by 6.8 percent. Although the Great Depression caused sales to drop precipitously in the 1930s, the success in Scotland ensured that Guinness continued extensive use of advertising.[130]

At least from the incorporation of the company in 1886, Guinness recognized that visitors enjoyed seeing the inner workings of the massive St. James's Gate Brewery. In 1887, 4,000 people toured Guinness.[131] By the early highpoint in 1919 this number had climbed to 19,600 visitors and the company had distributed almost 20,000 guidebooks.[132] Numbers declined thereafter as political tension increased with the onset of the War of Independence. Interested parties had only to "present a suitable letter or introduction" to receive a tour through St. James's Gate. Evidently a fair number of such letters existed because tours departed every fifteen minutes, Mondays to Fridays, from eleven A.M. to three P.M.[133]

Following the tourism boom after World War II and the news that Fianna Fáil was going to push through new tourism legislation, Guinness began planning to improve its tourism product. A memo was circulated that suggested that more guides be trained, enabling "more inexperienced men to see how a star performer puts across the patter to his audience." It was also noted that the company should conduct occasional visitor surveys in order to make certain that tourists were impressed by their visit.[134] In the following year a script was crafted in order to standardize the information provided to visitors, most of which covered the history of the brewery and the brewing process, but which also addressed the various benefits given to employees, including full medical support and inexpensive food. It was stressed that "although an old firm, we [Guinness] are not afraid to keep our plant modernised"—a claim that echoed the wider emphasis on Ireland's modernity in contemporary tourist guidebooks and the An Tóstal program.[135] Guides were even told how to answer many of the frequent questions asked by tourists, including the origin of the water used and the flavor of Guinness in the United Kingdom vis-à-vis Ireland. When asked about the water, guides were instructed to "kill the belief that Guinness is made from Liffey water"; instead, they were to inform visitors that the water is actually drawn from a special well in County Kildare. Those who asked about taste were to be told that "the results of tasting by our expert tasters do not show that Guinness brewed in one brewery is superior to Guinness brewed in another."[136] While the company's presentation for tourists was carefully considered, the organization did not expend any effort in mounting fancy displays. It was not an unsuccessful formula, and the brewery was attracting fifty thousand visitors per year by 1958 and sixty thousand in 1959. The brewery prided itself on its tour leaders, bragging that "our guides are prepared to meet all sorts of people, grave and gay, and to be ready for such jobs as lifting the Seven Dwarfs of 'Snow White' to enable them to see into a vessel, or finding another way round for the German wrestling giant, Gargantua, whose height of eight feet would not allow him to use the passenger tunnel to the lower level." The formula was so successful that "rarely is anybody disappointed."[137]

Besides staging the tours, Guinness continued to use its marketing budget to promote sporting events and festivals during the 1950s, often citing a perceived public obligation rather than advertising objectives. Likewise, in 1958 the company restored its windmill because of its "sense of public duty to preserve an historic landmark."[138] Support of the first Galway Oyster Festival in 1954 was justified in the same way, by the claim that the company was assisting a "wholly local, voluntary, and otherwise admirable organising committee."[139] While this may have been the case, there was undoubtedly a significant advertising and tourism benefit as well, giving Guinness every reason to support An Tóstal as well as the eventual catalog of festivals from Wexford to Cork that the company pulled under its wing.[140]

By 1960 the brewery tour had become so successful that tourists were carried along on a narrow-gauge railway called the "Planet," and in 1963 the company expanded its tourism efforts still further by opening a souvenir shop at the Victoria Quay stocked with glass tankards, penknives, glass cloths, and other collectables.[141] In 1966 the brewery inaugurated its first museum, though access was limited only to special parties. The museum represented a striking contrast with those of today. Rows of glass cases displayed various artifacts, including the "most interesting exhibit in the museum," a display of coopers' tools with illustrations of how they were used. Photographs, old bottles, a steam engine, and a Geoghegan narrow-gauge steam locomotive, old ledgers, and foreign labels filled out the exhibits.[142] It was a step toward providing still more attractions to tourists and was probably very much like other museum displays in Ireland at the time, showing objects and displaying a limited amount of written material but lacking the coherent narratives found in future efforts.

At the same time that the museum was opened on Waltling Street, a committee began to study the visitors' route through the brewery, looking for potential sanitation and safety problems, while also comparing the Guinness experience with those of the Carlsberg brewery in Copenhagen, the Heineken brewery in Amsterdam, and the Pripps brewery in Stockholm. It was hoped that the group would learn more about what Guinness was doing well while making it possible to adopt potentially attractive features used at these other breweries. Ultimately the committee reported "tours of brewery premises can be deadly dull," making the inclusion of entertainment at Pripps easily understandable. It was a message that was not lost on Guinness and that eventually came to dominate the thinking behind the company's tourism ventures. The committee was pleased to report that Guinness visitors were allowed access to a larger portion of the brewery than the other

Tourism and the Past | 171

6. Guinness operated a narrow-gauge train called "The Planet" as part of its brewery tour during the early 1960s. Courtesy of Guinness Ireland Archives, St. James's Gate, Dublin 8.

corporations allowed, but it noted that the bottling plant should be included and a larger effort made to interpret the facility through the use of models, as was being done at Carlsberg. Finally, it was felt that the museum should be opened to a larger number of visitors, although the committee was divided about the relative merits of doing so, given the cost of the improvements that would be required. Regardless of whatever changes might be made, "it is essential that a visitor leaving St. James's Gate should realise he has been to a brewery."[143]

By the 1980s the number of tourists had climbed still higher, and the leading of large numbers of tourists through the brewery was becoming ever more challenging. Furthermore, fashions had changed. Museums and heritage centers now demonstrated historical events or industrial processes using

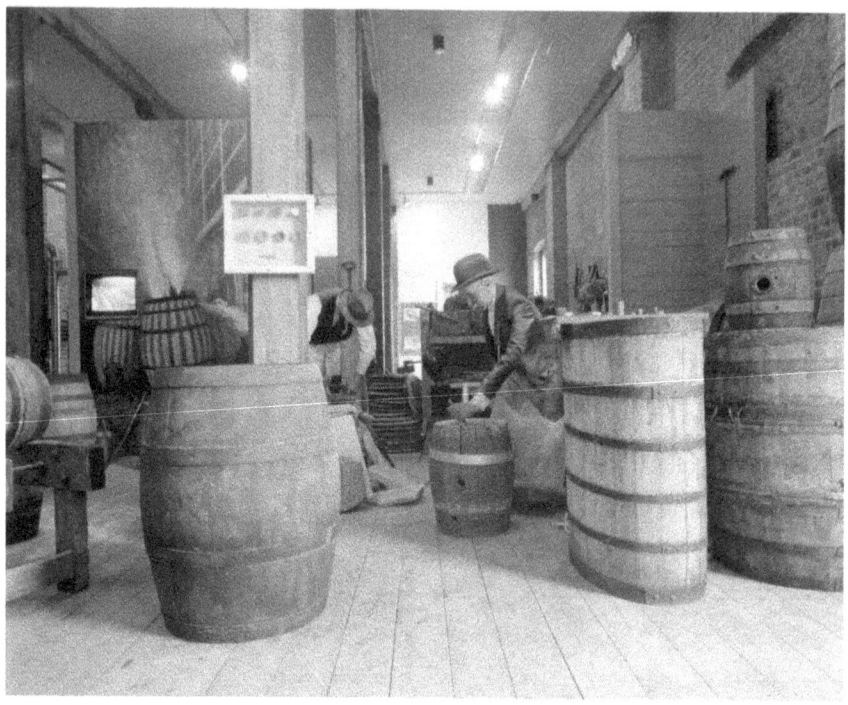

7. The Guinness Hopstore used the latest display technology to tell the story of Guinness stout during the 1980s and 1990s. Courtesy of Guinness Ireland Archives, St. James's Gate, Dublin 8.

manikins. Beginning in 1984, Guinness began constructing a new facility for tourists that fit new demands, investing £1.5 million in restoring and modifying the old hop-storage facility at St. James's Gate. When it finally opened on 27 July 1988, John Davies, the Guinness managing director, told gathered dignitaries that the exhibition "cleverly harnesses modern display technology to tell its story in a graphic and entertaining way"—the story being the evolution of Guinness as a company from its humble origins in the late 1750s among Dublin's many breweries of that day and the process used when making Guinness. Beginning on the first two floors, visitors were ushered through a display illustrating the making of beer, on through the original gates of the brewery, and into a collection of text panels, models, reconstructions, and bits of brewery equipment. Next, visitors learned about the history of the company, its place in the contemporary world, Guinness advertising, and the elaborate transport systems used to carry Guinness from the quay at Dublin to pubs around the world. The visit was completed with a pint of Guinness in the basement bar.[144] It was a site placed firmly at the forefront of museum design—it even smelled like a brewery, thanks to the aroma left after two hundred years of hop storage.

Storehouse

By the late 1990s, however, the Hopstore was obsolete. Inanimate reproductions and immobile text panels were out of date, and the three-floor facility was simply too small to handle the still growing number of tourists. Guinness made the decision in 1998 to abandon the Hopstore and to develop a massive six-story visitor facility in an old storehouse building—a large steel-beam structure originally built by A. H. Hignett in 1903.[145] The eighty-year-old Dublin-based architectural firm Robinson Keefe Devane completed the refurbishment at a cost of £24 million.[146] The steel-beam construction, still modern-looking one hundred years after its initial assembly, was augmented with a glass roof, endless escalators, and a glass elevator giving the upper floors an exceptionally bright and spacious feeling. The company used the steel-frame structure of the building, as well as assorted industrial equipment, to give the building a functional industrial feeling.[147] The new tourist facility also featured a 360-degree bar on the top level, two additional bars lower down, a visitor center, a cultural venue, the Guinness Ireland Archives, and a training facility for Guinness employees.[148] The "conceptualisation, identity, advertising, Web design, literature, and events programs" were all assigned to Imagination Group USA, a U.S.-based design and marketing company, at an additional cost of £6 million. When it was finally opened three years after work had begun, the Storehouse sought to "interpret one of the world's best known brands in a totally new and unexpected way," giving visitors a chance to learn "about the brewing process and the huge impact the business has made in Dublin and overseas."[149] This learning process was accomplished through "new set-piece exhibits and presentations in film, digital media, sound, and projections" in order to "fully immerse the visitor in the ongoing story of the famous brand."[150]

If nothing else, the Storehouse certainly was a change from past Guinness tourism efforts. Upon entering, visitors are greeted with a loud industrial-like noise and a massive waterfall designed to show the importance

8. Visitors to the Guinness Storehouse are greeted by a display featuring the ingredients used to make stout. Photograph by the author.

of water, as displays nearby describe hops, barley, and malt. Video screens depict Guinness as a central component of Irish culture, firmly linked to great moments in Gaelic football and hurling history as well as to memorable moments in Irish advertising. Further along, visitors sit on office furniture as images from the brewery's history are flashed on the walls around them and a voice recounts the story of Arthur Guinness's first purchasing an old brewery in order to establish his own, with the business gradually moving from the brewing of ales to that of stouts. As visitors ascend still higher, they reach an interactive advertising display that allows more patient tourists to view Guinness commercials dating from the 1950s to the present, reliving proud moments like an impressive drag-racing slug and talented bicycle-riding fish—both of which enjoy Guinness, despite the fact that Guinness is definitely *not* good for slugs! Finally, after climbing six floors, the tourist arrives at the Gravity Bar, where she can enjoy a pint while gazing on a 360-degree view of Dublin.

While the facility enjoyed a hugely successful launch and a significant boost when President Bill Clinton of the United States visited a few days later,[151] feelings about the site were mixed. *Irish Times* columnist Joe Humphreys was horrified by the company's attempt at "colonising our national heritage" and turned up his pen at the entire enterprise, declaring Guinness to be a "corporation that believes its own hype." It all seemed terribly impersonal to him because the visitor traverses the six-floor experience alone. "The idea seems to be to create a distance between the punter and the product in an effort to further heighten the mystique," he observed sourly, and then complained that many of the displays appealed little to adults while captivating the "under-sixes," inevitably creating battalions of Guinness drinkers and legions of alcoholics.[152] Guinness was disgusted at the reporter's comments, declaring that the company, at over 240 years of age and the drink of choice for millions, was every bit the major part of Irish culture suggested by the facility's narrative. Furthermore, the allegation that the Storehouse was little more than a giant sales pitch was wholly off the mark. This was a site that offered value for money because "visitors can easily spend several hours exploring the building" and enjoying their pint—or a glass of soda for those uninterested in Guinness. Moreover, it was incorrect to claim that the Storehouse might encourage underage drinking. After all, the company spokesperson asked rhetorically, "Does the Chamber of Horrors at Madame Tussaud's in London encourage young people to go on a rampage of torture and murder? We have to accept that parents with young families will quite reasonably try to satisfy their insatiable desire for knowledge by visiting attractive locations with a long history and tradition." Theirs was an authentic heritage site, an educational facility, and it was suitable for visitors of all ages.[153]

Humphries was not the only critic of the Storehouse. Shortly after the previously cited editorial appeared, Dr. Michael Loftus wrote to the *Irish Times* to express his agreement: "The most disturbing aspect is allowing youth of all ages to view the massive promotion of a potent, addictive drug. How sad. Where is the responsibility?"[154] Others disapproved of the near canonization of Guinness creator Arthur Guinness and the site's other "mawkish tributes" to the Irish brew.[155] The painful admission fee was also singled out for scorn; the *Irish Times,* for example, declared the facility to be the worst value in Ireland, saying, "Charges you 13.50 to watch some Guinness ads and have a pint. Yet gets more visitors than any other tourist attraction in Ireland. One word: suckers!"[156]

Ultimately, the Guinness story demonstrates the changing face of heritage, the increasingly international voices and fashions involved in translating it, and the almost inevitable conflict that develops as a result. Heritage is, after all, the most recent shape of historical debate both inside and outside of the nation. Although Humphreys did not explicitly say it, by questioning the brewer's right to "colonise" Irish heritage and the desirability of displaying the Guinness product to young people, he was challenging long-held stereotypes about the Irish and alcohol.[157] Is it desirable that Irishness be associated with a beer? Should the face of a nation be so closely linked to an opaque beverage? Is the success of Guinness advertising ultimately a horribly negative thing for the Irish image? The very success of the Guinness Storehouse, whether the facts it presents are accurate or not, makes these questions that much more prevalent, while continuing debate surrounding Irish heritage and history into a new millennium.

Conclusion

Since the foundation of the Irish Free State tourism has continually raised questions about the preservation, presentation, and exploitation of Irish history. What topics should be discussed and *how* should they be discussed? Is it permissible to present history that is contested, or to appropriate symbols to create links between certain products (especially when that product is an alcoholic beverage) and national identity? Should historical narratives be used to unify a people or as a way to reflect divisions that have made the nation what it is today?

This chapter reveals a long-standing uncertainty about the answers to the above questions. Irish people hoped to use the past to reflect well on modern Ireland by stressing earlier accomplishments while avoiding unpleasant recent memories. When the recent past was addressed, it was done in a manner that glossed over the more unpleasant realities, again presenting Ireland, both to foreign tourists and to the Irish themselves, in a positive light.

Perhaps it is unsurprising that the authorities and interested citizens tried to use the past to offer a pleasant image of Ireland, but the government's tendency to distance itself from the production of heritage, even "positive" heritage, is more striking. While money was certainly in short supply, the development of sites that celebrated Irish unity and achievement might have functioned to create strong feelings of national pride—much as the impressive structures built in nineteenth-century Germany were used to "nationalize the masses."[158] Instead, the government fostered a deeply ambivalent relationship with history, even as the tourist authorities recognized the value of the past for attracting tourists. Perhaps it is this ambivalence, as much as a lack of funds or the importance of landownership in nationalist thought, that has left authorities unwilling to make use of their powers to compulsorily acquire land or, at the very least, to "encourage" landowners to provide suitable access to important historic structures resting on their property.

6

Creating the Tourist Landscape

Territory and landscape make nations tangible. National landscapes are imagined to have unique characteristics that symbolically represent the native spirit of the *Volk*. While nationalists must develop national histories and culture, landscape requires the provision of a spatial knowledge of national geography that in turn enhances an exact understanding of what it is to be English, German, French, or Irish.[1] But nationalists often do more still, striving to preserve their landscape, to present it in a specific way, and to enhance access to the land so that it becomes possible to provide generation after generation, as well as foreigners and locals alike, with a personal understanding of the national territory.

Irish landscape is generally associated with the rugged western seaboard—an association that developed because it allowed Ireland to be defined against England, as well as against the eastern seaboard that was corrupted by Anglicization, urbanization, and industrialization.[2] Yet, given the important political role assigned to Irish scenery, Irish history does not abound with examples of the hiking clubs and healthy-living societies that developed as a way to teach those in places like Germany and England about their homelands.[3] Instead, tourist-related activity has partly substituted for the nationalist-minded hiking clubs.[4] The Irish Tourist Association, Bord Fáilte, and local authorities interested in tourism development actively worked to shape Ireland for both native and tourist consumption, an effort that was helped and hindered by groups and individuals outside of the tourist industry. The long history of conflict over land and the constitutional right to landownership ensured that tourist officials constantly had to deal with landowners. While officials could and did provide a nearly endless series of suggestions, advice, and even legislation, ultimately the creation of Irish landscape was the product of a horizontal dialogue that occurred across Irish society.

This chapter explores the interaction of the government, tourist authorities, and the Irish people themselves by addressing the importance of landscape in tourist discourse, questions about land access rights and ownership, efforts to develop and shape Irish landscapes and townscapes, Tourist Board attempts to redefine ecosystems to match perceived tourist demands, special undertakings to conserve environments, and the way in which landscapes have been manipulated through their photographic presentation. In the end readers should recognize the myriad factors involved in creating the way in which Ireland is visualized as well as the role that the negotiating of landscape has played in continually reimagining Irish national identity.

The Importance of Irish Landscape

Almost from the first moment that travelers visited Ireland, they were attracted to the scenery. Since the 1750s virtually every travel writer has voiced strong enthusiasm for the landscape, singing the praises of the Killarney lakes and gazing in awe at the rugged rocks and cliffs of the western seaboard. Archie Bell was so awestruck in 1928 that he urged visitors to travel slowly so that they might feel and absorb the beauty around them; the basic message has changed little since.[5] Of course there were also critical voices. In the early 1950s Heinrich Böll equated the greenness with forsakenness,[6] and in the late 1980s Eric Newby, who bravely rode around Ireland on a bicycle in January, complained often about the driving rain that obscured his view.[7] Most recently, Pete McCarthy protested bitterly about "slapdash construction of suburban housing in places where there are no suburbs."[8] Yet even this moaning reveals the powerful attraction of Irish scenery and the disappointment when it failed to meet expectations, a point further emphasized by the fact that virtually every major tourist market in Ireland cites landscape and scenery at or near the top of the list of the country's attractions.[9]

Members of the Irish Tourist Association recognized the strong pull of the landscape for tourists from the beginning. ITA guidebooks always stressed the many beauty spots of Ireland—the sheer quantity of which created a mecca for tourists.[10] During the initial push to establish local branches, areas like Dingle, Waterville, Kenmare, and Killarney were especially valuable focal points for ITA efforts precisely because of their scenic attractiveness. Representatives were fond of saying that Ireland's scenery was among the finest in the world, that there was little reason to visit America, France, or Switzerland when Ireland offered more diversity spread over a much smaller area, thus making it possible to really experience the whole instead of tidbits here and there.[11]

For the Irish Tourist Association it was not enough merely to feature attractive photographs or glowing textual accounts of Ireland's beauty; they also believed that it was necessary to protect the landscape from the visual signs of modernization while at the same time developing the land for consumers. As early as the 1920s, ITA leaders advocated the belief that it was important for Ireland to preserve and improve the landscape in order to attract visitors. Even as tourism advocates dreamed of a tourism-inspired modernity, they also sought to guarantee that development projects fit a specific set of aesthetic assumptions about what belonged in Irish landscapes and townscapes. Furthermore, the association worked to create a network of signposts around the country that would allow tourists to find their way through the labyrinth of narrow country lanes.

Beginning as early as 1925, the ITA lobbied for the improvement of urban areas, including the destruction of derelict sites. According to the association, "one such eyesore spoils the effects of an otherwise unkept secret. If councils have not powers to deal arbitrarily with such matters, they should take steps to secure them."[12] Simply removing abandoned buildings was not enough, and the Tourist Association touted the efforts of those areas that were pushing for urban cleanliness, applauding Clonmel, for example, for its effort to create cleaner streets and provide "a general brightening-up of the aspect of the town."[13]

The association also took an interest in urban development projects in other countries. For example, P. C. O'Mahony, a member of the Killarney branch of the ITA, enthusiastically pointed to the Yorkshire seaside resort at Scarborough as an example of what Irish towns should emulate. O'Mahony noted that the local corporation "controls practically everything" in order to ensure that the town remains clean, attractive, and inviting. Disused buildings were quickly disposed of or refurbished, beachside bungalows were kept in smart repair, and streets were looked after by a team of full-time staff.[14] Picture-postcard perfection was the rule, not the exception.

The ITA paid careful attention to the type of structures that were erected, hoping to make sure that Ireland did not develop buildings out of keeping with its image. Talk of constructing high-rise hotels to cater to American visitors, for example, was strongly questioned. "It would certainly look a bit odd to see a huge building in, say, O'Connell Street, Dublin, towering over the other houses like a giant looking down on a lot of dwarfs." It was not that skyscrapers were inherently bad or unaesthetic; after all, as the author pointed out, the Nelson Pillar was equally out of place on O'Connell Street. Rather, the point was that tourists seek unfamiliar sights. Only tourists completely unfamiliar with tall buildings would find such a structure interesting, and neither British nor American visitors fit such criteria.[15]

The association also pushed for major alterations to the modern Irish landscape. Beginning in 1926 the ITA lobbied for the implementation of a nationwide reforestation scheme. The group argued, "The necessity for a considerable amount of tree planting is an obvious one from the scenic point of view—trees are an essential part of inland scenery." Such a scheme would dramatically improve the national health, and the Irish climate would be "favourably affected by an increase in our areas under timber." Moreover, it was the government's duty to "repair the ravages of recent years by initiating a scheme of compulsory planting."[16] Once planted, trees should be cared for in a manner that ensured their aesthetic appeal. The association reported that tourists had already commented to ITA representatives about the "disfigurement of the countryside caused by careless lopping of trees." Trees should be planted, but at the same time the local authorities should be given the power to make certain that any and all pruning was "done more skillfully."[17] This scheme, if implemented, would have completely redefined the appearance of the areas into which it was introduced, altering Irish scenery to mirror more closely that of America or even continental Europe.

Given its tiny budget and its lack of statutory authority, the Irish Tourist Association was in no position to act as anything other than a lobby for environmental preservation and responsible development. The later statutory tourist boards, on the other hand, had more power to undertake landscape-altering schemes and devoted considerable energy to redefining Irish scenery. While more will be said about the board's various activities in a moment, suffice it to say here that at various points the Tourist Board undertook environmental studies, worked to redefine Irish townscapes, acted as a quasi-environmental watchdog organization, attempted to retrain the Irish people to accept a specific aesthetic of Irish spaces, forwarded an extensive signposting campaign, and even altered whole ecosystems in order to meet tourist desires.

The concern about Irish scenery extended beyond the efforts of tourist organizations. Newspaper letter-writers frequently used tourism as a reason for action or inaction on landscape-related concerns. In 1946, for example, one man wrote to the *Irish Times* to complain about widespread logging between Bray and Enniskerry, just south of Dublin. "We have become so obsessed by the profit motive that it is useless to suggest that Ireland's natural beauty is a thing worth preserving for its own sake," the author grumbled. Continuation of the current "orgy of destruction" would virtually assure the loss of tourism revenue.[18]

Lord Sligo of Westport, Co. Mayo, also cited tourism as a reason for careful consideration of how to treat the Irish landscape. In 1960, Lord Sligo opened Westport House to tourists for the first time, attracting some two thousand visitors in the first weeks of operation. The building was the first private "great house" in southern Ireland to open as a tourist attraction, and Lord Sligo had big plans, including a large-scale publicity campaign and a concerted effort to improve the amenities available to house visitors. Yet, just as he was set to develop his property as a major tourist attraction, efforts were well advanced to build a fifteen-acre factory adjacent to the house. Sligo insisted that he was not worried about the factory per se; indeed, he favored any project that would bring employment to his town. But he was concerned that it would severely alter the view from his estate, thus badly damaging its potential as a tourist attraction.[19] The danger was profound because it could not "be too strongly emphasised that the average tourist comes here [to the west of Ireland] partly because he does *not* have to look at factories—quite likely, he works in one employing several thousands." During 1961, Lord Sligo expected 10,000 visitors to Westport House, and "the possibility of explaining away a factory on our front-door step to 10,000 people, who might have paid to visit this house, causes us some concern."[20]

Among the people of Westport, Lord Sligo's plight received little sympathy. The Westport Urban Development Council unanimously passed a resolution calling for the factory's construction and declared the resolution their "best night's work yet." The community had long wanted a factory, and as far as the council was concerned, Sligo had no say in the matter. At certain points the language became heated and threatening. Members went so far as to say that Lord Sligo should not be permitted to walk on a public footpath near the harbor.[21] Within months the tone had gotten so unpleasant that the *Irish Times* referred to the debate as "the war at Westport." As far as the townspeople were concerned, tourism revenue would be beneficial, but they had seen precious little of it during the first year that the house was open to visitors, and they did not imagine that further wealth would be forthcoming. Meanwhile they believed that the factory would employ some five hundred local men, bringing "new life and business to Westport." The factory would "transform the town."[22]

The Westport situation is but one of many similar stories of conflict between proposed growth projects and the need to maintain an essentially premodern landscape for tourists—a dialogue that stretched even into the very heart of Irish tourism at Killarney. As far back as William Thackeray's visit in the 1840s, Killarney was notable for "a hideous row of houses" that informed the visitor that he had reached Killarney.[23] Today Killarney has expanded into a massive expanse of bed-and-breakfasts, hotels, and small homes. The travel writer Pete McCarthy describes the scene accurately and with much humor:

> "Killarney—Looking Good," says the sign, but whichever direction you approach from . . . you are greeted by rows and rows of B&Bs. Many are suburban semis [semi-detached] . . . that, Tardis-like, have miraculously created the space to accommodate big-boned American families reared on hormone-enriched all-you-can-eat buffets. Others are grander, executive-style homes that look like they were assembled last week from a doll's house kit. All are festooned with signs proclaiming their attractions. "All Rooms En-Suite! TV! Car Space! Tea and Coffee Making Facilities!" they shout. But why stop there? People shouldn't sell themselves short. Tourism's a cut-throat business. You need to get all your selling points up there on the board. "Sheets On All Beds!" "Legs Keep Bed Off Floor!" "Drawer To Put Underpants In!" "Walls!"[24]

The development that prompted the expansion of the town from Thackeray's row of ugly cottages into a holiday metropolis created strong feelings even among those interested in promoting Irish tourism. Just as with the Killarney boatmen's objections to motor-launches, the growth of holiday homes was often greeted with hostility. Dublin-born, London-based travel writer Leslie Daiken is a case in point. His articles urge an approach to Irish travel based on impulse and "Edwardian rhythms."[25] He was among the first writers to advocate a horse-drawn caravan tour of Cork—promoting Con Murphy's horse-drawn caravan business as an ideal source of the perfect Irish holiday and anticipating Bord Fáilte's recognition of the attractiveness of this type of vacation.[26] While Daiken was all for getting to one's holiday destination quickly, once there he asked, "Is there anything quite so good for the body, mind, and senses than to climb into an open barouche, nod to the coachman, and 'do the tour,' passing under those branches drooping with heady perfume, indifferent to the sun-intoxicated flies that follow the old nag's ears as, clop-clopping to the rhythm of the *Fiacre* ballad, he leads us in and out of streets and laneways that no limousine or motorcycle looks quite right in." There was no better way to see Ireland than in a jaunting car, exploring Dublin through its "Bloom's Cabs" or seeing Killarney or the Mountains of Mourne at a horse's pace.[27] He viewed jaunting cars as "a symbol of unchanging Ireland" and dreamed that they might "long continue so, as they have done all these years at Killarney," even as he tirelessly promoted tourism in Ireland and urged more and more visitors to make the trip.[28] In Daiken's mind Kerry represented the last place "in these islands where you can call for a wagonette and have a uniformed coachman drive you into breath-taking scenery."[29] As a result, he focused much of his energy on promoting the region.

Given Daiken's apparent dedication to tourism development,[30] the horror with which he reacted to the success of tourism is striking. In 1961, after doing research on the current tourism market in Killarney, proposing articles to a handful of publications about the area, and learning about the sale of a large portion of the lakes to an American (see below), Daiken became greatly disenchanted by the changes that he saw taking place in this tourism center. All at once, in an unpublished article, Daiken urged tourists to "see Killarney before they murder it." He grieved,

If you have tears, prepare to shed them now—for the "developers" are in. And you can imagine what that means. Most Irish people who love their country's natural beauty (and who used to nourish an honest hatred for the Saxon invader) now reserve their righteous anger and fury for this new menace—the soulless speculators and magnates who, by remote control, are turning the world-famed beauty spots of Éireann into "developed areas," replacing the dignified emblem of an Irish Wolfhound for that of a Hot Dog.

Daiken gave "Killarney ten years before it becomes a second Blackpool," and noted that he had once believed Killarney would escape the ravishes of the profit hounds, leaving the "ineffable, unspoilt, heavenly vistas of Killarney's lakes and fells" to "go on forever," but he now realized this was a mere pipedream. It was not only that an American had purchased Killarney (Daiken made no secret of his disgust about this fact); it was also the "Germanisation of Killarney," the disappearance of the area's former solitude, the omnipresent concern about "how many more beds can we squeeze into this region at 'x' hundred £ per bed per annum." Killarney was becoming little more than another European tourist center, and this "Europeanisation of Killarney" was "a death-blow to the very impulse that attracts the English-speaking-world."[31]

Whose Landscape?

Even as Daiken was being horrified by rapid and excessive growth in Killarney, a few miles away in Tuosist, Father John Scanlon desperately hoped to attract development and to replace the increasingly depopulated landscape of his parish with family homes and productive farms. In chapter 3, Scanlon's quest to attract tourism revenue during the early 1960s was explored as an example of a local voice actively trying to use tourism as a harbinger of modernity, wealth, and a barrier against the endless cycle of emigration. In 1971, Scanlon again contacted the government when he learned that one of the larger local farms was on the market. While tourists might see "unspoilt virgin scenery," the painful reality was that "old folk" and "lonely bachelors" were selling their "small rocky holdings to foreigners for a few thousand and then . . . [migrating] to the nearest town . . . or cross the seas." Scanlon was horrified. He could not fathom selling to foreigners, and he believed that tourism development would solve the problem.³² It was not enough that beautiful landscapes existed in Ireland; they should be owned, farmed, and enjoyed by the Irish themselves.

While Taoiseach Jack Lynch appreciated Scanlon's plea, he replied to the concerned priest that there was little chance of Bord Fáilte's or the government's purchasing the land. According to Lynch, "the right to private property enshrined in our constitution is interpreted as the right to dispose of it freely as well. It is only on very rare occasions . . . that this right can be invaded."³³ Scanlon was mortified and promptly replied that "we lovers of our country would have something to leave to posterity as a proof of our genuine patriotism" if the land were purchased by the state.³⁴ In Scanlon's mind the constitution was irrelevant. Only continued Irish ownership of Irish land really mattered.

Brian Lenihan, minister for transport and power, followed up the taoiseach's letter by noting that although Bord Fáilte had statutory authority to purchase property, it did so only through grants to local authorities in order to facilitate large-scale development. Tuosist was simply not "in a major resort" and therefore was not eligible for resort-development funds. While tourist authorities were in contact with the Kerry County Council and were willing to encourage preservation of the area, they simply could not provide any financial assistance.³⁵

The foreign threat perceived by Scanlon was not limited to rural farms. In 1962 an American businessman contacted the Office of the Taoiseach on behalf of a wealthy American investor asking to purchase Blarney Castle, a site long popular with tourists. The man argued that his employer "would use every means possible to bring to Ireland an enormous increase in visitors by creating a desire on the part of Americans to see Ireland and to kiss the Blarney Stone." Beyond making just a simple purchase, the investor hoped to restore the old castle and "build a great hotel" to cater to legions of American tourists.³⁶ Mercifully, the taoiseach dismissed the offer out of hand. The castle was considered a national monument, and the taoiseach was unwilling to apply the same legal criteria that he had urged for Tuosist.

The story was much more complicated at Killarney, however, where an American real-estate investor actually purchased the Kenmare estate, containing some 8,300 acres of Ireland's most beautiful scenery, including two of Killarney's three lakes, Ross Castle, and the old abbey of St. Finian Lobhar—for a mere £100,000. The investor, J. Stuart Robertson, was born in Glasgow, married a Killarney girl, and subsequently moved to the United States, where he attained considerable success in real estate. Robertson purchased the property in August 1956 amid concern from local interests that he might permanently alter time-honored agreements such as jarvey access to the Gap of Dunloe or the ban on motor-launches on the lake.[37] Robertson assured the locals that this would not be the case and added that he was interested in using the site to breed Irish horses for export.[38]

The sale sparked an immediate outcry from almost all sectors of Irish society. The Killarney Tourist Association started a fund to purchase the site, and Sinn Féin suggested that the descendants of evicted tenants should receive the land as compensation for the losses incurred by their relatives in the late nineteenth century.[39] Bord Fáilte suggested that the land should be purchased "on a national basis," and pointed out "this was an opportunity, which might not recur, of establishing the future of Killarney which is our best known tourist attraction." The land could easily be added to the previously existing Bourn Vincent Park that abutted it in many places.[40] Yet in spite of the various appeals by Sinn Féin, the Tourist Board, the ITA, the Royal Irish Academy, the Royal Dublin Society, the Irish Hotels Federation, and the Hotel and Restaurant Association, to say nothing of numerous individuals,[41] the government refused to consider purchasing the land because to do so would create "a most embarrassing precedent for them." Yet the political potency of the sale was not lost on government officials, and they promised to ensure that the "national interest" would not be undermined by the sale, and that no tawdry development would be allowed.[42] Legislation to protect beauty spots and tourist amenities, for example, might prove a viable way to guarantee the protection of "special areas" while not forcing the government to directly challenge the Irish constitution.[43]

As it happened, Robertson sold the estate early in 1961 to an Irish-American millionaire named John McShain, who no doubt pleased the citizens of Killarney by calling Robertson "a complete promoter" interested in little more than financial gain. McShain promised that he would not develop the site for commercial purposes, but would instead use the existing Kenmare family home as a private holiday residence. The only change would be the installation of a modern heating system and a complete refurnishing with Irish antiques purchased at sales in the area.[44]

No Unauthorized Entry

Private landownership often forces tourists in Ireland to confront "No Trespassing" signs, as Pete McCarthy discovered while searching for an ancient burial site in County Cork. After finding the site, McCarthy discovered a sign that read: "Notice is hereby given that the occupier of this property excludes the duty of care to all visitors. No unauthorised entry is allowed."[45] The travel writer considered climbing the gate, but he imagined "some beefy farmer lurking behind the net curtains, with ginger hair growing out of his ears and nostrils, just itching to exclude the duty of care to some trespassing English bastard," and he therefore decided to move on in search of a stone circle.[46] Once again he located the site with some difficulty, only to discover that it was located in a paddock marked with a warning about a bull. At every turn McCarthy was confronted with a view of land that emphasized private ownership and restricted access over public consumption and accessibility—a conflict that reflects two distinctly different readings of the "national interest," one giving primacy to attracting tourist dollars, the other projecting the politically charged nineteenth-century notions of the "three Fs" and peasant proprietorship.[47] These dueling views have placed tourism interests, the government, and local families in direct conflict since the 1920s.

The Irish government first tried to address the ownership dilemma in relationship to historic sites in the 1930 National Monuments Act, then again in the 1952 Tourist Traffic Act. Both of these laws authorized first the Office of Public Works, then An Bord Fáilte, to acquire land. From a preservation standpoint the 1930 Monuments Act worked fairly well, requiring only three amendments as of 2002, but the two acts did very little to solve ownership and access concerns because the government was rarely willing to fully use the powers of compulsory acquisition included in both pieces of legislation.[48] Little conflict resulted when this legislation functioned properly. For example, in 1938 it was reported that a cairn in Oldcastle Townland, Co. Cork, was in jeopardy because the landowner planned to remove the structure in order to facilitate more efficient plowing. The Office of Public Works responded by filing a preservation order that was subsequently approved. As was generally the case, the farmer accepted the order and no damage was done to the site.[49] In situations where the landowner was more intransigent, however, problems quickly arose because the government was unwilling to risk an expensive lawsuit. The battle of wills inherent in such a scenario inevitably raised questions about rights to Irish lands as well as to the historic sites found on the property. If the government was unwilling to demand control over the most beautiful areas of the country, or the most historic ones, did that ultimately mean that the country's scenic and historic gems were the private possessions of a privileged few rather than all Irish men and women?

The Battle for Poulnabrone

The questions of ownership and access were raised most prominently during a protracted struggle over ownership of the Poulnabrone dolmen in the Burren of County Clare during the 1980s and 1990s. The dolmen, a type of megalithic tomb in which several standing stones support one massive capstone, stands in a field of limestone pavement near the Corofin-Ballyvaughan road in the heart of the Burren. Poulnabrone is "one of Ireland's most photographed dolmens."[50]

The Poulnabrone story began in 1981 when Dr. Peter Harbison, then archeologist for Bord Fáilte, called the Office of Public Works in order to urge the speedy acquisition of the dolmen and its immediate surroundings so that a suitable car park could be constructed and the site preserved as an important national historic site.[51] Public Works quickly affirmed its willingness and began to determine how much land should be acquired.[52] The initial signs were positive and the needed steps were taken completely according to plan; the landowner, Thomas Byrnes, even agreed to hand the dolmen over to the state.[53] By May 1982, however, the situation began to spin out of control. First, the Clare Archaeological and Historical Society reported structural problems at the site. Smaller stones around the base of the monument had been moved, risking the structural integrity of the whole dolmen. Given Poulnabrone's "situation and its graceful appearance," the society urged immediate action.[54] Perhaps sensing that the level of alarm about the dolmen's condition might raise its market value if the process were slowed, Byrnes and his lawyer began to ignore Office of Public Works correspondence. Matters got worse still when a group of "visitors" locked ten of the farmer's cattle into a nearby shed, where they remained undiscovered for three days without access to food or water. The farmer was enraged, and correspondence between Bord Fáilte, the Office of Public Works, and the farmer became heated.[55] By 1985 the Office of Public Works was exceedingly frustrated by the lack of progress.[56]

Despite the setbacks, Public Works continued to push for state acquisition of Poulnabrone, a task made even more difficult because the government and the farmer had fundamentally different ideas about what ownership of the dolmen should mean. For Public Works the owning of a national monument entailed serious responsibility because the landowner was effectively a guardian of the nation's past. From the government's perspective the purchase offer of £2,000 was more than generous under the circumstances,[57] and would even provide the farmer with a certain existential equanimity by making him "happy in the knowledge that he was co-operating in the preservation of an important part of our heritage."[58] The offer held little promise for the disgruntled landowner, however. According to the farmer's lawyer, Jennifer Foley, Byrnes "was like any other person who owned property . . . ; he would not part with any of it except for a price, and the fact that it was a national monument meant absolutely nothing to him."[59] If Poulnabrone was to pass into government hands, the farmer was going to receive a fair market value for the land, payment of legal costs and applicable taxes, and assurances that the site would be fenced off so that tourists would not trespass on his land.[60]

At wits end and fearing reports that the dolmen's structural integrity was deteriorating still further, the government was forced to act.[61] The Office of Public Works applied for a "guardianship order" on 21 November 1985. Although the order did not change ownership of the site, it did allow Public Works to carry out all necessary restoration activity.[62]

Following the completion of a major restoration project at Poulnabrone, attempts to purchase the site continued and the price inched ever skyward, hitting £60,000 in 1989.[63] Byrnes and the government each hired firms to evaluate the value of the property and predictably reached vastly different conclusions: The Public Works set the value at £10,000, while the firm hired by Foley valued the land at £50,000 because it "could be very valuable" for "commercial development."[64]

From the tourism perspective things proceeded to get worse. Early in 1993, Thomas Byrnes's insurance company advised the farmer that the constant traffic of visitors to the dolmen presented a substantial insurance risk and instructed him to take "every possible precaution to prevent people from gaining access to his lands." It did not take long for the farmer to construct a barbed-wire fence to stop the invasion of his property "by trespassers for the purpose of viewing the dolmen." Although he promised not to interfere with the structure in any way, he would now use "every possible means" to prevent tourists from viewing it.[65] The Office of Public Works quickly contacted the Department of Agriculture in the hope of attaining a suitable insurance package that might protect Byrnes and others like him, while keeping the dolmen open to its adoring public.[66]

By 1994 the dolmen was again accessible to tourist traffic, but now a new challenge was present—Byrnes had decided to use the site as a means of generating profit by standing near the fence and demanding a contribution from all visitors. This action brought a series of complaints—especially when "a scruffily dressed man" began approaching women in their cars to demand money—but there was little that could be done.[67] The dolmen was privately owned and therefore out of government control; Byrnes was free to collect whatever fees he wished. The cost of public liability insurance was extremely high, and while the Office of Public Works hoped that "the few farmers who are charging admission fees will cease the practice," it was nevertheless understandable.[68]

Finally, after twenty years of dead-end negotiations and seemingly endless confrontations with the landowner, the sordid mess drew to a close in 2001 after Byrnes and his lawyers set the asking price at £300,000.[69] Exhausted by the long battle for Poulnabrone, the Office of Public Works, now called Dúchas, asked the Department of Finance for permission to purchase the property for the amount asked. Finance approved the purchase just four days after receiving the Dúchas request.[70] At last Poulnabrone was in state hands, leaving Dúchas to begin drafting a plan for proper development of the site.

Perhaps the most striking issue raised by the Poulnabrone dolmen story is the attitude taken by public and private interests toward the desirability of acquiring historic sites by compulsory purchase. Under the 1930 National Monuments Act and the 1952 Tourist Traffic Act, compulsory acquisition of important sites was legal, and both Bord Fáilte and the Office of Public Works expressed a desire to purchase Poulnabrone, but neither of the two bodies was willing to exercise the statutory muscle at their disposal to force the issue. Private landownership trumped national aspirations.

Developing Irish Landscapes

In spite of challenges involving ownership and access, from the 1950s onward there was rarely a moment when the statutory tourist authorities were not directly seeking to train the Irish people to accept a specific view of land, to reshape the landscape, and to protect particularly scenic areas while at the same time developing sites to make them more friendly to outsiders.

During the Emergency in the early 1940s the vast bulk of Irish Tourist Board activity was directed toward resort and hotel development, and relatively little attention was paid to worries about landscape preservation and improvement, unsightly buildings, or related concerns. This priority was primarily because the listing of "special areas," as covered in part IV of the 1939 Tourist Traffic Act, was suspended during the first part of the Emergency and only reconsidered for implementation in 1944.[71]

It was not until the early 1950s that statutory tourist authorities became overtly concerned with improving urban and rural landscapes. Beginning in 1951 the Tourism Development Board implemented a national signposting campaign, launched its program called "Tourism Is Everybody's Business, the Tourist Is Everybody's Guest," became increasingly involved in planning decisions, and even began an angling-development scheme that altered whole ecosystems to fit tourist demands—all of which were designed to improve the landscape for visitors.

Signposting

In one story in their famous collection about an English resident magistrate negotiating Irish country life, Edith Somerville and Martin Ross observed, "In that part of Ireland in which my lot is cast signposts do not exist. The residents, very reasonably, consider them to be superfluous, even ridiculous, in view of the fact that everyone knows the way, and as for strangers, "haven't they tongues in their heads as well as another?" It all tends to conversation and an increased knowledge of human nature."[72] This attitude was not limited to the stomping grounds of "the Irish R.M.," and the same state of Irish signage was found in much of the Irish countryside. From the 1920s onwards, the Irish Tourist Association encouraged the erection of signposts as "a necessary advancement for the development of motor touring."[73] The resulting program was funded by the central government but carried out by local authorities;[74] unfortunately, it did not prove far-reaching enough, and the majority of Irish roadways were left unsigned and therefore incomprehensible to tourists and nonlocals alike. By the 1950s, when the amount of motor traffic began to increase steadily, the perplexing Irish road network had become a growing tourism liability, prompting the Tourism Development Board to undertake a nationwide signage campaign designed to order the Irish countryside for tourist consumption.

Bord Fáilte was required by statute to undertake signposting activities in the Republic of Ireland, incurring expenditure for the creation of signs and any further activities "in connection with the signposting of roads and the designation of recognised tourist routes, as the board may consider desirable in the interests of the development of tourist traffic."[75] In addition, the Tourist Board was also expected to erect interpretive signs in the vicinity of national monuments, both pointing the way toward important sights/sites and explaining them upon the visitors' arrival.[76]

The Tourist Board began its signposting program in 1951 in conjunction with the Automobile Association, which had started its own signposting scheme in late 1950. By July 1951 the route between Dublin and Belfast, the Dublin-Killarney road, and the route to Waterford from Dublin were all clearly marked, and plans were made to complete a series of advance-direction signs between Waterford, Cork, and Killarney as well as along the Dublin-Sligo road.[77]

The Tourist Board's efforts were directed by Kevin O'Doherty, who was responsible for studying the best approaches to signage, the acquisition of signs, and the distribution of these signs to relevant local authorities for erection. O'Doherty's first activity was to travel to Windsor, near London, to learn everything that he could about road signage from the acknowledged experts. He quickly discovered that the best road signage available was far beyond the means of his organization to acquire. An Bord Fáilte amounted to a group of "very small boys with very small budgets," and the massive illuminated overhead signs then becoming popular in Britain were simply not viable in Ireland.[78] Regardless of the utility of the impressive British signs, Ireland was forced to adopt a more conservative approach. The Tourist Board acquired three types of signs, including "advance direction signs," "fingerpost indicators," and "signs to national monuments." The first of these warned travelers on Irish trunk roads about approaching turns and about the direction in which they would need to go so as to reach their destination. Fingerposts complemented these signs at the turns themselves. And finally, national-monument signs were "intended to be partly descriptive, the aim being . . . to enable visitors touring the country to select monuments which may be of interest to them." In each case signs were presented in both English and Gaelic, with Gaelic presented on top.[79]

From the outset the relationship between Bord Fáilte and local authorities on the signage issue was tense. From O'Doherty's perspective, although signage was essential for tourist development, it was the responsibility of local authorities, not the Tourist Board. For tourist authorities, however, the inclusion of signage in the Traffic Act represented a cynical ploy by the Department of Local Government to indulge local unwillingness to develop a signage network. It was not that local authorities were opposed to tourism, but rather that they lacked initiative. O'Doherty recalls needing to fight with local authorities to accept signs; then, because the signs originated from An Bord Fáilte and not their employer, the engineers responsible for installing the signs argued that the signage represented a tourist-development activity and should earn them additional wages. This demand directly clashed with the Tourist Board's belief that the installation of road signs was already a local responsibility. As a result, once local authorities began to install the signs, resentment about low pay and management issues guaranteed that the signs were not always installed correctly or in the right locations; the placement of mileage signs and directional signage often bore little in common with actual mileages or directions to given locations.[80]

Despite the challenges, the signposting efforts of Bord Fáilte gradually gathered steam. By March 1954, 3,360 fingerpost signs had been ordered, with almost 2,900 already having been distributed; 290 of them were for national monuments.[81] On 14 March 1956 the 10,000th signpost was erected to guide visitors to Our Lady's Church at Glendalough. Also by that time the variety of signs had been expanded to include mileage markers and town or village names.[82] The program ultimately continued through the 1960s, with some 36,000 signs having been posted by 1965.[83]

Everybody's Business

When tourist authorities first informed the Irish people "Tourism Is Everybody's Business" in 1952, they hoped to teach ordinary people about how they could help foster the tourism industry. The advice was to provide courteous and friendly service and to work tirelessly to make yards, hedges, and built structures presentable by planting flowers, trimming bushes, and painting buildings.[84] While this counsel had roots in the activities of the Irish Tourist Association, it was probably motivated by foreign influences as well. For example, when the Irish Tourist Board sent a committee to Germany to study the Kraft durch Freude (KdF) program in 1937, the committee observed the KdF's large-scale program to improve the attractiveness of German homes and villages by planting flowers and removing unsightly structures.[85] Likewise, tourism officials were also aware that the more recent Festival of Britain encouraged the improvement of people's surroundings by promoting the removal of damaged buildings and the redesign of bombed-out landscapes.[86] Given such inspiration, there was little doubt among tourism developers that aesthetic reform was desirable and that Ireland should seek to remove unfortunate reminders of past or present poverty.

In keeping with this opinion, the Tourist Board applauded the efforts of tourism interests in Arklow, who took the ITB's advice and launched a program "to beautify our town and make it a pleasant healthy place for ourselves and an attractive happy resort for visitors." Among their activities, the Arklow Tourist Association created lantern slides depicting the townscape in the way that it *should* look. Members of the group also contacted their local authority in order to demand improved street lighting, additional public seating, and improved signposting, along with regular Sunday street cleaning.⁸⁷ Arklow's response inspired Bord Fáilte to expand its effort, working to encourage individuals, societies, and clubs to plant trees along streets, create memorial groves, and develop communal woodlots and "decorative shelterbelts"—all in the hope of improving Irish scenery through the addition of more trees.⁸⁸

In the following year the government agreed to support the An Tóstal festival. The public was told that An Tóstal would bring people to Ireland, creating new friends for the country, but that to be successful, the effort demanded that "we must be proud of what we have to show and therefore we must plan and prepare. Everyone can help, by decorating homes, by removing eyesores, by writing to friends abroad, by showing courtesy to our visitors, [and] by aiding in the setting up and activities of local Tóstal committees."⁸⁹ Civic pride was essential and local committees were the "most effective weapon" for creating it.⁹⁰ Newspaper readers were urged to "trim your lawns and plant flowers," and were informed that An Tóstal would "result in the brightening up of towns and villages and the clearing away of eyesores."⁹¹

A number of towns energetically adopted Tourist Board suggestions. Cork city went to great lengths to provide visitors with an attractive display. Shields of important Munster families were mounted on lampposts in the city's main thoroughfare. Plots of flowers, shrubs, and other plants were laid throughout the city; flags and banners were flown, and there were even plans to attain a variety of special lighting fixtures to ensure that the city would be attractive after the sun had set.⁹² Even smaller towns were excited; for example, Portumna in County Galway enlisted the help of local schoolchildren to "brighten" and "decorate" the town.⁹³

The public-education component of An Tóstal was judged to be a resounding success, and Bord Fáilte strove to expand the ability of the festival to promote civic pride and the implementation of local improvements.⁹⁴ Under the direction of Jim O'Brien, a former ITA member, the Tourist Board launched a new "Tidy Towns and Villages Competition" as part of the 1958 An Tóstal. There were no large prizes and little publicity, yet the idea was popular enough to attract fifty-three entries in the first year alone.⁹⁵ O'Brien's enthusiasm was infectious and spread like a pandemic of aestheticism as he crisscrossed the countryside from village to village and town to town, making comments about each place into a cassette recorder and finally reporting on the winners.

The Tidy Towns concept extended local Tóstal activities, like painted window-box competitions in County Cork, to the whole of Ireland and promoted the idea that houses should be brightly painted, flowers planted, litter collected, and derelict buildings removed, all the while hastening the development of civic responsibility.[96] The Tidy Towns and Villages idea immediately resonated at both the local and national levels. The minister for local government was especially smitten by the idea and promptly encouraged "earnest consideration" of the project by each local authority and "the desirability of taking part in the competition." Participation was "clearly in the national interest . . . so that there may be widespread awakening of civic consciousness in the direction of making and keeping towns clean, tidy, and generally attractive." In keeping with the Tidy Towns idea, the Department of Local Government urged measures to clear derelict sites, improve sanitary conditions, remove litter, and otherwise embellish townscapes by providing litter receptacles, planting trees and shrubs, maintaining public sanitary conveniences, and painting public buildings, to say nothing of working closely with shopkeepers to make further improvements.[97]

Backed by strong support, the Tidy Towns Competition quickly took hold. There were 82 entries in 1959 and 213 in 1960, and officials fully expected more towns to enter in subsequent years.[98] By 1964 Bord Fáilte reported that "Irish villages and towns looked markedly neater and more colorful than at any time in the past," and it attributed the improvement to the Tidy Towns Competition.[99] When the annual event was first launched, most Irish towns were dirty and lacked color, having the personality of "wet cement," but the new competition sparked an aesthetic revolution in Ireland's urban spaces that left behind pastel-painted buildings, flower boxes, and carefully cropped vegetation.[100]

Recognizing the potential for still further improvement, the Tourist Board expanded the competition, adding categories for resorts and coarse-fishing centers as well as awarding a prize for rural roadside properties. The latter category is particularly interesting because "contestants" did not register to compete, as was true in the other categories; rather, Bord Fáilte officials simply noted particularly attractive properties "which set an example to others in the district" while driving around the country. It was a less than subtle way of encouraging rural dwellers, using peer pressure and competition, to maintain their land and houses in a manner acceptable to tourists and the tourist authorities. While the Tourist Board was not really able, despite holding the required statutory authority, to forcibly acquire land, its officials were capable of pushing landowners to comply with the "national interest" in aesthetic terms by offering prize money and the opportunity to upstage the neighbors—all at the bargain price of just £7,500 in 1963.[101] In the following year Bord Fáilte further expanded the number of "surprise prizes," recognizing the potential that the awards had to influence the appearance of rural homesteads.[102]

Many local authorities and community organizations caught the Tidy Town bug. Meetings were held in community centers around the country to discuss ways to improve the chances of winning the competition. Enthusiastic citizens in Clonakilty, Co. Cork, for example, met regularly in the late 1960s and early 1970s to discuss Tidy Town results and their tactics for improvement. In October 1970 members of the Clonakilty Town Council decided to use the Bord Fáilte report on their town to pressure "the owners of property mention[ed] in the report as being unsightly and to ask them for their co-operation for the coming year." In the same year the council also employed the report to press the post-office authorities to improve the aesthetic appeal of the post office and the space immediately surrounding it. The report was further used to identify specific hedges and other shrubs requiring attention.[103]

Towns elsewhere took a similar interest. The urban council in Ennis, for example, launched its 1986 Tidy Towns campaign by promoting a special environmental seminar in a local hotel that included speakers from the Shannonside RTO and the secretary of the Keep Kilkenny Beautiful Committee—the local group that spearheaded the "Marble City's" successful 1985 campaign.[104] By February 1986 the Ennis Urban Council further increased its efforts to win the coveted Tidy Town title by investing £250,000 in such improvements as twice-weekly trash collection, maintenance of open spaces, and a program of environmental works.[105]

Kilkenny's approach to the competition was not limited to a well-organized and hard-working committee or costly campaigns by the local council, but also included local competitions, including one that pitted storeowners against one another to determine the most attractive storefront in the city. The competition pushed banks to completely abandon unsightly plastic signage in favor of cut stone. Each year the committee met to develop a "plan of campaign" that included monthly targets and plans to carry them out. While the committee itself was comprised of volunteers, the Kilkenny County Council did what it could to assist these efforts. Indeed, the group went so far as to carefully plan council-housing schemes so as to include the provision of liberal amounts of open space, parks, and trees—an action that earned a special award from Bord Fáilte.[106]

The composition of Tidy Towns committees varied across Ireland. Sometimes they were entirely driven by local authorities and at other times they were voluntary. Local church leaders frequently conducted the campaigns. Even more often, Tidy Towns efforts were the domain of women anxious to demonstrate their organizational abilities on a public stage. They sought to show Ireland that its women were far more than just good housekeepers; they were stewards of Irish places and spaces, with control over the aesthetic appeal of their country. It was a way for women to express both local and national pride and to be rewarded accordingly.[107]

The Tidy Towns concept was so successful from Bord Fáilte's perspective that the organization continued adding additional categories to the competition. By the end of the 1970s prizes had been added for best estate village, market town, fishing village, historic town, seaside town, city village (areas like Clonskeagh or Rathmines in Dublin), and commuter town—not to mention the overall prize and the surprise prizes included previously.[108] In 1980 the authorities even introduced awards for primary and post–primary school grounds, hoping to make certain that even schoolyards personified the right view of Irishness.[109] The number of towns participating also increased dramatically. In 1979, 754 towns and villages took part.[110] By 1984 the number of entries had climbed to 804, while a similar National Gardens Competition attracted 1,300 entries.[111]

Although tourist authorities did not view all Irish towns and villages as identical, they did have ideas about the essence of these places. Irish towns were "disarming in their simplicity," sometimes hinted at when "a distant church spire or castle gives warning," but otherwise nestled cleanly into the landscape. Irish towns featured "gaily-painted" gateways, "rows of white-washed stones," and farmhouses "with pink-washed walls and slated roofs." Even petrol stations were painted in "gay colours."[112] On approach, visitors should experience a smooth transition between "the open countryside" and "the closed, contained spaces of the narrow streets or village square." Townscapes should provide a contrast with distant views of hills, mountains, lakes, and seas. In essence, a "village might be called the 'snug' of the countryside [a snug is a quiet corner of a pub where conversation and contacts flourish in sociable surroundings]." Expanding the concept of the warm and welcoming pub, villages should possess individuality, emphasized by the use of creative color schemes possessing "all the charm and confidence of folk art."[113]

When judging towns, Bord Fáilte adjudicators never wished to forget the unique attributes of any town while applying a range of common criteria. For example, while judges were particularly interested in the harbor in seaside towns, the river in riverside villages, and the juxtaposition of mountain and town in hilly regions, they were especially vigilant in the search for those attributes not acceptable in *any* Irish town. Checklist in hands, judges drove slowly into these towns, paying careful attention to the approach. Were there unkempt hedges or rock walls? Was litter strewn along the roadside? Once inside the village, the judges then explored the town, looking for public spaces, attractive paint, flowers, and the integration of appealing built spaces with natural features. Plastic signage or even overhead telephone and electricity wires might badly damage a competitor's chance of dominating the competition, and Bord Fáilte made a point of informing towns that the "mess of overhead wires" quickly destroyed the appearance of Irish streetscapes and should be dealt with quickly by urban-development boards and local councils: such outward displays of modernity were unacceptable. Signage should be "traditional" and avoid unsightly plastic. It was even better if Gaelic were integrated into signage texts. Modern conveniences, while required *inside* Irish hotels, bed-and-breakfasts, and guest houses, were to be kept invisible from those walking down an Irish street. After all, tourists visited Irish towns to find out what it means to be Irish, noted one Bord Fáilte Tidy Towns judge, and the presentation of these towns was therefore an essential means of transmitting the right image.[114]

The competition was not entirely about presenting an image to visitors, but also stressed the presentation of that same image to locals as well by creating "a better place in which to live." The challenge was to retrain Irish people to work with one another toward a common objective. For any Tidy Towns committee to function, the traditional Irish tendency toward "jealousy and bickering" must be avoided, allowing "everyone, from the smallest child to the most senior citizen," to take part in the national improvement effort. Sound leadership, cooperation, and solid community relations, combined with local pride and a desire for color, cleanliness, good repair, politeness, and friendliness to all, along with school and youth involvement and a desire to succeed—all could be combined to create both a tidy town and better Irish men and women.[115] By pushing people to join together to improve their towns for visitors, the Tourist Board hoped to reshape the Irish people themselves. Aesthetic sense had to be changed, mutual appreciation and toleration fostered, and a sense of local and national pride instilled. The work of creating a tidy town extended far beyond the pursuit of an ever-increasing cash prize to that of fostering a better national community—from the built environment on up. This important enterprise was not a project that ever ended, and at the outset of the 1970s Bord Fáilte commented approvingly on the record number of Tidy Towns entries before stressing the need for persistent effort by all bodies involved in managing Irish landscapes and cityscapes in order to guarantee the continued Irishization of Irish spaces.[116]

Altering Ecosystems for Tourism

Beyond promoting improvements to built environments, tourist authorities exerted considerable energy toward molding ecosystems to match the demands of tourism. Even in the 1920s the Irish Tourist Association recognized the potential of angling tourism.[117] In 1926 the association launched a program to improve trout fishing in Killarney's lakes, beginning with a letter to the Department of Fisheries asking about the best approach to enhancing trout fishing in the area. The minister suggested that the ITA ask local anglers about the stock in the lakes, the average size of fish available, and the ease of catching fish before actually undertaking fish-planting operations.[118] These activities were subsequently carried out, and eventually a hatchery program was implemented with assistance from the Department of Fisheries, including the initial hatching of twenty thousand trout ova.[119] Later the program was expanded and an additional forty thousand ova were purchased, composed primarily of white trout, as recommended by the minister.[120]

While these early ITA efforts differed very little from long-time fish-farming practices, Bord Fáilte had a different idea and undertook an expansive and dramatic campaign to improve angling facilities, especially along the border with Northern Ireland. It was widely felt that the counties of Cavan, Monaghan, Longford, and Roscommon offered little to tourists. There were no dramatic sea cliffs, no wave-battered beaches, and while there were great expanses of bogland, these places were viewed as fruitful areas for turf harvesting but not for tourist development. On the other hand, numerous lakes and rivers had never been developed for angling tourism. In addition, Erskine Childers, a member of the cabinet and a TD for Athlone-Longford, took a particular interest in the area, and in his energetic fashion he urged Lemass to allow the Tourist Board to pursue an angling-development program there.[121] The first such program was approved in January 1953 and was operated in partnership with the Inland Fisheries Trust.[122] It was noted that the number of coarse fish was causing a dramatic deterioration in the quality of trout angling as well as a reduction in the length of the angling season in larger lakes. Local angling associations made some effort to address the problem, but they were largely unsuccessful. The plan devised by An Bord Fáilte and Inland Fisheries was to take place over five years and involved "a partial scheme of coarse fish elimination and trout salvage on inflowing rivers and streams in Lough Corrib and Mask and a somewhat complete operation on Lough Arrow." The Inland Fisheries Trust initiated the program in January 1953 with financial support from the Tourism Development Board.[123] During 1956 alone, 10,000 pike (one of which weighed 46 pounds) and 276,000 perch were removed from the seven lakes covered by the scheme, killed, and buried next to the lake. Several million perch ova were also removed. As predators were reduced, trout stocks climbed.[124]

Ironically, at the very moment when the program was proving most successful, doubts began to surface about its wisdom. Not all fishermen enjoyed catching trout or salmon as did the Irish. For example, the French enjoyed pike fishing, while English anglers had a soft spot for perch and other coarse fish—in striking contrast to Irish and American anglers, who sought brown and rainbow trout respectively. These other markets might prove more lucrative if the predatory fish were *not* removed from Irish waters.[125] It was estimated that Britain alone was home to at least two million coarse fishermen. This realization brought a sudden change in policy. The new "long-term fishery development program," implemented in April 1957, designated some areas for coarse fishing while continuing to exterminate predatory fish in others. Initial activities included the expansion of available accommodation and increased access to fishing areas, as well as the restocking of lakes with coarse fish. Efforts were also made to improve game fishing on the Shannon.[126] In the first months of the program thirty-five coarse-fishing centers were established. Classes were offered to local women at vocational schools in Leitrim, Donegal, and Westmeath on the proper way to prepare coarse fish—courses made necessary because the Irish themselves had no experience actually cooking such fish.[127]

Two years after the new plan went into effect, fifty-five coarse-fishing centers had been established and a series of twelve sea-angling festivals had been organized.[128] A special guidebook devoted to marketing the new coarse-fishing holidays highlighted what had been accomplished. Officials did not

> guarantee that as soon as you come to Ireland, you will start catching numbers of big fish; we cannot even guarantee that you will catch a fish at all, for fish are queer, unpredictable creatures, as every angler knows, and we want to be perfectly straight with you. We do, however, declare without fear of contradiction that your chances will be better here than elsewhere, that you will have a vast number of well-stocked, almost virgin waters at your disposal, and that the Irish people will do their best to see you enjoy yourself. The size of the catch is up to you—and up to the fish.[129]

Anglers took the bait. In 1959 fish-mad tourists spent as much as £675,000, compared with the £431,500 they had spent just a year earlier—an impressive return on the £54,000 invested in the plan.[130]

Ultimately, what is vitally important about the angling-development programs, beyond the obvious economic yield, is the fact that the tourist authorities were not content merely to shape Ireland's towns and villages or to take part in the planning of such projects. In addition, they extended their interest to altering aspects of Ireland's natural environment. In this instance foreign tastes were wholeheartedly catered to, and Irish lakes were molded to match the tourist gaze. The Irish public does not appear to have expressed significant interest in the angling programs. Whereas there was great popular awareness of the Tidy Towns Competition and widespread interest in landownership issues, Ireland's fish were left to dangle, unloved except by those—a growing fraternity of foreign visitors—who would pursue and eat them.

Conservation, Planning, and Development

It would be incorrect to assume that tourist authorities have spent the past eighty years looking only for ways to alter Irish landscapes and townscapes to meet tourist demands without also exerting effort to conserve environmentally sensitive areas, limit pollution, and promote responsible development. During the 1970s and 1980s Bord Fáilte was particularly active in encouraging responsible planning decisions, lobbying for environmental conservation, and even working to define how developments should look.

Up to 1963, Irish planning initiatives were not terribly successful. Following the Civil War, planning was overshadowed by the need for survival. Unemployment was a much larger concern than responsible building and design; housing problems necessitated quick action, not an extended muddle over design issues.[131] Significant planning legislation was passed in 1934, but there was "an absence of an adequate will to implement it."[132] During the 1940s there were increasing calls, primarily from architectural groups, to consider organized planning programs when constructing new buildings in Irish cities, especially Dublin. In 1942 these demands spawned a National Planning Conference that included representatives from twenty-five different organizations, including the Irish Tourist Board. The conference demonstrated Irish capacity to produce a broad planning movement, but unfortunately it generated little lasting success owing to political and ministerial apathy and "the inability of the government to come to terms with such a radical movement with interdepartmental implications." By 1944 any drive to update planning legislation had all but dissolved.[133] The first widely implemented legislation was passed in 1963. It was designed to achieve certain major objectives; these included the development of a more flexible planning system operated by local authorities and the devising of the means that would better enable local authorities to promote industrial and commercial development, to preserve amenities in both town and country, and to fairly determine the compensation payable to landowners for the specific restrictions imposed on them.[134] In the present context it is especially noteworthy that the 1963 Planning and Development Act was intended to help preserve amenities as well as to develop them—a substantial change from past practice because nature reserves, the protection of animal and plant species, and the protection of natural environments simply were not major issues before the 1960s.[135]

The foundation of An Taisce, the National Trust for Ireland, in 1948 also represented a substantial shift in Irish thinking about conservation. An Taisce sought to "preserve, for the benefit of the nation, lands of natural beauty, buildings of national historic or artistic interest, and, as regards land, to preserve (as far as practicable) its natural aspect and features and animal and plant life."[136] Initially the group consisted of some 250 members and concerned itself with "nature conservation and matters such as the flora in the Burren, County Clare, the state of the area surrounding Killarney, Kanturk Castle in County Cork, [and] the possibility of using Powerscourt House as a Georgian museum."[137] As time passed, An Taisce acquired some lands, began to manage a handful of Ireland's "big houses," and functioned as a lobby for environmental concerns, pushing the government to consider the impact of development on both plant and animal life as well as the aesthetic appeal of the countryside. Still, the body had no statutory role and was thus limited in its ability to carry out major projects.

Although the Irish Tourist Board was included in the 1942 Planning Conference (it was represented there by J. P. O'Brien), the body does not appear to have shown significant concern for planning or conservation issues in its day-to-day practices until at least the 1960s.[138] The Tourist Board's planning role, however, was dramatically altered by the 1963 Local Government (Planning and Development) Act, which recognized a number of specified bodies—including An Taisce and Bord Fáilte—to oversee the conservation aspects of the legislation because its framers "recognised the close connections between the quality of the environment and the tourist industry"—an outgrowth of the new consensus about the national importance of tourism.[139] The Tourist Board and other designated bodies were given responsibility to review development plans that might have a detrimental environmental or aesthetic impact within certain limitations (there were special exemptions for agricultural development such as piggeries).[140] Should any objection be made to a specific development plan, it could be appealed to the assigned bodies for review.[141] The Tourist Board's inclusion not only ensured that planning questions were constantly on Bord Fáilte's plate; it also provided the board with some power to back up its growing interest in conservation and environmentalism.

By the early 1970s the Tourist Board was thoroughly absorbed in its planning role, and besides reviewing planning petitions under the 1963 Planning Act, it became involved in projects designed specifically to define the physical shape of Irish development. In 1972, Bord Fáilte joined with the International Council of Societies of Industrial Design, the Kilkenny Design Workshop, and Córas Trachtala (the Irish Export Board) to promote a seminar attended by designers from around the world; their job was to study Irish tourist areas and to make suggestions about ways to improve existing structures and the aesthetics of future tourist development. The seminar was based on the idea that tourism "should be seen as a continuing social and educational process" in which tourists are conditioned to read a landscape in a given way, and children and young adults are made to understand the land in a particular manner defined from above. Tourism itself was considered as a way to demonstrate to visitors how local people live, but at the same time tourism must "appear to remain" secondary to other activities. At no point should the Irish people feel themselves to be "inhabitants of a tourist museum."[142]

After the consortium completed a survey of the Irish countryside, it released a detailed report covering everything from the style and physical placement of accommodation to the most attractive and functional designs for road signs. Every aspect of correct design for tourism needed to be integrated into the Irish landscape without announcing itself. Colors and materials should be chosen to match the local scenery, and furnishings should be made locally to assure continuity—an activity that would require ongoing effort to train locals to "be aware of and protective of their natural resources."[143] The group advocated a variety of changes to Irish roadways in order to exploit their scenic potential, including the planting of vegetation to enhance particular views or to camouflage undesirable ones.[144] Footpaths were suggested as an ideal way to promote "greater appreciation of the countryside."[145] Road signs, so much a part of Tourist Board efforts to carefully translate the network of roadways into a form easily consumable by tourists, were to be made more easily readable. In particular, "directional, informational, and utility signs could include Irish characters for the sake of atmosphere and national morale, but they should be properly designed from the point of view of legibility and recognition."[146] Perhaps even more interesting, the committee advocated changing the green color of Irish postboxes to something more visible lest tourists be unable to find them[147]—a somewhat startling suggestion because the boxes, many still displaying the royal crest from the days before independence, had been hastily painted green after the Anglo-Irish Treaty of 1921 in order to proclaim Ireland's newfound freedom.[148] Ultimately the report furnished a comprehensive series of design suggestions that were intended to balance the need to present a uniquely national landscape, increased automotive traffic, and the constant growth of tourist demand.

The International Council of Societies of Industrial Design report, however, had relatively little, if any, real impact. In 1989, Bord Fáilte, in conjunction with An Taisce, published yet another document that covered much of the same ground, carefully detailing how buildings should be constructed and where they should be sited. This time special emphasis was placed on using whitewashed siding and thatched roofs—materials that would "help ensure that Ireland's landscapes continue to be a source of delight not only for those who live and work there but also for the visitors for whom they are a major attraction."[149] Traditional cottages should be refurbished to meet new demands while maintaining the timeless qualities of the Irish countryside.[150] New structures should be positioned in such a way as to carefully blend in—placed in the same careful manner that Irish builders had reputedly used for hundreds of years.[151]

In spite of the initiatives of tourism authorities, Irish efforts toward responsible development have been less than successful. Travel writer Pete McCarthy recently reiterated common criticisms:

> I am not the first to observe that the landscape of rural Ireland has been badly defaced these last thirty years by the slapdash construction of suburban housing in places where there are no suburbs. . . . But before sneering at Irish bad taste, smug outsiders who live in twee English villages, like me,

should bear in mind that the bungalow blight is simply the logical outcome of Ireland's history of poverty; a poverty for which English landlords living across the sea in their carefully preserved villages must shoulder their fair share of the blame.[152]

While McCarthy's view of history probably contains some truth, a lack of older homes has little to do with the blight of new developments—the very developments upon which he is commenting in this passage. These are the result of often inadequately exercised planning restrictions, not of English oppression. Since at least 1968 planning efforts have been burdened by allegations of corruption. Erskine Childers, for example, was forced in 1968 to refute allegations by one Dáil deputy who alleged that property values were being raised by corrupt use of the planning process.[153] More recently, during the months in which this book was being researched, Ireland was rocked by a series of allegations stemming from the Flood tribunal that clearly revealed corruption in the building industry, to say nothing of the government and civil service.[154]

Besides the presence of corruption (at least in recent years), there was often conflict between local authorities and central planning bodies like An Foras Forbartha (the National Planning Board), to say nothing of a certain amount of public apathy.[155] Even in the area of environmental controls the Irish public showed less inclination for concern than those in other European countries.[156] Even so, Bord Fáilte took an ever-increasing interest in the protection of the environment in the early 1970s. In 1972 the Tourist Board, in conjunction with An Foras Forbartha, released a massive study of Ireland's coastal areas. This study not only surveyed the natural characteristics and beauty of coastal areas but also assessed the potential of these areas to support tourism development, paying particular attention to Ireland's Gaelic-speaking districts. The report suggested ways in which such areas could best be used, noting especially those areas whose beauty warranted protection, but also identifying those best suited to industrial development or urban expansion. Foreign investment in coastal districts was also considered, but its scale and significance were downplayed—Ireland was not being purchased by Europeans as Father Scanlon had once feared.[157]

In the years following this report, and with the tourist authorities' expanding interest in planning, environmental concerns were seldom absent from Bord Fáilte's annual reports. In 1974 Bord Fáilte argued that industrial development should be kept well clear of scenic areas so that foreigners and Irish people alike need not see drab industrial structures while consuming the beauties of the Irish countryside; the landscape should be divided into development zones, with some areas carefully protected and others sacrificed to progress.[158] Annual reports also provided opportunities to raise awareness of environmental threats. For example, in 1979 Bord Fáilte insisted that

> an attractive environment is the cornerstone of the Irish tourist industry. While the main tourist areas are recognised as designated areas in the Tourist Development Plan and are a primary concern, there continue to be many threats to the rural and urban environment. There is often a widespread indifference to the whole issue of conservation. Changes in the use of land and water resources as a result of industrialisation, new agricultural techniques, urbanisation, etc., and the frequent low standards in the treatment of sewage and industrial waste, poor road standards, and inadequate management of public facilities such as toilets, public spaces, and refuse dumps, pose an ongoing threat to the environment and overall quality of life.
>
> The efforts of community and voluntary groups at national, regional, and local level in tackling such problems must be commended. Hopefully, it is a sign of the awakening of a general understanding of the benefits of a clear and healthy environment, but much remains to be achieved.[159]

The message had not changed in 1981, when the board reported some progress and increasing public awareness of environmental threats, or in 1985, when Bord Fáilte drew attention to the problem that pollution was more widespread than previously feared.[160] Between the late 1960s and early 1990s Bord Fáilte repeatedly stressed the need for careful management of the countryside and the protection of Ireland's natural amenities. As long as the environment remained "the cornerstone of Irish tourism," it was essential for tourism authorities, the government, and the Irish people to take green-space issues seriously.[161] Indeed, the 1994–99 *Tourism Development Plan* envisioned environmental protection as a centerpiece of the drive to create "sustainable tourism." While the report claimed that there now existed "an unprecedented level of environmental awareness in Ireland," it also conceded that there was "no room for complacency" because "our superior environment is mainly due to a historically low level of development rather than to any preconceived plan."[162]

Representations of Irish Landscape

Photographic and literary representations of Irish landscape offered for tourist consumption have changed remarkably little with time, yet this fact makes the particular framing or choice of subject in tourist photographs no less important. Whether captured in 1926, 1972, or the mid-1990s, images of the Gap of Dunloe near Killarney, for example, almost always feature the roadway meandering through the rugged, rocky mountains, taken from slightly up the hillside, and featuring a jaunting car.[163] Even so, images were often produced to match new marketing demands. For example, during the 1960s motor touring became a major emphasis of Tourist Board marketing efforts, and as a result, photos of automobiles were increasingly introduced into tourist guidebooks and advertising—generally showing a motor car in the foreground and a happy couple enjoying the scenery either from the car itself or from a slight distance. These images clearly demonstrated to potential visitors that Ireland's richest beauty spots could be easily reached in the comfort of an automobile, and the photos were further enhanced by texts stressing the relative dearth of motor traffic on Irish roadways.[164] Once motorcars became a standard part of the lexicon of tourism photography, they did not disappear; the fundamental ingredients remained largely the same. If there was any major shift in official Tourist Board photography, it had more to do with the skill of the photographers, the use of models rather than actual tourists (beginning in 1960 and probably influenced by the appearance of John Hinde Studios in the marketplace), and, of course, a much wider usage of color images as printing techniques improved during the 1960s and 1970s.

Ireland was perhaps best known through postcards produced by John Hinde Studios. Hinde possessed an unparalleled understanding of tourist tastes. In particular, he recognized the need for vivid color, clearly expressing the notion *"I wish I was there."*[165] Hinde's images presented an idealized Ireland, one that tourists inevitably wanted to remember, regardless of how often it had rained during their trip. From the publication of his first postcards in 1957, Hinde broke with photographic and artistic traditions:

Creating the Tourist Landscape | 211

9. and 10. Photographs of the Gap of Dunloe near Killarney were almost always shot from the same handful of vantage points, as these images from 1972 and 1996 illustrate. Courtesy of Bord Fáilte Éireann–Irish Tourist Board.

"By introducing bright foreground colours in his cards . . . He stuck primary colours prominently in the foreground to accentuate to viewers that, yes, they were looking at a COLOUR photograph . . . He was shrewd enough to realise that an audience used to seeing black and white pictures didn't just want to see a bit of colour tinting, it wanted to see A COLOUR PHOTOGRAPH."[166]

In order to make certain that his images matched his aesthetic objective, Hinde's photographers bent over backwards to *construct* images of Irish landscape, rather than simply presenting narrow views as was true in most travel photography. It was not a case of waiting days for the correct lighting, as photographers have done since the first camera appeared in the 1820s; rather, objects were introduced to each image based on what the photographer felt *should* be present. Hinde's photographers always carried foxglove in their cars so that it might be planted in the foreground of photographs, even when the flower would not grow naturally in the spot in question.[167] More striking still, models were carefully dressed to provide the necessary authenticity to an image. In the early 1990s, during an exhibition of Hinde postcards at the Museum of Modern Art in Dublin, David Noble, a well-known Hinde Studios photographer, recalled a ten-day photo shoot in the Aran Islands during which he hoped to capture a shot of fisherman carrying their currach into the sea while another mended his nets in the foreground. Despite telling the men what he hoped to capture, the local models arrived directly from church and dressed in their Sunday best: hardly the picture of rugged fishermen in wellies and Aran sweaters that Noble imagined. Making matters worse, when an effort was made to outfit one of the locals in a suitable sweater, the only such garment available in all of the Aran Islands was moth-eaten and too small.[168]

As in Hinde's photographs, where the touristic desire for color and authenticity was carefully catered to, stories in *Ireland of the Welcomes* were chosen to meet the demands of an external gaze. From the beginning, the magazine's designer, a Dutchman named Jan de Fouw, exerted considerable influence on content because "as an outsider, I had more of an open eye to what was interesting in Ireland than the Irish themselves."[169] There was a conscious effort to escape the "Killarney syndrome" and to cover other aspects of Irish scenery and culture, usually with a bent toward personal-interest stories.

The coverage of Ireland's extensive boglands provides a case in point. Before the 1960s and 1970s these areas were not presented to tourists as desirable places to visit. Many of the Irish themselves were deeply ambivalent. Those who grew up on the bog were viewed as little more than "bog-trotters" and represented "the symbol of poverty and backwardness," "ignorance and illiteracy." The bog was "itself in the Irish mind . . . a symbol of aridity and barrenness."[170] Beginning in the 1930s the great expanses of turf began to inspire a different set of ideas among a handful of officials, who increasingly viewed these areas as a potential source of fuel, even while others maintained a healthy dose of "amused skepticism."[171] In 1934 the government established the Turf Development Board, renamed Bord na Móna in 1946.[172] In subsequent years the Turf Board discovered how to efficiently mine Ireland's peat resources, constructed massive turf-burning power stations, and proudly presented the program as an Irish industrial-development success story, taking what was useless and making it into something exceedingly valuable.[173] The bogs were not romantic spaces and certainly were not worthy of the tourist gaze, unless it was to see Irish cleverness at work.

By the early 1970s, however, the bogs were increasingly romanticized, and they were seen more and more as uniquely Irish. In 1970, *Ireland of the Welcomes* published an issue featuring "a day on the bog" that dealt with the time-worn tools used by farmers to harvest turf for their fires, enthused about the wonderful conversations that might be had with farmers as they cut turf, and declared the bog to be "a grand place when the weather's right."[174] Another article in the same issue described the bogs as a "national liability for at least a thousand years" that was made useful only after the acceptance of nationalist demands that the bogs be used to promote Irish freedom. Today, the author enthused, "the patriot's dream has come true. Research and mechanisation have turned turf production into a large-scale national industry. Bord na Móna (the Turf Board) has had a more dynamic effect on Ireland than practically anything that has happened in its history."[175] The Tourist Board was beginning to understand that tourists, especially those from America, found bogs unique, romantic, and interesting, but at the same time there was a need to continue using them as a symbol of Ireland's modernity—in striking contrast to the bog-trotter stereotype.

Six years later, the romanticization of the bog continued apace. Irish poet Seamus Heaney was called on to write about his experiences on the bog. Though he acknowledged the great financial benefits of Bord na Móna, his prose reflected a far more romantic view of these places than was current previously. While Heaney admired the enterprise embodied by the exploitation of the bog, he maintained an "irrational attachment to the unspoiled wastes." The bog was not just beautiful; it was a catalogue of Ireland's long past, "Jungian ground" which functioned as a kind of "geological memory-bank," a "treasure trove" of objects "retrieved bit by bit by the turf-cutter." The bog was a "dark casket" containing "clues to our past and to our cultural identity."[176] For Heaney it was a conflict between his head and his heart, the old struggle between an Irish identity that was forward-looking and modern, and a sense of Irishness rooted in a timeless past of the imagination. No longer were bogs a liability; instead, they constituted a storehouse of the Irish past, a direct link to timeless ancestors, and a beautiful unspoiled retreat from the present. It would be wrong to portray Heaney's view as one defined by tourists—his extensive catalog of bog-related poetry clearly shows his personal connection with these spaces—but the fact that Bord Fáilte chose to publish the poet's comments illustrates the growing tourist interest in these places. Finally, in 1987, the editors of *Ireland of the Welcomes* devoted an entire issue to the bog. This time readers learned about the types of bog, read poetry celebrating these uniquely Irish places, perused accounts of unique bog flora and fauna, discovered the archeological inheritance provided to the Irish people, and were made aware of the back-breaking but romantic experience of hand-cutting turf. Bord na Móna did not inspire outright criticism, but the uneasy relationship between conservation and exploitation was acknowledged in more blunt fashion than in previous issues. This time an author wrote that the case for environmentalism was long a difficult one to "impress upon Irish people—especially those who live beside the peatlands." For them, the bog represented a resource to be exploited; their attitudes were "utilitarian." Abstract concepts such as "ecosystems and biotopes" held little sway. Yet, on the other hand, the author added that more bogs should be preserved intact, thus casting aside the notion that the only use for Ireland's peatlands was the generation of a few more megawatts.[177]

The bog has become an openly contested space, a symbol of Ireland's successful ability to straddle both ancient and modern living, to debate and discuss its places, spaces, and past. Bogland is no longer synonymous with backwardness; instead, it is thoroughly romanticized and celebrated for the ecosystem, history, and unique scenery available there. It was a transformation that had little to do with Bord na Móna propaganda and far more to do with the tourist gaze and with official desires not only to satisfy that gaze but also to bring tourist money into areas like Roscommon, which previously had little to offer tourists in the way of scenic grandeur or famous historic sites/sights.

Conclusion

From the first publications of the Irish Tourist Association to the most recent books and films by Bord Fáilte and Tourism Brand Ireland, Irish landscapes and townscapes have been one of the most important aspects of the tourism product. Tourists have flocked to places like Killarney in order to consume beautiful spaces, and tourist authorities have responded by working to physically shape Irish landscapes, whether through development and improvement projects or through conservation. Likewise, local voices like those of Father Scanlon and Lord Sligo, to say nothing of the numerous Tidy Towns committees, have also sought to ensure that Irish aesthetics and economics fell into line, presenting Irish landscapes and townscapes in a uniquely "Irish" way. Tourist guidebooks and postcards reflect a gradual trend toward niche-marketing (motor touring, for example), the growing importance of new technology (such as color photography), and even changing ideas about which landscapes are desirable and appealing (the bog).

From the 1920s the Irish looked upon their physical spaces as a way to portray Irishness to the world, and tourism developers encouraged their fellow citizens to actively consider the foreign gaze when building new structures or maintaining old ones. Most expressed a palpable desire not only to attract tourism income but also to show Ireland in the most positive light possible. The alteration or preservation of physical spaces was viewed in nationalist terms every bit as much as in economic ones. At the same time attitudes about the importance of earning a living *in* Ireland, as in the case of the Gaelic language revival, were never far from the surface for many groups. Landownership represented a potential source of revenue, a fact that could produce behavior that was either selflessly patriotic or an outright insult to the greater good, as in the case of Poulnabrone, depending on circumstances.

In the final analysis this chapter suggests that the Irish landscape has been an important area of debate about Irishness. The active effort by many Irish people to shape their physical space had the effect of melding environmental and aesthetic trends with economic concerns and long-standing attitudes toward landownership; the result was a long-running dialogue about uniquely Irish places and spaces.

7
Tourism and the Tiger, 1994–2007

Beginning in 1987, Ireland experienced arguably the most dramatic transformation in the country's entire economic history; the "Celtic Tiger" of the mid- and late 1990s sparked hitherto unimaginable economic development, construction, and job growth. Unemployment, once the bane of Irish life, virtually disappeared. Beginning in 1994, some one thousand jobs were added each week, more than fifty thousand per year. By 2000, Ireland was *importing* workers while attracting many of its native sons and daughters home from "exile." The change was so dramatic that when this book was being researched, potential immigrants faced long lines at the immigration office, many opting to camp out, joining the queue in the earliest hours of the morning in order to assure service. Job growth reflected stunning economic expansion. Irish growth rates exceeded all others in Europe and often surpassed the four "Asian Tigers." In 1995, the country enjoyed a 10 percent increase in gross domestic product (GDP), while in 1996 the gross national product (GNP) was three times higher than at any point in the previous decade, averaging 5.4 percent in the four years to 1997. Growth rates were the highest in the world, some 7.5 percent per year, and inflation was low. The national debt was reduced to 69 percent of the GNP in 1997. Irish living standards soon rose to match the European average for the first time.[1] Although tourist postcards continued to feature the slogan "Rush Hour in Ireland" atop a sheep-strewn roadway, life actually moved at a pace closer to the speed of now nearly ubiquitous BMWs.

The tourist industry both contributed to and was altered by the Celtic Tiger. By 1994, the debates about how to present Ireland to visitors and the desirability of doing so had established an efficient and modern tourist industry. Tourism products were in place. Marketing was sophisticated. The Irish image was welcoming and friendly. The Irish people built it; now the tourists came in unimaginable numbers. From 1994 onward Irish tourism expanded by as much as 18 percent each year—staggering when compared with the international average of only 4.5 percent during the same period.[2] Although England was always Ireland's largest single source of tourism revenue, profound growth in the English market continued during the boom period. Between 1993 and 1997, for example, the number of British tourists increased by 17 percent, from 1,783,000 to 2,590,000.[3] These numbers reached 3,494,000 in 2000. At the same time, revenue increased from £401.6 million in 1993 to £873.4 million in 2000.[4] Growth in the North American market was equally impressive with revenue growing 18 percent between 1993 and 1997, while the number of American visitors increased by 16 percent. While just 422,000 North Americans visited Ireland in 1993,[5] by 2000 this number grew to 1,058,000. The increase in North American earnings was notable, moving from £316.6 million in 1996 to £541.8 million in 2000.[6] The numbers were similarly positive from Europe, which had only become a substantial segment of the Irish tourist market in the 1980s.[7] In 1987, 382,000 Europeans, mostly from France and Germany, visited Ireland.[8] By 1997 this number reached 1,168,000,[9] and by 2000 it hit 1,451,000. Earnings increased from £457.7 million to £578.1 million during the same period.[10]

The Irish made Ireland Irish and then successfully sold their new identity to the world, but there was nothing fixed about the new product. The two great tourism-related debates remained. What does it mean to be Irish and how should Irishness be balanced with the nation's interests? This concluding chapter examines both the continued transformation of the Irish tourism industry since 1994 and the struggle to reconcile Irishness with economic demands. After examining why tourist numbers increased so dramatically during the 1990s, the chapter outlines continued government efforts to reformulate the tourist industry to more closely meet the national interest. The final section illustrates that the challenge of balancing culture, economic need, and disparate ideas about the meaning of Irishness remain an important part of Irish national discourse.

Coming of the Golden Horde

It is virtually impossible to identify any single cause for the explosive increase in tourist traffic to Ireland during the 1990s. Instead, several specific conditions of possibility combined to create an environment ripe for dramatic growth. These include: the long-term effort of tourism advocates and others to create a successful tourist industry (see chapters 1–6); the advent of government spending commensurate with the industry's significance (see chapter 3); increased political stability in Northern Ireland; the sudden "pop culture" notoriety that resulted from a proliferation of popular Irish rock bands and Irish-themed films; and the significant increase in the number of Irish pubs and products around the world. When these factors combined with a favorable economic situation in the United States and Britain, as well as with a continued expansion of Irish tourist products and accommodation, the pump was primed for previously unimagined expansion. The country had something to sell and the infrastructure necessary to sell it. It is worth examining several of these factors in turn.

The End of Violence

Despite a general trend after World War II toward tourism growth, Irish tourism suffered a series of severe difficulties in the 1970s related to two oil crises (1973 and 1979) and, more important, violence in Northern Ireland.[11] In the years after partition, tourism tended to draw Northern Ireland and the Republic closer together. The Irish Tourist Association and its Northern counterpart, the Ulster Tourist Development Association (UTDA) had close ties during the 1920s and 1930s.[12] During the 1940s, cross-border tourism cooperation was in contrast to the official "cold war" that raged between North and South and represented a rare *public* display of collaboration during a period when the two states were officially divided by a deep chasm of mutual antagonism.[13] Cooperation continued, albeit behind closed doors during the 1950s,[14] and tourism topped the agenda during the famous meetings between Irish Taoiseach Seán Lemass and Northern Ireland Prime Minister Terence O'Neill in January 1965. The two men agreed on the value of developing cross-border tourism links, and it was decided to explore several areas for cooperation; these included the possibility of joint promotion abroad, the encouragement of "inter-flow between the two parts of Ireland," the abolition of the *triptyque* system for private cars at the border, and consideration of permitting the free passage of hired cars through border checkpoints.[15] It was critical to eliminate any hassles that travelers might encounter.[16] There was also discussion of launching a joint venture to develop Enniskillen Airfield, a regional airport that would facilitate more efficient travel to Sligo, Donegal, and Leitrim, as well as attracting more tourists to Fermanagh and Tyrone.[17] Finally, the two leaders affirmed that their respective ministers with authority for tourism development, Erskine Childers in the South and Brian Faulkner in the North, should hold joint talks in the near future.[18] This promising state of affairs lasted until the onset of the Troubles in 1968.

Throughout the 1970s and 1980s, there were regular meetings between officials from both North and South; tourism was almost entirely at the mercy of the political situation, however. After the IRA cease-fire took effect in August 1994, the road was cleared for an increased tourism push in Northern Ireland as well as for an expansion of North-South tourism cooperation. In November of that year authorities from both countries announced that a £6million cross-border marketing campaign would be launched in 1995 in the hope of attracting an additional 92,000 tourists. While details were not immediately announced, it was agreed that the two tourist boards would collaborate on an "Ireland Vacations" television campaign in Britain, America, France, Germany, and Holland. As always, the campaign would include houses, gardens, literary tours, museums, castles, and heritage and cultural attractions. The cease-fire represented what Charlie McCreevy, Dublin's minister for tourism and trade, called an opportunity to "maximise the island's greatest asset—the natural beauty and heritage." McCreevy's Northern counterpart agreed, predicting, "tourism has the capability and imagination necessary to seize the opportunities which now present themselves." And opportunities there were: by October 1994 the Northern Ireland Tourist Board (NITB) had already experienced an increase of over 90 percent in visitor inquiries as compared with the previous year.[19]

In the following year a more significant program was announced that called for an integrated island-wide "Tourism Brand for Ireland" to be launched in 1997. It was anticipated that the plan would cost £5 million to kick off and some £20 million to £30 million annually thereafter. Bord Fáilte and the NITB would collaborate on the project[20]—ultimately reaching a level of cooperation that was celebrated by a special award granted by England's *Observer* newspaper in 1996; the award recognized the two boards as "a model of cross-border cooperation, as they have combined their respective strengths to promote an industry that remains central to Ireland's long-term economic development."[21]

Bord Fáilte was very excited about the new program, envisioning it as "a critical change in focus for the marketing of the island of Ireland over the next five years." Tourism Brand Ireland represented the first time that "all of Irish tourism will be able to unify behind a single market initiative, a tourism brand which will contain the same central message, with variations and modifications which meet the needs and expectations of individual markets and cultures." The program, it was argued, would provide a powerful tool, strengthening the island's market position and allowing Ireland to attain its ultimate tourist potential.[22]

On 11 November 1996, Tourism Brand Ireland was launched, eighteen months after the initial market research had commenced. I have already described the emotionally evocative video that represented the first installment of the new marketing program (see introduction); it was only one part of a "complete portfolio" of materials compiled to communicate the central message of the campaign—that Ireland was not so much a place as "an emotional experience." In all cases the term "Ireland" was used, always in English, without denoting North or South.[23] It was as though past conflicts between the two Irelands never existed, as though sectarianism was not even a memory.

The development of the new program brought the long period of Troubles-related pessimism to an abrupt halt. In Northern Ireland, for example, tourism numbers began climbing very soon after the first announcement of the cease-fire, and a new spirit of cooperation between North and South on tourism matters arose shortly thereafter. Despite occasional outbreaks of violence, the new environment even caused tourism officials in Belfast to be buoyant with optimism after tourism shot up 67 percent in just one year,[24] and these officials subsequently launched a campaign to promote the proliferation of bed-and-breakfasts on the Falls Road, the working-class neighborhood most closely associated with the IRA.[25] As far as many tourists were concerned, there were no longer any reasons *not* to travel to Ireland. Crossing the border no longer required special paperwork as it had before 1965, Northern Ireland was safe for visitors, and there was little reason to fear traveling freely across the whole island—a fact that tourism authorities could publicize widely.

Even so, there were further challenges. While decommissioning and the creation of a new policing body attracted most of the news coverage, establishing cross-border groups to handle tourism, fishing, and the rest also proved controversial. In April 1998, John Bruton, leader of the Fine Gael party, explained that the purpose of these efforts was to build a "structure of co-dependence which makes conflict impossible" by replacing the "traditional aspirations which made conflict inevitable up to now." The problem was that the various parties involved could read efforts toward this end differently. When unionists proposed developing joint cooperative ventures with Scotland, nationalists viewed the suggestion as a clear attempt to strengthen the union, while nationalist efforts to develop cross-border ventures were seen as an extension of Lemass's original policy to use cooperation to move toward a united Ireland. The "game of suspicion would gradually corrode the new institutions."[26]

At the end of November 1998, Tony Blair, the British prime minister and one of the driving forces behind the process that led to the Good Friday Agreement, flew to Ireland to launch a joint British-Irish council that would address issues spanning the Irish Sea as laid out in the agreement. Blair used the meeting to begin pushing for the establishment of cross-border cooperative bodies. Although there was considerable enthusiasm for the possibility of expanded all-Ireland marketing,[27] tourism and transport were already proving problematic because the Ulster Unionist Party (UUP) was unwilling to accept all-Ireland distribution of European development funds—money that would invariably benefit the Republic disproportionately.[28] Unionists insisted that tourism be removed from the list of cross-border bodies in favor of the development of separate organizations that would work together in the same manner that had been in place since the mid-1960s.[29] During their discussions Blair and Trimble left tourism on the table, but when they agreed to the establishment of six cross-border bodies on 24 November 1998, tourism was omitted from the list.[30]

By 1 December all consensus had eroded and there was talk that the devolution of powers called for by the Good Friday Agreement might not take place. Challenges existed on both sides of the border. While nationalists in Northern Ireland viewed North-South bodies as a "counter-weight" to the unionist majority, unionists were reluctant to agree to extensive cooperation for the same reason. Meanwhile, the government in Dublin resisted the establishment of cross-border bodies out of a reluctance to restrict departmental authority.[31] Two days later, Tony Blair returned to Belfast to find a solution to the impasse.[32] By the following morning, 4 December, a tentative agreement was reached on four North-South implementation bodies: trade and business development, transport, EU programs, and tourism. The plan was certainly not complete, and the deadlock was not yet forgotten, but progress did seem to be at hand.[33] The parties reached a final agreement on 18 December, following yet another eighteen-hour series of negotiations ending in what one delegate called "a victory for common sense." This time six cross-border bodies were agreed, with one more now included as "an unofficial seventh cross-border body to regulate tourism." This seventh body would be created through the merger and privatization of the Northern Ireland Tourist Board and Bord Fáilte.[34]

Relatively little changed in 1999 in terms of cross-border tourism cooperation. To be sure, Northern Ireland enjoyed a dramatic tourism expansion, showing growth of almost 20 percent between 1999 and 2000. Further growth was predicted following the establishment of the new cross-border company.[35] Tourism Ireland Ltd. was incorporated in December 2000 after the circulation of a memorandum outlining the functions of the North/South tourism company,[36] and it was given responsibility for all international marketing beginning in 2002. The new publicity body comprised one hundred former Bord Fáilte employees and thirty from the Northern Ireland Tourist Board, with another twenty to be hired by the Northern authorities. The new company acquired "ownership and management of Tourism Brand Ireland, strategic all-island destination marketing in all markets outside the island of Ireland, and responsibility for the entire overseas office network." Although Tourism Ireland Ltd. was assigned the task of delivering international marketing materials, Bord Fáilte and the Northern Ireland Tourist Board remained in charge of developing the underlying products. The two national boards also retained control over marketing domestic tourism, research and planning, niche marketing, regional marketing, the implementation of sports-tourism initiatives, festivals and cultural events, the grading of hotel premises, and the development of sustainable tourism.³⁷

With North and South working together, there was no longer any reason for tourists to stay away. The new structure would pose challenges and the success of the new venture would depend on a "positive attitude and a willingness to co-operate," but in the short term Irish tourism was freed of a significant stumbling block.³⁸

Popular Culture and Irish Products

Ireland's growing status as a center of popular culture, in contrast to its earlier obscurity, aided the new publicity effort. Following the foundation of Bord Fáilte in the 1950s, it became painfully obvious to tourism promoters that Ireland was largely unknown beyond the shores of Éire: "Ireland didn't exist outside Ireland." Americans, of course, celebrated St. Patrick's Day, but tourist authorities believed that there was little Irish about the American version of the holiday; even the whiskey consumed was Scottish. From a tourism standpoint continental Europeans often confused Ireland with Iceland, a cold, dreary, and frozen rock somewhere in the Atlantic Ocean.³⁹ In an attempt to correct this misunderstanding, the Export Board, Fógra Fáilte, Aer Lingus, and the Department of External Affairs formed a cultural relations section during the 1950s in order to "get Irish things better known." The group worked to market Irish products like Jameson's whiskey and Guinness stout; they strove to create a widespread belief in the "genuine Irish welcome" and to make it clear that Ireland was not a desolate rock in the North Atlantic, but rather a green, vibrant, and quickly developing yet timelessly rustic country.

As it happened, the group's efforts proved remarkably successful. Guinness and Jameson's whiskey are now ubiquitous. Surveys conducted by Bord Fáilte consistently show that tourists overwhelmingly cite the "Irish people" as one of the highlights of their travels and primary reasons for traveling.⁴⁰ And, of course, prefabricated Irish pubs now dispense their libations in virtually every city around the world, made to order by a Dun Laoghaire–based company specializing in selling all the right kitsch.⁴¹

Ireland also received a dramatic boost as a prospective tourist destination when filmmakers started to represent the country in popular films. John

Ford's *Quiet Man* (1952) inspired untold numbers of American tourists to visit Cong, County Mayo, after initial release of the movie. Subsequent showings on television and eventually VHS and DVD further enhanced the picture's impact. Some years later, David Lean's *Ryan's Daughter* (1970) sparked a similar increase in tourism around the Dingle Peninsula. Yet these early Irish-centered films represented only the tip of a much larger iceberg.

In 1973, the Arts Council of Ireland was empowered to assist the creation of an Irish film industry. In 1977, the Arts Council took advantage of this power by providing film script awards to indigenous writers. The film *Poitín* (1978), directed by Bob Quinn, was the first beneficiary of the new monies and helped inspire the creation of the Irish Film Board in 1981. Between 1981 and 1987 the Film Board helped fund work by major directors such as Neil Jordan and John Boorman, establishing them as significant figures in cinema and going some way toward making Ireland an attractive location for and subject of major films. Between 1988 and 1992, the government further increased efforts to attract filmmakers by offering special incentives to those willing to make their movies in Ireland, with significant results; movies included: *The Courier* (1988), *Reefer and the Model* (1988), *The Field* (1990), *The Commitments* (1991), *Into the West* (1992), and *Far and Away* (1992). Although the box office for these films was not always huge, they helped further establish Ireland as a film center.[42] More movies followed, including blockbusters such as Mel Gibson's Oscar-winning epic *Braveheart* (1994) that was set in Scotland but largely filmed in the Wicklow Mountains outside of Dublin. More often than not, movie audiences found a rustic, simple, friendly Ireland that was little removed from the tourist board image that was by now well established. The impact on Irish tourism was dramatic. Naoise Barry, film commissioner for the Irish Film Board, summed up the situation by saying, "Irish cinema has a huge impact on Ireland's tourism industry. [Major films] will be seen by millions around the world for years to come. Ireland's rural landscape has enormous appeal to film-maker and tourist alike."[43] In 2007, Fáilte Ireland (see below) estimated that film and television representations of Ireland were responsible for as much as €250 million in tourism revenue annually.

At the same time, especially among a younger audience, the popularity of rock bands like U2 and The Corrs should not go unnoticed. Quite simply, during the 1990s, U2 became the most popular rock band in the world. Their records and CDs sold many millions of copies, their songs received staggering airplay, and their concerts packed massive stadiums and outdoor venues around the world—each show resembling a gargantuan revival meeting, a tribal gathering, more than merely a rock concert. In the present context the group's success is important because

> it is difficult to read or hear anything relating to U2 without confronting sooner or later that they are an "Irish" band. If individual members do not raise the issue, commentators, journalists, or fans feel compelled to. Although it is impossible to define the category of "Irishness," a large part of the band's significance and impact depends specifically upon its national status in an increasingly multinational world, and particularly on the great variety of connotations which trail that identity into the twenty-first century.[44]

Unlike most Irish bands, U2 remains based in Dublin—Bono (Paul Hewson) and The Edge (Dave Evans) living just south of the city in the wealthy suburb of Killiney.[45]

For music fans across Europe and America the country of U2, the Pogues, The Corrs, Van Morrison, Enya, Sinéad O'Connor, the Chieftains, and Riverdance represented a significant cultural draw throughout the 1990s—something on which Dublin Tourism has tried to capitalize in recent years with a Dublin music-scene walking tour that traverses the city from one important musical site to the next. Rock music and the continuing popularity of traditional Irish music have made Ireland "hip," and when combined with the Celtic Tiger image of Ireland as a country on the make, it is unsurprising that young people flooded in. The Emerald Isle is no longer a destination purely for families and the more mature, but now exerts a strong attraction for younger visitors—a fact that makes itself abundantly clear when wandering Dublin's streets or traveling around the country.

Fáilte Ireland

In contrast to the 1990s, the first years of the new millennium were difficult ones for the Irish tourist industry. The initial "crisis descended from the skies" and had "the potential to torpedo much of the economy and much of what has been achieved in growth."[46] Foot-and-mouth disease, a viral infection that causes high fever as well as blisters on the tongue and feet of cloven-hoofed animals, struck Great Britain with a vengeance beginning on 20 February 2001. Because the disease spreads quickly and is virtually untreatable, the only recourse is to destroy whole herds of livestock. The first outbreak was in Essex, England, and within weeks 2,024 more farms were afflicted.[47] The Countryside Agency put the cost at between £800 million and £2.4 billion in livestock losses, while British tourism suffered a still worse fate, losing between £2 billion and £3 billion.[48] Ireland was spared the horrors of widespread destruction—only one farm, in Proleek, County Louth, was actually hit by the disease—but tourism still suffered. To avoid a widespread epidemic, the Irish government shut down the countryside and many attractions. Livestock could not be moved, hill walking was banned, national parks were closed, angling was stopped, equestrian sports were forbidden. In effect, the country was closed to tourism. Forty-one days after the outbreak, the government finally announced that the country was open again.[49] By August authorities were breathing a sigh of relief. Tourism numbers were down by 2.4 percent, largely because of a significant drop in English tourists, but overall "it could have been worse."[50]

Yet natural disaster was not the only threat to the tourist industry. The September 11 terrorist attacks in New York City, in the skies over western Pennsylvania, and in Washington, D.C., sent shock waves around the world. It was not simply that nearly three thousand people were dead for reasons that most people did not understand, but that passenger planes were used as weapons. The image of planes flying into buildings was like something drawn from a Hollywood action film and it was more than many travelers could stomach—even when world governments, especially the United States, dramatically enhanced airline security. The impact was severe; in the United States alone, the airline sector lost 20 percent of its value overnight. Flights were cut, jobs were eliminated, and travelers stayed home—at least initially. Expanded airline security only made travel seem that much less desirable.[51]

For tourism officials in Ireland, the horror was twofold. Just as was true for millions of people around the world, the attack prompted shock and grief. Closer to home, the second horror was the reality that the devastation at Ground Zero in New York "will resonate in the Irish industry well into next year." Bord Fáilte predicted "big losses" for the Irish tourism sector,[52] and Dr. James McDaid, the minister responsible for tourism development, predicted as much as a 17 percent drop in tourist traffic extending well into 2002.[53] A drop in tourism revenue, in turn, meant lost jobs and lost livelihoods.

While foot-and-mouth disease and terror attacks were visible threats, the Irish tourist industry faced another challenge as well: the Irish were slowly losing their reputation for friendliness, especially in Britain. Always the largest market for Ireland's tourist product, the number of British holidaymakers dropped slightly in 1999 from 970,000 tourists to 940,000. Faced with what authorities hoped was not a long-term downward trend, Bord Fáilte hired an Edinburgh consultancy firm to examine the problem. The firm's report was worrying.[54] As far as tourism authorities were concerned, "nothing in the entire array of the Irish tourist product is more important than the quality of the Irish welcome," yet the report made clear that many prospective tourists no longer felt the same welcome they had come to expect.[55]

The problem was probably not a fundamental shift in Irish character, but rather the collective impact of daunting change. As noted above, Ireland went from being poor and backward to relative affluence almost overnight. At the same time, tourist numbers far exceeded the actual population of the country itself. With the world turned upside down, it hardly seems surprising that the people of Ireland needed time to adjust. They needed to undergo the kind of dialogue detailed in these pages. They needed to collectively assess what it meant to be Irish in a land of BMWs, widespread tourism, and the sudden availability of a hitherto unimaginable standard of living.

Finally, there was at least one other factor that required the attention of authorities: the reality that tourism marketing in both Northern Ireland and the Republic was, for the first time, to be conducted by the same organization: Tourism Ireland Ltd. As noted, the creation of a single body to handle all foreign marketing of Ireland was a symbol of peace and cooperation, and the developments that prompted the creation of Tourism Ireland played an important role in the tourism boom of the 1990s. Yet Tourism Ireland had another effect as well, this one more worrisome for those still working for Bord Fáilte. Specifically, Tourism Ireland Ltd. assumed one of the tourist board's most important tasks—overseas marketing, raising the not insignificant question of whether the old structure for Irish tourism development was still relevant in the twenty-first century.

As foot-and-mouth disease, the disappearing welcome, the impending launch of Tourism Ireland Ltd., and eventually 9/11 struck home, government and tourism officials considered how best to address the challenge of developing tourism in a new millennium. Minister for Tourism Dr. James McDaid asked himself an unsurprising question: was it time to shake up the bureaucratic structure of Irish tourism? Bord Fáilte was a more professional and sophisticated organization than it had been in 1953, but was it suited to new realities? The desire to centralize control by creating Dublin-led Regional Tourism Organisations had gone wrong almost immediately during the mid-1960s; was it now time to assume *real* centralized control? Could a new organization reverse the perception problem while developing new marketing strategies that would continue to expand Ireland's tourism marketplace? Might a new tourism organization, freed from its history and armed with a new structure, ultimately create new attractions and new plans? Now that Tourism Ireland handled overseas marketing, was Bord Fáilte structured in the most productive fashion for handling domestic tourism development? For McDaid, the answer seemed overwhelming: it was time to create a new tourism organization and time to retire Bord Fáilte.

For their part, Bord Fáilte officials and staff were content to proceed as they had always done, setting goals, striving to achieve them, and, when faced with a problem such as the disappearing welcome, looking for ways to quietly encourage changed behavior. As a case in point, to solve the problem of the disappearing welcome, Bord Fáilte used the same strategy that so successfully redefined the Irish landscape: they launched a new competition, the "Irish Welcome Awards," which rewarded those who truly embodied the old "Céad Míle Fáilte" as opposed to the new "Frosty Fáilte."[56] As far as many in Bord Fáilte were concerned, the old structure was far from broken and the evidence to support this view was clear to see; in 2001 British travel agents voted to award Bord Fáilte the prestigious Travel Trade Gazette Award for top tourist/destination board in the world.[57]

Neither awards nor the status quo was acceptable to McDaid and his colleagues in the Department of Arts, Sport, and Tourism. In late August or early September 2001, the government contacted the directors of Bord Fáilte and CERT, the Council for Education, Recruitment and Training, suggesting that the two organizations amalgamate.[58] Like Bord Fáilte, CERT was a product of the staggering tourism development efforts of the 1950s and 1960s. The government formed the council thirteen years after the Christenberry report (see chapter 2) had recommended a formalized structure for training hotel workers, thus taking responsibility for training away from Bord Fáilte and so freeing the tourist board to single-mindedly pursue development and promotion work.[59] As time passed, CERT established training centers around Ireland at Killybegs, Sligo, Galway, Limerick, Tralee, Cork, Waterford, Tallaght, Dublin, and Athlone. Students could pursue courses in cooking, waitressing, housekeeping, tourism, bartending, reception, and management, among other careers.[60] Given the striking lack of government records or Dáil debate about the organization, as well as a surprising lack of contentious news coverage, CERT apparently sparked relatively little controversy and was successful in reaching a large client base. In 1992 alone CERT provided training to some 10,000 students.[61] In 1995, during the first years of the Celtic Tiger, no fewer than 98 percent of CERT graduates found employment, despite the fact that the number of students rose to 11,500.[62] The organization was the very model of accomplishment.

Successful or not, McDaid was convinced that "one agency, capable of delivering more integrated, streamlined programs and services, might provide the best delivery model for supporting the future development of the industry in line with Government objectives." On 5 September 2001 officials from both the tourist board and from CERT notified McDaid that they accepted the new initiative.[63] At the same time the two bodies released a statement noting that they would spend the coming weeks carefully studying how best to effect the merger.[64] On the surface, everything appeared entirely copasetic.

Behind the scenes and off the record, fear was widespread among tourist board staffers. As the majority of research for this book was completed, tourist board officials worried about what jobs would be allotted the planned "National Tourism Development Authority" (more commonly called "Fáilte Ireland") and whether they and their friends would have a place in the new body. Many were unclear about the division of labor between Tourism Ireland and the development authority. At the same time, Tourism Ireland acquired roughly one-half Bord Fáilte's staff and these men and women worried about whether the move from a semistate body to a private one would negatively impact their incomes and pensions.[65] For many who had given their lives to tourism development, nothing seemed certain anymore.

The staffs were left to worry for roughly a year before the minister presented any significant new information. Finally, in September 2002, a new minister for arts, sport and tourism, John O'Donoghue, announced that legislation creating the new tourism body would receive fast-track treatment so that the new board would be in place in time for the 2003 tourist season.[66] The minister presented his bill on 21 November 2002. While Fáilte Ireland would not handle international marketing, it nevertheless maintained many of Bord Fáilte's old responsibilities. The new board would "encourage, promote and support the development and marketing of tourist facilities within the state" by overseeing education (CERT's former role), developing tourism products, grading and registering hotels, engaging in research and planning, pursuing advertising and publicity activities within the Republic, and providing advice and consultancy services. Of particular interest, Fáilte Ireland would also have the ability to establish tourism-related companies—a risky role that had caused considerable problems during the Fáilte Hotels controversy that nearly destroyed Irish tourism during the late 1940s.[67]

The legislation passed easily through the Seanad, although questions were raised about ministerial authority and the process for selecting Fáilte Ireland officials.[68] The bill was subsequently presented to the Dáil on 12 February 2003 where it received a warm welcome. One by one Dáil ministers expressed their approval of the new legislation, while also noting the successes of Bord Fáilte and CERT. As Jack Wall, a Labour TD, put it, "Bord Fáilte and CERT deserve to be congratulated for their work over many years. Bord Fáilte did an amazing amount of work to promote tourism in Ireland. CERT has had a major influence with regard to the training of personnel in the tourism industry."[69] Unlike past argument over the creation of new tourism bodies, Fáilte Ireland simply did not inspire very much debate. At the dawn of the new millennium, almost all considered tourism to be a national interest and few doubted that changed circumstances might warrant a new development board.

Now four years old, Fáilte Ireland appears to be a success. Armed with more funding than any previous Irish tourist board, the new body is tremendously active in sponsoring events, pursuing environmental initiatives, lobbying for the construction of facilities such as conference centers and sports complexes, and developing new tourism products. On the training front, CERT's remit to oversee training programs also continues, complete with regular workshops to help train those already active in the industry. Even competitions such as the Irish Welcome Awards continue, attempting to assure that Ireland's tourism product is safe.[70] Far from the revolution that many in Bord Fáilte feared as they awaited legislation in 2002, in many respects Fáilte Ireland represents striking continuity with the past.

"The Dingle Wrangle"

Despite the creation of a new tourist board and widespread consensus about the importance of tourism, the long-running debates about national identity and the national interest continued unabated during the first years of the twenty-first century. Not only does tourism remain a nexus for debate and discussion, national discourse continues to involve many of the issues described in these pages.

There is no better example of this still ongoing dialogue than the heated conflict over the name ascribed to the town of Dingle, the little fishing village that, as early as 1924, ITA advocates believed had the potential to become a major tourist draw. As described in chapter 1, most Dingle residents were ambivalent about tourism at first. In fact, the only way that Irish Tourist Association officials were able to establish a local branch was to promise that tourism was synonymous with the improvement of infrastructure. During the 1920s better roads, drainage, and sewerage trumped all other concerns. The national interest, at least as far as Dingle residents were concerned, was closely tied to an improvement in the standard of living. Although the notion that tourists might actually flood into Dingle was impossibly abstract to most residents, the townspeople were anxious to get whatever they could from the ITA and the central government.

During the 1960s tourism and government officials earmarked monies to develop hotels, resort facilities, and beach access for tourists[71]—a timely investment because the release of David Lean's film *Ryan's Daughter* in 1970, filled with beautiful area scenery, quickly attracted the attention of an ever-increasing tide of visitors and prompted the construction of still more facilities. The appearance, in 1983–84, of a friendly dolphin, which area entrepreneurs soon named Fungie, prompted Dingle's final rush toward tourism greatness. In 1987, just one sailor carried tourists out to see Fungie, twelve passengers at a time. By 1991 the number of boats, which varied widely in size, reached fifteen. Tourism was now the town's largest source of income. "Dingle" was a tourist brand, synonymous with beautiful scenery, a fun-loving porpoise, and a higher density of ancient sites than virtually anywhere else in the world.[72] If the people of Dingle doubted the significance of tourism in 1924, by 2004 public skepticism was virtually nonexistent.

Consensus did not mean an absence of debate about either the national interest or national identity. During the spring of 2005 Dingle catapulted into the national and international spotlight as the result of a heated, sometimes nasty, debate about precisely what to call the town. The incident started in 2003 when the Oireachtas passed the Official Languages Act. Just as politicians during the early days of Irish independence sought to save the Irish language by promoting its use in government offices and in schools, and by considering the creation of Gaelic language preserves free of tourists (see chapter 4), the new legislation was intended to "promote the use of the Irish language for official purposes in the state."[73] One section of the act stipulated that English language place names would no longer be acceptable in Gaeltacht areas, so the minister for community, rural, and Gaeltacht affairs, Éamon Ó Cuív—Éamon de Valera's grandson—insisted that the town of Dingle change its name to "An Daingean," an Irish word meaning "fort." The name "Dingle" would no longer appear on "maps, road signs, statutory instruments and official correspondence." As far as the minister was concerned, the legislation was clear and there was little room for discussion. When asked about the change, Ó Cuív huffed, "It is An Daingean, full stop. The days of walking both sides of the street are over. It's a nonsense not having linguistic criterion attached to the Gaeltacht."[74]

Despite the minister's definitive sense of closure, by changing the name from "Dingle" to "An Daingean," Ó Cuív reignited debates about core versus periphery, urban versus rural, Ireland's relationship to its colonial history, and the importance of tourism relative to a uniquely Gaelic Irishness.

While the monetary stakes were much higher than at any previous point in the history of Irish tourism, the fundamental debate about Irishness was little changed.

For those living in Dingle town, about 1,800 residents, the name change represented a direct attack by Dublin authorities on both the villagers' sense of identity and their primary source of income. One pub owner told the *New York Times* that the change "was thrown upon us with the stroke of a pen." For many, such top-down management inspired memory of English rule from Dublin. For the editorial board of the *Irish Examiner*, the change was "not only an intolerable subversion of our democracy but a show of contemptible arrogance by Government and local authorities, that has not been witnessed since the days when we were ruled from Dublin Castle."[75]

The historical value of the Dingle name also captured the imagination of some townspeople. One group of activists formed an informational campaign to fight the change: the Dingle Name Campaign. While combating centralized control and a perceived attack on democracy was at the heart of their argument, history was also a factor. The group took pains to trace the history of "Dingle" from the twelfth century forward, pleading, "The Minister and his department have said that Dingle is a corrupted place name, and that it doesn't mean anything. Dingle has been known as Dingle for the past 750 years. How long must a town have its name before it has meaning?"[76] Every native resident grew up in a place called "Dingle"; for these people the word meant "home."

Above all, campaigners argued that the name change would cripple Dingle's tourist industry. From the beginning, local tourism officials feared that Gaelic language signs would confuse tourists and lead to disaster. Tourists were "getting dizzy in the head" trying to make sense of new road signs. A local west Kerry councilor, Michael O'Shea, added, "We might write to Minister Ó Cuív and tell him that foreigners do not understand the Irish language. Perhaps a new sign should now be put up on the N86: 'If you don't understand Irish, don't go beyond this point.'"[77] Justifying their fear, the Dingle Name Campaign conducted a survey over the St. Patrick's Day bank holiday in 2007 and found that eight of every ten visitors had trouble finding Dingle town.[78] Activists argued that businesses were dying and Americans were unable to find the town—even the time-honored act of asking directions did not work as many Kerrymen had yet to internalize the name change.⁷⁹ Dingle faced a significant problem. Lost tourists meant lost livelihood. Tourism had helped stop emigration from Dingle; now the old specter loomed again. For what? The government "spent millions promoting the Dingle Peninsula brand" and they were now willing "to throw it away."⁸⁰

For those in favor of the name change, inconvenience and short-term confusion were a small price to pay for saving the Irish language and Irish heritage. Sean Ó Cathasaigh, a native Gaelic speaker from Dingle living in Maynooth, County Kildare, wrote to the *Irish Times* to express his support for the change. While many might "denigrate our native language," the Irish should take pride in acknowledging "our native treasure."⁸¹ Finian McGrath, an Independent TD from Dublin, expressed a similar sentiment, noting that he would not expect the French or Spanish to provide Anglicized versions of their place names, so why should the Irish bow to tourist pressure? For McGrath, the tourist industry faced little threat because "clever and sensible marketing will brand 'An Daingean' internationally in a matter of weeks."⁸² Raé Kearns, of Trim, County Meath, lamented the loss of authentic Gaelic names in favor of "bland, soulless inventions that have usually no historical or environmental relevance to the area." Anglicized names represented the loss of "a very important part of our linguistic and environmental heritage."⁸³ Kearns did not agree that changing the name "Dingle" was desirable, but he nevertheless advocated a careful consideration of naming—deliberation that was not given to the small Kerry town. Finally, the minister behind the change, Éamon Ó Cuív, weighed in to insist on the correctness of the conversion. The name change would simplify matters for tourists because only a Gaelic name would appear on signs and maps. Answering the anti-change activists' question about how long it takes for a name to develop meaning, the minister admitted that the name "Dingle" has a long history, but insisted that "An Daingean" represents the "authentic" name for the community. Evidently 750 years is not enough time to establish authenticity for a "foreign" word. Ó Cuív went on to insist that tourism would not suffer from the change; indeed, the display of national pride and the marketing of authentic Gaelic Irishness might actually increase tourist interest.

In short, most of the old notions of Irish identity were represented in the debate. For some, authentic Ireland should be understood as pre-Norman;

for others, it is the product of history. The idea that Ireland is defined by common economic interests, especially tourism, was prevalent in the anti-name-change arguments, while the idea that Ireland is more culturally defined dominated the pro-change view. Ultimately the two views represented polar opposites and, for the debate participants, it was a zero sum game.

The Dingle Wrangle seemed largely insoluble. Name change opponents fought using every tool at their disposal. First, they sought to control the media. The Dingle Name Campaign published a website in order to make their position as widely known as possible. The tone of this site was calm and serious. It featured a history of Dingle, presented a reasoned anti-change argument, republished newspaper articles and letters to the editor, and reassured language campaigners by providing Irish-language material to interested readers. Anti-change advocates readily gave interviews. Editorial pages disproportionately reflected an anti-change position. Perhaps most damning, foreign papers took a negative view of the change. For example, Melbourne, Australia's *Sunday Herald Sun* began an article on the debate with the line "Tourists, beware"—precisely the opposite of the welcoming and friendly view of Ireland that tourism advocates spent the better part of a century developing.[84]

But the anti-change campaign's most significant action was to demand a plebiscite about the name change. In October 2005 the Kerry County Council agreed to hold an election and they subsequently did so one year later.[85] Roughly 1,222 residents were allowed to vote, mostly inhabitants of the town itself, and 1,095 of these opted to do so. Of those who voted, 1,005 voted in favor of a bilingual name: Dingle Daingean Uí Chúis. The vote cost €10,000, but for anti-change campaigners it seemed well worth the expense.

Despite the overwhelming vote, Ó Cuív continued to insist that no bilingual name would be legally acceptable under the Official Placenames Act.[86] The villagers were not amused. Angry letters appeared on the letters pages of Irish newspapers, ministers got an earful from constituents, and editorial writers decried the government's "subversion of democracy."[87]

After considerable ministerial wrangling, it was finally reported that a deal was struck on 20 June 2007 between Jackie Healy-Rae, TD, and An Taoiseach Bertie Ahearn to reinstate the town's bilingual name. Healy-Rae, fresh off a narrow election victory in May, was anxious to deliver on a campaign promise. Ahearn was almost certainly well aware that "people are sick of the whole situation."[88] After three years of fighting, the democratic process won out, but the debate itself was not, nor could it be, solved. For more than eighty years tourism inspired debate about the nature of Irishness and Irish interests; the Dingle Wrangle was yet another chapter in this debate and the existence of a new tourism authority did nothing to stop dialogue.

Conclusion

All too often we forget that history is not simply about a few great men or about the results of high-level political squabbling. Authors write within the context of their times. Artists and musicians respond to or react against contemporary trends. To a large degree, politicians must act within the confines of public opinion. Yet despite these realities, there is a tendency to discuss national identity as though Wizard of Oz–like characters control society while sitting in offstage control booths. Critics often present tourism as an unstoppable force that robs social groups of agency and leaves permanently altered societies in its wake. Scholars often present national identity as the creation of a few educated elites. The narrative of Irish history is dominated by a handful of nationalists, groups, and writers while everyday men and women, who have also played an important role in shaping Irish history, are forgotten.

The story told here offers a different narrative. Through tourism-inspired discourse, government officials, rural priests, community groups, foreign governments, tourists, and others came together to develop and create the image of Ireland that is presented to visitors today. Each group played an important role and none of the developments described in these pages would have been possible without the combined effort of all. In many ways, the development of the tourist industry was a significant triumph for the Irish people, who created their own identity and offered it to the world largely on their own terms. This is not the story of a people locked in a postcolonial prison as some suggest; it is the story of a nation actively involved in creating its own past, present, and future.

From the Irish Civil War to the present, tourism facilitated debate about Irish national identity along two separate but closely related axes. First, there was debate about the shape of Ireland's "national interest." While social scientists and historians have tended to dismiss the notion of a national interest as little more than an indication of the importance of the *rhetoric of nationalism* in an age of nation-states, the concept is actually more fundamental than that. Having a single "national" interest perpetuates an idea of unity by fostering dialogue. In Ireland there was often little agreement about precisely what the Irish nation wanted or needed, in spite of an underlying assumption of unanimity. From government officials all the way to parish priests, there were myriad opinions about what was best for the Irish people. At the local level, concerns like the need for sanitation or road improvements and the expansion of employment opportunities often seemed to overwhelm other concerns. If roads were made better, Irish towns more livable, and Irish people employed, then the community as a whole would benefit. In the halls of power, the national interest tended to revolve around growing the economy, filling the dollar gap, saving the Irish language, and placating Marshall Plan officials.

The question of modernization loomed large on both sides of the national interest debate. While improved transportation and the influx of tourists might have dramatic benefits, so too it could potentially destroy traditional culture such as the language or timeless fairs and festivals. Motor-launches on the Killarney lakes might bring benefits to the community, but they might also destroy a way of life. The development of tourist hotels might improve the economy but the new structures might also blight the landscape. Pro-modernization forces eventually won the battle for tourism, but even then the challenge of balancing the realities of modernity with the need for timelessness forced debate about the country's national interest.

Even as tourism prompted the debates noted above, it also led to discussion about the very things most often cited as core components of national identity. Whether the issue was landscape, culture, or history, virtually all Irish men and women wanted Ireland to be presented in the best possible way, and this required deciding precisely what "way" that was. Traditionally, Irish townscapes existed in black and white, derelict sites littered the landscape, and there was little attention paid to clearing away trash—all attributes that would negatively impact any tourism program, to say nothing of foreign attitudes toward the Irish people. Tourist authorities, local groups, architects, and others combined their efforts to alter the appearance of Irish landscapes, redefining townscapes as brightly colored and clean, promoting the removal of derelict sites, and urging anti-litter campaigns. Likewise, traditional Irish fairs and festivals were coarse and sometimes violent affairs—qualities that would lend weight to negative stereotypes of Irishness rather than promote the more jovial and pleasant depictions of the national character preferred by many in the Tourist Board and beyond. Once again tourist authorities and local committees addressed the problem by creating new traditions while casting their gaze into antiquity for inspiration. Irish history provided a very similar problem. Much of the recent Irish past was defined by struggle and conflict, including agonizing civil war. The narrative that was developed for historical sites—both for tourist and local consumption—glossed over these divisions, even when the site was intimately associated with partisanship and conflict as at Kilmainham Jail. Ireland's past was most often viewed in terms of saints and scholars while ancient historic sites assumed greater value than more recent monuments. Tourism created a dialogue about the Gaelic language revival as well, an issue that went to the very heart of the notion of a Gaelic Ireland. Was Irishness better served by protecting the language from foreign influences and by keeping tourists at bay, or by attracting visitors to the Gaeltachts? Would the rural Irish benefit more by developing a revenue stream or maintaining a distinctive language-culture in an essentially premodern form? Then, in the past few years, should economic considerations or a desire to save the language triumph in places like Dingle?

In all of these cases, the various participants prioritized aspects of identity, ultimately determining the "official" form that Irishness would take, a shape that was to be presented to the Irish and their visitors alike. While the discussion might have been about a tourist product, it was never possible to limit the material results of these discussions to a narrow imaginary space, a sort of tourist museum. When landscapes were changed, regardless of the reason, the alteration could not help but modify the relationship of those living in close contact with these spaces. When new festivals were created, people quickly became invested in them, whether as participants or observers. When a narrative of Irish history was decided upon, its historic sites became the destination for school field trips as well as the tourist gaze, educating Irish children and their parents, domestic tourists, and foreign visitors alike about Ireland's past. When tourism development was prioritized over self-conscious language protection, the impact was profound in Gaeltacht communities like Dingle that were transformed from communities in decline to internationally known tourism centers, only to continue being the focus of heated discussion over the merits of money versus culture.

None of this is to say "tourism changed the Irish people." The reality was never so simple, nor so vulgar. At every turn Irish groups and individuals made decisions, hashed out their thoughts on a public stage, made determinations about how they viewed themselves and how others should view them. As noted above, the interpretations of Irishness discussed here were not entirely imposed from above, nor were they merely colonial fragments hung like cowbells around the necks of Ireland's men and women. The Irish people were active participants in the creation of their own identity, not the victims of a relentless tourist gaze or the unyielding drive of policy-makers.

While not every voice has been included in these pages, the stories that have been are representative and reveal an impressive level of participation across social groups and geographic space. To be sure, after the advent of the Irish Tourist Board, most (though not all) tourism initiatives came from the "top," but proposals were not necessarily accepted and always required willing participation by local groups. Central tourism authorities could not "go it alone" and constantly had to concern themselves with developing effective ways to work with local realities. Dublin could create plans, but it was groups and individuals in Cork, Kerry, Galway, Mayo, Waterford, Sligo, Wexford, Tipperary, and all of Ireland's other counties who had to carry them out. The Tidy Towns Competition would have failed had it not been for local interest. Language preservation would more than likely have trumped Gaeltacht development schemes were it not for calls from rural and Gaeltacht areas for financial help. Kilmainham Jail would have been destroyed in the early 1960s if a group of nationalist-minded volunteers had not stepped in to refurbish it, rewriting the site's historical narrative in the process. Ultimately the negotiation of Irishness and Irish interests that occurred as a result of tourism was a horizontal and perpetually recurring process.

Of course, dialogue was not entirely internal. Even as identity was debated across Irish society it was also partly defined through dialogue with outsiders. At the heart of tourism, after all, are tourists. Visitor expectations had to factor into discussion. If American tourists wanted to find long lost relatives, expected to experience historic sites, and dreamed of purchasing Irish products, and if English tourists were more interested in the scenery and a quick getaway, both tastes had to be taken into consideration. Likewise, as tourism spending increased, so too did the need to consider what French, German, Italian, Spanish, and other groups of European tourists wanted to find. Foreign voices were not only those of tourists—foreign governments also had comments to make, pressures to apply. From the Marshall Plan to European Development Grants, international interests have concerned themselves with the Irish identity and the Irish national interest, helping to push the notion that Ireland needs tourism and to pay attention to what is required to attract tourists. The Irish could pick and chose which voices to hear, which initiatives to implement, which products to produce, but they did so while in constant contact with the outside world—a contact that tourism did a great deal to promote.

The story told in *Making Ireland Irish* is a complicated one and it does not lend itself to a clear summation of continuities and changes. Over the time-span covered by this study there was a general trend toward consensus about the importance of tourism, the need for increased government spending, and the idea that everybody should play a role, however small, in making the national tourism project work. As time passed, there was also a diversification of Ireland's tourism products that have, among other things, expanded to include a greater recognition of the country's long struggle for independence, suggesting a growing acceptance of the past.

There is more to see in Ireland than ever before, but old issues persist. No Trespassing signs still mar the landscape. Puck Fair continues to take place every August, even if in an altered form. Litter proliferates like proverbial rabbits. Regional concerns still plague central tourism authorities. Heritage sites remain primarily ancient and religious in nature, though more "nationalist" sites have appeared in the last fifteen years. The language question still makes international headlines. But, through it all, the Irish scenery continues to dominate tourism marketing just as Céad Míle Fáilte has remained a perpetual component of advertising materials.

Rather than reading the narrative presented here as a relentless march toward the present, or even in terms of specific continuities and changes, we should read this story as one of continual discussion and we should place the utmost importance on the dialogue itself. As early as the 1930s there were those who wanted to see more sites devoted to Irish martyrs: they did not mysteriously emerge in the late 1950s to urge restoration of Kilmainham. Rather they gradually earned a more dominant voice as conditions changed. Likewise, as early as the 1920s there were calls to remove derelict sites and to clean up litter, though what success was attained had to wait until ecological concern attracted widespread attention and financial resources increased. And, of course, there are still those who fear that tourism will destroy the Gaeltachts. This is a story about opinions whose fortunes wax and wane. Different understandings of Irish national identity rise in prominence at various points only to diminish in importance later on. It follows that self-identification changes as well as people redecide exactly what it means to be Irish.

Notes

Bibliography

Index

Notes

Introduction

1. Neil Steedman, "£3m Tourism Brand Ireland Is Launched," *Irish Travel Trade News*, Nov. 1996, 13.

2. Irene Furlong, "Frederick W. Crossley: Irish Turn-of-the-Century Tourism Pioneer," in *Irish History: A Research Yearbook*, no. 2 (Dublin: Four Courts Press, 2003), 162.

3. Hartmut Berghoff and Barbara Korte, "Britain and the Making of Modern Tourism: An Interdisciplinary Approach," in *The Making of Modern Tourism: The Cultural History of the British Experience, 1600–2000*, ed. Barbara Korte, Hartmut Berghoff, Ralf Schneider, and Christopher Harvie (Basingstock, UK: Palgrave, 2002), 1–20.

4. Jeremy Black, *The British Abroad: The Grand Tour in the Eighteenth Century* (New York: St. Martin's Press, 1992).

5. Gerhard Stilz, "Heroic Travellers—Romantic Landscapes: The Colonial Sublime in Indian, Australian and American Art and Literature," in Korte et al., *Making of Modern Tourism*, 85–107, especially page 85.

6. Alain Corbin, *The Lure of the Sea* (Berkeley: Univ. of California Press, 1994).

7. Peter Womack, *Improvement and Romance: Constructing the Myth of the Highlands* (London: Macmillan Press, 1989). Also see Charles Withers, "The Historical Creation of the Scottish Highlands," in *The Manufacture of Scottish History*, ed. Christopher Whatley and Ian Donnachie (Edinburgh: Polygon, 1992), 143–56.

8. Ian Ousby, *The Englishman's England: Taste, Travel and the Rise of Tourism* (Cambridge, UK: Cambridge Univ. Press, 1990), see chap. 3.

9. Penelope Durell and Cornelius Kelly, eds., *The Grand Tour of Kerry* (Allihies, Beara, Co. Cork: Cailleach Books, 2001), 21.

10. Durell and Kelly, *Grand Tour of Kerry*, 23.

11. Ibid., 29.

12. Melissa Fegan, "The Traveller's Experience in Famine Ireland," *Irish Studies Review* 9, no. 3 (2001): 161–372, see page 361.

13. Orvar Löfgren, *On Holiday: A History of Vacationing* (Berkeley: Univ. of California Press, 1999), 16–17.

14. Shelley Baranowski and Ellen Furlough, eds., *Being Elsewhere: Tourism, Consumer Culture, and Identity in Modern Europe and North America* (Ann Arbor: Univ. of Michigan Press, 2001), 6.

15. Löfgren, *On Holiday*, 19.

16. Piers Brendon, *Thomas Cook: 150 Years of Popular Travel* (London: Secker and Warburg, 1991). For a short summary, see W. H. Bradley, "Around the World with Thomas Cook," *British Heritage*, 1988, 56–61.

17. Furlong, "Frederick W. Crossley," 163; Donal Horgan, *The Victorian Visitor in Ireland: Irish Tourism, 1840–1910* (Cork: Imagimedia, 2002), 23.

18. English numbers are drawn from P. J. G. Ransom, *The Victorian Railway and How It Evolved* (London: Heinemann, 1990), 79 and 110. Irish numbers are drawn from Donal Horgan, *Victorian Visitor*, 24–27.

19. Brendon, *Thomas Cook*, 64–65 and 167–68.

20. Furlong, "Frederick W. Crossley," 173–74.

21. Ibid., 174–75.

22. This account of Crossley's activities is based on Furlong's superb article, one of the very few scholarly treatments of nineteenth-century Irish tourism. It should be of interest to anybody anxious to learn more about early Irish tourist development.

23. Quoted in Joe J. Lee, *Ireland, 1912–1985: Politics and Society* (Cambridge: Cambridge Univ. Press, 1989), 56.

24. For Finnish numbers, see ibid., 69; Spanish Civil War statistics are available in Stanley G. Payne, *The Spanish Civil War, the Soviet Union, and Communism* (New Haven: Yale Univ. Press, 2004), 336n. 14.

25. Baranowski and Furlough, *Being Elsewhere*, 1.

26. Louis Turner and John Ash, *The Golden Hordes: International Tourism and the Pleasure Periphery* (London: Constable and Co., 1975).

27. James Buzard, *The Beaten Track: European Tourism, Literature, and the Ways to Culture, 1800–1918* (Oxford: Clarendon Press, 1993).

28. Paul Fussell, as quoted in Baranowski and Furlough, *Being Elsewhere*, 3.

29. Dean MacCannell, *The Tourist: A New Theory of the Leisure Class* (Berkeley: Univ. of California Press, 1999), 45.

30. Walter Benjamin, *Illuminations: Essays and Reflections* (New York: Schocken Books, 1968), 217–52.

31. Rudy Koshar, "'What Ought to Be Seen': Tourists' Guidebooks and National Identities in Modern Germany and Europe," *Journal of Contemporary History* 33, no. 3 (1998): 323–40.

32. Michel Peillon, "Tourism—the Quest for Otherness," *Crane Bag* 8 no. 2 (1984): 165–68.

33. Tom Selwyn, ed., *The Tourist Image: Myths and Myth Making in Tourism* (Chichester, UK: John Wiley and Sons, 1996), 23.

34. Robert E. Wood, "Tourist Ethnicity: A Brief Itinerary," *Ethnic and Racial Studies* 21, no. 2 (1998): 218–41.

35. Catherine A. Palmer, "Tourism and Colonialism: The Experience of the Bahamas," *Annals of Tourism Research* 21, no. 4 (1994): 792–811. Spurgeon Thompson makes a similar argument about Irish tourism. See his "The Postcolonial Tourist: Irish Tourism and Decolonization since 1850" (Ph.D. diss., Univ. of Notre Dame, 2000).

36. Simon Abram, "Performing for Tourists in Rural France," in *Tourists and Tourism: Identifying with People and Places,* ed. Simon Abram, Jacqueline Waldren, and Donald V. L. Macleod (Oxford: Berg, 1997), 31.

37. Moya Kneafsey, "Tourism and Place Identity: A Case-Study in Rural Ireland," *Irish Geography* 31, no. 2 (1998): 111–23, see page 121.

38. Moya Kneafsey, "Rural Tourism and Identity: Stories of Change and Resistance from the West of Ireland and Brittany," in *New Directions in Celtic Studies,* ed. Amy Hale and Philip Payton (Exeter: Univ. of Exeter Press, 2000), 167–96, see page 172.

39. Thompson, "The Postcolonial Tourist," 3–4.

40. Frank O'Connor was a pseudonym for Michael O'Donovan. He was born in Cork and raised in poverty by a loving mother. His father served in the British army and was largely absent from O'Donovan's life. As a young man, he fought as a Republican in the Civil War and was eventually interned in Gormanstown in 1923. O'Donovan's first collection of short stories, *Guests of the Nation,* recounted his wartime experiences, contrasting the ideals he fought for with the painful realities of war. O'Donovan was harshly censored during the 1940s and became increasingly bitter as a result. This bitterness extended to the Clare County Council, which refused to build a monument to Marriman, one of O'Donovan's favorite poets. He emigrated to the United States in 1951, after his marriage collapsed and life in Ireland became unbearable. While in the United States, he lectured widely at American universities and produced three critical works on Irish literature. He returned to Ireland in 1960 and died six years later. See Brian Ó Dalaigh, ed., *The Stranger's Gaze: Travels in County Clare, 1534–1950* (Dublin: Clasp Press, 1998).

41. "IRA Protest on O'Connor's Article," *Irish Press,* 21 Jan. 1950.

42. Letter from John J. Byrne, [?] Dec. 1949, Department of the Taoiseach [hereafter cited as DT], S14716A, National Archives of Ireland, Dublin.

43. "US Magazine Asked to Apologise," *Irish Independent,* 7 Jan. 1950.

44. Letter from Killarney Urban District Council Resolution and letter to the Taoiseach, 23 Jan. 1950, DT, S14716A, National Archives of Ireland, Dublin.

45. "Libeling a People," *Catholic News,* 26 Nov. 1949.

46. While O'Connor's accuracy does not matter in our context, much of what he wrote was relatively correct. The Catholic Church did hold considerable power (as became very clear during the Mother and Child controversy just four years later). Poverty was appalling. Dublin was in such poor shape that Georgian buildings literally collapsed upon themselves. Infant mortality was horrendous. There was little in the way of industry. A vast number of men and

women fled Ireland in search of better prospects during the 1950s. Of course, O'Connor made a number of not insignificant errors as well. His discussion of Irish history, for example, was riddled with inaccuracy. The Civil War was not caused by partition and the Allies did not maintain essential military bases in southern Ireland during the Second World War (although they certainly wanted to).

47. Francis McCoy, "Backstage with Mr. Frank O'Connor," Dec. 1949, DT, S14716A, National Archives of Ireland, Dublin.

48. "How O'Connor Article Was Concocted," *Irish Press,* 21 Jan. 1949.

49. Department of External Affairs, memorandum, 18 Jan. 1950, Department of Foreign Affairs [hereafter cited as DFA], 366/117, National Archives of Ireland, Dublin.

50. Department of External Affairs, article draft and letter, 25 Sept. 1950, DFA, 366/117/1, National Archives of Ireland, Dublin.

51. Ernest Gellner, *Nations and Nationalism* (Ithaca, N.Y.: Cornell Univ. Press, 1983); and E. J. Hobsbawm, *Nations and Nationalism since 1780* (Cambridge: Cambridge Univ. Press, 1990).

52. Partha Chatterjee, *The Nation and Its Fragments* (Princeton, N.J.: Princeton Univ. Press, 1993).

53. Benedict Anderson, *Imagined Communities: Reflections on the Origin and Spread of Nationalism* (London: Verso, 1991). See also Alan Williams, ed. *Film and Nationalism* (Piscataway, N.J.: Rutgers Univ. Press, 2002).

54. Michael Billig, *Banal Nationalism* (London: Sage Publications, 1995).

55. Tim Edensor, "National Identity and the Politics of Memory: Remembering Bruce and Wallace in Symbolic Space," *Environment and Planning* 29 (1997): 175–94.

56. Oliver Zimmer, *A Contested Nation: History, Memory and Nationalism in Switzerland, 1761–1891* (Cambridge: Cambridge Univ. Press, 2003).

57. Stuart B. Schwartz, ed., *Implicit Understandings: Observing, Reporting, and Reflecting on the Encounters Between Europeans and Other Peoples in the Early Modern Era* (Cambridge: Cambridge Univ. Press, 1994), 3.

1. Introducing a National Interest, 1922–1939

1. Tom Garvin, *1922: The Birth of Irish Democracy* (New York: St. Martin's Press, 1996), 83; and Michael Farry, *The Aftermath of Revolution: Sligo 1921–23* (Dublin: Univ. College Dublin Press, 2000), 205.

2. Michael Hopkinson, *Green Against Green: The Irish Civil War* (Dublin: Gill and Macmillan, 1988), 273.

3. Terence Brown, *Ireland: A Social and Cultural History, 1922 to the Present* (Ithaca, N.Y.: Cornell Univ. Press, 1985), 15.

4. D. George Boyce, *Nationalism in Ireland* (London: Routledge, 1995), 340.

5. Quoted in Boyce, *Nationalism in Ireland,* 339.

6. "The Cobh Outrage: Hopes of Capture; Hunting for Missing Men; Free State Forces in the South," *Kerryman*, 5 Apr. 1924.

7. Farry, *Aftermath of Revolution*, 202.

8. C. S. Andrews, *Man of No Property: An Autobiography*, vol. 2 (Dublin: Mercier Press, 1982), 26.

9. Jeffrey Prager, *Building Democracy in Ireland: Political Order and Cultural Integration in a Newly Independent Nation* (Cambridge: Cambridge Univ. Press, 1986), 99.

10. Garvin, *1922*, 88.

11. Sasha David Pack, "Spain in the Age of Mass Tourism, Modernization, and Dictatorship, 1945–1975" (Ph.D. diss., Univ. of Wisconsin-Madison, 2004), 24–25, 53–58, especially page 56.

12. Brown, *Ireland*, 16.

13. "Tribute to a Senator," *Irish Independent*, 7 Jan. 1924.

14. "Tourist Traffic, An All-Ireland Movement: What Other Places Have Done," *Kerryman*, 26 Apr. 1924.

15. Irish Tourism Memorandum and Association Articles of Association, 1924, Dissolved Companies, D7282, National Archives of Ireland, Dublin.

16. "Obituary. Death of Former President of ITA, the Late Mr. J. C. Foley, LL.D.," *Irish Travel*, June–July 1933, 123.

17. "Activities of the ITA," *Irish Travel*, Sept. 1925, 9–10.

18. "Mr. Howard S. Harrington: Appreciation by His Old Staff," *Kerryman*, 11 Sept. 1926.

19. Irish Tourism Memorandum and Association Articles.

20. Michael Kevin O'Doherty, interview by author, Dublin, 29 Apr. 2002. Also see C. S. Andrews, *Man of No Property*, 67.

21. C. S. Andrews, *Man of No Property*, 66 and 71.

22. Harvey Levenstein, *We'll Always Have Paris: American Tourists in France since 1930* (Chicago: Univ. of Chicago Press, 2004), x. See also Pack, "Spain in the Age of Mass Tourism," 58.

23. Dáil Debate, 5 (12 Dec. 1923), 1802. All Dáil and Seanad debates are available online at <http:\\www.oireachtas.ie>.

24. Dáil Debate, 6 (19 Mar. 1924), 2175.

25. Dáil Debate, 9 (20 Nov. 1924), 1322.

26. According to Mary E. Daly, the role of government was seriously debated in the first twenty-five years after the Anglo-Irish Treaty. Some believed that the state should not interfere with industrial development, while others felt that such intervention was necessary and desirable. Daly argues that a new industrial elite emerged in the 1920s and 1930s that was intensely dependent on government assistance. Mary E. Daly, *Industrial Development and Irish Society: 1922–1939* (Syracuse, N.Y.: Syracuse Univ. Press, 1992), 177–80.

27. "Tourist Plans: Conference Called by the Minister of Industry," *Kerryman*, 20 Dec. 1924.

28. Dáil Debate, 10 (10 Mar. 1925), 847.

29. *Irish Independent*, 7 Jan. 1924.

30. Dáil Debate, 10 (10 Mar. 1925), 847.

31. *Local Government Act, 1925* (Dublin: Government Publications, 1925).

32. "Tourist Development: National Association," *Kerryman*, 24 Jan. 1925.

33. "Notes and News," *Irish Travel*, Sept. 1925, 2–4.

34. "Irish Tourist Association: Killarney Branch Formed," *Kerryman*, 26 Jan. 1924.

35. "Dingle Doings: The Tourist Trade," *Kerryman*, 27 Dec. 1924.

36. "Dingle Rural Council: Tourist Development," *Kerryman*, 13 Dec. 1924.

37. "Irish Tourist Association: Dingle Branch," *Kerryman*, 23 May 1925.

38. "Dingle Doings: Sewerage," *Kerryman*, 17 Oct. 1925.

39. "Irish Tourist Association: Dingle Branch," *Kerryman*, 20 Feb. 1926.

40. "Dingle Branch, Irish Tourist Association: Committee Appointed," *Kerryman*, 27 Feb. 1926.

41. "Tourist Development Association, Dingle Branch: Condition of Streets; Question of Urbanizing," *Kerryman*, 13 Mar. 1926.

42. "Dingle Doings," *Kerryman*, 27 Mar. 1926.

43. "Dingle Doings," *Kerryman*, 24 July 1926.

44. Cork-Kinsale Road, 23 Apr. 1930, Kinsale Development Association [hereafter cited as KDA], U274/6, Cork Archives Institute, Cork, Ireland.

45. L. O'Connell to ITA, 3 Apr. 1930, KDA, U274/6, Cork Archives Institute, Cork.

46. J. P. O'Brien to L. O'Connell, 14 Apr. 1930, KDA, U274/6, Cork Archives Institute, Cork.

47. Clipping from unknown newspaper, "Main Road Grants," 20 Feb. 1931, KDA, U274/6, Cork Archives Institute, Cork.

48. L. O'Connell to Secretary of Roads Board, Department of Local Government, 31 May 1933, KDA, U274/6, Cork Archives Institute, Cork; and "Kinsale Notes: Kinsale Tourist Development and Water Scheme," [?]1938, KDA, U274/2, Cork Archives Institute, Cork.

49. "Advertising Tourist Resorts," *Kerryman*, 24 Dec. 1926.

50. "Killarney Tourist Association," *Kerryman*, 1 Jan. 1927.

51. "Tourist Development," *Kilkenny People*, 7 Nov. 1925.

52. "Kilkenny County Rates," *Kilkenny People*, 5 Mar. 1927.

53. "Tourist Association: Directors from Local Bodies," *Kilkenny People*, 29 Jan. 1927; and "Tourist Traffic: Irish Association's Important Decision," *Kerryman*, 29 Jan. 1927.

54. "Tourist Trade: Preparing for the Coming Season," *Kerryman*, 19 Feb. 1927.

55. During his varied career, Todd Andrews established Bord na Móna (the Turf Board), acted as chairman of Córas Iompair Éireann (Irish rail), and was a director of Radio Telefís Éireann (RTÉ).

56. C. S. Andrews, *Man of No Property*, 67–68.

57. Ibid., 71–72.

58. Ibid., 67–68.

59. Ibid., 70–71.

60. Ibid., 73–74.

61. Daly, *Industrial Development*, 10–11.

62. Cu Uladh, "Gaeltacht and Tourists," *Irish Press*, 31 Sept. 1938.

63. "Irish Tourist Association," *Kerryman*, 1 Nov. 1924.

64. *Irish Travel*, Sept. 1925, 2–5.

65. T. C. O'Reilly, letter, Jan. 1926, Seamus Fitzgerald Papers [hereafter cited as SFP], PR6/673 (1) and (2), Cork Archives Institute, Cork.

66. "Killarney Tourist Association: Proposed Motor Boat Service," *Kerryman*, 24 Oct. 1925.

67. "Kerryisms," *Kerryman*, 17 Oct. 1925.

68. "Killarney Lakes: Boatmen Against Motor Boats," *Kerryman*, 17 May 1924.

69. "Killarney Tourist Association," *Kerryman*, 24 Oct. 1925.

70. "Launches on the Lakes: The Reply of the Boat-Men's Association," *Kerryman*, 31 Oct. 1925.

71. "Kerryisms," *Kerryman*, 7 Nov. 1925.

72. "Kerryisms," *Kerryman*, 17 Oct. 1925.

73. Republished as "Success of the Tourist Season: Killarney Pleased, All Expectations Beaten," *Kerryman*, 31 Oct. 1925.

74. "Killarney and Motor Launches: Letter from Mr. Wm. Ahern, UDC," *Kerryman*, 14 Nov. 1925.

75. "Motor Launches on Killarney Lakes: Letter from Lord Kenmare," *Kerryman*, 21 Nov. 1925.

76. "Activities of the ITA," *Irish Travel*, Feb. 1929, 128–29.

77. *Ireland: Official Publication* (Dublin: Irish Tourist Association, 1929). One-third of the ITA's annual income came from contributions made by local authorities. The rest was made up of subscriptions by hotel and rail companies, dues paid by two hundred members, and grants from a handful of other companies. C. S. Andrews, *Man of No Property*, 70.

78. Board Memo No. 4345, 9 July 1925, GDB/C009/0405, Guinness Ireland Archives, Dublin.

79. While no comprehensive history of the first Irish Tourist Association has been written, interested readers should consult the organization's major publication: the *Irish Tourist*. Donel Horgan's *Victorian Visitor in Ireland* also contains limited information as does Irene Furlong's "Frederick W. Crossley."

80. Moran owned both Moran's Hotel and the Dolphin Hotel. He also served on the Ports and Docks Board.

81. Board Memo No. 4345.

82. General Purposes Sub-Committee Minutes, 17 Aug. 1926, GOB/C006/0121, Guinness Ireland Archives, Dublin.

83. Board Memo No. 4345.

84. "Notes and News," *Irish Travel*, Aug. 1926, 291.

85. "Ireland as a Tourist Resort," *Kerryman*, 21 Aug. 1926.

86. Marguerite S. Shaffer, *See America First: Tourism and National Identity, 1880–1940* (Washington D.C.: Smithsonian Institution Press, 2001).

87. J. Booth, letter, 8 May 1925, Department of Finance [hereafter cited as DF], S041/0012/25, National Archives of Ireland, Dublin.

88. H. P. Boland to J. Booth, 27 May 1925, DF, S041/0012/25, National Archives of Ireland, Dublin.

89. After the assassination of Kevin O'Higgins, the government called a second general election following passage of an aggressive Public Safety and Electoral Act. The new legislation required all members of the Oireachtas (Irish legislature) to take an oath of allegiance—a clever way to press de Valera to either accept constitutional politics or return to the political wilderness. The new legislation also allowed Cosgrave to take an aggressive and democratic stand against continued Republican violence. Fianna Fáil agreed to the new requirement and entered the Oireachtas in August 1927. For a very readable account, see Stephen Collins, *The Cosgrave Legacy* (Dublin: Blackwater Press, 1996); see also John Horgan, *Seán Lemass: The Enigmatic Patriot* (Dublin: Gill and Macmillan 1997), 46.

90. For a fairly typical example of O'Sullivan's campaign rhetoric, see "Mr. Eugene O'Sullivan's Candidature: Meeting at Kenmare," *Kerryman*, 28 May 1927. O'Sullivan briefly mentioned tourism on 21 May, arguing, "Our neglected fisheries and our tourist trade are amongst the nation's prime assets, and must be attended to in a competent and business-like way." "Mr. Eugene O'Sullivan. Chairman Killarney Urban District Council to Stand for Kerry as an Independent Candidate," *Kerryman*, 21 May 1927.

91. Seanad Debate, 14 (6 May 1931), 896–97.

92. Income during the period 1926–30 was as follows:

1926—£2,227
1927—£5,169
1928—£8,827
1929—£10,245
1930—£10,222.

Letter to James McNeill, 1931, DT, S5482, National Archives of Ireland, Dunlin.

93. Seanad Debate, 14 (6 May 1931), 896–97.

94. O'Doherty interview, 29 Apr. 2002.

95. Roy Foster, *Modern Ireland: 1600–1972* (London: Penguin, 1988), 540.

96. John Horgan, *Enigmatic Patriot*, 52.

97. Dáil Debate, 38 (22 Apr. 1931), 19–20.

98. Collins, *Cosgrave Legacy*, 53. See also Lee, *Ireland, 1912–1985*, 175–78, for more details about the campaign.

99. Lee, *Ireland, 1912–1985*, 178.

100. Tourist traffic numbers are far from precise until at least the 1950s; however, it is fair to assume that the trends represented in early figures are accurate. In 1926, estimates were that 184,320 Britons visited Ireland. By 1932, this number had increased to 245,468, and by 1936 the estimate had risen to 317,979. The number of American visitors also rose, moving from just over 8,000 in 1926 to 10,840 in 1936. "The 1936 Tourist Season Has Set New Records," *Irish Travel*, Nov. 1936, 26.

101. Brian Farrell, *Seán Lemass* (London: Gill and Macmillan, 1983), 41.

102. See John Horgan, *Enigmatic Patriot*, 88.

103. Quoted in ibid., 88–89.

104. Bernard Share, *The Flight of the Iolar: The Aer Lingus Experience, 1936–1986* (Dublin: Gill and Macmillan, 1986), 7.

105. Quoted in John Horgan, *Enigmatic Patriot*, 88–89.

106. O'Doherty interview, 29 Apr. 2002.

107. John Horgan, *Enigmatic Patriot*, 87.

108. Farrell, *Seán Lemass*, 41.

109. John Leydon, letter, 18 May 1938, DFA, S084/0020/38 (Main File), National Archives of Ireland, Dublin.

110. Memo by Sean Ua Morain, 1938, DFA, S084/0020/38 (Part 2), National Archives of Ireland, Dublin.

111. Minute from Mr. Lynd, 22 May 1938, DFA, S084/0020/38 (Part 1), National Archives of Ireland, Dublin.

112. Minute by C. S. Almond, 6 May 1938, DFA, S084/0020/38 (Main File), National Archives of Ireland, Dublin.

113. Minute from Mr. Lynd, 22 May 1938.

114. Minute by C. S. Almond, 6 May 1938.

115. "Tourist Traffic Board for Ireland," *Cork Evening Echo*, 25 Oct. 1938.

116. "Killarney Discusses Tourists: New Government Bill Examined by UDC," *Cork Evening Echo*, 5 Nov. 1938.

117. *Tourist Traffic Act, 1939* (Dublin: Government Publications, 1939).

118. "The Irish Tourist Board: New Appointment by Government Recognizes Importance of Irish Tourist Industry," *Irish Travel*, Sept. 1939, 313.

2. Developing Irish Tourism, 1939–1958

1. Brian Garvin and Geoffrey Roberts, eds., *Ireland and the Second World War: Politics, Society and Remembrance* (Dublin: Four Courts Press, 2000), 11.

2. Garvin and Roberts, *Ireland and the Second World War*, 13.

3. Donal Ó Drisceoil, *Censorship in Ireland 1939–1945: Neutrality, Politics, and Society* (Cork: Cork Univ. Press, 1996), 3.

4. Lee, *Ireland, 1912–1985*, 259–60.

5. Ibid., 265.

6. Ó Drisceoil, *Censorship in Ireland*, 6.

7. Tony Gray, *The Lost Years: The Emergency in Ireland, 1939–45* (London: Little, Brown and Co., 1997), 7.

8. Ronan Fanning, *The Irish Department of Finance, 1922–58* (Dublin: Institute of Public Administration, 1978), 312.

9. John Horgan, *Enigmatic Patriot*, 100–101.

10. Garvin and Roberts, *Ireland and the Second World War*, 32 and 34.

11. Tourist Traffic Act, 1939—Question of Suspension, 7 Sept. 1939, DT, S10946, National Archives of Ireland, Dublin.

12. J. P. O'Brien to J. Leydon, 5 Sept. 1939, DT, S10946, National Archives of Ireland, Dublin.

13. Tourist Traffic Act, 1939—Question of Suspension.

14. Memorandum for the Government from J. P. O'Brien, 20 Nov. 1939, DT, S10946, National Archives of Ireland, Dublin.

15. Department of Industry and Commerce Memorandum, 29 Jan. 1940, DT, S10946, National Archives of Ireland, Dublin.

16. Ibid.

17. Department of Finance Memorandum, circa Jan. 1940, DT, S10946, National Archives of Ireland, Dublin.

18. Fanning, *Irish Department of Finance*, 626.

19. Lee, *Ireland, 1912–1985*, 572.

20. Ibid., 573.

21. Fanning, *Irish Department of Finance*, 627.

22. Irish Tourist Board Annual Report and Accounts, Year Ended 31st March 1941, 25 June 1941, Tourism, Transport, and Communications [hereafter cited as TTA], 5/1/2, National Archives of Ireland, Dublin.

23. Cabinet Minutes. G.C. 3/49, 29 Feb. 1944, DT, S10946, National Archives of Ireland, Dublin. See also Department of Industry and Commerce Memorandum, 18 Feb. 1944, DT, S10946, National Archives of Ireland, Dublin.

24. Fanning, *Irish Department of Finance*, 629.

25. Ibid., 631.

26. Irish Tourist Association memorandum to Minister for Industry and Commerce, 16 Apr. 1941, DT, S10946, National Archives of Ireland, Dublin.

27. "Holidays in 1941," *Irish Travel*, Feb. 1941, 86.

28. Department of Local Government, *Department of Local Government Report, 1940–41* (Dublin: Government Publications, 1941), 20.

29. Department of Local Government, *Department of Local Government Report, 1943–44* (Dublin: Government Publications, 1944), 20.

30. For the most thorough discussion of English savings clubs, see Susan Barton, *Working-Class Organisations and Popular Tourism, 1840–1970* (Manchester: Manchester Univ. Press, 2005). Interested readers should also see John K. Walton, *Blackpool* (Edinburgh: St. Martin's Press, 1998), 53–54.

31. Account of Success of Holiday Savings Clubs Established by Irish Tourist Association in Industrial and Commercial Concerns, [?] 1948, Ms 33, 718/H (231), National Library of Ireland, Dublin. Cited with the permission of the Board of the National Library of Ireland.

32. "With the ITA Holiday Savings Clubs: Close of the Cork Campaign," *Irish Travel*, Mar. 1942, 92.

33. "Irish Tourist Holiday Savings Club Scheme," *Irish Travel*, Jan. 1941, 66.

34. Account of Success. Cited with the permission of the Board of the National Library of Ireland. See also Irish Tourist Association's Twentieth Anniversary Issue: 1925–45, 1945, Todd Andrews Papers [hereafter cited as TAP], P91/B/10, University College Dublin Archives, Dublin.

35. List of ITA Accomplishments, 1963, DT, S13087G/63, National Archives of Ireland, Dublin. By the early 1950s, the savings club program was no longer viable. Even as the Organization for European Economic Cooperation advocated forming European-wide savings clubs, An Bord Fáilte declared that such savings clubs "would not meet with success in this country as Irish people generally like to make individual holiday arrangements." See Debate summary, 3 Feb. 1953, TTA 3/1/7, National Archives of Ireland, Dublin.

36. "Irish Hotels Federation Report of the Third Annual General Meeting," *Irish Travel*, Dec. 1940, 63.

37. "Irish Tourist Association Annual General Meeting, Thursday, Oct. 23rd, 1941," *Irish Travel*, Nov. 1941, 19.

38. Memo: The Tourist Industry, 10 Feb. 1945, DT, S13087A, National Archives of Ireland, Dublin.

39. Irish Tourist Board Annual Report and Accounts, Year Ended 31st March, 1943, 23 June 1943, TTA 5/1/2, National Archives of Ireland, Dublin.

40. Industry and Commerce Memorandum, 18 Feb. 1944.

41. Irish Tourist Board Annual Report and Accounts, Year Ended 31st March, 1945, 28 June 1945, TTA 5/1/2, National Archives of Ireland, Dublin.

42. Industry and Commerce Memorandum, 18 Feb. 1944. For additional information about the Portmarnock, Bundoran, and Lisdoonvarna plans, see J. P. O'Brien memorandum, 10 Feb. 1945, DT, S13087A, National Archives of Ireland.

43. O'Doherty interview, 29 Apr. 2002.

44. C. S. Andrews, *Man of No Property*, 76.

45. "Death of Mr. Edward T. Keane," *Kilkenny People*, 19 May 1945.

46. Ó Drisceoil, *Censorship in Ireland*, 181.

47. "Where Jobs Accumulate and Men Decay," *Kilkenny People*, 21 Mar. 1942.

48. "Here We Are Again!" *Kilkenny People*, 18 Apr. 1942.

49. "The Playboys of the Western World," *Kilkenny People*, 23 Jan. 1943.

50. "The Irish Tourist Board," *Kilkenny People*, 31 Mar. 1945.

51. "Let Us Praise Famous Men: Tourist Bigwigs on Parade; Sausages and Highbrows," *Kilkenny People*, 4 Nov. 1944.

52. "Really, Mr. Condon!" *Kilkenny People*, 2 Sept. 1944.

53. "The Tourist Ramp Costs," *Kilkenny People*, 25 Mar. 1944.

54. "Staggered Holidays," *Kilkenny People*, 26 Feb. 1944.

55. "A Square Deal for the Taxpayers," *Kilkenny People*, 24 July 1943. Also see "The Tourist Ramp," *Kilkenny People*, 4 May 1946.

56. *Kilkenny People*, 2 Sept. 1944.

57. C. S. Andrews, *Man of No Property*, 76.

58. Michael Kevin O'Doherty, interview by author, Dublin, 30 July 2002.

59. Michael Gorman, interviews by author, Dublin, 6 Aug. 2002 and 11 Oct. 2002.

60. The cost of these properties averaged roughly £12,000 each. For a detailed accounting, see National Archives of Ireland, DF, F200/7-14/45.

61. Tourist Development Program, 29 June 1946, TTA 5/1/2, National Archives of Ireland, Dublin.

62. Irish Tourist Board Annual Report and Accounts, Year Ended 31st March 1947, 27 June 1947, TTA 5/1/2, National Archives of Ireland, Dublin.

63. "Killarney Discusses Tourists. New Government Bill Examined by UDC," *Cork Evening Echo*, 5 Nov. 1938.

64. C. S. Andrews, *Man of No Property*, 76.

65. "The Tourist Ramp," *Kilkenny People*, 27 Jan. 1945.

66. *Kilkenny People*, 4 May 1946.

67. "More Vital Than Luxury Hotels," *Kilkenny People*, 15 June 1946.

68. "Tourist Board and Tourists," *Irish Independent*, 1 May 1946.

69. "The Future of Irish Tourism," *Irish Press*, 12 Oct. 1950.

70. Preliminary Report of the Irish Hotels Commission, 30 Sept. 1950, DT, S13087C, National Archives of Ireland.

71. "Tourism a Major Asset of Nation," *Irish Independent*, 27 Oct. 1950.

72. "Heavy Tourist Spending Will Increase Living Costs," *Irish Times*, 18 Apr. 1946.

73. "The Tourist Ramp," *Kilkenny People*, 19 Apr. 1947.

74. Memorandum: Killarney, 16 Jan. 1948, DT, S13087A, National Archives of Ireland, Dublin.

75. KTA chairman's address to Killarney Tourist Association annual general meeting, 12 Dec. 1947, DT, S13087A, National Archives of Ireland, Dublin.

76. Memorandum: Killarney, 16 Jan. 1948.

77. Photographs K.1/48–K.107/48 include the Killarney area. Another two hundred photographs, running to K.301/48, cover remaining Killarney-area tourist sites in the Dingle and Ring of Kerry areas. (The archive's indexing system uses the first number to define the photograph's position on a roll and the second number to denote the year in which the image was taken.)

78. Shelley Baranowski, *Strength Through Joy* (Cambridge: Cambridge Univ. Press, 2004), 62. Nazi Germany's Kraft durch Freude (Strength Through Joy) program was designed to raise "the productivity and political loyalty" of workers by improving factory conditions, encouraging development of the Volkswagon (People's Car), and promoting a holiday program that, at its height, accounted for nearly ten million overnight stays in German hotels during 1936—11 percent of total bednights for the year. The program went a long way toward helping to structure leisure time by providing inexpensive outings to workers. See Rudy Koshar, *German Travel Cultures* (Oxford: Berg, 2000), 121, 123–25.

79. ITB memorandum, "Towards an Irish Recreational Policy," Feb. 1944, DT, S13087A, National Archives of Ireland, Dublin, emphasis mine.

80. See Peter Bailey, *Leisure and Class in Victorian England: Rational Recreation and the Contest for Control* (Buffalo, N.Y.: Univ. of Toronto Press, 1978); Robert W. Malcolmson, *Popular Recreations in English Society, 1700–1850* (Cambridge: Cambridge Univ. Press, 1973); also see Walton, *Blackpool.*

81. See Baranowski, *Strength Through Joy.*

82. Minister of Local Government and Public Health memorandum, 29 Apr. 1944, DT, S13087A, National Archives of Ireland, Dublin.

83. Share, *Flight of the Iolar,* 106.

84. Mícheál Ó Rain, *Are Lingus: 1936–1986: A Business Monographic* (Dublin: Magill Print/Aer Lingus, 1986), 13–14.

85. Ó Rain, *Are Lingus,* 14.

86. Ibid., 14–15.

87. Share, *Flight of the Kolar,* 104–5.

88. Ó Rain, *Are Lingus,* 15.

89. O'Doherty interview, 29 Apr. 2002.

90. Memorandum: Fáilte Téoranta, 21 Nov. 1949, DT, S13904B, National Archives of Ireland, Dublin.

91. Minute, 30 Nov. 1949, DFA, 366/115 Pt. 1, National Archives of Ireland, Dublin.

92. Fanning, *Irish Department of Finance,* 397.

93. First Interim Report on Tourism of the Inter-Departmental Working Party on Dollar Earnings, 1950, DT, S13087C, National Archives of Ireland, Dublin.

94. Bernadette Whelan, *Ireland and the Marshall Plan, 1947–57* (Dublin: Four Courts Press, 2000), 17.

95. Levenstein, *We'll Always Have Paris,* 114–19.

96. "Colonel Pozzi in Ireland," *Irish Travel,* July 1949, 198.

97. O'Doherty interview, 29 Apr. 2002.

98. "Colonel Pozzi in Ireland."

99. Interim Report, 1950, DT, S13087C, National Archives of Ireland, Dublin.

100. Memo to Mr. McCarthy, 30 Dec. 1949, TTA 5/2/14, National Archives of Ireland, Dublin.

101. DFA Memorandum, 27 July 1950, DT, S13087C, National Archives of Ireland, Dublin.

102. Dáil Debate, 22 Apr. 1931.

103. Department of External Affairs, Memorandum for the Government: Cultural Publicity Abroad, 2 June 1947, DT, S13773A, National Archives of Ireland, Dublin.

104. Summary of Meeting with Michael Gorman, 18 June 1959, DFA, 366/263, National Archives of Ireland, Dublin.

105. "Christenberry Report," July–Aug. 1950, DT, S13087D, National Archives of Ireland, Dublin.

106. Denis O'Hearn, *Inside the Celtic Tiger: The Irish Economy and the Asian Model* (London: Pluto Press, 1998), 37.

107. Department of Industry and Commerce memorandum, 15 Feb. 1950, TTA 5/2/14, National Archives of Ireland, Dublin.

108. Department of Finance memorandum, 16 Feb. 1950, TTA 5/2/14, National Archives of Ireland, Dublin.

109. Briefs for Minister of Industry and Commerce, Feb. 1951, TTA 2/4, National Archives of Ireland, Dublin; and O'Doherty interview, 29 Apr. 2002.

110. Preliminary Report of the Irish Hotels Commission for American Tourism, 30 Sept. 1950, DT, S13087C, National Archives of Ireland, Dublin.

111. James Deegan and Donal Dineen devote three pages to the Christenberry report in their twenty-five-page summary of Irish tourism development between 1922 and 1960. They acknowledge that the report's influence on government policy is difficult to determine. See James Deegan and Donal Dineen, *Tourism Policy and Performance: The Irish Experience* (London: International Thompson Business Press, 1997), 17–19. Linda King is far less guarded and argues that the report had a profound impact, especially in the area of advertising content. Linda King, "'Guaranteed Irish'—Aer Lingus and the Representation of Ireland" (paper presented at *Ireland's Heritages: Critical Perspectives on Consumption, Method and Memory,* Galway-Mayo Institute of Technology, Castlebar, 19 Oct. 2002).

112. Christenberry report. Tourist guides took this scattered approach as a result of the ITA's close connection to local authorities and the need to universally please all counties, not the belief that everything and every place in Ireland was equally important to tourists. Areas like Killarney were able to exert more pressure than the Roscommons or Cavans of the country, but minor regions *also* contributed to the Association's small budget and could not be ignored.

113. Quinlan was appointed primarily for his pro–Fine Gael politics and he seems to have lacked any substantial tourism background.

114. Much of the graphic design work done in Ireland during the 1950s and 1960s was by Dutch designers like Jan de Fouw who produced, among other things, *Ireland of the Welcomes* from 1952 into the 1990s. De Fouw and his fellow countrymen were encouraged to keep a low profile and to avoid putting their name on their publications because doing so sparked negative commentary in the pages of Irish newspapers. *Home Movie Nights: Jan de Fouw*, directed by Alan Gilsenan, Dublin: RTÉ, 2001; and also Jan de Fouw, interview by author, Dublin, 14 Oct. 2002. For a more complete outline of the story of Dutch influence on Irish design, including an account of de Fouw's influence, see Conor Clarke, *Oranje and Green: Holland-Ireland, Design Connections 1951–2002* (Amsterdam: BIS Publishers, 2002).

115. Christenberry report.

116. DFA Minutes, 31 Jan. 1951, DFA, 366/115 Pt. 1, National Archives of Ireland, Dublin.

117. Report of Cabinet Subcommittee on Tourism, 10 July 1950, DT, S13087C, National Archives of Ireland, Dublin.

118. Memorandum: The Irish Tourist Board and Tourist Publicity, 1950, DT, S13087C, National Archives of Ireland, Dublin.

119. Ibid.

120. Memorandum from Irish Tourist Board to Minister for Industry and Commerce, 13 Dec. 1950, DT, S13087C, National Archives of Ireland, Dublin.

121. Memo to Mr. McCarthy, 30 Dec. 1949, TTA 5/2/14.

122. "Tourist Board Scheme Delayed by Minister," *Irish Times,* 9 Oct. 1950.

123. O'Doherty interview, 29 Apr. 2002.

124. "Irish Tourist Association Annual General Meeting and Luncheon," *Irish Travel,* Nov. 1950, 27–33.

125. *Irish Press,* 12 Oct. 1950. This is a reference to a leadership shake-up at the Tourist Board that took effect on 1 October during which J. A. Nugent was made the new chairman. As noted above, there were not, however, any massive changes to board structure or responsibilities. See Annual Reports and Accounts, Year Ended 31st Mar. 1951, 1951, DT, S13904C, National Archives of Ireland, Dublin.

126. "The Future of Irish Tourism Part II," *Irish Press,* 14 Oct. 1950.

127. DFA Minutes, 31 Jan. 1951.

128. DFA Minutes, 1 Feb. 1951, DF, 366/115 Pt. 1, National Archives of Ireland, Dublin.

129. DFA Minutes, 7 Feb. 1951, DFA, 366/115 Pt. 1, National Archives of Ireland, Dublin.

130. DFA Minutes, 14 Mar. 1951, DFA, 366/115 Pt. 1, National Archives of Ireland, Dublin.

131. Draft of Tourist Traffic (Amendment) Bill, 1951, TTA 2/4, National Archives of Ireland, Dublin.

132. Dáil Debate, 129 (27 Feb. 1952), 1120–22.

133. Liam Cosgrave was the only minister to make veiled reference to the personal reasons behind the formation of the publicity board. Cosgrave commented that "[i]t is essential in a matter of this kind to avoid any merely personal considerations or any question of personalities and to recognize that the interests of the tourist industry transcend both personalities and the importance of any of these organizations, however long established or however well-intentioned the members of them may be. The industry is far too important to allow it to be handled in a way which will result in either confusion or overlapping of functions." Part of Cosgrave's statement referred to the perpetuation of the Irish Tourist Association; however the "personal considerations" mentioned were undoubtedly a reference to the friendship between Lemass and O'Brien. Ibid.

134. Dáil Debate, 129 (27 Feb. 1952), 1136–39.

135. Dáil Debate, 219 (6 Mar. 1952), 1608. Actually, Lemass was responding to a powerful ITA effort to preserve "the identity of the ITA." See ITA Directors Are Perturbed, 26 Oct. 1951, TTA 14/2, National Archives of Ireland, Dublin; and Industry and Commerce Memorandum, Nov. 1951, TTA 5/2/3, National Archives of Ireland, Dublin.

136. Department of Industry and Commerce Minutes, 6 Dec. 1951, TTA 2/7 vol. 1, National Archives of Ireland, Dublin.

137. Report of Inter-Departmental Meeting, 1 Dec. 1951, TTA 5/2/3, National Archives of Ireland, Dublin.

138. Note to McElligott from D. P. Shanagher, 19 Dec. 1951, TTA 2/7 vol. 1, National Archives of Ireland, Dublin.

139. This finding contradicts Joe J. Lee's suggestion that Finance was able to dramatically handicap Industry and Commerce efforts to forward tourist development [Lee, *Ireland, 1912–1985*, 308].

140. D. P. Shanagher to J. A. Nugent, 18 Dec. 1951, TTA 2/7 vol. 1, National Archives of Ireland, Dublin.

141. The idea that a new name was required for the Irish Tourist Board was one of the few suggestions made in the Christenberry report that was wholeheartedly adopted by the government. This acceptance was owing to the need to distance the new body from the failed board of the 1940s. Given the speed with which the publicity board was launched, it is hardly surprising that out of a desire to begin work O'Brien began using stationary headed "Tourist Publicity Board of Ireland" without receiving official sanction first. O'Brien's action sparked immediate anger in the Department of Industry and Commerce, and the publicity chief was quickly ordered to cease using the English-language letterhead because Lemass wanted to use an Irish name for the new board. See Note from Agnew to Slattery, 8 Oct. 1951, TTA 2/7 vol. 1, National Archives of Ireland, Dublin. The minister felt that it was "desirable that we should get away from the unimaginative kind of name that we established in 1939," no doubt because

such "unimaginative" names were all too closely associated with the failed 1939 board. See Dáil Debate, 129 (27 Feb. 1952), 1124.

142. At the end of October, O'Brien suggested that the name "Fógra Fáilte" might be ideal. J. Agnew, a civil servant at Industry and Commerce, replied that "fógra" was unsuitable because it translated as "notice" or "warning"; the numerous other names that were suggested, however, including Fáilte Éireann and Forás Fáilte, failed to generate substantial support. The names offered for the Tourist Board itself, including Turas Éireann, Cuaird Éireann, Forás Taisteal, and Taisteal Éireann, likewise proved unpopular. See Memo from Agnew to Slattery, 20 Oct. 1951, TTA 2/7 vol. 1, National Archives of Ireland, Dublin; and Points in Regard to the Attached Draft Heads, 1951, TTA 2/7 vol. 1, National Archives of Ireland, Dublin.

143. Dáil Debate, 129 (6 Mar. 1952), 1607.

144. For a detailed discussion of the background and content of An Tóstal, see chapter 4. The festival's profound impact on Irish landscapes is addressed in detail in chapter 6.

145. "An Tóstal," *Irish Tourist Bulletin,* Nov. 1952, DT, S14995A, National Archives of Ireland, Dublin.

146. Taoiseach's Speech at Opening of Tóstal at Cork, 8 May 1955, DT, S15297B, National Archives of Ireland, Dublin.

147. "An Tóstal: A Word of Advice," *Dublin Opinion,* Dec. 1953. This "advice" was contained in an advertisement placed by the tourist board in the satirical magazine *Dublin Opinion.* There was nothing satirical about the advertisement, however, and it succinctly states what the board was saying in its own publications and press statements.

148. According to the booklet, tourism was responsible for £28 million in total exports. As a whole agriculture brought in £40.5 million but the board's figures divided this into specific categories, the largest of which were cattle exports valued at £20 million. Exports were further divided into "other live animals" (£7 million), "eggs" (£5 million), "drink" (£5 million), and "poultry" (£3.5 million). *What Does Tourism Mean to You?* 1952, DT, S14995A, National Archives of Ireland, Dublin.

149. *What Does Tourism Mean to You?*

150. *Tourism Is Everybody's Business,* produced by Joe Byrne, Aiden O'Hanlon, and Brian Keogh for Bord Fáilte Éireann, 1978, Irish Film Center Archives, Dublin.

151. Gorman interviews, 6 Aug. 2002 and 11 Oct. 2002. O'Brien passed away in 1956. See Acknowledgement of a Subscription to the J. P. O'Brien Memorial Fund, May 1956, SFP, PR6/1027, Cork Archives Institute, Cork.

152. O'Doherty interview, 29 Apr. 2002; Gorman interview, 11 Oct. 2002.

153. Dáil Debate, 148 (9 Feb. 1955), 48.

154. Memorandum, 21 July 1955, TTA 14/4, National Archives of Ireland, Dublin. Following the 1952 Tourist Traffic Act, the ITA was primarily responsible for running tourist bureaus in Ireland and no longer published its own guidebooks, magazines, or other materials.

155. Resolution from County Council Chambers, 12 Feb. 1955, DT, S15766, National Archives of Ireland, Dublin.

156. Dáil Debate, 148 (9 Feb. 1955), 48.

157. O'Doherty interview, 30 July 2002.

158. Gorman interview, 11 Oct. 2002.

159. Memorandum, 11 Feb. 1959, DT, S16596A, National Archives of Ireland, Dublin.

160. BFÉ Press Release, 17 Sept. 1964, DT, S13087H/95, National Archives of Ireland, Dublin.

3. Change and Continuity, 1958–1994

1. Tony Varley, Thomas A. Boylan, and Michael P. Cuddy, eds., *Rural Crisis: Perspectives on Irish Rural Development* (Galway: Center for Development Studies, Univ. College Galway, 1991).

2. J. W. O'Hagan, *The Economy of Ireland: The Performance of a Small European Country* (London: Macmillan, 1995), 27.

3. Tom Inglis, *Moral Monopoly: The Rise and Fall of the Catholic Church in Modern Ireland* (Cork: Cork Univ. Press, 1998).

4. Brian Fallon, *An Age of Innocence: Irish Culture, 1930–1960* (Dublin: Gill and Macmillan, 1998), especially page 257.

5. See O'Hearn, *Inside the Celtic Tiger*; and O'Hagan, *Economy of Ireland*. The unemployment statistic cited here is found in O'Hagan, *Economy of Ireland*, 40.

6. It has often been suggested that the 1960s represented a "quantum leap into modernity"; however, Brian Fallon argues that developments in the 1950s and even the 1940s were far more profound. Fallon's view is definitely borne out in tourism development. While there was dramatic growth in the 1960s, the foundation was laid earlier and changes that took place during the 1960s and 1970s seldom had the profound impact of the institutional developments covered in chapter 2. See Fallon, *An Age of Innocence*, especially 257–71.

7. No legislation after 1955 attempted to accomplish anything as dramatic as the 1939, 1952, or 1955 acts had done and instead covered budgetary increases and minor issues such as the grading of caravan parks. See Deegan and Dineen, *Tourism Policy and Performance*, 38 and 41.

8. Pack, "Spain in the Age of Mass Tourism," 106.

9. Father John Scanlon to Erskine Childers, 29 July 1963, DT, S17316/63, National Archives of Ireland, Dublin.

10. John B. Keane, "A Matchmaker Wanted for the Deserted Village," *Sunday Press*, 10 Nov. 1963.

11. Father John Scanlon to Erskine Childers.

12. Keene's sympathy with the plight of bachelor farmers was recorded in *The Chastitute*, a humorous story of John Bosco's unsuccessful attempts to hire a matchmaker able to help end his fifty-three-year battle with religiously inspired sexual guilt, social ineptitude, bad luck,

and virginity. See John B. Keane, *The Chastitute: A Play In Two Acts* (Dublin: Mercier Press, 1981).

13. *Sunday Press,* 10 Nov. 1963.

14. Runai Aire to Father John Scanlon, 1 Sept. 1963, DT, S17316/63, National Archives of Ireland, Dublin.

15. Ó Cearbhaill from Father John Scanlon, 18 Sept. 1963, DT, S17316/63, National Archives of Ireland, Dublin.

16. Seán Lemass to Father John Scanlon, 26 Sept. 1963, DT, S17316/63, National Archives of Ireland, Dublin; and 18 Sept. 1963, DT, S17316/63.

17. Father John Scanlon to Electricity Supply Board, 7 Jan. 1964, DT, S17316/95, National Archives of Ireland, Dublin.

18. Note from Electricity Supply Board, 18 Feb. 1964, DT, S17316/95, National Archives of Ireland, Dublin.

19. Memorandum: Problems of Small Western Farms, 29 July 1963, DT, 98/6/149, National Archives of Ireland, Dublin.

20. Memorandum: Father Scanlon's letter, 24 Sept. 1963, DT, S17316/63.

21. Tourism brochure: "Take a Holiday 'Away from It All' in Tuosist," circa 1970, DT, 2002/8/299, National Archives of Ireland, Dublin.

22. For a detailed discussion of cross-border tourism dialogue, see Eric G. E. Zuelow, "'Ingredients for Cooperation': Irish Tourism in North-South Relations, 1924–1998," *New Hibernia Review* 10, no. 1 (2006): 17–39.

23. "Hoteliers and Catering People Upset by Bord Fáilte Booklet," *Clare Champion,* 10 Nov. 1972.

24. "Angling—The Saviour of Clare Tourism," *Clare Champion,* 25 Mar. 1983.

25. "Bord Fáilte Accused of Neglecting East Clare," *Clare Champion,* 24 May 1985.

26. Department of Transport and Power Information Sheet: Irish Tourist Association, Feb. 1963, DT, S13087G/63, National Archives of Ireland, Dublin.

27. Michael R. Boland to Erskine Childers, 11 Mar. 1963, DT, S13087H/63, National Archives of Ireland, Dublin.

28. Department of Transport and Power Information Sheet.

29. Erskine Childers to Seán Lemass, 21 Mar. 1963, DT, S13087G/63, National Archives of Ireland, Dublin.

30. J. Fitzpatrick to Erskine Childers, 4 Jan. 1963; Note from Irish Tourist Association to Department of Transport and Power, 1963, DT, S13087H/63, National Archives of Ireland, Dublin.

31. Erskine Childers to Seán Lemass, 21 Mar. 1963.

32. Seán Lemass to Erskine Childers, 28 Mar. 1963, DT, S13087G/63, National Archives of Ireland, Dublin.

33. Statement by Erskine Childers to Deputation from Irish Tourist Association, 11 Apr. 1963, DT, S13087G/63, National Archives of Ireland, Dublin.

34. Erskine Childers to Seán Lemass, 19 Apr. 1963, DT, S13087G/63, National Archives of Ireland, Dublin.

35. The paper was designed to be both a party newspaper—De Valera remained on the paper's board of directors throughout his career in politics—and a commercial enterprise. Following Seán Lemass's tenure as the paper's managing director, it began to reflect an ideological split within Fianna Fáil. The paper sided against the party's protectionist wing and supported the new Whitaker/Lemass belief in free trade and the promotion of outside investment. Given the paper's new forward-looking direction, it is interesting that it did not immediately welcome the demise of the ITA in favor a more efficient and modern tourism development structure. See John Horgan, *Irish Media: A Critical History since 1922* (London: Routledge, 2001), 28 and 68.

36. "Talks to Be Held on Fate of ITA," *Irish Press*, 19 Apr. 1963.

37. "Bord Fáilte to Take over ITA," *Irish Press*, 16 Oct. 1963.

38. "New Tourist Plan Is Vital to Economy," *Irish Press*, 18 Oct. 1963.

39. O'Doherty interview, 30 July 2002. Also see Minutes, ITA Council of Director's Meeting, 20 Feb. 1964, SFP, PR6/1031(2), Cork Archives Institute, Cork.

40. Minutes, ITA Council of Director's Meeting, 20 Feb. 1964.

41. O'Doherty interview, 30 July 2002.

42. Minutes, ITA Council of Director's Meeting, 20 Feb. 1964.

43. "ITA Says No Closing Down Yet," *Irish Press*, 7 May 1964.

44. Bord Fáilte, *Bord Fáilte Annual Report and Accounts, Year Ending 31st March 1959* (Dublin: Bord Fáilte, 1959).

45. Bord Fáilte, *Bord Fáilte Annual Report and Accounts, Year Ended 31st March 1961* (Dublin: Bord Fáilte, 1961).

46. Bord Fáilte, *Bord Fáilte Report for the Year Ended 31 March 1962* (Dublin: Bord Fáilte, 1962).

47. Bord Fáilte, *The Irish Tourist Board Report for the Year Ended March 31 1964* (Dublin: Bord Fáilte, 1964).

48. Bord Fáilte Press Release, 17 Sept. 1964, DT, S13087H/95, National Archives of Ireland, Dublin.

49. Bord Fáilte, *The Irish Tourist Board Report for the Year Ended March 31, 1965* (Dublin: Bord Fáilte, 1965).

50. Department of Transport and Power Memorandum, 12 June 1970, DT, 2001/6/316, National Archives of Ireland, Dublin.

51. Bord Fáilte, *The Irish Tourist Board Report for the Year Ended 31 March 1962*.

52. Bord Fáilte, *The Irish Tourist Board Report for the Year Ended March 31, 1966* (Dublin: Bord Fáilte, 1966); Bord Fáilte, *The Irish Tourist Board Report for the Year Ended March 31, 1970* (Dublin: Bord Fáilte, 1970).

53. Department of Transport and Power Memorandum.

54. "Targets Are Set High: Third Programme Issued," *Irish Travel Trade News*, Feb. 1969, 1 and 8.

55. "Bord Fáilte Hit by Big Financial Set Back in '66," *Irish Travel Trade News*, Feb. 1966, 1.

56. *Tourist Traffic Act, 1966* (Dublin: Government Publications, 1966).

57. "Is Rate of Investment in Irish Tourism Sufficient?" *Irish Travel Trade News*, Oct. 1966, 2.

58. "Rate of State Investment in Tourism Too Low," *Irish Travel Trade News*, Dec. 1968, 10.

59. *Tourist Traffic Act, 1968* (Dublin: Government Publications, 1968).

60. "Tourism Being Starved to Death by Lack of Financial Support," *Irish Travel Trade News*, May 1970, 18.

61. *Tourist Traffic Act, 1972* (Dublin: Government Publications, 1972).

62. *Tourism Traffic Act, 1975* (Dublin: Government Publications, 1975).

63. *Tourism Traffic Act, 1983* (Dublin: Government Publications, 1983).

64. *Tourism Traffic Act, 1987* (Dublin: Government Publications, 1987).

65. Bord Fáilte, *The Fáilte Business 2000: The Role of Tourism in Economic Growth* (Dublin: Bord Fáilte, 2000), 32.

66. Frank McNally, "All Ireland Tourism Campaign Launched," *Irish Times*, 12 Nov. 1996.

67. "Allocation for Tourism up 21 Percent," *Irish Times*, 12 Nov. 1999.

68. Bord Fáilte, *Fáilte Business*, 2.

69. Deegan and Dineen, *Tourism Policy and Performance*, 156–65.

70. Gerry Smyth, *Space and the Irish Cultural Imagination* (New York: Palgrave, 2001), 82.

71. "'Old Dublin' Must Be Developed as Tourism Centre," *Irish Travel Trade News*, May 1989, 44–45.

72. Smyth, *Space*, 82.

73. Bord Fáilte, *Bord Fáilte Report for the Year Ended March 1993* (Dublin: Bord Fáilte, 1993).

74. "Matt McNulty Is New Temple Bar Chairman," *Irish Travel Trade News*, Aug./Sept. 1999, 29.

75. An Taisce, *Grafton Street Sustaining the Magic. What Future for Dublin's Favorite Shopping Street?* (Dublin: An Taisce, 1995).

76. Ruth McManus, "Dublin's Changing Tourism Geography," *Irish Geography* 34, no. 2 (2001): 103–23, see page 107.

77. Transport, Fuel, and Power, Transfer of Administration and Ministerial Functions Order, No. 2, 28 Oct. 1961, DT, S13987G/61, National Archives of Ireland, Dublin.

78. "Should Tourism Have a Government Spokesman Queries NTC Chairman," *Irish Travel Trade News*, July/Aug. 1973, 6.

79. "Minister Blamed at Tourism Meeting," *Irish Travel Trade News*, Nov. 1974, 1 and 4.

80. "Tourism Industry Gets Ministerial Recognition," *Irish Travel Trade News*, Oct. 1977, 1.

81. "Ahern Makes Substantial Changes in Departmental Responsibilities," *Irish Times*, 27 June 1997.

82. Mark Hennessy, "Lobbying Saves Walsh, Smith: Five New Faces to Figure at Cabinet Table as Ahern Sacks Four Ministers," *Irish Times*, 7 June 2002.

83. Thompson, "The Postcolonial Tourist," 4–5.

84. "British Pressmen Visit Killarney. Address of Welcome," *Kerryman*, 23 May 1925.

85. *Kerryman*, 5 Apr. 1924.

86. P. J. Courtney, "Railways and Tourists," *Kerryman*, 19 Jan. 1924.

87. "Killarney Tourist Development. Great Western of England Representatives at Killarney," *Kerryman*, 26 Sept. 1925.

88. Department of Justice to Maurice Moynihan, 19 July 1939, DT, S11345, National Archives of Ireland, Dublin.

89. Seán Lemass to Erskine Childers, 6 Aug. 1964, DT, S13087H/95, National Archives of Ireland, Dublin.

90. "Kerryisms," Kerryman, 23 May 1925.

91. "English Firm Leaves Tourist Board in Shade," *Kilkenny People*, 22 Sept. 1951.

92. "The Tourist Board," *Kilkenny People*, 22 Sept. 1951.

93. "ITA and English Company," *Kilkenny People*, 24 Nov. 1951.

94. See [?] McCarthy, Minute, 16 Feb. 1953, TTA 12/3, National Archives of Ireland, Dublin; and [?] O'Riordain, Minute, 19 Nov. 1952, TTA 12/3, National Archives of Ireland, Dublin.

95. De Fouw interview, 14 Oct. 2002.

96. Gilsenan, *Home Movie Nights*.

97. De Fouw interview, 14 Oct. 2002.

98. Points for the Minister on the Memorandum dated 16th February submitted to the Government by the Minister for Finance in regard to Tourist Industry, [?]1950, TTA 5/2/14, National Archives of Ireland, Dublin; and A New Approach? 28 Sept. 1950, DT, S13087C, National Archives of Ireland, Dublin.

99. Department of External Affairs, British Travel and Holidays Association, [?]1955, DFA, 366/215, National Archives of Ireland, Dublin.

100. *Le Guinness: Son Brassage, Ses Properties, Ses Qualities* (Dublin: Guinness, 1932), 14 and 17, Guinness Ireland Archives, Dublin. See also *Guinness, Brasserie de Renommée Mondiale: L'histoire du Célèbre Stout aux Cinq Millions Hectolitres de Ventes Annuelles* (Dublin, circa 1950), 5 and 17, Guinness Ireland Archives, Dublin.

101. *Guinness Dublin* (Dublin, 1939, 1948, 1955), Guinness Ireland Archives, Dublin.

102. Gorman interview, 11 Oct. 2002.

103. "Irish Tourist Association: Meeting in Cork, Work in America, Branch Formed in Dingle," *Kerryman*, 13 Dec. 1924.

104. See "Ireland for Tourists: The Whole Country Organised; Elaborate Publicity Work," *Kerryman*, 2 May 1925; and "Killarney Tourist Association: Election of Officers,

Future Town Clerk to Be Secy, Killarney in the Films, Delightful Pictures of Killarney," *Kerryman*, 23 Jan. 1926.

105. "Irish Tourist Association: Bureau in New York," *Kerryman*, 24 Dec. 1927.

106. "Christenberry Report."

107. Bord Fáilte, *Bord Fáilte Éireann Newsletter* (Mar.–Apr. 1956), 1.

108. Seanad Debate, *Tourist Traffic Bill, 1938—Fifth Stage*, 20 July 1939.

109. Gorman interview, 11 Oct. 2002.

110. "Big Success for BFÉ Benelux Promotion," *Irish Travel Trade News*, Mar. 1968, 1.

111. For an example, see Bord Fáilte, *Urlaub Made in Ireland* (Frankfurt: Bord Fáilte, 1969).

112. "Importance of German Market Emphasized by Frankfurt Workshop," *Irish Travel Trade News*, June 1971, 2.

113. Bord Fáilte, *Bord Fáilte Éireann Newsletter* (Nov.–Dec. 1955), 1.

114. Levenstein, *We'll Always Have Paris*, 145 and 207.

115. Bord Fáilte, *Newsletter* (Nov.–Dec. 1955), 1.

116. Bord Fáilte, *Bord Fáilte Éireann Newsletter* (July–Aug. 1956), 1.

117. Bord Fáilte, Survey of Visitors, Summer 1956, DF, F120/1/57, National Archives of Ireland, Dublin.

118. Bord Fáilte, *Attitudes of American and English Tourists Towards Shopping in Ireland and Irish Merchandise: A Qualitative Investigation* (Dublin: Bord Fáilte, 1973).

119. Bord Fáilte, *Know Your Market: Italy* (Dublin: Bord Fáilte, 1997).

120. Bord Fáilte, *Know Your Market: France* (Dublin: Bord Fáilte, 1998).

121. Bord Fáilte, *Know Your Market: North America* (Dublin: Bord Fáilte, 1998).

122. There has been a tendency in some of the scholarly literature to claim that government interest in tourism did not develop until the late 1980s because the industry was not a spending priority. (Desmond Gillmor, "Recent Trends and Patterns in Irish Tourism," in *Irish Tourism Development*, ed. Proinnsias Breathnach [Maynooth: Geographical Society of Ireland, 1994], 3.) Although it is true that grants for tourism development were often smaller than the industry wanted and that really substantial government investment had to wait until the late 1980s, I hope that it has been clear that gauging government interest should not be based entirely on the amount of money allocated for development. It is more precise to consider financial allocations in conjunction with a willingness to include tourism in government development programs, the government role in tourism policy development, and the position afforded tourism in the cabinet. The resulting picture shows a growing recognition of tourism's important role as a national interest spanning some forty years, not as a sudden epiphany in 1988.

4. Culture, Language, and Tourism

1. Miroslav Hroch, "From National Movement to the Fully-formed Nation: The Nation-building Process in Europe," in *Mapping the Nation*, ed. Gopal Balakrishnan (New York: Verso, 1996), 78–97, especially page 79.

2. Anthony D. Smith, *The Ethnic Origins of Nations* (Oxford: Blackwell, 1986).

3. Gellner, *Nations and Nationalism*; and Eric Hobsbawm and Terence Ranger, eds., *The Invention of Tradition* (Cambridge: Cambridge Univ. Press, 1986).

4. Gellner, *Nations and Nationalism*; and Anderson, *Imagined Communities*.

5. Catalan nationalists base their claim for independence on the issue of linguistic rights, believing that the very definition of "Catalan" would lose any clarity if the language were to disappear. See Daniele Conversi, "Language or Race?: The Choice of Core Values in the Development of Catalan and Basque Nationalisms," *Ethnic and Racial Studies* 13, no. 1 (1990): 50–70, see pages 53 and 57. Flemish nationalists stress their language rather than shared values, dress, or other markers of national difference. See Jan Blommaert, "Language and Nationalism: Comparing Flanders and Tanzania," *Nations and Nationalism* 2, no. 2 (1996): 235–56, see pages 237–38. Finally, Quebecois nationalism emphasizes language as a primary marker of identity—a stance that won concessions from the Canadian government and assured that Quebec remains effectively a unilingual state within a state. See Milton Taras, "Nations and Language-Building: Old Theories, Contemporary Cases," *Nationalism and Ethnic Politics* 4, no. 3 (1998): 79–101, especially 87–89.

6. Colman Ó Huallachain, *The Irish and Irish: A Sociolinguistic Analysis of the Relationship between a People and Their Language* (Dublin: Irish Franciscan Provincial Office, 1994); Reg Hinley, *The Death of the Irish Language* (London: Routledge, 1990).

7. Mike Cronin, *Sport and Nationalism in Ireland: Gaelic Games, Soccer and Irish Identity since 1884* (Dublin: Four Courts Press, 1999).

8. Timothy Gerard McMahon, "The Social Bases of the Gaelic Revival, 1893–1910," (Ph.D. diss., Univ. of Wisconsin-Madison, 2001).

9. Central Statistics Office, *Statistical Abstract, 1990* (Dublin: Government Publications, 1990), 55.

10. It is very likely that a large percentage of those who claim to be Irish speakers actually know only a few words or phrases. In other words, the census data probably *overestimates* the strength of the language revival, and these numbers are worthy of caution.

11. "Dingle as Tourist Centre. Inch—Ireland's Finest Strand," *Kerryman*, 3 Oct. 1925.

12. "Kerry Roads and Hotels," *Kerryman*, 28 Aug. 1926.

13. "Tourist Development," *Kerryman*, 29 Jan. 1927.

14. Irish Tourist Association, *Ireland: Official Publication* (Dublin: Irish Tourist Association, 1929).

15. Gavon Campbill to Department of Finance, 14 July 1930, DF, E109/31/30, National Archives of Ireland, Dublin; and J. P. O'Brien to government, 12 June 1930, DF, E109/31/30, National Archives of Ireland, Dublin.

16. Irish Tourist Association, "Holidays in the Gaeltacht: See Ireland First," circa 1930, DF, E109/31/30, National Archives of Ireland, Dublin.

17. Archie Bell, *The Spell of Ireland* (Boston: L. C. Page and Co., 1928), 75.

18. Sean MacEntee, Memorandum: Development of the Tourist Industry in the Gaeltacht, 20 Nov. 1934, DT, S7839A & B, National Archives of Ireland, Dublin. The memorandum to which MacEntee was responding is missing from the National Archives and the relevant Taoiseach file.

19. Máire Cruise O'Brien, *The Same Age as the State* (Madison: Univ. of Wisconsin Press, 2004), 50, 78–79, 80, and 115.

20. MacEntee, Memorandum: Development of the Tourist Industry in the Gaeltacht, 20 Nov. 1934.

21. *Irish Press,* 31 Sept. 1938, emphasis mine.

22. R. Jacob, "Gaeltacht and Tourists," *Irish Press,* 5 Oct. 1938.

23. Cu Uladh, "Gaeltacht and Tourists," *Irish Press,* 3 Oct. 1938.

24. "Tourist Bill Will Benefit Gaeltacht," *Irish Press,* 1 Oct. 1938.

25. "Kilarney Discusses Tourists. New Government Bill Examined by UDC," *Cork Evening Echo,* 5 Nov. 1938.

26. This term was used by Donnchadh Ó hEaluighthe during debate about the bill in the Seanad. See Seanad Debate, *Tourist Traffic Bill, 1938—Fifth Stage,* 20 July 1939. It is not clear whether the anti-tourism authors were members of the Gaelic League or whether the Gaelic League took any official stance on the legislation.

27. Ibid.

28. C. S. Almond, Minute, 25 May 1938, DFA, S084/0020/38, National Archives of Ireland, Dublin.

29. ITA Memorandum to Minister for Industry and Commerce, 16 Apr. 1941, DT, S10946, National Archives of Ireland, Dublin.

30. Irish Tourist Association, *Official Guide to the "Kingdom of Kerry"* (Dublin: Irish Tourist Association, [?]1940).

31. O'Doherty interview, 30 July 2002.

32. Department of Finance Note, 1 Feb. 1944, DF, F200/17/44, National Archives of Ireland, Dublin.

33. Inter-Departmental Committee on Development of Gaeltacht Resorts, Report on Development of Gaeltacht Resorts, Feb. 1948, DF, F200/17/44, National Archives of Ireland, Dublin.

34. Irish Tourist Board, Gaeltacht Summer Colleges, 6 Jan. 1944, DF, F200/17/44, National Archives of Ireland, Dublin.

35. Ibid.

36. Nuala C. Johnson, "Making Space: Gaeltacht Policy and the Politics of Identity," in *In Search of Ireland: A Cultural Geography,* ed. Brian Graham (London: Routledge, 1997), 181.

37. Cabinet Minutes, 28 Oct. 1952, DT, S13087E1, National Archives of Ireland, Dublin.

38. Minute from Donnelly to Hayes, 8 Mar. 1959, TTA 2/27, National Archives of Ireland, Dublin.

39. Department of Finance, Memorandum for the Government: Observations of the Minister for Finance on the Memorandum of the Minister for Transport and Power Regarding Proposals for Assisting the Economies of Small Farm Areas in the West of Ireland through Tourism, 7 Apr. 1965, DT, 98/6/149, National Archives of Ireland, Dublin.

40. Lee, *Ireland, 1912–1985,* 671.

41. Ibid., 673.

42. "Tourism Is Not Good for the Irish Language—DJ at Dingle Court," *Kerryman,* 29 Nov. 1958.

43. L. Perry Curtis, Jr., *Apes and Angles: The Irishman in Victorian Caricature* (Washington, D.C.: Smithsonian Institution, 1997), x–xxxi and 157; Richard Stivers, *Hair of the Dog: Irish Drinking and Its American Stereotype* (New York: Continuum, 2000), see pages 1–10 for a brief summary of the drunken Irish stereotype.

44. Maureen Waters, *The Comic Irishman* (Albany: State Univ. of New York Press, 1984), 1–6.

45. Seamus Deane, *Strange Country: Modernity and Nationhood in Irish Writing since 1790* (Oxford: Clarendon Press, 1997), 54–56.

46. Michael de Nie, "'A Medley Mob of Irish-American Plotters and Irish Dupes': The British Press and Transatlantic Fenianism," *Journal of British Studies* 40, no. 2 (2001): 213–40, especially page 239. For more on British colonial ideas about the people of India, see Thomas R. Metcalf, *Ideologies of the Raj* (Cambridge: Cambridge Univ. Press, 1995).

47. Roy Foster, *Paddy and Mr. Punch: Connections in Irish and English History* (London: Oxford Univ. Press, 1995), 281–305.

48. *Kerryman,* 21 Aug. 1926.

49. Irish Tourist Association, "The Irish Elections, 1927," *Irish Travel,* June 1927, 197.

50. "Genuine Irish Welcome," *Irish Travel,* May 1932, 191.

51. Jack Lynch, Address by the Taoiseach, 13 Aug. 1968, DT, 99/1/131, National Archives of Ireland, Dublin.

52. Will Rogers, "American Tribute. Ireland's Welcome for the Tourist," *Kerryman,* 21 Aug. 1926.

53. Bell, *The Spell of Ireland,* 29.

54. Tony Hawks, *Round Ireland with a Fridge* (New York: St. Martin's Griffin, 1988), 93.

55. "Kerryisms," *Kerryman,* 15 Oct. 1927.

56. Bord Fáilte, *Ireland: Fairies* (Dublin: Bord Fáilte, 1976).

57. Draft letter from Michael Kevin O'Doherty to [?], Apr. 1950, Michael Gorman private collection.

58. Report of Cabinet Sub-Committee on Tourism.

59. Bord Fáilte, *Bord Fáilte Éireann Newsletter,* Nov. 1957, 3.

60. Gilsenan, *Home Movie Nights*.

61. Brown, *Ireland*, 75.

62. Roy Foster, *W. B. Yeats, A Life, Part Two: The Arch-Poet* (Oxford: Oxford Univ. Press, 2003), 332–35.

63. Brown, *Ireland*, 113.

64. Cuddy, 33–34.

65. Ibid., 42.

66. Quinn and Keane, 190.

67. Ibid., 192.

68. Bord Fáilte, *Developing Sustainable Tourism: Tourism Development Plan 1994–1999* (Dublin: Bord Fáilte, 1995), 3.

69. Denis A. Cronin, Jim Gilligan, and Karina Holton, eds., *Irish Fairs and Markets, Studies in Local History* (Dublin: Four Courts Press, 2001), 14.

70. D. Cronin, Gilligan, and Holton, *Irish Fairs and Markets*, 135.

71. Ibid., 16.

72. Ibid., 124. See also Patrick Logan, *Fair Day: The Story of Irish Fairs and Markets* (Belfast: Appletree Press, 1986), 65.

73. Logan, *Fair Day*, 20.

74. Rukeyser describes how a ten-year-old girl, the Green Queen, crowns Puck (69–70), then proceeds to stress the extraordinary sexuality of the girl's royal partner: "The huge white balls were before my eyes, great in their power and whiteness . . . Energy bulged here, a double bulge robed in the smoothness of white fur, hidden and trumpeting, open and recondite, worlds creating worlds, something secret and understood . . . He swung there, strong, white, the crowned world rising up through worlds, crowned by a girl's arm, still and held in his kingship, with the great bells slung between his horns, the great testicles slung between his legs." Muriel Rukeyser, *The Orgy* (New York: Coward-McCann, 1965), 71–72.

75. During a conversation I had while researching this book, one local publican proudly told me about his approach to the event. He boasted that all stools and tables were removed from his bar before the fair; it was simple geometry: more people could be plugged into the pub than would be possible if furniture were present. He went on to say that he would stock up on huge quantities of extra alcohol, hire a substantial short-term staff, and forego sleep for the entire event. It is a very lucrative, if exhausting, weekend for local public houses.

76. Logan, *Fair Day*, 56–57.

77. D. Cronin, Gilligan, and Holton, *Irish Fairs and Markets*, 136.

78. In the front space of the original 1965 edition of *The Orgy*, Rukeyser's publisher inserted the following disclaimer: "The goat is real, Puck Fair is real; the orgy is real. All the characters and the acts of this book, however, are—of course—a free fantasy on the event." The author steadfastly denied the publisher's statement, however, claiming that the work was "a documentary account of three days of living under an extraordinary power." According to Rukeyser, she drew all of her reporting directly from the notes taken during her August 1958 trip. Indeed,

"The only thing in it I did not write and I cannot vouch for is the publishers' disclaimer." See Murial Rukeyser, "Not a Novel," *New York Review of Books* 4, no. 9 (3 June 1965).

79. Rukeyser, *Orgy*, 25.

80. Ibid., 28.

81. Ibid., 104.

82. Ibid., 184.

83. I would like to thank Dr. Aoife Bhreatnach for sharing her research on changing perceptions of Irish Travellers with me during numerous conversations in the winter/spring of 2002. Interested readers should see Aoife Bhreatnach, *Becoming Conspicuous: Irish Travelers, Society and the State, 1920–70* (Dublin: Univ. College Dublin Press, 2007).

84. Logan, *Fair Day*, 113.

85. Irish Tourist Association, *Official Guide to "Kingdom of Kerry"* (Dublin: Irish Tourist Association, 1934), 95.

86. "Souvenir of Your Visit to Puck Fair, Killorglin," circa 1946, MS 33,488, List 34, National Library of Ireland, Dublin. Cited with the permission of the Board of the National Library of Ireland.

87. Sean O'Faolain, *An Irish Journey* (London: Reader's Union, 1941), 128. Leslie Daiken, "Fair at Killorglin," newspaper clipping, MS 33,488, List 34, National Library of Ireland, Dublin. Cited with the permission of the Board of the National Library of Ireland.

88. Fógra Fáilte, *Ireland Guide* (Dublin: Fógra Fáilte, [?]1953.

89. Bord Fáilte, *Ireland: Calendar of Events, 1958* (Dublin: Bord Fáilte, 1958).

90. Bord Fáilte, *Ireland: Calendar of Events, 1961* (Dublin: Bord Fáilte, 1961).

91. Bord Fáilte, *Ireland: Calendar of Events, 1973* (Dublin: Bord Fáilte, 1973).

92. Bord Fáilte, *Ireland: 1980* (London: Bord Fáilte, 1980).

93. Logan, *Fair Day*, 113.

94. Rukeyser, *Orgy*, 15.

95. Daiken, "Fair at Killorglin."

96. Leslie Daiken, *Where Puck Is King*, script for BBC radio broadcast, London, 1960, MS 33,483 (48), National Library of Ireland, Dublin. Cited with the permission of the Board of the National Library of Ireland.

97. Leslie Daiken, "Kerry in August: Where Puck Is King," *Ocean Times*, 8 July 1962. See also Leslie Daiken, "Puck Fair (Synopsis)," 1 Feb. 1960, MS 33,483 (48), National Library of Ireland, Dublin. Cited with the permission of the Board of the National Library of Ireland.

98. Michael Gorman to Leslie Daiken, 4 Sept. 1959, MS 33, 472 box 3, folder 11, National Library of Ireland, Dublin. Cited with the permission of the Board of the National Library of Ireland.

99. O'Doherty interview, 29 Apr. 2002. The administration of An Tóstal is covered by Irene Furlong, "Tourism and the Irish State in the 1950s," in *The Lost Decade: Ireland in the 1950s*, ed. Dermot Keogh, Finbarr O'Shea, and Carmel Quinlan (Douglas Village, Cork: Mercier, 2004).

100. Subcommittee on Tourism memorandum, 1950, DT, S13087C, National Archives of Ireland, Dublin.

101. The Festival of Britain served many roles beyond those listed here. For example, it was also designed to reflect the Labour Party's agenda for the country and was held as a centennial commemoration of the Great Exhibition of 1851. Becky E. Conekin, *'The Autobiography of a Nation': The 1951 Festival of Britain* (Manchester: Manchester Univ. Press, 2003), 2, 4, 8, and 28.

102. An Tóstal Proposal, [?]1951, DT, S15297A, National Archives of Ireland, Dublin.

103. Conekin, *Autobiography*.

104. "An Tóstal" (Ireland at Home): April 5th–26th, 1953, TTA 12/1, National Archives of Ireland, Dublin.

105. P. W. Joyce, *A Social History of Ancient Ireland*, vol. 2 (New York: B. Blom, 1968 [1913]).

106. Fógra Fáilte, *An Tóstal: Official Souvenir Guide* (Dublin: Fógra Fáilte, 1953), 96, in Michael Gorman private collection.

107. O'Doherty interview, 29 Apr. 2002.

108. De Fouw interview, 14 Oct. 2002.

109. Fógra Fáilte, "An Tóstal: Ireland at Home Brochure," 1953, DT, S15297A, National Archives of Ireland, Dublin.

110. Conekin, *Autobiography*.

111. An Bord Fáilte, An Tóstal Proposal, [?]1951.

112. Conekin, *Autobiography*.

113. An Bord Fáilte, *Irish Tourist Bulletin*, Dec. 1952, 6, DT, S14995A, National Archives of Ireland, Dublin.

114. Colm O'Laoghaire, *Ireland Invites You*, 16 mm, 20 min., 1953, distributed by Universal Irish News, Irish Film Center Archives.

115. An Bord Fáilte, *Irish Tourist Bulletin*, June 1952, 3, DT, S14995A, National Archives of Ireland, Dublin.

116. An Bord Fáilte, *Irish Tourist Bulletin*, Dec. 1952, DT, S14995A.

117. Aodh O'Neill, "Pageant of St. Patrick," 7 Dec. 1953, DT, S15297B, National Archives of Ireland, Dublin.

118. An Bord Fáilte, *Irish Tourist Bulletin*, Feb. 1954, 3–4, DT, S14995B, National Archives of Ireland, Dublin.

119. O'Doherty interview, 29 Apr. 2002.

120. Report of Meeting, 2 Sept. 1954, TTA 12/5, National Archives of Ireland, Dublin.

121. Bord Fáilte, *Some Highlights of An Tóstal, 1955* (Dublin: Bord Fáilte, 1955). While the Tóstal guide did not mention it, all three of these individuals were born in England. McMaster was born in Birkenhead, Cheshire, in 1891. He began acting in 1911 and founded a touring Shakespeare company in 1925. This group ventured widely, especially in areas often neglected by theatre groups such as the Near East and Irish provinces. During World War

II, McMaster's company toured Ireland, then traveled to Australia following the war. He returned to Dublin in 1951 where he again led a traveling theater group around Ireland. He has been described as the "last of the great Irish actor-managers." McMaster died in 1962. MacLiammóire (1899–1978) was born in London. While at school in London, he became interested in Gaelic and joined the London Gaelic League. He eventually moved to Ireland in 1927. Edwards (1903–1982) was also born in London. He first toured Ireland in 1920 with Anew McMaster's Shakespeare company and then returned to London where he joined the Old Vic. In 1927 Edwards returned to Dublin to perform once more with McMaster and then decided to open his own theatre, the Peacock in Abbey Street. He joined the Gate Theatre in 1930 and went on to direct more than four hundred productions. Henry Boylan, *A Dictionary of Irish Biography,* 3rd ed. (Niwot, Colo.: Robert Rinehart, 1998).

122. Bord Fáilte, *Bord Fáilte Éireann Newsletter,* Jan.–Feb. 1956, 3.

123. *An Tóstal: Official Souvenir Guide,* 98–100.

124. *An Tóstal,* 102.

125. Ibid., 34–38.

126. Ibid., 53.

127. Ibid., 56.

128. "Kilkenny's Industrial Exhibition," *Kilkenny People,* 4 Apr. 1953.

129. "An Tóstal Closes in Kilkenny," *Kilkenny People,* 2 May 1953.

130. Diarmuid O Braoin, "Comhairle Tostail Corchaighe," 1954, Organising Secretary's Report, 30 June 1954, SFP, PR6/1325 (14), Cork Archives Institute, Cork.

131. "Industrial Parade Will Be Bigger Than Ever," *Limerick Leader,* 16 Mar. 1955. I would like to thank Dr. Aoife Bhreatnach for bringing this reference to my attention.

132. O'Connor argues that Irish people are represented as prone to talking, drinking, laughing, and playing music, but certainly not to working. When work is represented, she claims, "it is transformed into something very different from the alienated experience which it very often is through a process of romanticisation." Labor is made organic, boiled down to milking cows or cutting turf. She claims that this imagery is a result of colonization and that the prevalence of country people in tourist imagery is a trait Ireland shares with many other "'primitive' societies" in which the peasant is turned into a tourist attraction. Barbara O'Connor, "Myths and Mirrors: Tourist Images and National Identity," in *Tourism in Ireland: A Critical Analysis,* ed. Barbara O'Connor and Michael Cronin (Cork: Cork Univ. Press, 1993), 72–73.

133. *An Tóstal: Official Souvenir Guide,* 70.

134. *An Tóstal,* 74.

135. Ibid., 64.

136. Malachy Hynes, "A Foretaste of Tóstal," *Ireland of the Welcomes,* Nov.–Dec. 1952, 3–8.

137. Éamon de Valera, Speech Draft, 5 Apr. 1953, DT, S15197A, National Archives of Ireland, Dublin.

138. Braoin, "Comhairle Tostail Corchaighe."

139. Bord Fáilte, *Ireland of the Festivals* (Dublin: Bord Fáilte, 1959).

140. "An Tóstal—Latest News," *Leinster Express,* 2 Aug. 1958.

141. (1) Future of An Tóstal (2) Commencement Date in 1954 and Subsequent Years, [?]1954, TTA 12/5, National Archives of Ireland, Dublin.

142. Bord Fáilte Éireann Favored 6th–21st May for the 1956 Tóstal, [?]1955, TTA 12/5, National Archives of Ireland, Dublin.

143. Industry and Commerce Minute, 3 Sept. 1955, TTA 12/5, National Archives of Ireland, Dublin.

144. Confidential Memorandum on An Tóstal Review, 24 July 1958, TTA 12/5, National Archives of Ireland, Dublin.

145. Bord Fáilte, *Ireland of the Festivals.*

146. "Probe: The Festivals—What Now?" *Irish Travel Trade News,* May 1965, 2.

147. "Bord Fáilte to Spend £30,000 on 11 Festivals," *Irish Travel Trade News,* Sept. 1965, 7.

148. "Week-Long Festival Celebration Plans," *Irish Travel Trade News,* Mar. 1970, 18. For a more detailed overview of Dublin Tourism's handling of the Dublin Saint Patrick's Parade, see Mike Cronin and Daryl Adair, *The Wearing of the Green: A History of St. Patrick's Day* (London: Routledge, 2002), 184–85.

149. Cronin and Adair, I>Wearing of the Green," 241.

150. Eithne Donnellan, "Manager Mick Becomes Green Marshal for St. Patrick's Day," *Irish Times,* 31 Jan. 2002.

151. *The Rose of Tralee: The Truth in Her Eyes,* produced by Celtic Production/Telegael for Bord Fáilte, 1991, Bord Fáilte Photographic Archives.

5. Tourism and the Past

1. Prasenjit Duara, *Rescuing History from the Nation: Questioning Narratives of Modern China* (Chicago: Univ. of Chicago Press, 1995), 3.

2. Duara, *Rescuing History,* 4. As early as 1320, Scottish nobles and clerics drew on history to explain why Scotland was distinct from England. The "Declaration of Arbroath" traced the Scots from "Greater Scythia" through Spain and finally to Scotland, all the while unified as a people and governed by good qualities that were constantly under attack by outsiders. Even today, Scots look back on the "Declaration" as a clear statement of their proud past. Of course, not every "nation" can look back on fourteenth-century expressions of nationalism; some have had to work much harder. See James G. Kellas, *The Politics of Nationalism and Ethnicity* (New York: St. Martin's Press, 1991), 23–28, especially page 28. After the Second World War, for example, Austrians felt compelled to differentiate their sense of identity from that of the Germans in order to distance themselves from a legacy of mass murder and imperialism. For Austrian nationalists, it was not enough "to promote a distinctly Austrian national present"; it was required that they

draw on evidence from the past to reinforce difference. Nationalist historians focused on ancient demarcations from Germany, working to show that they had never really been part of the German nation. See Peter Thaler, "National History—National Imagery: The Role of History in Postwar Austrian Nation-Building," *Central European History* 32, no. 3 (1999): 277–310.

3. Anthony D. Smith, "Nationalism and the Historians," in *Mapping the Nation*, ed. Gopal Balakrishnan (London: Verso, 1996), 175.

4. Anthony D. Smith, "Gastronomy or Geology? The Role of Nationalism in the Reconstruction of Nations," *Nations and Nationalism* 1, no. 1 (1994): 18.

5. Bord Fáilte, *Report for the Year Ended 31 March 1962*, 13.

6. G. J. Ashworth, "Is Heritage a Globalisation of the Local or a Localisation of the Global?" (paper presented at *Ireland's Heritages: Critical Perspectives on Consumption, Method and Memory*, Castlebar, Co. Mayo, Ireland, 19 Oct. 2002); and Michael Hunter, ed., *Preserving the Past: The Rise of Heritage in Modern Britain* (Stroud, Gloucestershire: Alan Sutton Publishing, 1996), 1.

7. Maxine Feifer, *Tourism in History: From Imperial Rome to the Present* (New York: Stein and Day, 1985), 7–26.

8. Irish Tourist Association, *Ireland*, 1929, 12.

9. For a discussion of the beginnings of the Victorian fascination with ruins, see Ousby, *Englishman's England*.

10. Bell, *The Spell of Ireland*, 29–30 and 52.

11. "'Kuklos,' Awheel in Kerry: 'The Most Beautiful County in the British Isles'; English Writer's Cycle Trip through the 'Kingdom'; Interesting Impressions and High Appreciation," *Kerryman*, 29 Oct. 1927 (originally published in the *London Daily News*).

12. Department of Education Memorandum, [?]1925, DT, S5004A, National Archives of Ireland, Dublin.

13. Gerald Baldwin-Brown, *The Care of Ancient Monuments* (Cambridge: Cambridge Univ. Press, 1905), 128.

14. Baldwin-Brown, *Care of Ancient Monuments*, 73–74.

15. Rudy Koshar, *Germany's Transient Pasts: Preservation and National Memory in the Twentieth Century* (Chapel Hill: Univ. of North Carolina Press, 1998).

16. Baldwin-Brown, *Care of Ancient Monuments*, 74–75.

17. Koshar, *Germany's Transient Pasts*, 31.

18. Professor R. A. S. MacAlister was perhaps the most vocal Irish advocate of preservation in Ireland. Born in Dublin in 1870, he attended school in both Rathmines and Germany before attending Cambridge University. MacAlister edited the journal of the Royal Society of Antiquaries between 1910 and 1918, then served as the society's president between 1924 and 1928. His archeological experience extended beyond the British Isles; he served as director of excavations for the Palestine Explorations fund between 1900 and 1909. Following his time in the Middle East, MacAlister returned to Ireland, where he became the first professor

of Celtic archaeology at University College Dublin—a post he held until 1943. He was also the first chairman of the National Monuments Advisory Council in the Free State following passage of the Monuments Act in 1930. MacAlister was in Germany at the very moment that calls for preservation were growing louder, and he was at Cambridge when the first preservation legislation was passed in England. When this familiarity with the larger preservation discourse is combined with his own interest in Celtic archaeology and languages, it is hardly surprising that MacAlister began warning against the destruction of Irish monuments as early as the 1890s. For more, see Boylan, *Dictionary of Irish Biography*, 230. Irene Furlong briefly describes MacAlister's late-nineteenth-century preservationist concerns in her article "Frederick W. Crossley: Turn-of-the-century Tourism Pioneer."

19. R. A. S. MacAlister, *Ancient Ireland: A Study in the Lessons of Archaeology and History* (London: Methuen and Co., 1935), x.

20. Andrew Saint, "How Listing Happened," in Hunter, *Preserving the Past*, 115–33.

21. Baldwin-Brown, *Care of Ancient Monuments*, 156–57.

22. Memorandum, [?]1925, DT, S5004A).

23. R. A. S. Macalister to the Department of the Taoiseach, 19 May 1926, DT, S5004A, National Archives of Ireland, Dublin.

24. Gavin Stamp, "The Art of Keeping One Jump Ahead: Conservation Societies in the Twentieth Century," in Hunter, *Preserving the Past*, 82–85.

25. Ancient Monuments Protection Act Draft, [?]1925, DT, S5004A, National Archives of Ireland, Dublin.

26. After cabinet consideration, the definition of *ancient monuments* changed relatively little in chronological terms, but dropped much of the initial specificity. *National Monuments Act, 1930* (Dublin: Government Publications, 1930).

27. *National Monuments Act, 1930*.

28. O'Doherty interview, 30 July 2002.

29. *ITA Twentieth Anniversary Issue*, TAP, P91/B/10, University College Dublin. Also see Kinsale Development Association Special Meeting Transcript, 10 Aug. 1942, KDA, U274/5, Cork Archives Institute, Cork.

30. *Anniversary Issue*, TAP, P91/B/10. Very little of the original ITA photographic collection remains, though a handful of undated glass plates are stored in the Bord Fáilte archive that are probably the remnants of the ITA collection. Bord Fáilte acquired the ITA's photo library during the early 1950s.

31. *Anniversary Issue*, TAP.

32. "Christenberry Report."

33. "Preliminary Report of the Irish Hotels Commission," 30 Sept. 1950, DT, S13087C.

34. Report of Meeting, 1 Dec. 1951, TTA 2/7 vol. 1, National Archives of Ireland, Dublin.

35. An Bord Fáilte, *Irish Tourist Bulletin*, July 1951, 3–4, DT, S14995A, National Archives of Ireland, Dublin.

36. O'Doherty interviews, 29 Apr. and 30 July 2002.

37. In his book *The Past Is a Foreign Country* (Cambridge: Cambridge Univ. Press, 1997), David Lowenthal makes a similar point, noting that the placement of signs around castle ruins leads visitors to read the site/sight as a particular historical narrative, defining the castle in a specific way that has little to do with the actual past of the monument. See pages 265–70.

38. An Bord Fáilte, *Irish Tourist Bulletin*, Dec. 1953, 8–9, DT, S14995B, National Archives of Ireland, Dublin.

39. E. M. Fahy to Paddy [?], 27 Sept. 1960, Cork Public Museum [hereafter cited as CPM], U180, Cork Archives Institute, Cork.

40. See note 48 in chapter 6.

41. "The War at Westport," *Irish Times*, 18 Jan. 1961.

42. Arts Council to the Taoiseach, [?], DT, 97/6/380, National Archives of Ireland, Dublin.

43. *Bord Fáilte Éireann Newsletter*, Nov. 1957, 4.

44. *Irish Tourist Bulletin*, Feb. 1954, 6, DT, S14995B.

45. O'Doherty interview, 30 July 2002.

46. Brian Callanan, *Leaders, Visions, and Networks, Ireland's Shannon Story: A Case Study of Local and Regional Development* (Dublin: Irish Academic Press, 2000), 58–64. A far more detailed, if less scholarly, account of the development of Bunratty Castle can be found in Bernard Share, *Bunratty: Rebirth of a Castle* (Dingle, Ireland: Brandon, 1995).

47. An Bord Fáilte, *Irish Tourist Bulletin*, Nov. 1953, 12–13; *Bord Fáilte Éireann Newsletter*, Mar. 1958, 2; Bord Fáilte, *The Irish Tourist Board Annual Report for the Year Ended 31 March 1962* (Dublin: Bord Fáilte, 1962); and O'Doherty interview, 29 Apr. 2002. Dúchas finally developed the Hill of Tara in the 1990s. The new installation includes an impressive multimedia presentation in a converted church. Amusingly, in the late 1960s, an Irish-American named William E. P. O'Donnell proposed that the Irish government should develop Tara, not as a tourist site but as a new site for the Oireachtas and an Irish college. O'Donnell argued that a long boulevard should be constructed between Tara and Slane to host massive St. Patrick's Day parades. "'Save Tara' Plea by American," *Irish Press*, 22 Jan. 1969.

48. Gorman interview, 11 Oct. 2002.

49. Donal Horgan, *Victorian Visitor*, 66.

50. See Irish Tourist Association, *Introducing Ireland* (Dublin: Irish Tourist Association, 1950); Fógra Fáilte, *Ireland: An Illustrated Guide to the Counties of Ireland* (Dublin: Fógra Fáilte, [?]1953); and Bord Fáilte, *Ireland: The Heritage of the Past* (Dublin: Bord Fáilte, 1968). The Bord Fáilte Photographic Archive maintains an extensive collection of early images of Glendalough in all seasons.

51. An Bord Fáilte, *Irish Tourist Bulletin*, Dec. 1951, 6–7, DT, S14995A, National Archives of Ireland, Dublin.

52. Thomas Bodkin, Extract from Report to the Government of Ireland on various Institutions and Activities concerned with the Arts in Ireland, 30 Sept. 1949, DT, S8488B, National Archives of Ireland, Dublin.

53. Peadar S. Doyle, Question for the Taoiseach, 31 Oct. 1951, DT, S8488B, National Archives of Ireland, Dublin.

54. *Irish Tourist Bulletin,* July 1951, 3–4, DT, S14995A.

55. "Ireland's Ancient Monuments, Lack of Interest by Schools Is Deplored," *Irish Independent,* 3 Oct. 1952.

56. *Irish Tourist Bulletin,* Nov. 1953, 12–13, DT, S14995B; and An Bord Fáilte, Annual Report and Accounts, Year Ended 31st March 1954, DT, S15647B, National Archives of Ireland, Dublin. See also An Bord Fáilte, *Irish Tourist Bulletin,* Aug. 1953, 5–6, DT, S14995B, National Archives of Ireland, Dublin.

57. O'Doherty interview, 29 Apr. 2002.

58. Erskine Childers to Seán Lemass, 16 May 1962, DT, S17301/62, National Archives of Ireland, Dublin.

59. Seán Lemass to Erskine Childers, 15 June 1962, DT, S17301/62, National Archives of Ireland, Dublin.

60. In many ways, the development of the Garden of Remembrance chronologically mirrors the restoration of Kilmainham Jail. The Old IRA first proposed a monument at the Rotunda Gardens during the mid-1930s but government action was put on hold by the Emergency. After the war, the site was converted into a tuberculosis hospital and it was not until Noël Browne, minister for health during the interparty government between 1948 and 1951, was able to locate an alternate site at which to base anti-TB efforts that the Remembrance proposal was actualized. Unlike Kilmainham, the Garden of Remembrance was an entirely government-led project. Like Kilmainham, it was formally opened during the fiftieth anniversary commemorations in 1966, but was not completed until the early 1970s. See the following Taoiseach files: S8114A-C/61, 96/6/193, 96/6/159, and 2000/6/83.

61. Anne Dolan, *Commemorating the Irish Civil War: History and Memory, 1923–2000* (Cambridge: Cambridge Univ. Press, 2003), 200.

62. "Muckross House," newspaper clipping, 13 Dec. 1963, DT, S6355C/63, National Archives of Ireland, Dublin.

63. E. Myers to Seán Lemass, 23 Sept. 1963, DT, S6355C/63, National Archives of Ireland, Dublin.

64. Erskine Childers to Seán Lemass, 16 May 1962.

65. Erskine Childers to Seán Lemass, 20 Nov. 1963, DT, S6355C/63, National Archives of Ireland, Dublin.

66. Ibid.

67. L. P. Leech, "The Bourne-Vincent Memorial Park," *Irish Press,* 3 Dec. 1963.

68. R. C. MacMillan, "Why Not the Lakes of Killarney for All?" newspaper clipping, 29 Nov. 1963, DT, S6355C/63, National Archives of Ireland, Dublin.

69. E. Myers to Seán Lemass, 23 Sept. 1963.

70. The Royal Hospital was eventually turned into the National Gallery of Modern Art and many of the artifacts originally planned for display in the Georgian building were moved to the Collins Barracks just down the Liffey.

71. Department of Finance, Memorandum for the Government, 20 Apr. 1963, DT, S6355C/63, National Archives of Ireland, Dublin.

72. "20,000 See Muckross House," *Irish Press,* 31 Oct. 1964.

73. Newspaper clipping, 3 Dec. 1968, DT, 96/6/150, National Archives of Ireland, Dublin; "Muckross Gate to Remain Closed," *Cork Examiner,* 9 Aug. 1968.

74. Bord Fáilte, *Tourism Plan 1981–85: Marketing and Development Guide Lines for the Irish Tourist Industry* (Dublin: Bord Fáilte, 1980).

75. "How to Sell Killarney," *Irish Travel Trade News,* May 1989, 46–47.

76. Gorman interview, 11 Oct. 2002.

77. Department of External Affairs, Memorandum, 20 July 1960, DFA, 366/263, National Archives of Ireland, Dublin.

78. See folder DFA, 366/166/1, National Archives of Ireland, Dublin.

79. See detailed records in file sequence: DFA, 366/166/1-15, National Archives of Ireland, Dublin.

80. Conor Cruise O'Brien to E. F. Bozman, 22 May 1952, DFA, 366/175, National Archives of Ireland, Dublin.

81. E. F. Bozman to Conor Cruise O'Brien, 26 May 1952, DFA, 366/175, National Archives of Ireland, Dublin.

82. Memorandum, 24 Feb. 1939, DT, S8114A, National Archives of Ireland, Dublin.

83. While the construction of the Garden of Remembrance sparked little controversy, there was considerable debate about the inscription that was to be included. This conflict extended the completion of the memorial long past its formal inauguration in 1966. After a text was finally agreed—no easy task (see letter from [?] to Jack Lynch, 10 Apr. 1969; Government Meeting Report, 5 Sept. 1969; Garden of Remembrance: Inscriptions on Carved Wall, 21 Sept. 1969, DT, 2000/6/83, National Archives of Ireland, Dublin)—there was a great deal of concern about what languages to use. Although the initial plan was to present a poem in Gaelic, chosen by a government-run contest, there was objection at both public and government level. See letter from [?] to Seán Lemass, 10 Apr. 1969, DT, 2000/6/83, National Archives of Ireland, Dublin. Although the Garden of Remembrance had never been considered as a potential tourist attraction, the idea of a Gaelic-only inscription troubled at least one reporter, who advocated translations of the poem in English, French, and "whatever other languages are considered necessary," because most would be unable to understand the Gaelic—a fact that was nowhere more true than for tourists. See Desmond Rushe, "How Many Could Really Translate It?" *Irish Independent,* 2 Nov. 1971. After all, the Garden would be "one of the very few attractions of its type we have for visitors" and "if only as a gesture of courtesy,

whatever inscription is there should be available in understandable languages." See Desmond Rushe, "The Winning," *Irish Independent,* 12 Nov. 1971.

84. *Ghosts of Kilmainham* (Dublin: Kilmainham Jail Restoration Society, 1963).

85. Pat Cooke, *A History of Kilmainham Gaol* (Dublin: Dúchas, 2001).

86. Letter from [?] to A. D. Codling, 27 Apr. 1928, DF, S002/0003/28, National Archives of Ireland, Dublin.

87. Department of Justice to [?], 2 Feb. 1929, DF, 13/9/29, National Archives of Ireland, Dublin.

88. Memorandum for the Government. Disposal of Kilmainham Jail, 17 June 1946, DF, S102/017/53, National Archives of Ireland, Dublin.

89. Reflecting the growing republican interest in the prison, the Irish Tourist Association drew attention to Kilmainham in 1938 by publishing an article in its monthly magazine, *Irish Travel,* entitled "A Visit to Kilmainham Jail, Dublin: The Bastille of Ireland." The article detailed the role played by the prison in Irish nationalist history, though it limited mention of the Civil War to a short note about female prisoners in 1923 without using the words "Civil War." See C. F. Ridgway, "A Visit to Kilmainham Jail, Dublin: The Bastille of Ireland," *Irish Travel,* Nov. 1938, 34; "Kilmainham Memorial Plans," *Sunday Press,* 4 May 1958.

90. The Invincibles were an offshoot of the Irish Republican Brotherhood who advocated political assassination. They are most significant for carrying out the Phoenix Park murders in 1882.

91. *Sunday Press,* 4 May 1958.

92. Memorandum for the Government. Disposal of Kilmainham Jail, 17 June 1946.

93. M. O. Muimhneachain to [?], 26 Aug. 1953, DFA, S102/017/53, National Archives of Ireland, Dublin.

94. Manuscript by Lorcan C. G. Leonard, "The Kilmainham Project as I Dreamt It and Lived It," 1960, Kilmainham Jail Archives, Dublin.

95. Lorcan C. G. Leonard to John Dowling, 9 June 1958, 1/G/1/2/14, Kilmainham Jail Archives, Dublin.

96. Leonard, "Kilmainham Project."

97. In 1956, Dublin Corporation received a planning application for a cinema to be constructed immediately adjoining the jail. The corporation declared that "it is of the utmost importance that its amenity ground be strictly preserved," and advocated using the jail as a museum. It was urged that "every precaution should be taken to safeguard the amenities of the hospital-jail complex in light of possible future fruition of these schemes." See Letter Regarding Kilmainham Jail, 15 Oct. 1956, DFA, S102/017/53, National Archives of Ireland, Dublin.

98. *Sunday Press,* 4 May 1958.

99. Old IRA Literary and Debating Society to Éamon de Valera, 27 Oct. 1958, DT, S6512D/63, National Archives of Ireland, Dublin.

100. When the Restoration Society's plan was received, the government was again considering the Graves Association proposal in a slightly modified form. The estimated cost had risen to £20,000. See Proposal Submitted Concerning Jail by Cabinet Committee, 29 Oct. 1958, DT, S6512D/63, National Archives of Ireland, Dublin.

101. Outline Proposals for Restoration of Kilmainham Jail, 1958, DT, S6512D/63, National Archives of Ireland, Dublin.

102. Minute to Dr. O'Sullivan from [?Slavery], 1963, DT, S6512D/63, National Archives of Ireland, Dublin.

103. Seán Dowling to *Irish Times,* 27 Oct. 1966, Kilmainham Jail Archives, Dublin.

104. George Gilmore, "Connolly Plaque," *Irish Times,* 26 Oct. 1966.

105. J. P. Anderson, "Kilmainham Jail," *Irish Times,* 26 Oct. 1966.

106. Seán Lemass to Seán Dowling, 18 May 1966, DT, 96/6/193, National Archives of Ireland, Dublin.

107. Dáil Éireann, "Dáil Question Regarding Cost of Kilmainham Jail," DT, 96/6/159, National Archives of Ireland, Dublin.

108. Seán Lemass to Donogh O'Malley, 20 Feb. 1969, DT, 96/6/159, National Archives of Ireland, Dublin.

109. Seán Dowling to Seán Lemass, 15 Mar. 1969, DT, 96/6/159, National Archives of Ireland, Dublin.

110. Bord Fáilte, *Annual Report for the Year Ended 31 March 1962.*

111. *Kilmainham News,* 1960, Kilmainham Jail Archives, Dublin.

112. "Taoiseach's Sentimental Jail Visit—Pay Tribute to the Work of Renovators," *Sunday Press,* 3 May 1964.

113. "The 'Rising' Returns to Kilmainham," *Dublin Evening Mail,* 2 Jan. 1962.

114. Newspaper clipping, "Idealism Lives Again Among Workers at Kilmainham," n.d., Kilmainham Jail Archives, Dublin.

115. Cooke, *History of Kilmainham Gaol,* 41.

116. O'Hearn, *Inside the Celtic Tiger,* 38.

117. Ibid., 49.

118. Paul Connerton, *How Societies Remember* (Cambridge: Cambridge Univ. Press, 1989).

119. *Ireland of the Welcomes,* July–Aug. 1986, 39–40.

120. O'Doherty interview, 29 Apr. 2002.

121. David Brett, *The Construction of Heritage* (Cork: Cork Univ. Press, 1996), 131.

122. Quoted in Sean Browne, "Heritage in Ireland's Tourism Recovery," in *Cultural Tourism,* ed. J. M. Fladmark (London: Donheal Publishing, 1994), 14.

123. Browne, "Heritage," 14–15.

124. Ibid., 16 and 18.

125. Wiendu Nuryanti, "Heritage and Postmodern Tourism," *Annals of Tourism Research* 23, no. 2 (1996): 249–60, see page 253.

126. Nuryanti, "Heritage and Postmodern Tourism," 253–54.

127. When asked, Guinness declined to supply current visitor statistics. According to Bord Fáilte figures, the Guinness Hopstore—replaced by the Storehouse in December 2000—drew nearly 500,000 tourists in 2000. By 16 September 2001, the company reported that its new facility had welcomed one million visitors and expected another 180,000 by year's end. See "1m Visit Guinness Storehouse," *Irish Times,* 16 Sept. 2002.

128. S. R. Dennison and Oliver MacDonagh, *Guinness 1886–1939: From Incorporation to the Second World War* (Cork: Cork Univ. Press, 1998), 180.

129. Dennison and MacDonagh, *Guinness 1886–1939,* 185.

130. Ibid., 176.

131. "Viewing the Brewery," *The Guinness Harp,* May–June 1959, 17, in Guinness Ireland Archives, Dublin.

132. Registry Department, Board Yearly Reports, 1919–1924, Guinness Ireland Archives, Dublin.

133. *Guinness Dublin* (1939).

134. G. P. Adams, Memorandum: Guides' Talks to Visitors, 29 June 1951, GDB/PE03.01/0365, Guinness Ireland Archives, Dublin.

135. J. A. Mackeown, Guides' Talk (text), 7 Feb. 1952, GDB/PE03.01/0365, Guinness Ireland Archives, Dublin.

136. J. A. Mackeown, Memorandum: Guides' Talks—Supplementary Points, 1 July 1952, GDB/PE03.01/0365, Guinness Ireland Archives, Dublin.

137. "Guests of St. James's Gate," *Guinness Harp,* Mar.–Apr. 1958, 4, Guinness Ireland Archives, Dublin; R. T. Mooney, "Our Visitors: Sixty Thousand People Have Seen the Brewery During This Year," *Guinness Harp,* Oct.–Dec. 1959, 26, Guinness Ireland Archives, Dublin.

138. "Our Windmill Will Remain," *Guinness Harp,* Mar.–Apr. 1958, 3, Guinness Ireland Archives, Dublin.

139. L. A. Luke, "Galway Oyster Festival," *Guinness Harp,* Nov.–Dec. 1958, 15, Guinness Ireland Archives, Dublin.

140. "Laughter by the Liffey: Ireland's Annual Festival, An Tóstal, Meant Laughter and Music by Liffey-Side," *Guinness Harp,* July–Sept. 1959, 49, Guinness Ireland Archives, Dublin.

141. "Souvenir Shop," *Harp,* Autumn 1965, 49, Guinness Ireland Archives, Dublin.

142. H. S. Corran, "The Brewery Museum," *Harp,* Autumn 1966, 16–17, Guinness Ireland Archives, Dublin.

143. F. Edmundson, Report of the Committee on the Visitors' Route, Mar. 1971, Guinness Ireland Archives, Dublin.

144. *The World and His Wife* (Dublin: [?]1961), Guinness Ireland Archives, Dublin. See also *Your Guide to the World of Guinness at the Guinness Hopstore* (Dublin, circa 1990); and *Discover What's Brewing at the Guinness Hopstore* (Dublin: circa 1990).

145. "Ireland's New Golden Age," *Building Design*, 11 July 1997, 12.

146. "Refurbishment of Guinness Storehouse," *Building Design*, 1 Dec. 2000, 4.

147. Imagination Group USA, *Guinness Storehouse*, 2003, <http://www.imagination.com/usa/work/guinness.html> (accessed 9 Apr. 2003).

148. *Building Design*, 11 July 1997.

149. "Imagination Pulls Guinness Pint," *Design Week*, 22 Sept. 2000, 3.

150. Imagination Group USA, *Guinness Storehouse*.

151. "Storehouse Gets Celebrity Start," *Irish Marketing and Advertising Journal*, 1 Jan. 2001.

152. Joe Humphreys, "An Irishman's Diary," *Irish Times*, 10 Mar. 2001.

153. Pat Barry, "The Guinness Storehouse," *Irish Times*, 16 Mar. 2001.

154. Michael Loftus, "Letter to the Editor," *Irish Times*, 16 Mar. 2001.

155. David Abel, "Guinness Tour a Tough Swallow, Till the End," *Boston Globe*, 28 May 2003.

156. ". . . and the Worst Value," *Irish Times*, 12 Aug. 2003.

157. For an excellent discussion of these stereotypes, both in America and in Ireland, see Stivers, *Hair of the Dog*.

158. George L. Mosse, *The Nationalization of the Masses: Political Symbolism and Mass Movements in Germany from the Napoleonic Wars through the Third Reich* (Ithaca, N.Y.: Cornell Univ. Press, 1991).

6. Creating the Tourist Landscape

1. Pieter M. Judson, "Frontiers, Islands, Forests, Stones: Mapping the Geography of a German Identity in the Hapsburg Monarchy, 1848–1900," in *The Geography of Identity*, ed. Patricia Yaeger (Ann Arbor: Univ. of Michigan Press, 1996), 382.

2. Catherine Nash, "'Embodying the Nation': The West of Ireland Landscape and Irish Identity," in O'Connor and Cronin, *Tourism in Ireland*, 86–87.

3. David Matless, *Landscape and Englishness* (London: Reaktion, 1998); Scott Moranda, "Maps, Markers, and Bodies: Hikers Constructing the Nation in German Forests," The Nationalism Project, 2000, <http://nationalismproject.org/articles.html> (accessed 7 Aug. 2003); and Judson, "Frontiers."

4. Patrick J. Duffy, "Writing Ireland: Literature and Art in the Representation of Irish Place," in *In Search of Ireland: A Cultural Geography*, ed. Brian Graham (London: Routledge, 1997), 81. For those interested in related discussion of the visual representation of Ireland, see Adele M. Dalsimer, ed., *Visualizing Ireland: National Identity and the Pictorial Tradition* (Boston: Faber and Faber, 1993); and Fintan Cullen, *Visual Politics: The Representation of Ireland, 1750–1930* (Cork: Cork Univ. Press, 1997).

5. Bell, *The Spell of Ireland*, vii.

6. Heinrich Böll, *Irish Journal*, trans. Leila Vennewitz (New York: McGraw-Hill, 1967), 24.

7. Eric Newby, *Round Ireland in Low Gear* (London: Viking, 1987).

8. Pete McCarthy, *McCarthy's Bar* (Edinburgh: Hodder and Stoughton, 2000), 116.

9. Bord Fáilte, *Know Your Market: Britain* (Dublin: Bord Fáilte, 1998), 32–33; *Know Your Market: Switzerland/Austria* (Dublin: Bord Fáilte, 1994); *Know Your Market: Australia/New Zealand* (Dublin: Bord Fáilte, 1998); *Know Your Market: Austria/Switzerland/Eastern Europe* (Dublin: Bord Fáilte, 1998); *Know Your Market: Benelux 1997–1998* (Dublin: Bord Fáilte, 1997); *Know Your Market: Britain* (Dublin: Bord Fáilte, 1993, 1998); *Know Your Market: France* (Dublin: Bord Fáilte, 1998).

10. "Irish Tourist Development: Meeting at Waterville," *Kerryman,* 5 Dec. 1925.

11. For an example of this sort of comment, see "Tourist Development: Visit of English Railway Directors; Southern Beauty Spots; Reception at Parknasilla, Glengariff and Killarney," *Kerryman,* 9 July 1927.

12. "Notes and News," *Irish Travel,* Nov. 1925, 50.

13. "Notes and News," *Irish Travel,* Oct. 1925, 26–28.

14. "An Example for Ireland," *Irish Travel,* Oct. 1925, 42–43.

15. "Castles or Skyscrapers?" *Irish Travel,* Sept. 1925, 15. The author's negative comment about the Nelson Pillar is another indication of strong Republican feeling at the staff level in the Irish Tourist Association.

16. "Notes and News," *Irish Travel,* Jan. 1926, 94. Also "Notes and News," *Irish Travel,* May 1926, 187.

17. "Notes and News," *Irish Travel,* Apr. 1926, 162.

18. "Tourist Traffic," *Irish Times,* 25 Apr. 1946.

19. Marquis of Sligo to Seán Lemass, 30 Sept. 1960, DT, S13087F, National Archives of Ireland, Dublin.

20. Marquis of Sligo to national daily newspapers, 8 Dec. 1960, DT, S13087F, National Archives of Ireland, Dublin.

21. "'Green Light' for £2m. Factory on Council Site," *Mayo News,* 24 Sept. 1960.

22. *Irish Times,* 18 Jan. 1961.

23. McCarthy, *McCarthy's Bar,* 151.

24. Ibid., 151–52.

25. Leslie Daiken, "Strictly Personal. . . . " (manuscript), [?] June 1956, MS33,481(46), National Library of Ireland, Dublin. Cited with permission of the Board of the National Library of Ireland.

26. C. M. Murphy to Leslie Daiken, 28 May 1956, MS33,481(46), National Library of Ireland, Dublin. Cited with permission of the Board of the National Library of Ireland.

27. Leslie Daiken, "Vintage Vehicles," *GO Holiday Magazine,* Jan.–Feb. 1957, 23–25, MS33,488, National Library of Ireland, Dublin. Cited with permission of the Board of the National Library of Ireland.

28. Leslie Daiken, "Leslie Daiken Tells of His Boyhood Days in Ireland—and Re-Captures His Memories of Them—Round Trap Roundabout" (manuscript), 16 Jan. 1957,

MS33,487 box 5, National Library of Ireland, Dublin. Cited with permission of the Board of the National Library of Ireland.

29. Daiken, "Boyhood Days."

30. Daiken actively campaigned for an appointment as Bord Fáilte's principal representative in London so that he might improve the Board's effectiveness in the English marketplace. See Leslie Daiken to Niall Sheridan, 3 June 1956, MS33,485(50), National Library of Ireland, Dublin; Leslie Daiken to Niall Sheridan, 21 Mar. 1956, MS33,485(50), National Library of Ireland, Dublin; and Leslie Daiken to Niall Sheridan, 21 July 1956, MS33,485(50), National Library of Ireland, Dublin. All cited with permission of the Board of the National Library of Ireland.

31. Leslie Daiken, "By Killarney's Lakes and Fells: 'Heaven's Reflex'—or Hell's Perspex?" (manuscript), [?]1961, MS33,514, box Add. folder 51, National Library of Ireland, Dublin. Cited with permission of the Board of the National Library of Ireland.

32. John Scanlon to Jack Lynch, 2 Jan. 1971, DT, 2002/8/299, National Archives of Ireland, Dublin.

33. Jack Lynch to John Scanlon, 5 Jan. 1971, DT, 2002/8/299, National Archives of Ireland, Dublin.

34. John Scanlon to Jack Lynch, 21 Jan. 1971, DT, 2002/8/299, National Archives of Ireland, Dublin.

35. Brian Lenihan to Jack Lynch, 26 Feb. 1971, DT, 2002/8/299, National Archives of Ireland, Dublin.

36. Alvin Mansfield Owsley to Seán Lemass, 30 Mar. 1962, DT, S5004 E/62, National Archives of Ireland, Dublin.

37. This was not the first time that the sale of land at Killarney raised substantial concern. In 1899 the Muckross estate was placed on the market, sparking profound concern both in Ireland and in the Irish-American community. Irish-Americans, inspired by the recent creation of the first national parks in America, urged the Irish government to acquire the Muckross property and to declare it a national park rather than allow it to pass into foreign hands. As it happened, Guinness acquired the land, only to sell it to an American investor in 1910. See Marion R. Casey, "Ireland, New York and the Irish Image in American Popular Culture, 1890–1960" (Ph.D. diss., New York Univ., 1998), 233. The property subsequently passed through various American owners until it was finally bequeathed to the Irish government.

38. "American Has Bought Killarney Estate, Privileges to Be Continued," *Irish Independent,* 11 Aug. 1956.

39. Untitled newspaper clipping, *Kerryman,* 11 Aug. 1956, DT, S16047A, National Archives of Ireland, Dublin.

40. Bord Fáilte, Memorandum: Proposed Sale of the Kenmare Estate (Secret), 7 Aug. 1956, DT, S16047A, National Archives of Ireland, Dublin.

41. "National Appeal Advocated," *Irish Times,* 7 Aug. 1956.

42. Department of the Taoiseach and Killarney Tourist Association, 1956, DT, S16047A, National Archives of Ireland, Dublin.

43. M. O. Muimhneaohain, memorandum, 2 Aug. 1956, DT, S16047A, National Archives of Ireland, Dublin.

44. "Killarney Estate Not to Be 'Commercialized,'" *Irish Times*, 3 Feb. 1961.

45. McCarthy, *McCarthy's Bar*, 30. *Duty of Care* is a legal term that refers to the obligation imposed on an individual to adhere to a reasonable standard of care while performing acts that could be harmful. In this case, the term refers to harm that may result from unsupervised wandering on farmland and the owner's unwillingness to hazard the risk of allowing such access.

46. Ibid., 34.

47. In the nineteenth century, nationalists struggled to gain the "Three F's"—fair rent, fixity of tenure, and free sale—while nationalist leaders like Charles Stewart Parnell told Irishmen to "keep a firm grip on your homesteads and lands," creating a close link between political nationalism and the interests of Irish peasants. See Laurence M. Geary, "Parnell and the Land Question," in *Parnell: The Politics of Power*, ed. Donal McCartney (Dublin: Wolfhound Press, 1991), 90–101, especially page 95. For a concise overview of Parnell's relationship to the land question, as well as his larger political career, see: F. S. L. Lyons, *Parnell* (Dundalk, Ireland: Dundalgan Press, 1963).

48. Specifically, the Monuments Act provides: "The Commissioners may, with the consent of the Minister, acquire compulsorily or by agreement any national monument which they consider it expedient to acquire, and the Commissioners may so acquire a national monument whether they or a local authority are or are not the guardians thereof and whether a preservation order is or is not in force in regard thereto." *National Monuments Act, 1930* (Dublin: Government Publications, 1930).

Section 19 of the 1939 Tourist Traffic Act allowed the Irish Tourist Board to: "If and whenever the Board thinks proper to acquire compulsorily any land for the purpose of the exercise of any of the powers or the performance of any of the duties or functions conferred or imposed on it by this Act, the Board may, with the consent of the Minister, by order declare its intention so to acquire such land and every such order shall operate to confer on the Board full power to acquire compulsorily the land mentioned therein under and in accordance with this section." *Tourist Traffic Act, 1939* (Dublin: Government Publications, 1939).

The 1952 Tourist Traffic Act, sect 7, part 1, allowed: "Where the Board proposes to erect a notice or fence at, or to provide or improve means of access to, any historic building, site or shrine, or other place which, in the opinion of the Board is likely to be of particular interest to the public, and the owner refuses to permit the Board to carry out the proposed work, the Board shall have power to acquire, under section 19 of the Act of 1939, such land as the Board thinks proper to enable the work to be carried out." *Tourist Traffic Act, 1952* (Dublin: Government Publications 1952).

49. Cairn in Oldcastle Townland, Co. Cork—Issue of Preservation Orders, 1938, DF, S200/2/38, National Archives of Ireland, Dublin.

50. Peter Harbison, *Guide to National and Historic Monuments of Ireland* (Dublin: Gill and Macmillan, 1992), 68.

51. Phone record, 30 Nov. 1981, 94/3500/1, Office of Public Works, Dublin.

52. R. Nic Raighine to Peter Harbison, 10 Dec. 1981, 94/3500/1, Office of Public Works, Dublin.

53. Martin Bradley (Shannonside Tourism) to Office of Public Works, 20 Oct. 1981, 94/3500/1, Office of Public Works, Dublin.

54. John Costello to Secretary of the Office of Public Works, 11 May 1982, 94/3500/1, Office of Public Works, Dublin.

55. Martin Bradley to John Berkery, 31 May 1983, 94/3500/1, Office of Public Works, Dublin.

56. Martin Bradley to John Mahony, 22 Apr. 1985, 94/3500/1, Office of Public Works, Dublin.

57. Draft letter from M. Molloy to Jennifer Foley, 15 July 1985, 94/3500/1, Office of Public Works, Dublin.

58. Joan Phillips to Jennifer Foley, 13 Aug. 1985, 94/3500/1, Office of Public Works, Dublin.

59. Joan Phillips, memorandum, 23 Oct. 1985, 94/3500/1, Office of Public Works, Dublin.

60. Jennifer Foley to Office of Public Works, 29 Nov. 1985, 94/3500/1, Office of Public Works, Dublin.

61. J. Kevin Vaughn (Clare Co. Development Team) to Office of Public Works, 19 Feb. 1985, 94/3500/1, Office of Public Works, Dublin; "Guardianship Order for Poulnabrone Dolmen," *Clare Champion,* 10 Jan. 1986.

62. National Monuments: Acquisition Criteria and Information Check, 25 Oct. 1985, 94/3500/1, Office of Public Works, Dublin.

63. Jennifer Foley to Office of Public Works, 29 Jan. 1987 (OPW, 94/3500/3); [?] McMahon, memorandum, 8 Nov. 1989, 94/3500/3, Office of Public Works, Dublin.

64. Cyril de Courcy, "Report and Valuation of Lands at Poulnabrone Dolmen, Co. Clare," 1993, 94/3500/3, Office of Public Works, Dublin. Given the dolmen's location far from any other development, adequate transportation routes (the roadway that passes by is narrow and inefficient), or water sources, one wonders how this conclusion was reached. Indeed, the presence of a "national monument" would have made any such development illegal.

65. Jennifer Foley to Office of Public Works, 13 Mar. 1993, 94/3500/3, Office of Public Works, Dublin.

66. Report of Meeting Held at Ballyvaughn, Co. Clare on Friday 12th March 1993, Mar. 1993, 94/3500/3, Office of Public Works, Dublin. The monument's closure did not prevent Bord Fáilte from continuing to include photographs of the site in its various guidebooks—a

fact that certainly did little to reduce the tourist traffic climbing the farmer's barbed wire fence in order to make the "dangerous" trek across the limestone pavement. See Bord Fáilte, *Ireland Guide* (Dublin: Bord Fáilte, 1993), 256; and Bord Fáilte, *Ireland* (Dublin: Bord Fáilte, 1994), 12–13. There has been little effort by tourist officials to assure that sites presented in guidebooks and visitor centers are actually accessible to the general public. For example, the Burren visitor's center at Kilfenora uses images of a Penal-era painted red hand that likely served as a direction marker to a hedge school or hidden chapel in its multimedia presentation and display. When I went looking for the site, however, I soon discovered that the red hand appears to be located in the backyard of a local homeowner, surrounded by an eight-foot wooden fence with numerous "No Trespassing" signs posted along the full length of the wall.

67. Leslie J. Dlugokinski to Office of Public Works, 7 May 1999, 94/3500/3, Office of Public Works, Dublin.

68. Gerry Murray to Ms. McCann, 4 Nov. 1994, 94/3500/3, Office of Public Works, Dublin.

69. Note from Martin Luby, 30 July 2001, 94/3500/3, Office of Public Works, Dublin.

70. Martin Luby, 26 Jan. 2001, 94/3500/3, Office of Public Works, Dublin.

71. Department of Industry and Commerce Memorandum, 18 Feb. 1944, DT, S10946.

72. E. Æ Somerville and Martin Ross, *The Irish R.M.* (London: Abacus, 2000 [1928]), 458.

73. "Notes and News," *Irish Travel*, Feb. 1926, 114.

74. "Activities of the ITA," *Irish Travel*, July 1927, 240.

75. Draft Heads of Tourist Traffic (Amendment) (No. 2. Bill 1951, [?] July 1951, TTA 2/6, National Archives of Ireland, Dublin.

76. Report of Interdepartmental Meeting Held on 1st December 1951, to Discuss the Heads of the Proposed Tourist Traffic Bill. Amendments Requested by the Commissioners of Public Works, 1 Dec. 1951, TTA 2/7 vol. 1, National Archives of Ireland, Dublin.

77. *Irish Tourist Bulletin*, July 1951, 3–4, DT, S14995A.

78. O'Doherty interview, 29 Apr. 2002.

79. An Bord Fáilte, *Irish Tourist Bulletin*, Sept. 1953, 4–5, DT, S14995B, National Archives of Ireland, Dublin.

80. O'Doherty interview, 29 Apr. 2002.

81. An Bord Fáilte, *Annual Report and Accounts, Year Ended 31st March 1954*, Apr. 1954, DT, S15647B, National Archives of Ireland, Dublin.

82. Bord Fáilte, *Bord Fáilte Éireann Newsletter*, May–June 1956, 2.

83. Bord Fáilte *Irish Tourist Board Report for the Year Ended March 31 1965* (Dublin: Bord Fáilte, 1965).

84. An Bord Fáilte, *Irish Tourist Bulletin*, June 1951, 4–5, DT, S14995A, National Archives of Ireland, Dublin.

85. Baranowski, *Strength Through Joy*, 62. The third chapter of *Strength Through Joy*, "The Beauty of Labor," details the KdF's factory and community development programs.

86. Conekin, *Autobiography*, 153.

87. An Bord Fáilte, *Irish Tourist Bulletin*, Aug. 1951, 13–14, DT, S14995A, National Archives of Ireland, Dublin.

88. An Bord Fáilte, *Irish Tourist Bulletin*, Apr. 1951, 9, DT, S14995A, National Archives of Ireland, Dublin.

89. An Bord Fáilte, *Irish Tourist Bulletin*, Sept. 1952, 1, DT, S14995A, National Archives of Ireland, Dublin.

90. An Bord Fáilte, *Irish Tourist Bulletin*, Aug. 1952, 2, DT, S14995A, National Archives of Ireland, Dublin.

91. "An Tóstal," *Kilkenny People*, 14 Mar. 1953; "An Tóstal," *Kilkenny People*, 21 Mar. 1953.

92. "Decoration Plans for An Tóstal: City Streets Will Be Gay and Colourful," *Evening Echo* (Cork), 26 Mar. 1954.

93. An Bord Fáilte, *Irish Tourist Bulletin*, Dec. 1952, 6, DT, S14995A, National Archives of Ireland, Dublin.

94. Confidential memorandum on An Tóstal Review, 19 Feb. 1958, TTA 12/5, National Archives of Ireland, Dublin. Also Gorman interview, 11 Oct. 2002.

95. Bord Fáilte, *Annual Report and Accounts, Year Ending 31st March 1958* (Dublin: Bord Fáilte, 1958). Also O'Doherty interview, 30 July 2002.

96. O'Doherty interview, 30 July 2002.

97. Department of Local Government, *Department of Local Government Report, 1958–1959* (Dublin: Government Publications, 1959), 114–15. I would like to thank Dr. Aoife Bhreatnach for bringing this reference to my attention.

98. Bord Fáilte, *Annual Report and Accounts, Year Ending 31st March 1959*; and Bord Fáilte, *Annual Report and Accounts, Year Ended 31st March 1961*.

99. Bord Fáilte, *Report for the Year Ended March 31 1964*.

100. O'Doherty interview, 30 July 2002.

101. Bord Fáilte, *Board Report for the Year Ended March 31 1964*.

102. Bord Fáilte, *Report for the Year Ended March 31 1965*.

103. Records of Clonakilty Town Council, 1968–72, 6 Oct. 1968, Clonakilty Town Council Records, UDC1/10, Cork Archives Institute, Cork.

104. "New Approach to the Tidy Towns," *Clare Champion*, 14 Feb. 1986.

105. "On Target for a Tidier Ennis," *Clare Champion*, 28 Feb. 1986.

106. Kieran Hickey, ed., *Working to Win*, videocassette, circa 1988, distributed by Bord Fáilte, Bord Fáilte Photographic Archives, Dublin. The use of the phrase "plan of campaign" is particularly interesting as it draws a parallel line between the national work of creating tidy towns and the fight for land ownership during the late-nineteenth-century Land War.

107. O'Doherty interview, 30 July 2002.

108. Kieran Hickey, ed., *Our Tidy Towns—21 Years of Community Effort*, 16mm, 39 min., 1979, distributed by Bord Fáilte, Irish Film Center Archives, Dublin.

109. "Tidy Town," *Clare Champion,* 9 May 1980.

110. Bord Fáilte, *Bord Fáilte Report and Accounts for the Year Ended December 1979* (Dublin: Bord Fáilte, 1979).

111. Bord Fáilte, *Bord Fáilte Report and Accounts for the Year Ended December 1984* (Dublin: Bord Fáilte, 1984).

112. Dermot O'Toole, "Improving Our Towns," *Ireland of the Welcomes,* Nov.–Dec. 1961, 13–16.

113. George Bagnall, "Town and Village: Happy 21st Birthday, Tidy Town Scheme," *Ireland of the Welcomes,* Sept.–Oct. 1978, 10–15.

114. Eamon De Buitlear, ed., *There's Work to Be Done,* videocassette, unknown length, 1992, distributed by Bord Fáilte, Bord Fáilte Photographic Archive, Dublin.

115. Hugh Weir, "Making a Tidy Town," *Clare Champion,* 30 Oct. 1981.

116. Bord Fáilte, *Bord Fáilte Report for the Year Ended March 1973* (Dublin: Bord Fáilte, 1973).

117. *Kerryman,* 5 Dec. 1925.

118. "Killarney Tourist Association: Improving Killarney Lakes Fishing; Letter from Minister," *Kerryman,* 11 Dec. 1926.

119. "Killarney Tourist Association," *Kerryman,* 12 Mar. 1927; "Killarney Tourist Association," *Kerryman,* 9 Apr. 1927; and "Killarney Tourist Association," *Kerryman,* 21 May 1927.

120. "Killarney Tourist Association," *Kerryman,* 12 Nov. 1927.

121. O'Doherty interview, 30 July 2002.

122. Ibid. The Inland Fisheries Trust was a private organization and not officially recognized by the state. Nevertheless, it was supported by James Dillon, then minister for agriculture, and received some state funding as a tourism interest.

123. An Bord Fáilte, *Annual Report and Accounts, Year Ending 31st March 1953* (Dublin: Bord Fáilte, 1953).

124. Bord Fáilte, *Annual Report and Accounts, Year Ending 31st March 1957* (Dublin: Bord Fáilte, 1957).

125. O'Doherty interview, 30 July 2002.

126. Bord Fáilte, Angling Development and Exploitation Summary Details of Five-Year Plan, 1957, DF, F120/2/57, National Archives of Ireland, Dublin.

127. Industry and Commerce Memorandum for the Government. *Annual Report and Accounts, Year Ended 31st March 1958* (Dublin: Bord Fáilte, 1958); and Bord Fáilte, *Annual Report, 1957.* It is worth noting that a similar, though less expansive, program was also implemented in 1957 to destroy "vermin" responsible for the reduction of game animals and birds.

128. Industry and Commerce Memorandum for the Government. Bord Fáilte and Fógra Fáilte Reports and Accounts for the Year Ended 31st March, 1959, 11 Nov. 1959, DT, S15647B, National Archives of Ireland, Dublin.

129. Bord Fáilte, *Ireland for Coarse Fishing Holidays* (Dublin: Bord Fáilte, 1959), 5 and 15.

130. Department of Industry and Commerce Memorandum for the Government: Bord Fáilte and Fógra Fáilte: Reports and Accounts for the Year Ended 31st March 1960, 24 Oct. 1960, DT, S15647B, National Archives of Ireland, Dublin.

131. Michael J. Bannon, Kevin I. Nowlan, John Hendry, and Ken Mawhinney, eds., *Planning: The Irish Experience 1920–1988* (Dublin: Wolfhound Press, 1989), 13.

132. Bannon et al., *Planning*, 47 and 71–85.

133. Ibid., 64–65.

134. Department of Local Government, Explanatory Memorandum: Local Government (Planning and Development) Bill, 1962, DT, S16968C/63, National Archives of Ireland, Dublin.

135. Bannon et al., *Planning*, 91.

136. An Taisce, *The National Trust for Ireland* (Dublin: An Taisce, [?]1961), 2.

137. Bannon et al., *Planning*, 94.

138. National Planning Conference folder, 1943, DT, S 13469, National Archives of Ireland, Dublin.

139. Bannon et al., *Planning*, 99.

140. Bord Fáilte, *Bord Fáilte Report for the Year Ended December 1975* (Dublin: Bord Fáilte, 1975).

141. Bannon et al., *Planning*, 99.

142. Michael Gorman, Frank Height, Mary V. Mullin, and W. H. Walsh, eds., *Design for Tourism: An ICSID Inter Design Report* (Oxford: Pergamon Press, 1977), 10–11. I would like to thank Michael Gorman for providing me with a copy of this publication.

143. Gorman et al., *Design for Tourism*, 16–17.

144. Ibid., 33.

145. Ibid., 35.

146. Ibid., 40.

147. Ibid., 41.

148. *Seven Ages: Story of the Irish State (Program 1)*, RTÉ Online, 2000, <http://www.rte.ie/tv/sevenages/prog1.html> (accessed 13 Aug. 2003).

149. Philip Geoghegan, *Building Sensitively in Ireland's Landscapes* (Dublin: Bord Fáilte and An Taisce, 1989), 5–6.

150. Geoghegan, *Building Sensitively*, 9.

151. Ibid., 16–43.

152. McCarthy, *McCarthy's Bar*, 116.

153. Erskine Childers to Jack Lynch, 22 Mar. 1968, DT, 99/1/521, National Archives of Ireland, Dublin.

154. Although it had little to do with tourism, the Flood Report—released in September 2002, five years after it was launched in October 1997 following former Fianna Fáil TD Ray Burke's resignation over bribery allegations—revealed extensive corruption including

payments made by JMSE, an Irish construction company, to Burke. While the report certainly does not prove the long-running allegations of planning corruption, it does hint that there may have been at least a grain of truth in these rumors.

155. Bannon et al., *Planning*, 136.

156. Ibid., 139.

157. Niall Hyde, *National Coastline Study*, vol. 1 (Dublin: Bord Fáilte and Foras Forbartha, 1972).

158. Bord Fáilte, *Report for the Year Ended December 1974* (Dublin: Bord Fáilte, 1974).

159. Bord Fáilte, *Report and Accounts for the Year Ended December 1979* (Dublin: Bord Fáilte, 1979).

160. Bord Fáilte, *Report and Accounts for the Year Ended December 1981* (Dublin: Bord Fáilte, 1981); Bord Fáilte, *Report and Accounts for the Year Ended December 1985* (Dublin: Bord Fáilte, 1985).

161. Bord Fáilte, *Bord Fáilte Report for the Year Ended March 1992* (Dublin: Bord Fáilte, 1992).

162. Bord Fáilte, *Developing Sustainable Tourism*, 29.

163. Although the images included here are from a later period, the following photo series at the Bord Fáilte Photographic Archives further illustrate the point: K3/37, K.3A/37, K39–40/48, K42–47/48, K48–55/48, K8/57, K11/62–K34/62. There were some variations from later photographs, images taken from road level or from a jaunting cart itself, for example; the continuity is striking nevertheless.

164. Irish Tourist Board, *Ireland: Carefree Motoring* (Dublin: Bord Fáilte, 1969).

165. Luke Gibbons, *Transformations in Irish Culture* (Cork: Cork Univ. Press, 1996), 40.

166. *Hindesight* (Dublin: Irish Museum of Modern Art, 1993), 18–19.

167. *Hindesight*, 36.

168. Ibid., 38.

169. De Fouw interview, 14 Oct. 2002.

170. C. S. Andrews, *Man of No Property*, 114.

171. Ibid., 128.

172. Ibid., 130 and 133.

173. Turf harvesting was frequently included in tourism publications in this light. For an example, see the photographs in Irish Tourist Association, *Introducing Ireland* (Dublin: Irish Tourist Association, 1950). Similarly, Bord Fáilte declared that Irish bogs are a "valuable asset" that "yield turf for fuel and electric power." See Fógra Fáilte, "Ireland Invites You" (draft), 1953, DT, S15498, National Archives of Ireland, Dublin.

174. John Reader, "A Day on the Bog," *Ireland of the Welcomes*, Mar.–Apr. 1970, 8–11.

175. Stephen Rynne, "The Bog Transformed," *Ireland of the Welcomes*, Mar.–Apr. 1970, 12–15.

176. Seamus Heaney, "The Bog," *Ireland of the Welcomes*, May–June, 1976, 20–25.

177. "Bogland Special Edition," *Ireland of the Welcomes*, May–June 1987, 43.

7. Tourism and the Tiger, 1994–2007

1. Paul Sweeney, *The Celtic Tiger: Ireland's Economic Miracle* (Dublin: Oak Tree Press, 1998), 1–5.

2. Bord Fáilte, *Bord Fáilte Report and Financial Statements 2000* (Dublin: Bord Fáilte, 2000), 3.

3. Bord Fáilte, *Bord Fáilte Report for the Year Ended March 1993* (Dublin: Bord Fáilte, 1993), 12; and Bord Fáilte, *Markets: Perspectives on Irish Tourism 1993–97* (Dublin: Bord Fáilte, 1999), 7.

4. Bord Fáilte, *Report and Financial Statements 2000*, 17.

5. Bord Fáilte, *Markets*, 94.

6. Bord Fáilte, *Report and Financial Statements 2000*, 17.

7. Bord Fáilte, *Markets*, 17.

8. Bord Fáilte, *Bord Fáilte Report for the Year Ended March 1987* (Dublin: Bord Fáilte, 1987), 8.

9. Bord Fáilte, *Markets*, 17.

10. Bord Fáilte, *Report and Financial Statements 2000*, 17.

11. J. W. O'Hagan and M. J. Harrison, "UK and US Visitor Expenditure in Ireland," *The Economic and Social Review* 15, no. 3 (1984): 195–207.

12. "Notes and News," *Irish Travel*, [?]1926, 236–37.

13. For a detailed discussion of the North/South tourism relationship, see Zuelow, "'Ingredients for Cooperation.'" See also Michael Kennedy, *Division and Consensus: The Politics of Cross-Border Relations in Ireland, 1925–1969* (Dublin: Institute of Public Administration, 2000), 3.

14. Gorman interview, 11 Oct. 2002.

15. Report of Taoiseach's Visit to Belfast, 14 Jan. 1965, DT, 98/6/429. A "triptyque" was a complicated document that provided authorities with proof that the visitor's reason for travel was legitimate. It was often extremely frustrating to tourists, especially Americans, and was abolished throughout the rest of Europe during the early 1950s.

16. Report of Press Conference by Taoiseach, 16 Jan. 1965, DT, 98/6/149.

17. Jim Flanagan, "Cross Border Air Link," *Sunday Press*, 31 Jan. 1965.

18. Report of Taoiseach's Visit to Belfast.

19. "£6m Boost for North-South Tourism Drive," *Irish Travel Trade News*, Dec. 1994, 14.

20. "Ireland to Launch Tourism Brand in 1997," *Irish Travel Trade News*, Oct. 1995, 12.

21. "Joint Award for Bord Fáilte/NITB," *Irish Travel Trade News*, Nov. 1996, 19.

22. Bord Fáilte, *Bord Fáilte Report for the Year Ended March 1996* (Dublin: Bord Fáilte, 1996).

23. Steedman, 13.

24. Jane O'Sullivan, "Belfast Agreement Could Pave Way to Peace Payoff," *Irish Times*, 15 May 1998.

25. Dani Garavelli, "A Suitable Place for a Tourist?" *Scotland on Sunday*, 28 Mar. 1999.

26. John Bruton, "Agreement Must Be Focus of a New Loyalty," *Irish Times*, 20 Apr. 1998.

27. Frank Fitzgibbon, "Ireland Tourism Industry Confederation," *Sunday Times (London)*, 8 Nov. 1998.

28. John Murray Brown, "Blair Flies to Ulster in Bid to Rescue Deadlocked Talks: Move to Secure Agreement on Setting up Cross-Border Bodies," *Financial Times (London)*, 3 Dec. 1998.

29. Liam Clarke, "Blair Unveils UK-Irish Body in Dublin," *Sunday Times (London)*, 22 Nov. 1998. The removal of tourism from the list of cross-border bodies came after early indications that tourism would be uncontroversial. See Jane O'Sullivan, "All-Island Body May Replace Bord Fáilte," *Irish Times*, 6 June 1998.

30. Martin Fletcher, "Trimble and Ahern Agree on Cross-Border Bodies," *Times (London)*, 25 Nov. 1998.

31. John Murray Brown, "Mallon Urges Agreement on Cross-Border Bodies," *Financial Times (London)*, 1 Dec. 1998, 11.

32. *Financial Times (London)*, 3 Dec. 1998.

33. Clare Murphy, "Mallon Claims Deal Was Brokered by Blair," *Irish Times*, 4 Dec. 1998; and John Mullin, "Ulster Parties' Haggling Renewed as Blair Leaves," *Guardian (London)*, 4 Dec. 1998.

34. Alison Hardie, "Ulster Parties Agree Power-Sharing Structure," *Scotsman*, 19 Dec. 1998. Some pundits declared the solution to be a slap in the face for Sinn Féin because the party had hoped for eight official bodies including tourism development. For nationalists, cross-border bodies represented a counterbalance to the dominance of unionist parties in the Northern executive.

35. John Murray Brown, "Peace Accord Benefits Tourism in Ireland," *Financial Times (London)*, 28 Sept. 2000.

36. Implementation Group, *Establishment of New Tourist Development Authority* (Dublin: Department of Tourism, Sport, and Recreation, 2002), 30.

37. Implementation Group, *New Tourist Development Authority*, 6–7.

38. Ibid., 30.

39. Gorman interview, 11 Oct. 2002.

40. Bord Fáilte, *Tourism Plan 1981–85: Marketing and Development Guidelines for the Irish Tourist Industry* (Dublin: Bord Fáilte, 1980).

41. Cited in McCarthy, *McCarthy's Bar*, 365–66. Other companies, such as Bellatopia.com, offer items to "decorate your Irish pub or to entertain guests in your Ireland-themed rec room." *Ireland/Irish Pub Themed Items*, Bellatopia.com, 2003, <http://www.bellatopia.com/themes_irish_pub.shtml> (accessed 4 Aug. 2003).

42. Lance Pettitt, *Screening Ireland: Film and Television Representation* (Manchester: Manchester Univ. Press, 2000), 37–45.

43. Kate Homquist, "Shaking Up Our Quiet Movie Image," *Irish Times*, 3 Aug. 2006.

44. Smyth, *Space*, 164.

45. Ibid., 169.

46. Ella Shanahan, "Sending Out the Right Signals to Keep the Visitors Coming," *Irish Times*, 31 Mar. 2001.

47. "Origin of the UK Foot and Mouth Disease Epidemic in 2001," Department for Environment, Food and Rural Affairs (United Kingdom), <http://www.defra.gov.uk/foot-andmouth/pdf/fmdorigins1.pdf> (accessed 27 July 2007).

48. Alex Kirby, "F&M: The Rural Nemesis," BBC News World Edition, <http://news.bbc.co.uk/2/hi/in_depth/world/2001/review_of_2001/1697976.stm> (accessed 27 July 2007).

49. Sean MacConnell and Declan Fahy, "Foot-and-mouth Restrictions to Be Eased on Tourist Attractions," *Irish Times*, 2 May 2001.

50. Joe Humphreys, "A Bad Year but It Could Have Been Worse," *Irish Times*, 20 Aug. 2001.

51. Robert Looney, "Economic Costs to the United States Stemming from the 9/11 Attacks," *Strategic Insights* 1, no. 6 (Aug. 2002), <http://www.ccc.nps.navy.mil/si/aug02/homeland.asp> (accessed 27 July 2007).

52. Una McCaffrey, "Bord Fáilte Forecasts Big Losses in Already Ailing Tourism Industry," *Irish Times*, 13 Sept. 2001.

53. Dáil Debate, "Other Questions: Tourism Industry," 14 Nov. 2001.

54. Jim Dunne, "British Holidaymakers Think Irish Less Friendly," *Irish Times*, 20 Feb. 2001.

55. "Céad Míle Fáilte," *Irish Times*, 22 Feb. 2001.

56. Regina Daly, "Fáilte Ireland Search for Embodiment of Warm Irish Welcome," *Irish Times*, 3 Aug. 2004.

57. "Bord Fáilte Gets Top UK Award," *Irish Times*, 2 Nov. 2001.

58. Dáil Debate, "Written Answers," 14 Nov. 2001.

59. Deegan and Dineen, *Tourism Policy and Performance*, 19.

60. *Tourism and Travel in Ireland* (Dublin: Gill and Macmillan, 1993), 164–68.

61. "10,000 Trained in Tourism," *Irish Times*, 4 Jan. 1993.

62. "Work Found by 98 Percent of CERT Students," *Irish Times*, 17 Feb. 1995.

63. Dáil Debate, 14 Nov. 2001.

64. Jim Dunne, "Bord Fáilte and CERT Urged to Amalgamate," *Irish Times*, 6 Sept. 2001.

65. Jim Dunne, "Bord Fáilte Staff Seek Jobs and Pensions Assurances," *Irish Times*, 10 Dec. 2001.

66. Miriam Donohoe, "New Tourism Authority Bill to get Dáil Priority," *Irish Times,* 4 Sept. 2002.

67. *National Tourism Development Authority Bill, 2002, Explanatory Memorandum* (Dublin: Government Publications, 2002).

68. Seanad Debate, *National Tourism Development Authority Bill, 2002* 3 Dec. 2002.

69. Dáil Debate, *National Tourism Development Authority Bill, 2002,* 12 Feb. 2003.

70. Fáilte Ireland, *Annual Report 2005* (Dublin: Fáilte Ireland, 2005).

71. Department of the Taoiseach Memorandum, [?]1967, DT, 98/6/890, National Archives of Ireland, Dublin; and Bord Fáilte to the Department of the Taoiseach, 4 Mar. 1960, DT, S13087F, National Archives of Ireland, Dublin.

72. Steve MacDonogh, *The Dingle Peninsula* (Dingle, Ireland: Brandon, 2000), 77 and 80.

73. *Official Languages Act 2003* (Dublin, 2003).

74. Anne Lucey, "Minister Insists on Irish Version of Dingle," *Irish Times,* 20 May 2005.

75. "Alterations Subvert Democracy," *Irish Examiner,* 11 Jan. 2007.

76. *Dingle Name Campaign,* Dingle Name Campaign, 2007, <http://www.dinglename.com> (accessed 21 July 2007).

77. Lucey, "Minister Insists."

78. Eoin English, "Eight-in-ten Tourists Struggle to Find Dingle over St. Patrick's Weekend," *Irish Examiner,* 2 Apr. 2007.

79. "West Kerry 'Suffering Dramatic Fall in Business,'" *Kerryman,* 2 Feb. 2007.

80. Owen Bowcott, "Dingle Fights to Keep Its Name: Port Holds Referendum on Switch to Irish Version Change Could Confuse Tourists, Locals Claim," *Guardian,* 19 Oct. 2006.

81. Sean O Cathasaigh to the *Irish Times, Irish Times,* 18 June 2005.

82. Finian McGrath, TD, to the *Irish Times, Irish Times,* 22 July 2005.

83. Raé Kearns to the *Irish Times, Irish Times,* 4 Mar. 2006.

84. Shawn Pogatchnik, "Signs of the Irish Times," *Sunday Herald,* 4 Sept. 2005.

85. Anne Lucey, "Plebiscite to Be Held on Daingean or Dingle," *Irish Times,* 18 Oct. 2005; and Anne Lucey, "Ballot Includes 160 Not Living in An Daingean," *Irish Times,* 22 Aug. 2006.

86. Anne Lucey, "An Daingean Votes for Bilingual Name," *Irish Times,* 21 Oct. 2006.

87. *Irish Examiner,* 11 Jan. 2007.

88. Marian O'Flaherty, "Dingle Deal Struck—Healy-Rae Strikes Deal with Taoiseach to Restore Dingle Name," *Kerry's Eye,* 20 June 2007.

Bibliography

Archives

Bord Fáilte Photographic Archive

    Ancient Sites and Monuments List, 1953– (black-and-white negatives)
    Bord Fáilte Photographic Library color prints, 1990s, CD-ROM, vol. 3, 2002
    Bord Fáilte Photographic Library Video Collection
    Co. Kerry List, 1934–1985 (black-and-white negatives)
    Types List, Pre-1960 (black-and-white negatives)

Cork Archives Institute

    Clonakility Town Council
    Cork Corporation Civic Reception Committee
    Cork Public Museum
    Kinsale Development Association
    Seamus Fitzgerald Papers

Guinness Brewery Archives

    Accounting Office Records
    Annual Reports
    Magazine/Guidebook Collection
    Photographic Collection

Kilmainham Jail Archives

    Kilmainham Jail Restoration

National Archives of Ireland

    Department of Finance
    Department of Foreign Affairs (Department of External Affairs)

Department of the Taoiseach

Department of Tourism and Transport/Industry and Commerce/Transport and Power

National Film Centre of Ireland

Bord Fáilte travel and training films

National Library of Ireland Manuscript Collection

Dr. Sean Cooney Papers
Leslie Daiken Papers
Dillion Family Postcards, 1900–1940
Jacob Rosamond Papers

National Photographic Archives of Ireland

Lawrence Comparative Study
Wiltshire Collection

Public Records Office Northern Ireland, Belfast

Cabinet Minutes
Northern Ireland Tourist Board Annual Reports

University College Dublin Archives

Todd Andrews Papers

Department of Public Works/Dúchas—The Heritage Service

Poulnabrone Dolmen, Co. Clare. Tenure—Preservation Order, Guardianship

Private Collections

Michael Gorman, Dublin, Ireland

Libraries

Boole Library, University College Cork, Cork, Ireland
Cork City Library, Cork, Ireland
Madison Public Library, Madison, Wisconsin
National Library of Ireland, Dublin, Ireland
Trinity College Library, Dublin, Ireland
University of Washington Libraries, Seattle, Washington

University of Wisconsin-Madison Libraries, Madison, Wisconsin

Interviews

Clive Brooks, Bord Fáilte Photographic Library. Dublin, 17, 18, 22, 23 July 2002.
Jan de Fouw, graphic designer, *Ireland of the Welcomes*. Dublin, 15 Oct. 2002.
Michael Gorman, Bord Fáilte, retired. Dublin, 6 Aug. 2002 and 11 Oct. 2002.
Michael Kevin O'Doherty, Bord Fáilte, retired. Dublin, 29 Apr. and 30 July 2002.

Newspapers

Australian Financial Review (Australia)
Belfast and Irish News (Northern Ireland)
Belfast News Letter (Northern Ireland)
Belfast Telegraph (Northern Ireland)
Calgary Herald (Canada)
Catholic News (Ireland)
Clare Champion (Ireland)
Cork Examiner (Ireland)
Cork Evening Echo (Ireland)
Daily Telegraph (England)
Evening Herald (Ireland)
Financial Times (England)
Grand Rapids Press (United States)
Guardian (England)
Herald (Scotland)
Independent (England)
Irish Times (Ireland)
Irish Independent (Ireland)
Irish Press (Ireland)
Irish Weekly (Ireland)
Leinster Express (Ireland)
Limerick Leader (Ireland)
Kerryman (Ireland)
Kerry's Eye (Ireland)
Kilkenny People (Ireland)
Mayo News (Ireland)
Munster Express (Ireland)
New York Times (United States)

New York Review of Books (United States)
Ocean Times (Cunard Line)
Picture Post (England)
Toronto Star (Canada)
Seattle Times (United States)
Scotsman (Edinburgh)
Scotland on Sunday (Scotland)
Sunday Herald Sun (Australia)
Sunday Press (Ireland)
Sunday Times (England)
USA Today (United States)
Washington Post (United States)
Western People (Ireland)

Magazines

Building Design (England)
Design Week (England)
Dublin Opinion (Ireland)
Go (Britain)
Guinness Harp (Ireland)
Holiday Magazine (United States)
Irish Digest (Ireland)
Irish Marketing and Advertising Journal (Ireland)
Ireland of the Welcomes (Ireland)
Irish Travel (Ireland)
Irish Travel Trade News (Ireland)
Sunset Magazine (United States)
Traveltrade (Australia)

Videocassettes/Movies/Radio Transcripts

Byrne, Joe, Aiden O'Hanlon, and Brian Keogh. *Tourism Is Everybody's Business*. 16 mm, 14 min., 1978. Distributed by Bord Fáilte.

Daiken, Leslie. *Where Puck Is King*. Script, 1960. Broadcast on BBC Radio.

De Buitlear, Eamon, ed. *There's Work to Be Done*. Videocassette, unknown length, 1992. Distributed by Bord Fáilte.

Engel, Larry, and Steven Engel. "Ireland." *Going Places*. Videocassette, 58 min., 1998. Distributed by Thirteen/WNET Production.

Flaherty, Robert J., dir. *Man of Aran.* Videocassette, 75 min., 1934. Distributed by Academy Video.

Gilsenan, Alan, ed. *Home Movie Nights: Jan De Fouw.* Television broadcast, 2001. Distributed by RTÉ.

Hatton, Buddy. *Song of Ireland.* Videocassette, 60 min., 1990. Distributed by Quantum Communications.

Hickey, Kieran, ed. *Ireland—The Heritage of the Past.* 16 mm, unknown length, 1974. Distributed by Bord Fáilte.

———, ed. *Our Tidy Towns—21 Years of Community Effort.* 16 mm, 39 min., 1979. Distributed by Bord Fáilte.

———, ed. *Working to Win.* Videocassette, unknown length, circa 1988. Distributed by Bord Fáilte.

Hirshelwood, Simon. *The Beauty of Ireland: Donegal and Cork.* Videocassette, 52 min., 1997. Distributed by American Home Treasures.

———. *The Beauty of Ireland: Dublin and Kerry.* Videocassette, 52 min., 1997. Distributed by American Home Treasures.

Le Tour de France en Irlande. Videocassette, unknown length, 1998. Distributed by Bord Fáilte.

Marcus, Louis, prod. *Discovering Ireland.* Videocassette, unknown length, 1984. Distributed by Bord Fáilte.

———, prod. *Ireland Ours.* 16 mm, unknown length, 1973. Distributed by Bord Fáilte.

McAleese, Mary. *President's Message for St. Patrick's Day.* Videocassette, unknown length, 1998. Distributed by Bord Fáilte.

Mulkenrs, James, prod. *Ireland Invites You.* 16 mm, 13 min., [?]1966. Distributed by Bord Fáilte.

Nairn, Richard. *Ireland Naturally.* Videocassette, unknown length, 1991. Distributed by Bord Fáilte.

Nolan, Liam. *Return to the Island.* Videocassette, unknown length, 1964. Distributed by Bord Fáilte.

Ó Mordha, Seán, dir. *Seven Ages.* Videocassette, seven episodes, 2000.

O'Laoghaire, Colm. *Ireland Invites You.* 16 mm, 20 min., 1953. Distributed by Universal Irish News.

Steves, Rick. *Western Ireland, Dublin, and Belfast.* Videocassette, 51 min., 1997. Distributed by Small World Production.

St. Patrick's Festival, 1998. Videocassette, unknown length, 1998. Distributed by Bord Fáilte.

Williams, John, ed. *Ireland: Bird's Eye View*. Videocassette, unknown length, 1983. Distributed by Bord Fáilte.

Published Primary Sources

Andrews, C. S. *Man of No Property: An Autobiography*. Vol. 2. Dublin: Mercier Press, 1982.

An Taisce. *An Taisce—Annual Report, 1976*. Dublin: An Taisce, 1976.

———. *An Taisce—Annual Report, 1977*. Dublin: An Taisce, 1977.

———. *An Taisce—Annual Report, 1978*. Dublin: An Taisce, 1978.

———. *An Taisce—Annual Reports, 1979–1980*. Dublin: An Taisce, 1979–80.

———. *Grafton Street Sustaining the Magic. What Future for Dublin's Favorite Shopping Street?* Dublin: An Taisce, 1995.

———. *Heritage at Risk*. Dublin: An Taisce, 1977.

Authority and to Town Commissioners—Model Byelaws for Streets. Dublin: Department of Local Government, 1959.

Bell, Archie. *The Spell of Ireland*. Boston: L. C. Page and Co., 1928.

Böll, Heinrich. *Irish Journal*. Translated by Leila Vennewitz. New York: McGraw-Hill, 1967.

Bord Fáilte. *Access Dining in Ireland Guide 1995*. Dublin: Bord Fáilte Éireann, 1995.

———. *Accommodation Guide*. Dublin: Bord Fáilte Éireann, 1991, 1994.

———. *Advertising Supplement to Ireland 1980*. London: Bord Fáilte Éireann, 1980.

———. *The Angler's Guide to Ireland*. 5th ed. Dublin: Bord Fáilte Éireann, 1957.

———. *Annual Report and Accounts, Year Ending 31st March 1953*. Dublin: Bord Fáilte Éireann, 1953.

———. *Annual Report and Accounts, Year Ending 31st March 1956*. Dublin: Bord Fáilte Éireann, 1956.

———. *Annual Report and Accounts, Year Ending 31st March 1957*. Dublin: Bord Fáilte Éireann, 1957.

———. *Annual Report and Accounts, Year Ending 31st March 1958*. Dublin: Bord Fáilte Éireann, 1958.

———. *Annual Report and Accounts, Year Ending 31st March 1959*. Dublin: Bord Fáilte Éireann, 1959.

———. *Annual Report and Accounts, Year Ended 31st March 1961*. Dublin: Bord Fáilte Éireann, 1961.

———. *Attitudes of American and English Tourists Towards Shopping in Ireland and Irish Merchandise: A Qualitative Investigation*. Dublin: Bord Fáilte Éireann, 1973.

———. *Be Our Guest Hotels and Guesthouses: Illustrated Guide*. Dublin: Bord Fáilte Éireann, 1989, 1991, 1992, 1993.

———. *Bord Fáilte Corporate Profile*. Dublin: Bord Fáilte Éireann, [?]2000.

———. *Bord Fáilte Diary and Tourism Directory*. Dublin: Bord Fáilte Éireann, 1994, 1995, 1996.

———. *Bord Fáilte Report and Accounts for the Year Ended December 1978*. Dublin: Bord Fáilte Éireann, 1978.

———. *Bord Fáilte Report and Accounts for the Year Ended December 1979*. Dublin: Bord Fáilte Éireann, 1979.

———. *Bord Fáilte Report and Accounts for the Year Ended December 1980*. Dublin: Bord Fáilte Éireann, 1980.

———. *Bord Fáilte Report and Accounts for the Year Ended December 1981*. Dublin: Bord Fáilte Éireann, 1981.

———. *Bord Fáilte Report and Accounts for the Year Ended December 1982*. Dublin: Bord Fáilte Éireann, 1982.

———. *Bord Fáilte Report and Accounts for the Year Ended December 1983*. Dublin: Bord Fáilte Éireann, 1983.

———. *Bord Fáilte Report and Accounts for the Year Ended December 1984*. Dublin: Bord Fáilte Éireann, 1984.

———. *Bord Fáilte Report and Accounts for the Year Ended December 1985*. Dublin: Bord Fáilte Éireann, 1985.

———. *Bord Fáilte Report for the Year Ended December 1974*. Dublin: Bord Fáilte Éireann, 1974.

———. *Bord Fáilte Report for the Year Ended December 1975*. Dublin: Bord Fáilte Éireann, 1975.

———. *Bord Fáilte Report for the Year Ended December 1976*. Dublin: Bord Fáilte Éireann, 1976.

———. *Bord Fáilte Report for the Year Ended December 1977*. Dublin: Bord Fáilte Éireann, 1977.

———. *Bord Fáilte Report for the Year Ended March 1972*. Dublin: Bord Fáilte Éireann, 1972.

———. *Bord Fáilte Report for the Year Ended March 1973*. Dublin: Bord Fáilte Éireann, 1973.

———. *Bord Fáilte Report for the Year Ended March 1974*. Dublin: Bord Fáilte Éireann, 1974.

———. *Bord Fáilte Report for the Year Ended March 1986*. Dublin: Bord Fáilte Éireann, 1986.

———. *Bord Fáilte Report for the Year Ended March 1987*. Dublin: Bord Fáilte Éireann, 1987.

———. *Bord Fáilte Report for the Year Ended March 1988*. Dublin: Bord Fáilte Éireann, 1988.

———. *Bord Fáilte Report for the Year Ended March 1989*. Dublin: Bord Fáilte Éireann, 1989.

———. *Bord Fáilte Report for the Year Ended March 1990*. Dublin: Bord Fáilte Éireann, 1990.

———. *Bord Fáilte Report for the Year Ended March 1991*. Dublin: Bord Fáilte Éireann, 1991.

———. *Bord Fáilte Report for the Year Ended March 1992*. Dublin: Bord Fáilte Éireann, 1992.

———. *Bord Fáilte Report for the Year Ended March 1993*. Dublin: Bord Fáilte Éireann, 1993.

———. *Bord Fáilte Report for the Year Ended March 1994*. Dublin: Bord Fáilte Éireann, 1994.

———. *Bord Fáilte Report for the Year Ended March 1995*. Dublin: Bord Fáilte Éireann, 1995.

———. *Bord Fáilte Report for the Year Ended March 1996*. Dublin: Bord Fáilte Éireann, 1996.

———. *Bord Fáilte Report for the Year Ended March 1998*. Dublin: Bord Fáilte Éireann, 1998.

———. *Brochures on Irish Holidays, Holy Places, Ancient Monuments, and Battle of the Boyne*. Dublin: Bord Fáilte Éireann, 1962.

———. *Calendars of Events Including An Tóstal 1954–58*. Dublin: Bord Fáilte Éireann, 1954–58.

———. *Caravan and Camping in Ireland*. Dublin: Bord Fáilte Éireann, 1973, 1974, 1976, 1979, 1980, 1981, 1982, 1987.

———. *Caravan Sites, 1961*. Dublin: Bord Fáilte Éireann, 1961.

———. *Christmas Programmes in Ireland, 1970*. Dublin: Bord Fáilte Éireann, 1970.

———. *Coarse Fishing in Ireland. Fisherman! Clare-Lakelands for the Fishing Experience of a Lifetime*. Dublin: Bord Fáilte Éireann, [?]1979.

———. *Coarse Fishing in Ireland. Limerick. It's Child's Play!* Dublin: Bord Fáilte Éireann, [?]1979.

———. *Connemara Makes It Good to Have Holidays*. Dublin: Bord Fáilte Éireann, [?]1979.

———. *Cork, City, and County: Official Guide*. Dublin: Bord Fáilte Éireann, 1957.

———. *Developing Sustainable Tourism: Tourism Development Plan 1994–1999.* Dublin: Bord Fáilte Éireann, 1995.
———. *Direct Marketing and the Internet Marketing for Success: A Practical Guide for Tourism Businesses.* Dublin: Bord Fáilte Éireann, 1997.
———. *Discover Ireland: Holiday Breaks.* Dublin: Bord Fáilte Éireann, 1995 and 1997.
———. *Discover Ireland: Spring Guide '73: Inclusive Weekends, Breakaway Holidays.* Dublin: Bord Fáilte Éireann, 1972.
———. *Dublin 1991 Events.* Dublin: Bord Fáilte Éireann, 1991.
———. *EMU—A Simple Guide for Tourism Businesses.* Dublin: Bord Fáilte Éireann, 1998.
———. *Erriff and Delphi Fisheries.* Dublin: Bord Fáilte Éireann, [?]1979.
———. *The Fáilte Business 2000: The Role of Tourism in Economic Growth.* Dublin: Bord Fáilte Éireann, 2000.
———. *A Glimpse of Ireland.* Dublin: Bord Fáilte Éireann, 1992.
———. *Golf.* Dublin: Bord Fáilte Éireann, 1993.
———. *Grand Canal Festa.* Dublin: Bord Fáilte Éireann, 1971.
———. *Gulliver Ireland's Tourism Information and Reservations System.* Dublin: Bord Fáilte Éireann, 1992.
———. *Ireland.* Dublin: Bord Fáilte Éireann, 1994.
———. *Ireland: 1980.* London: Bord Fáilte Éireann, 1980.
———. *Ireland: 1981.* London: Bord Fáilte Éireann, 1981.
———. *Ireland. Accommodation for Anglers. Coarse Fishing and Sea Angling Centres.* Dublin: Bord Fáilte Éireann, 1962.
———. *Ireland: Angling Accommodation, Coarse and Sea Angling Centres.* Dublin: Bord Fáilte Éireann, 1964.
———. *Ireland: Books of Irish Interest.* Information Sheet No. 18. Dublin: Bord Fáilte Éireann, 1977.
———. *Ireland: Calendar of Events, 1958.* Dublin: Bord Fáilte Éireann, 1958.
———. *Ireland: Calendar of Events, 1959.* Dublin: Bord Fáilte Éireann, 1959.
———. *Ireland: Calendar of Events, 1960.* Dublin: Bord Fáilte Éireann, 1960.
———. *Ireland: Calendar of Events, 1961.* Dublin: Bord Fáilte Éireann, 1961.
———. *Ireland: Calendar of Events, 1962.* Dublin: Bord Fáilte Éireann, 1962.
———. *Ireland: Calendar of Events, 1963.* Dublin: Bord Fáilte Éireann, 1963.
———. *Ireland: Calendar of Events, 1964.* Dublin: Bord Fáilte Éireann, 1964.
———. *Ireland: Calendar of Events, 1965.* Dublin: Bord Fáilte Éireann, 1965.
———. *Ireland: Calendar of Events, 1970.* Dublin: Bord Fáilte Éireann, 1970.

———. *Ireland: Calendar of Events, 1973*. Dublin: Bord Fáilte Éireann, 1973.
———. *Ireland: Calendar of Events, 1974*. Dublin: Bord Fáilte Éireann, 1974.
———. *Ireland: Calendar of Events, 1976*. Dublin: Bord Fáilte Éireann, 1976.
———. *Ireland: Calendar of Events, 1979*. Dublin: Bord Fáilte Éireann, 1979.
———. *Ireland: Calendar of Events, 1980*. Dublin: Bord Fáilte Éireann, 1980.
———. *Ireland: Calendar of Events, 1981*. Dublin: Bord Fáilte Éireann, 1981.
———. *Ireland: Carefree Motoring*. Dublin: Bord Fáilte Éireann, 1969.
———. *Ireland: Carefree Motoring*. Dublin: Bord Fáilte Éireann, 1972.
———. *Ireland: Climate*. Information Sheet No. 2. Dublin: Bord Fáilte Éireann, 1977.
———. *Ireland for Coarse Fishing Holidays*. Dublin: Bord Fáilte Éireann, 1959.
———. *Ireland: Eighteenth Century Ireland Dublin*. Dublin: Bord Fáilte Éireann, 1976.
———. *Ireland: Fairies*. Dublin: Bord Fáilte Éireann, 1976.
———. *Ireland of the Festivals*. Dublin: Bord Fáilte Éireann, 1959.
———. *Ireland Guide*. Dublin: Bord Fáilte Éireann, 1993.
———. *Ireland: The Heritage of the Past*. Dublin: Bord Fáilte Éireann, 1968.
———. *Ireland. List of Caravan Sites, 1963*. Dublin: Bord Fáilte Éireann, 1963.
———. *Ireland. List of Caravan Sites, 1964*. Dublin: Bord Fáilte Éireann, 1964.
———. *Ireland: A Golfer's Paradise*. Dublin: Bord Fáilte Éireann, 1968.
———. *Ireland: Hill Walking and Rock Climbing*. Dublin: Bord Fáilte Éireann, 1976.
———. *Ireland: Holy Places*. Dublin: Bord Fáilte Éireann, 1976.
———. *Ireland: Horse Drawn Caravans*. Information Sheet No. 14. Dublin: Bord Fáilte Éireann, 1977.
———. *Ireland: Horse Riding Holidays*. Dublin: Bord Fáilte Éireann, 1976.
———. *Ireland: Hotels and Guest Houses 1964*. Dublin: Bord Fáilte Éireann, 1964.
———. *Ireland: Irish Crafts*. Dublin: Bord Fáilte Éireann, 1976.
———. *Ireland: Irish Recipes*. Information Sheet No. 29. Dublin: Bord Fáilte Éireann, 1977.
———. *Ireland: Land Arrangements for Travel Agents, 1972*. Dublin: Bord Fáilte Éireann, 1971.
———. *Ireland: Libraries, Art Galleries, Museums*. Dublin: Bord Fáilte Éireann, 1976.
———. *Ireland: Newspapers*. Dublin: Bord Fáilte Éireann, 1976.
———. *Ireland: Official List 1955: Hotels, Guest Houses, Holiday Camps, Holiday Hostels, Youth Hostels*. Dublin: Bord Fáilte Éireann, 1955.

———. *Ireland: Official List 1956: Hotels, Guest Houses, Holiday Camps, Holiday Hostels, Youth Hostels*. Dublin: Bord Fáilte Éireann, 1956.
———. *Ireland: Official List 1957: Hotels, Guest Houses, Holiday Camps, Holiday Hostels, Youth Hostels*. Dublin: Bord Fáilte Éireann, 1957.
———. *Ireland: Sailing in Ireland*. Information Sheet No. 9. Dublin: Bord Fáilte Éireann, 1977.
———. *Ireland. Seaside Resorts*. Dublin: Bord Fáilte Éireann, 1959.
———. *Ireland: Theatre and Historic Pageantry*. Information Sheet No. 19. Dublin: Bord Fáilte Éireann, 1977.
———. *Ireland: Tracing Your Ancestors*. Information Sheet No. 8. Dublin: Bord Fáilte Éireann, 1977.
———. *Ireland: Traditional Music*. Dublin: Bord Fáilte Éireann, 1976.
———. *Ireland West: Galway and Mayo*. Dublin: Bord Fáilte Éireann, [?]1979.
———. *Ireland, Your Holiday Guaranteed*. Dublin: Bord Fáilte Éireann, 1974.
———. *Ireland's Ancient Monuments*. Dublin: Bord Fáilte Éireann, [?]1964.
———. *Ireland's Ancient Monuments*. Dublin: Bord Fáilte Éireann, [?]1966.
———. *The Irish Tourist Board Report for the Year Ending 31st March 1960*. Dublin: Bord Fáilte Éireann, 1960.
———. *The Irish Tourist Board Report for the Year Ended 31 March 1962*. Dublin: Bord Fáilte Éireann, 1962.
———. *The Irish Tourist Board Report for the Year Ended 31st March 1963*. Dublin: Bord Fáilte Éireann, 1963.
———. *The Irish Tourist Board Report for the Year Ended March 31 1964*. Dublin: Bord Fáilte Éireann, 1964.
———. *Irish Tourist Board Report for the Year Ended March 1970*. Dublin: Bord Fáilte Éireann, 1970.
———. *Irish Tourist Board Report for the Year Ended March 31 1965*. Dublin: Bord Fáilte Éireann, 1965.
———. *Know Your Market: Australia/New Zealand*. Dublin: Bord Fáilte Éireann, 1998.
———. *Know Your Market: Austria/Switzerland/Eastern Europe*. Dublin: Bord Fáilte Éireann, 1998.
———. *Know Your Market: Benelux 1997–1998*. Dublin: Bord Fáilte Éireann, 1997.
———. *Know Your Market: Britain*. Dublin: Bord Fáilte Éireann, 1993.
———. *Know Your Market: Britain*. Dublin: Bord Fáilte Éireann, 1998.
———. *Know Your Market: France*. Dublin: Bord Fáilte Éireann, 1998.

———. *Know Your Market: Germany*. Dublin: Bord Fáilte Éireann, 1993.
———. *Know Your Market: Italy*. Dublin: Bord Fáilte Éireann, 1997.
———. *Know Your Market: North America*. Dublin: Bord Fáilte Éireann, 1998.
———. *Know Your Market: Spain*. Dublin: Bord Fáilte Éireann, 1993.
———. *Know Your Market: Spain*. Dublin: Bord Fáilte Éireann, 1997.
———. *Know Your Market: Switzerland/Austria*. Dublin: Bord Fáilte Éireann, 1994.
———. *Markets*. Dublin: Bord Fáilte Éireann, 1999.
———. *Miscellaneous Tourist Information Literature, Including the 'Discover Ireland' and 'Ireland: Information Sheet Seers,' 1967–73*. Dublin: Bord Fáilte Éireann, 1967–73.
———. *National Monuments of Ireland in Charge of the Commissioners of Public Works in Ireland*. Dublin: Bord Fáilte Éireann, 1964.
———. *Perspectives on Irish Tourism, Irish Travel Market 1994: A Report on Trip Taking in Ireland and Abroad by Irish Residents*. Dublin: Bord Fáilte Éireann, 1997.
———. *Perspectives on Irish Tourism Visits to Tourist Attractions 1996*. Dublin: Bord Fáilte Éireann, 1997.
———. *Pricing and Yield Management Marketing for Success—a Practical Guide for Tourism Businesses*. Dublin: Bord Fáilte Éireann, 1997.
———. *Reaching the Customer, Marketing for Success—A Practical Guide for Tourism Businesses*. Dublin: Bord Fáilte Éireann, 1997.
———. *Regions*. Dublin: Bord Fáilte Éireann, [?]1999.
———. *Relationship Marketing, Marketing for Success—A Practical Guide for Tourism Businesses*. Dublin: Bord Fáilte Éireann, 1998.
———. *Report and Financial Statements 2000*. Dublin: Bord Fáilte Éireann, 2000.
———. *Sea Fishing: Ireland*. Dublin: Bord Fáilte Éireann, n.d.
———. *Some Highlights of An Tóstal, 1955*. Dublin: Bord Fáilte Éireann, 1955.
———. *Spring Weekends 1975*. Dublin: Bord Fáilte Éireann, [?]1974.
———. *Tourism in the Irish Economy*. Dublin: Bord Fáilte Éireann, 1989.
———. *Tourism Plan 1974–77: A Four-Year Working Document for the Irish Tourist Industry. This Plan Is Supplementary to the Tourism Plan 1973–76*. Dublin: Bord Fáilte Éireann, 1974.
———. *Tourism Plan 1981–85: Marketing and Development Guidelines for the Irish Tourist Industry*. Dublin: Bord Fáilte Éireann, 1980.
———. *Tourism Towards 2000: Marketing Plan for Irish Tourism 1999*. Dublin: Bord Fáilte Éireann, 1999.

———. *Tourist Development Plan, 1976–80: Dublin Regional Tourism*. Dublin: Bord Fáilte Éireann, 1976.

———. *Tourist Development Plan, 1976–80: Eastern Region*. Dublin: Bord Fáilte Éireann, 1976.

———. *Tourist Development Plan, 1976–80: Midland Region*. Dublin: Bord Fáilte Éireann, 1976.

———. *Tourist Development Plan, 1976–80: Mid-Western Region*. Dublin: Bord Fáilte Éireann, 1976.

———. *Tourist Development Plan, 1976–80: National Plan*. Dublin: Bord Fáilte Éireann, 1976.

———. *Tourist Development Plan, 1976–80: North-Western Region*. Dublin: Bord Fáilte Éireann, 1976.

———. *Tourist Development Plan, 1976–80: South Eastern Region*. Dublin: Bord Fáilte Éireann, 1976.

———. *Tourist Development Plan, 1976–80: Southern Region (Cork/Kerry) Tourism*. Dublin: Bord Fáilte Éireann, 1976.

———. *Tourist Development Plan, 1976–80: Western Region*. Dublin: Bord Fáilte Éireann, 1976.

———. *Tramore Resort Plan*. Dublin: Bord Fáilte Éireann, 1971.

———. *Urlaub Made in Ireland*. Frankfurt: Bord Fáilte Éireann, 1969.

———. *Welcome to Ireland*. Dublin: Bord Fáilte Éireann, 1976 and 1979.

———. *Where to Eat in Ireland: A Traveller's Guide to 100 Selected Restaurants*. Dublin: Bord Fáilte Éireann, 1973.

BP Touring Service of Ireland. *Touring Guide to Ireland: Cork*. Dublin: BP, n.d.

British Tourist Authority. *Britain and Ireland, Car Ferry Routes*. London: British Tourist Authority, 1979.

CaraIreland Tours. London: Cara, 1973.

Central Statistics Office. *Statistical Abstract*. Dublin: Government Publications, 1990.

CIÉ Tours International, Inc.: Europe, Ireland, Great Britain. Dublin: CIÉ, 1971.

Clark, Gordon. *Tourist Trail: A Signposted Walking Tour of Dublin*. Dublin: Dublin Tourism, [?]1985.

Comeback for Erin? Dublin: National Tourism Council of Ireland, 1977.

Come Cruising on Ireland's River Shannon, the Most Wonderful Waterway in Europe. Dublin: Penguin, 1969.

Convery, Frank, and Sheila Flanagan. *Investing for Tourism in Ireland. Proceedings of the Tourism Investment Conference Held at University College Dublin, March*

29–31, 1994. Dublin: Dublin Environmental Institute, University College Dublin, 1994.

Cooke, Pat. *A History of Kilmainham Gaol*. Dublin: Dúchas, 2001.

Co-ordinating Committee for Killarney Tourist Industry. *See Killarney First*. Dublin: Bord Fáilte, 1972.

Cork/Kerry Tourism Organisation. *Cork/Kerry Tourism Marketing Plan as of 26/2/98*. Cork: Cork/Kerry Tourism, 1998.

Corrigan Kearns, Kevin. *Georgian Dublin—Ireland's Imperiled Architecture*. Newton Abbot, UK: David and Charles, 1983.

Coughlan, Stephen. *Tóstal Corcai. Festival of Cork, Souvenir Programme*. Cork: n.p., 1956.

Dalaigh, Brian O., ed. *The Stranger's Gaze: Travels in County Clare, 1534–1950*. Dublin: Clasp Press, 1998.

Department of Local Government. *Department of Local Government Report, 1939-40*. Dublin: Government Publications, 1940.

———. *Department of Local Government Report, 1940-41*. Dublin: Government Publications, 1941.

———. *Department of Local Government Report, 1941-2*. Dublin: Government Publications, 1942.

———. *Department of Local Government Report, 1942–3*. Dublin: Government Publications, 1943.

———. *Department of Local Government Report, 1943–4*. Dublin: Government Publications, 1944.

———. *Department of Local Government Report, 1944–5*. Dublin: Government Publications, 1945.

———. *Department of Local Government Report, 1945–47*. Dublin: Government Publications, 1947.

———. *Department of Local Government Report, 1947–48*. Dublin: Government Publications, 1948.

———. *Department of Local Government Report, 1948–49*. Dublin: Government Publications, 1949.

———. *Department of Local Government Report, 1949–50*. Dublin: Government Publications, 1950.

———. *Department of Local Government Report, 1950–51*. Dublin: Government Publications, 1951.

———. *Department of Local Government Report, 1951–1952*. Dublin: Government Publications, 1952.

———. *Department of Local Government Report, 1952–1953.* Dublin: Government Publications, 1953.

———. *Department of Local Government Report, 1953–1954.* Dublin: Government Publications, 1954.

———. *Department of Local Government Report, 1955–1956.* Dublin: Government Publications, 1956.

———. *Department of Local Government Report, 1956–1957.* Dublin: Government Publications, 1957.

———. *Department of Local Government Report, 1958–1959—Roads.* Dublin: Government Publications, 1959.

———. *Department of Local Government Report, 1958–1959. Appendix xxiii, Circular Letter No. L2/1959 of 2nd Feb. 1959 to Each Sanitary.* Dublin: Government Publications, 1959.

"Dingle Name Campaign." *Dingle Name Campaign, 2007,* <http://www.dingle-name.com,> accessed 21 July 2007.

Discover What's Brewing at the Guinness Hopstore. Dublin: Guinness Brewing Company, circa 1990.

Drumshanbo An Tóstal Committee. *Twenty-Second An Tóstal Druimseanbhoth.* Dublin: Bord Fáilte, 1974.

Dublin Corporation. *Dublin City Development Plan 1991.* Dublin: Dublin Corporation, 1991.

———. *Dublin City Development Plan 1999.* Dublin: Dublin Corporation, 1999.

Duff, Chris. *On Celtic Tides: One Man's Journey around Ireland by Sea Kayak.* New York: St. Martin's Griffin, 1999.

Durell, Penelope, and Cornelius Kelly, eds. *The Grand Tour of Beara.* Allihies, County Cork, Ireland: Cailleach Books, 2000.

———, eds. *The Grand Tour of Kerry.* Allihies, County Cork, Ireland: Cailleach Books, 2001.

Feehan, John, ed. *Tourism on the Farm. Proceedings of Two Conferences on Farm Tourism in Ireland: University College, Dublin, March 1992; Enniskillen Fermanagh, May 1992.* Dublin: Dublin Environmental Institute, University College Dublin, 1992.

Fine Gael. *Time for Action for the Repedestrianisation of Grafton Street.* Dublin: Fine Gael, 1976.

Fógra Fáilte. *An Tóstal: Ireland at Home, 1953. National Programme.* Dublin: Fógra Fáilte, 1953.

———. *An Tóstal: Official Souvenir Guide.* Dublin: Fógra Fáilte, 1953.

———. *Ireland Guide*. Dublin: Fógra Fáilte, [?]1953.

———. *Ireland: An Illustrated Guide to the Counties of Ireland*. Dublin: Fógra Fáilte, [?]1953.

———. *Ireland: Official List 1953: Hotels, Guest Houses, Holiday Camps, Holiday Hostels, Youth Hostels*. Dublin: Fógra Fáilte, 1953.

———. *Ireland: Official List 1954: Hotels, Guest Houses, Holiday Camps, Holiday Hostels, Youth Hostels*. Dublin: Fógra Fáilte, 1954.

Geoghegan, Philip. *Building Sensitively in Ireland's Landscapes*. Dublin: Bord Fáilte and An Taisce, 1989.

Ghosts of Kilmainham. Dublin: Kilmainham Jail Restoration Society, 1963.

Gorman, Michael, Frank Height, Mary V. Mullin, and W. H. Walsh, eds. *Design for Tourism: An ICSID Inter Design Report*. Oxford: Pergamon Press, 1977.

Guinness Dublin. Dublin: Guinness Brewing Co., 1939, 1948, 1955.

Guinness. Brasserie De Renommée Mondiale. L'Histoire du Célèbre Stout aux Cinq Millions d'Hectolitres de Ventes Annuelles. Dublin: Guinness Brewing Company, circa 1950.

The Guinness Brewery. Dublin: Guinness Brewing Company, circa 1955.

Harbison, Peter. *Guide to National and Historic Monuments of Ireland*. Dublin: Gill and Macmillan, 1992.

Harrington, John P., ed. *The English Traveller in Ireland: Accounts of Ireland and the Irish through Five Centuries*. Dublin: Wolfhound Press, 1991.

Hawks, Tony. *Round Ireland with a Fridge*. New York: St. Martin's Griffin, 1988.

Hooper, Glenn. *The Tourist's Gaze: Travellers to Ireland, 1800–2000*. Cork: Cork Univ. Press, 2002.

Imagination Group USA. "Guinness Storehouse," <http://www.imagination.com/usa/work/guinness.html,> accessed 9 Apr. 2003.

Implementation Group. "Memorandum of Understanding on the North/South Tourism Company." In appendix 6 of *Establishment of New Tourist Development Authority*. Dublin: Department of Tourism, Sport, and Recreation, 2002.

———. *Establishment of New Tourist Development Authority*. Dublin: Department of Tourism, Sport, and Recreation, 2002.

Inland Fisheries Trust. *Salmon and Sea Trout Fishing in Ireland*. Compiled by the Inland Fisheries Trust for Bord Fáilte Éireann. Dublin: Inland Fisheries Trust, 1966.

Ireland Flyaway Holidays 70. Dublin: Aer Lingus and BEA, 1970.

"Ireland/Irish Pub Themed Items," Bellatopia.com, <http://www.bellatopia.com/themes_irish_pub.shtml,> accessed 4 Aug. 2003.

Irish Tourist Association. *Angling and Golf*. Dublin: Irish Tourist Association, 1946.

―――. *Cork Official Guide.* Dublin: Irish Tourist Association, 1932.

―――. *Cork: A Short Survey of the Attractions and Holiday Facilities of Cork City and County.* Dublin: Irish Tourist Association, [?]1928.

―――. *Dublin: Official Guide.* Dublin: Irish Tourist Association, 1933.

―――. *Hike It or Bike It.* Dublin: Irish Tourist Association, [?]1944.

―――. *Hotels and Boarding Houses in Cork City and County.* Dublin: Irish Tourist Association, 1927.

―――. *Hotels, Restaurants and Garages in the Irish Free State: A Detailed List with Particulars of Accommodation and Charges.* Dublin: Irish Tourist Association, n.d.

―――. *Introducing Ireland.* Dublin: Irish Tourist Association, 1950.

―――. *Ireland: Official Guide.* Dublin: Irish Tourist Association, 1938 and 1947.

―――. *Ireland: Official Publication.* Dublin: Irish Tourist Association, 1929.

―――. *Ireland: Official Publication of the Irish Tourist Association.* Dublin: Irish Tourist Association, 1930 and 1932.

―――. *Irish Curiosities. A Collection of Strange, Fascinating, Puzzling or Picturesque Oddities of Ireland Pictured and Described in This New I.T.A. Book.* Dublin: Irish Tourist Association, 1944.

―――. *Irish Tourist Directory Comprising Hotels, Boarding Houses, Restaurants, Garages, and Other Business in the Irish Free State.* Dublin: Irish Tourist Association, 1934.

―――. *Killarney: Beauty's Home: Official Guide.* Dublin: Irish Tourist Association, [?]1934.

―――. *Killarney: Cill Airne/I.T.A. Official Guide.* Trallee, Ireland: Irish Tourist Association, [?]1949.

―――. *Killarney: The Official Publication of the Irish Tourist Association.* Dublin: Irish Tourist Association, 1946.

―――. *The Kingdom of Kerry: The Official Publication of the Irish Tourist Association.* Dublin: Irish Tourist Association, [?]1946.

―――. *A Morning in Dublin.* Dublin: Irish Tourist Association, n.d.

―――. *Official Guide to "Kingdom of Kerry."* Dublin: Irish Tourist Association, 1934, [?]1940.

―――. *Welcome to Cork: A Short Survey of the Attractions and Holiday Facilities of Cork City and County.* Cork: Irish Tourist Association, [?]1927.

Irish Tourist Board. *Official List of Registered Premises for 1944. Hotels, Guest Houses, Holiday Hostels, Youth Hostels, Holiday Camps.* Dublin: Irish Tourist Association, 1944.

Kellogg's Fruit 'N Fibre Farmhouse B&B Guide. Huntingdon, UK: Kellogg, 1993.

Kerryweb Ireland. *"Cloghane and Brandon,"* <http://www.kerryweb.ie/destination-kerry/cloghane/cloghane.html,> accessed 12 Sept. 2000.

Kilmainham: The Bastille of Ireland. Dublin: Kilmainham Jail Restoration Society, 1970.

Le Guinness. Son Brassage, Ses Properties, Ses Qualities. Dublin: Guinness Brewing Company, 1932.

Living City Group. *Dublin—A Living City?* Dublin: The Living City Group, 1972.

Loughlin, Paul. *Product 1992. Getting the Product Right! A Presentation on the Progress Being Made in the Development of New Tourism Infrastructure. Bord Fáilte Tourism Industry Meeting, Burlington Hotel, Dublin*. Dublin: Bord Fáilte, 1991.

MacDonogh, Steve. *The Dingle Peninsula*. Dingle: Brandon, 2000.

McCarthy, Pete. *McCarthy's Bar*. Edinburgh: Hodder and Stoughton, 2000.

McKenna, Fionnuala. "Sunningdale Agreement, 8 January 1973," <http://cain.ulst.ac.uk/events/sunningdale/agreement.htm,> accessed 19 Mar. 2003.

National Coastline Study. Vol. 1. Dublin: S.N., 1972.

National Rehabilitation Board. *Guide to Accessible Accommodation in Ireland*. Dublin, 1998.

Neeson, Geraldine. *Our Heritage—Cork*. Dublin: Bruce Spicer, 1970.

Nelson, Justin, ed. *Faces and Places*. Dublin, circa 1987.

Newby, Eric. *Round Ireland in Low Gear*. London: Viking, 1987.

Northern Ireland Assembly. "Good Friday Agreement," <http://www.studiperlapace.org,> accessed 20 Mar. 2003.

O'Cahill, Donal, ed. *Killarney: Land and Lake*. 13th ed. Tralee: Donal O'Cahill, [?]1963.

O'Faolain, Sean. *An Irish Journey*. London: Reader's Union, 1941.

O'Sullivan, John F. *Glimpses of Paradise: A Guide History of Killarney*. Illfracombe: Stockwell, 1969.

Pictures and Answers: Things People Ask About Guinness. Dublin: Guinness Brewing Company, 1950.

Robertson, Manning. *Cautionary Guide to Dublin with 64 Illustrations*. Dublin: Royal Institute of the Architects of Ireland, 1933, 1934.

'Round Ballycotton Bay. Skibbereen: Star Printing, [?]1933.

Rukeyser, Muriel. *The Orgy*. New York: Coward-McCann, 1965.

Somerville-Large, Peter. *The Grand Irish Tour*. London: Hamish Hamilton, 1982.

Southern Regional Tourism Organisation. *Ivernia Interim Report—1971: Embodying End of Season Review 1971*. Cork: Southern Regional Tourism Organisation, 1972.

———. *Ivernia: Cork—Kerry.* Cork: Southern Regional Tourism Organisation, 1972.
"Storehouse Gets Celebrity Start." *Irish Marketing and Advertising Journal* 1 (Jan. 2001).
Taibln, Colm, and Bernard Loughlin, eds. *The Guinness Book of Ireland.* Enfield, Middlesex: Guinness and Bord Fáilte, 1995.
"Tourism—A Record." *The* Irish Times *Annual Review* 3 (Jan. 1966): 74–76.
Visitor's Guide to Dublin. Dublin: General Publications, [?]1969.
Walsh, Brendan. *Cycle Touring Ireland.* Dublin: Gill and Macmillan, 1997.
The World and His Wife. Dublin: Guinness Brewing Company, circa 1961.
Your Guide to the World of Guinness at the Guinness Hopstore. Dublin: Guinness Brewing Company, circa 1990.
Your Very Own Visitor Guide. The World of Guinness, Guinness Hopstore. Dublin: Guinness Brewing Company, circa 1990.

Secondary Sources

Unpublished Dissertations/Theses

Beyn, F. Emma. "Tourists, Travelers and Transients: Hostel Culture in Southwestern Ireland." Division III examination, Hampshire College, 1996.
Casey, Marion R. "Ireland, New York and the Irish Image in American Popular Culture, 1890–1960." Ph.D. diss., New York Univ., 1998.
De Nie, Michael William. "The Eternal Paddy: Irish Identity and the British Press, 1798–1882." Ph.D. diss., Univ. of Wisconsin-Madison, 2001.
Dolan, Anne. "Commemorating the Irish Civil War, 1924–2000." Ph.D. diss., Cambridge Univ., Cambridge, 2001.
Dunne, Paul. "Is Ireland the Ideal International Golfing Holiday Destination?" Master of Business Studies, Dublin Business School, 1995.
McMahon, Timothy Gerard. "The Social Bases of the Gaelic Revival, 1893–1910." Ph.D. diss., Univ. of Wisconsin-Madison, 2001.
Thompson, Spurgeon. "The Postcolonial Tourist: Irish Tourism and Decolonization since 1850." Ph.D. diss., Univ. of Notre Dame, 1999.
Zuelow, Eric G. E. "'Invasion of the Celts': The King's Visit and the Formation of Scottish National Identity." Master of Arts, Univ. of Wisconsin-Madison, 1999.

Other Unpublished Secondary Sources

Ashworth, G. J. "Is Heritage, a Globalisation of the Local or a Localisation of the Global?" Paper presented at *Ireland's Heritages: Critical Perspectives on*

Consumption, Method and Memory, Galway-Mayo Institute of Technology, Castlebar, Co. Mayo, Ireland, 19 Oct. 2002.

King, Linda. "'Guaranteed Irish'—Aer Lingus and the Representation of Ireland." Paper presented at *Ireland's Heritages: Critical Perspectives on Consumption, Method and Memory.* Galway-Mayo Institute of Technology, Castlebar, Co. Mayo, Ireland, 19 Oct. 2002.

Marcuse, Harold. "Shaping the Visitor Experience in Dachau, 1938–1968." In "Tourism, War and the Commemoration of Atrocity," ed. Rudi Hartmann, unpublished, 1999.

Published Secondary Sources

Abram, Simon. "Performing for Tourists in Rural France." In *Tourists and Tourism: Identifying with People and Places,* ed. Jacqueline Waldren, Simon Abram, and Donald V. L. Macleod, 29–50. Oxford: Berg, 1997.

Agnew, John. "European Landscape and Identity." In *Modern Europe: Place, Culture and Identity,* ed. Brian Graham, 213–35. London: Arnold, 1998.

Anderson, Benedict. *Imagined Communities: Reflections on the Origin and Spread of Nationalism.* London: Verso, 1991.

Arel, Dominique. "Language Politics in Independent Ukraine: Towards One or Two State Languages?" *Nationalities Papers* 23, no. 3 (1995): 597–624.

Ashworth, G. J., and P. J. Larkham, eds. *Building a New Heritage: Tourism, Culture and Identity in the New Europe.* London: Routledge, 1994.

Azaryahu, Maoz, and Aharon Kellerman. "Symbolic Places of National History in Zionist Mythical Geography." *Transactions of the Institute for Geography* 24 (1999): 109–23.

Bailey, Peter. *Leisure and Class in Victorian England: Rational Recreation and the Contest for Control.* Buffalo, N.Y.: Univ. of Toronto Press, 1978.

Balakrishnan, Gopal, ed. *Mapping the Nation.* London: Verso, 1996.

Baldwin-Brown, Gerald. *The Care of Ancient Monuments.* Cambridge: Cambridge Univ. Press, 1905.

Bannon, Michael J., Kevin I. Nowlan, John Hendry, and Ken Mawhinney, eds. *Planning: The Irish Experience 1920–1988.* Dublin: Wolfhound Press, 1989.

Baranowski, Shelley, and Ellen Furlough, eds. *Being Elsewhere: Tourism, Consumer Culture, and Identity in Modern Europe and North America.* Ann Arbor: Univ. of Michigan Press, 2001.

Barrington, Ruth, and Jim Dooge, eds. *A Vital National Interest: Ireland in Europe, 1973–1998.* Dublin: Institute of Public Administration, 1999.

Basch, Linda G., Nina Gleck Schiller, and Cristina Szanton Blanc. *Nations Unbound: Transnational Projects, Postcolonial Predicaments and Deterritorialized Nation-States.* Laughone, Pa.: Gordon and Breach, 1994.

Benjamin, Walter. *Illuminations: Essays and Reflections.* New York: Schocken Books, 1968.

Billig, Michael. *Banal Nationalism.* London: Sage, 1995.

Black, Jeremy. *The British Abroad: The Grand Tour in the Eighteenth Century.* New York: St. Martin's Press, 1992.

Blommaert, Jan. "Language and Nationalism: Comparing Flanders and Tanzania." *Nations and Nationalism* 2, no. 2 (1996): 235–56.

Boyce, D. George. *Nationalism in Ireland.* London: Routledge, 1995.

Boylan, Henry. *A Dictionary of Irish Biography.* 3rd ed. Niwot, Colo.: Robert Rinehart, 1998.

Bradley, W. H. "Around the World with Thomas Cook." *British Heritage,* 1988, 56–61.

Breathnach, Proinnsias, ed. *Irish Tourism Development.* Maynooth: Geographical Society of Ireland, 1994.

Brendon, Piers. *Thomas Cook: 150 Years of Popular Travel.* London: Secker and Warburg, 1991.

Brett, David. *The Construction of Heritage.* Cork: Cork Univ. Press, 1996.

Brown, Terence. *Ireland: A Social and Cultural History, 1922 to the Present.* Ithaca, N.Y.: Cornell Univ. Press, 1990.

Browne, Lance, and Kenneth A. Wright. *A Future for Dublin.* Bedford: Architectural Press, 1975.

Browne, Sean. "Heritage in Ireland's Tourism Recovery." In *Cultural Tourism,* ed. J. M. Fladmark, 13–25. London: Donheael Publishing, 1994.

Bruce, Steve. *The Edge of Union: The Ulster Loyalist Political Vision.* Oxford: Oxford Univ. Press, 1994.

Brunn, Stanley D., Ute Wardenga, and Anne Buttimer, eds. *Text and Image: Social Construction of Regional Knowledges.* Leipzig: Institut für Länderkunde, 1999.

Butler, R. W. "Evolution of Tourism in the Scottish Highlands." *Annals of Tourism Research* 12 (1985): 371–91.

Buzard, James. *The Beaten Track: European Tourism, Literature, and the Ways to Culture, 1800–1918.* Oxford: Clarendon Press, 1993.

Callanan, Brian. *Leaders, Visions, and Networks, Ireland's Shannon Story: A Case Study of Local and Regional Development.* Dublin: Irish Academic Press, 2000.

Cater, Erlet, and Stuart McMinn. "Tourist Typology: Observations from Belize." *Annals of Tourism Research* 25, no. 3 (1998): 675–99.
Chatterjee, Partha. *The Nation and Its Fragments: Colonial and Postcolonial Histories.* Princeton, N.J.: Princeton Univ. Press, 1993.
Chris Curtin, and Tony Varley. "Brown Trout, 'Gentry' and Dutchmen: Tourism and Development in South Mayo." In *Ireland from Below: Social Change and Local Communities,* ed. Thomas M. Wilson and Chris Curtin, 207–23. Galway: Galway Univ. Press, 1987.
Chubb, Basil. *The Politics of the Irish Constitution.* Dublin: Institute of Public Administration, 1991.
Clark, W., and B. O'Cinneide. *Tourism in the Republic of Ireland and Northern Ireland.* Belfast: Co-operation North, 1981.
Clarke, Conor. *Oranje and Green: Holland-Ireland, Design Connections 1951–2002.* Amsterdam: BIS Publishers, 2002.
Clifford, James. *Routes: Travel and Translation in the Late Twentieth Century.* Cambridge, Mass.: Harvard Univ. Press, 1997.
Cohrane, Feargal. *Unionist Politics and the Politics of Unionism since the Anglo-Irish Agreement.* Cork: Cork Univ. Press, 1997.
Colley, Linda. *Britons: Forging the Nation, 1707–1837.* New Haven, Conn.: Yale Univ. Press, 1992.
Collins, Stephen. *The Cosgrave Legacy.* Dublin: Blackwater Press, 1996.
Conekin, Becky E. *"The Autobiography of a Nation": The 1951 Festival of Britain.* Manchester: Manchester Univ. Press, 2003.
Confino, Alon. *The Nation as a Local Metaphor.* Chapel Hill: Univ. of North Carolina Press, 1997.
Connerton, Paul. *How Societies Remember.* Cambridge: Cambridge Univ. Press, 1989.
Connolly, S. J. "Popular Culture: Patterns of Change and Adaptation." In *Conflict, Identity, and Economic Development: Ireland and Scotland, 1600–1939,* ed. R. A. Houston, S. J. Connolly, and R. J. Morris, 103–13. Cambridge: Carnegie Publishing, 1995.
Conversi, Daniele, ed. *Ethnonationalism in the Contemporary World: Walker Connor and the Study of Nationalism.* London: Routledge, 2002.
Conversi, Daniele. "Language or Race?: The Choice of Core Values in the Development of Catalan and Basque Nationalisms." *Ethnic and Racial Studies* 13, no. 1 (1990): 50–70.
Corbin, Alain. *The Lure of the Sea.* Berkeley: Univ. of California Press, 1994.

Cormack, Mike. "Minority Languages, Nationalism and Broadcasting: The British and Irish Examples." *Nations and Nationalism* 6, no. 3 (2000): 383–98.
Cosgrove, Denis E. *Social Formation and Symbolic Landscape.* Madison: Univ. of Wisconsin Press, 1998.
Cronin, Denis A., Jim Gilligan, and Karina Holton, eds. *Irish Fairs and Markets.* Dublin: Four Courts Press, 2001.
Cronin, Michael. *Across the Lines: Travel, Language, Translation.* Cork: Cork Univ. Press, 2000.
Cronin, Mike. *Sport and Nationalism in Ireland: Gaelic Games, Soccer and Irish Identity since 1884.* Dublin: Four Courts Press, 1999.
Cronin, Mike, and Daryl Adair. *The Wearing of the Green: A History of St. Patrick's Day.* London: Routledge, 2002.
Cronin, Sean. *Frank Ryan: The Search for the Republic.* Dublin: Repsol Publishers, 1980.
Cullen, Fintan. *Visual Politics: The Representation of Ireland 1750–1930.* Cork: Cork University Press, 1997.
Curtis, L. Perry Jr. *Apes and Angles: The Irishman in Victorian Caricature.* Washington: Smithsonian Institution Press, 1997.
Dalby, Andrew. *Language in Danger.* New York: Penguin Press, 2002.
Dalsimer, Adele M., ed. *Visualizing Ireland: National Identity and the Pictorial Tradition.* Boston: Faber and Faber, 1993.
Daly, Mary E. *Industrial Development and Irish Society: 1922–1939.* Syracuse, N.Y.: Syracuse Univ. Press, 1992.
Darby, John. *Scorpions in a Bottle: Conflicting Cultures in Northern Ireland.* London: Minority Rights Group Publications, 1997.
De Nie, Michael. "'A Medley Mob of Irish-American Plotters and Irish Dupes': The British Press and Transatlantic Fenianism." *Journal of British Studies* 40, no. 2 (2001): 213–40.
Deane, Seamus. *Strange Country: Modernity and Nationhood in Irish Writing since 1790.* Oxford: Clarendon Press, 1997.
Deegan, James, and Donal A. Dineen. *Tourism Policy and Performance: The Irish Experience.* London: International Thomson Business Press, 1997.
Delany, Patrick, ed. *Dublin—A City in Crisis.* Dublin: Royal Institute of the Architects of Ireland, 1975.
Dennison, S. R., and Oliver MacDonagh. *Guinness 1886–1939: From Incorporation to the Second World War.* Cork: Cork Univ. Press, 1998.

Dillon, Michele. *Divorce: Moral Conflict in Ireland*. Lexington: Univ. of Kentucky Press, 1993.

Drisceoil, Donal Ó. *Censorship in Ireland 1939–1945: Neutrality, Politics, and Society*. Cork: Cork Univ. Press, 1996.

Duncan, A. A. M. *The Nation of the Scots and the Declaration of Arbroath*. Glasgow: Historical Association, 1970.

Durara, Prasenjit. *Rescuing History from the Nation: Questioning Narratives of Modern China*. Chicago: Univ. of Chicago Press, 1995.

Durie, Alastair J. "Tourism and Commercial Photography in Victorian Scotland: The Rise and Fall of G. W. Wilson and Co., 1853–1908." *Northern Scotland* 12 (1992): 89–104.

Edensor, Tim. "National Identity and the Politics of Memory: Remembering Bruce and Wallace in Symbolic Space." *Environment and Planning* 29 (1997): 175–94.

———. "Reading Braveheart: Representing and Contesting Scottish Identity." *Scottish Affairs* 21 (1997): 135–58.

Fallon, Brian. *An Age of Innocence: Irish Culture, 1930–1960*. Dublin: Gill and MacMillan, 1998.

Fanning, Ronan. *The Irish Department of Finance, 1922–58*. Dublin: Institute of Public Administration, 1978.

Farrell, Brian. *Seán Lemass*. London: Gill and Macmillan, 1983.

Farry, Michael. *The Aftermath of Revolution: Sligo 1921–23*. Dublin: Univ. College Dublin Press, 2000.

Fegan, Melissa. "The Traveller's Experience in Famine Ireland." *Irish Studies Review* 9, no. 3 (2001): 361–72.

Feifer, Maxine. *Going Places: The Ways of the Tourist from Imperial Rome to the Present Day*. London: Macmillan, 1985.

———. *Tourism in History: From Imperial Rome to the Present*. New York: Stein and Day, 1986.

Fishman, Joshua A. *Language and Nationalism: Two Integrative Essays*. Rowley, Mass.: Newberry House Publishers, 1973.

Fitzpatrick, David. *The Two Irelands: 1912–1939*. Oxford: Opus, 1998.

Forshee, Jill, Christina Fink, and Sandra Cate, eds. *Converging Interests: Traders, Travelers, and Tourists in Southeast Asia*. Berkeley: Univ. of California Press, 1999.

Foster, Roy. *Modern Ireland: 1600–1972*. London: Penguin, 1988.

———. *Paddy and Mr. Punch: Connections in Irish and English History*. London: Oxford Univ. Press, 1995.

———. "Remembering 1798." In *History and Memory in Modern Ireland*, ed. Ian McBride, 67–94. Cambridge: Cambridge Univ. Press, 2001.

———. *W. B. Yeats, A Life, Part II: The Arch-Poet*. Oxford: Oxford Univ. Press, 2003.

Fraser, T. G. *Ireland in Conflict: 1922–1998*. London: Routledge, 2000.

Fussell, Paul. *Abroad: British Literary Traveling between the Wars*. Oxford: Oxford Univ. Press, 1980.

Furlong, Irene. "Frederick W. Crossley: Irish Turn-of-the-Century Tourism Pioneer." *Irish History: A Research Yearbook*. No. 2, 162–76. Dublin: Four Courts Press, 2003.

Garrad, Larch S. "The Industrial Archaeology of Tourism." *Industrial Archaeology* 17, no. 1 (1982): 19–26.

Garvin, Tom. *1922: The Birth of Irish Democracy*. New York: St. Martin's Press, 1996.

Geary, Laurence M. "Parnell and the Land Question." In *Parnell: The Politics of Power*, ed. Donal McCartney, 90–101. Dublin: Wolfhound Press, 1991.

Geertz, Clifford. *The Interpretation of Cultures*. New York: Basic Books, 1973.

Gellner, Ernest. *Nations and Nationalism*. Ithaca, N.Y.: Cornell Univ. Press, 1983.

Gellner, Ernest, and Anthony D. Smith. "The Nation: Real or Imagined?: The Warwick Debates on Nationalism." *Nations and Nationalism* 2, no. 3 (1996): 357–70.

Gibbons, Luke. *Transformations in Irish Culture*. Cork: Cork Univ. Press, 1996.

Gillis, John R., ed. *Commemorations: The Politics of National Identity*. Princeton, N.J.: Princeton Univ. Press, 1994.

Gillmor, Desmond, ed., *The Irish Countryside: Landscape, Wildlife, History, People*. Dublin: Wolfhound Press, 1989.

———. "Republic of Ireland: An Expanding Tourism Sector." In *Tourism and Economic Development: European Experiences*, ed. G. Shaw and A. M. Williams, 221–41. Chichester, N.Y.: John Wiley and Sons, 1998.

———. *A Systematic Geography of Ireland*. Dublin: Gill and Macmillan, 1971.

Gold, John R., and Margaret M. Gold. *Imagining Scotland: Tradition, Representation and Promotion of Scottish Tourism since 1750*. Hampshire: Scholar Press, 1995.

Graham, Brian. "Historical Conservation and Revisionist Nationalism in Ireland." In *Building a New Heritage: Tourism, Culture and Identity in the New Europe*, ed. G. J. Ashworth and P. J. Larkham, 135–58. London: Routledge, 1994.

———, ed. *In Search of Ireland: A Cultural Geography*. London: Routledge, 1997.

Gray, Tony. *The Lost Years: The Emergency in Ireland, 1939–45.* London: Little, Brown and Company, 1997.

Gruffudd, Pyrs. "Back to the Land: Historiography, Rurality and the Nation in Interwar Wales." *Transactions of the Institute for Geography* 19 (1994): 61–77.

———. "Remaking Wales: Nation-Building and the Geographical Imagination, 1925–50." *Political Geography* 14, no. 3 (1995): 219–39.

Hall, C. M., and S. J. Page. *The Geography of Tourism and Recreation.* London: Routledge, 2000.

Hechter, Michael. *Internal Colonialism: The Celtic Fringe in British National Development, 1536–1966.* Berkeley: Univ. of California Press, 1975.

Heneghan, Philip. *Resource Allocation in Tourism Marketing.* London: Tourism International Press, 1976.

Hennessey, Thomas. *Dividing Ireland: World War I and Partition.* London: Routledge, 1998.

———. *A History of Northern Ireland.* New York: St. Martin's Press, 1997.

Hepburn, A. C. *The Conflict of Nationality in Modern Ireland.* New York: St. Martin's Press, 1980.

Herbert, David T., ed. *Heritage, Tourism and Society.* London: Mansell Publishing, 1995.

Hewison, Robert. *The Heritage Industry: Britain in a Climate of Decline.* London: Methuen London, 1987.

Hindesight. Dublin: Irish Museum of Modern Art, 1993.

Hindley, Reg. *The Death of the Irish Language.* London: Routledge, 1990.

Hopkinson, Michael. *Green Against Green: The Irish Civil War.* Dublin: Gill and Macmillan, 1988.

Horgan, Donal. *The Victorian Visitor in Ireland: Irish Tourism 1840–1910.* Cork: Imagimedia, 2002.

Horgan, John. *Irish Media: A Critical History since 1922.* London: Routledge, 2001.

———. *Seán Lemass: The Enigmatic Patriot.* Dublin: Gill and Macmillan, 1997.

Howe, Stephen. *Ireland and Empire.* Oxford: Oxford Univ. Press, 2002.

Huallachain, Colman Ó. *The Irish and Irish: A Sociolinguistic Analysis of the Relationship between a People and Their Language.* Dublin: Irish Franciscan Provincial Office, 1994.

Hunter, Michael, ed. *Preserving the Past: The Rise of Heritage in Modern Britain.* Stroud Gloucestershire: Alan Sutton Publishing, 1996.

Inglis, Tom. *Moral Monopoly: The Rise and Fall of the Catholic Church in Modern Ireland.* Cork: Cork Univ. Press, 1998.

Joyce, P. W. *A Social History of Ancient Ireland.* Vol. 2. New York: B. Blom, 1968 [1913].

Keane, John B. *The Chastitute: A Play in Two Acts.* Dublin: Mercier Press, 1981.

Kellas, James G. *The Politics of Nationalism and Ethnicity.* New York: St. Martin's Press, 1991.

Kelly, Deirdre. *Hands Off Dublin.* Dublin: O'Brien Press, 1976.

Kelly, Freida. *A History of Kilmainham Gaol: The Dismal House of Little Ease.* Cork: Dublin Mercier, 1988.

Kennedy, Michael. *Division and Consensus: The Politics of Cross-Border Relations in Ireland, 1925–1969.* Dublin: Institute of Public Administration, 2000.

Kirby, Alex. "F&M: The Rural Nemesis." *BBC News World Edition,* <http://news.bbc.co.uk/2/hi/in_depth/world/2001/review_of_2001/1697976.stm,> accessed 27 July 2007.

Kneafsey, Moya. "Rural Tourism and Identity: Stories of Change and Resistance from the West of Ireland and Brittany." In *New Directions in Celtic Studies,* ed. Philip Payton and Amy Hale, 167–96. Exeter: Univ. of Exeter Press, 2000.

———. "Tourism and Place Identity: A Case-Study in Rural Ireland." *Irish Geography* 31, no. 2 (1998): 111–23.

Kockel, Ullrich, ed. *Culture, Tourism, and Development: The Case of Ireland.* Liverpool: Liverpool Univ. Press, 1994.

Kofos, Evangelos. "National Heritage and National Identity in Nineteenth- and Twentieth-Century Macedonia." *European History Quarterly* 19, no. 2 (1989): 229–68.

Korte, Barbara, Hartmut Berghoff, Ralf Schneider, and Christopher Harvie, eds. *The Making of Modern Tourism: The Cultural History of the British Experience, 1600–2000.* London: Palgrave, 2002.

Koshar, Rudy. *German Travel Cultures.* Oxford: Berg, 2000.

———. *Germany's Transient Pasts: Preservation and National Memory in the Twentieth Century.* Chapel Hill: Univ. of North Carolina Press, 1998.

———. "'What Ought to Be Seen': Tourists' Guidebooks and National Identities in Modern Germany and Europe." *Journal of Contemporary History* 33, no. 3 (1998): 323–40.

Krapauskas, Virgil. *Nationalism and Historiography: The Case of Nineteenth Century Lithuanian Historicism.* New York: Columbia Univ. Press, 2000.

Krippendorf, Jost. *The Holiday Makers: Understanding the Impact of Leisure and Travel.* Oxford: Butterworth-Heinemann, 1987.

Krotz, Larry. *Tourists: How Our Fastest Growing Industry Is Changing the World.* Boston: Faber and Faber, 1996.

Kugelmass, Jack. "Bloody Memories: Encountering the Past in Contemporary Poland." *Cultural Anthropology* 10, no. 3 (1995): 279–301.

———. "The Rites of the Tribe: American Jewish Tourism in Poland." In *Museums and Communities,* ed. Ivan Karp, Christine Mullen Kreamer, and Steven D. Lavine, 382–427. Washington: Smithsonian Institution Press, 1992.

Kugelmass, Jack, and Annamaria Orla-Bukowska. "'If You Build It They Will Come': Recreating an Historic Jewish District in Post-Communist Kraków." *City and Society,* 1998, 315–53.

Kymlicka, Will. *Politics in the Vernacular: Nationalism, Multiculturalism, and Citizenship.* Oxford: Oxford Univ. Press, 2001.

Laitin, David. *Language Repertoires and State Construction in Africa.* Cambridge: Cambridge Univ. Press, 1992.

Lee, J. J. *Ireland 1912–1985, Politics and Society.* Cambridge: Cambridge Univ. Press, 1989.

Leed, Eric J. *The Mind of the Traveler.* New York: Basic Books, 1992.

Lloyd, David. *Ireland after History.* Cork: Cork Univ. Press, 1999.

Löfgren, Orvar. *On Holiday: A History of Vacationing.* Berkeley: Univ. of California Press, 1999.

Logan, Patrick. *Fair Day: The Story of Irish Fairs and Markets.* Belfast: Appletree Press, 1986.

Looney, Robert. "Economic Costs to the United States Stemming from the 9/11 Attacks." *Strategic Insights* 1, no. 6 (Aug. 2002), <http://www.ccc.nps.navy.mil/si/aug02/homeland.asp,> accessed 30 July 2007.

Loughlin, James. *The Ulster Question since 1945.* New York: St. Martin's Press, 1998.

Lowenthal, David. *The Past Is a Foreign Country.* Cambridge: Cambridge Univ. Press, 1985.

Lyons, F. S. L. *Parnell.* Dundalk, Ireland: Dundalgan Press, 1963.

MacAlister, R. A. S. *Ancient Ireland: A Study in the Lessons of Archaeology and History.* London: Methuen and Co., 1935.

MacCannell, Dean. *Empty Meeting Grounds: The Tourist Papers.* London: Routledge, 1992.

———. *The Tourist: A New Theory of the Leisure Class.* Berkeley: Univ. of California Press, 1999.

MacDonogh, Steve. *The Dingle Peninsula*. Dingle, Ireland: Brandon, 2000.
Malcolmson, Robert W. *Popular Recreations in English Society, 1700–1850*. Cambridge: Cambridge Univ. Press, 1973.
Massey, Doreen B. *Space, Place, and Gender*. Minneapolis: Univ. of Minnesota Press, 1994.
Matless, David. *Landscape and Englishness*. London: Reaktion, 1998.
Mazanec, Josef A., ed. *International City Tourism: Analysis and Strategy*. London: Pinter, 1997.
Mazon, Patricia, "Germania Triumphant: The Niederwald National Monument and the Liberal Moment in Imperial Germany." *German History* 18, no. 2 (2000): 162–92.
McCartney, Clem, and Lucy Bryson. *Clashing Symbols: A Report on the Use of Flags, Anthems and Other National Symbols in Northern Ireland*. Belfast: Institute for Irish Studies for the Community Relations Council, 1994.
McCrone, David, Angela Morris, and Richard Kiely. *Scotland—The Brand: The Making of Scottish Heritage*. Edinburgh: Edinburgh Univ. Press, 1995.
McDonald, Frank. *The Destruction of Dublin*. Dublin: Gill and Macmillan, 1985.
McIntosh, Gillian. *The Force of Culture: Unionist Identities in Twentieth-Century Ireland*. Cork: Cork Univ. Press, 1999.
McManus, Ruth. "Dublin's Changing Tourism Geography." *Irish Geography* 34, no. 2 (2001): 103–23.
———. "Heritage Tourism in Ireland—An Unholy Alliance?" *Irish Geography* 30, no. 2 (1997): 90–98.
McVeagh, John. *Irish Travel: A Bibliography*. Dublin: Wolfhound Press, 1996.
Melaugh, Martin. "The Sunningdale Agreement: Chronology of Events." *CAIN Web Service* (2002), <http://cain.ulst.ac.uk/events/sunningdale/chron.htm,> accessed 19 Mar. 2003.
Metcalf, Thomas R. *Ideologies of the Raj*. Cambridge: Cambridge Univ. Press, 1995.
Moranda, Scott. "Maps, Markers, and Bodies: Hikers Constructing the Nation in German Forests." *The Nationalism Project* (2001), <http://nationalismproject.org/articles.html,> accessed 7 Aug. 2003.
Mosse, George L. *Nationalism and Sexuality: Middle-Class Morality and Sexual Norms in Modern Europe*. Madison: Univ. of Wisconsin Press, 1985.
———. *The Nationalization of the Masses: Political Symbolism and Mass Movements in Germany from the Napoleonic Wars through the Third Reich*. Ithaca, N.Y.: Cornell Univ. Press, 1991.

National and Regional Tourism Planning: Methodologies and Case Studies. London: Routledge, 1994.

Nora, Pierre. "Between Memory and History: *Les Lieux de Mémoire.*" *Representations* 26 (1989): 7–25.

Nuryanti, Wiendu. "Heritage and Postmodern Tourism." *Annals of Tourism Research* 23, no. 2 (1996): 249–60.

O'Barr, William M., and Jean F. O'Barr, eds. *Language and Politics.* The Hague: Mouton and Co., 1976.

O'Beirne, J. W. *Romantic Story of Ireland's Greatest Park—The Phoenix.* Dublin: Bray Printing Co., 1934.

O'Brien, Harvey. "The Chastitute by John B. Keene." *Culture Vulture* (2002), <http://www.culturevulture.net/Theater/Chastitute.htm,> accessed 15 Apr. 2008.

———. "Culture, Commodity, and *Céad Míle Fáilte:* U.S. and Irish Tourist Films as a Vision of Ireland." *Éire-Ireland* 37, no. 1/2 (2002): 58–73.

O'Connor, Barbara, and Michael Cronin, eds. *Tourism in Ireland: A Critical Analysis.* Cork: Cork Univ. Press, 1993.

O'Hagan, J. W., ed. *The Economy of Ireland: Policy and Performance of a Small European Country.* London: Macmillan, 1995.

O'Hagan, J. W., and M. J. Harrison. "UK and US Visitor Expenditure in Ireland." *The Economic and Social Review* 15, no. 3 (1984): 195–207.

O'Hearn, Denis. *Inside the Celtic Tiger: The Irish Economy and the Asian Model.* London: Pluto Press, 1998.

O'Neill, Padraig. *Geographical Aspects of Tourism in the Republic of Ireland.* Galway: Social Sciences Research Center, Univ. College, Galway, 1979.

"Origin of the UK Foot and Mouth Disease Epidemic in 2001." Department for Environment, Food and Rural Affairs (United Kingdom), <http://www.defra.gov.uk/footandmouth/pdf/fmdorigins1.pdf,> accessed 27 July 2007.

Ousby, Ian. *The Englishman's England: Taste, Travel and the Rise of Tourism.* Cambridge: Cambridge Univ. Press, 1990.

Owen, Charles. *Britons Abroad: A Report on the Package Tour.* London: Routledge and Kegan Paul, 1968.

Paasi, Anssi. *Territories, Boundaries, and Consciousness: The Changing Geographies of the Finnish-Russian Border.* Chichester, UK: John Wiley and Sons, 1996.

Palmer, Catherine A. "Tourism and Colonialism: The Experience of the Bahamas." *Annals of Tourism Research* 21, no. 4 (1994): 792–811.

Patterson, Henry. *The Politics of Illusion: Republicanism and Socialism in Modern Ireland.* London: Hutchinson Radius, 1989.

Peillon, Michel. "Tourism—The Quest for Otherness." *Crane Bag* 8, no. 2 (1984): 165–68.

Pettitt, Lance. *Screening Ireland: Film and Television Representation.* Manchester: Manchester Univ. Press, 2000.

Pollard, John. "Patterns in Irish Tourism." In *Ireland: A Contemporary Geographical Perspective,* ed. A. J. Parker and R. W. G. Carter, 301–30. London: Routledge, 1989.

Prager, Jeffrey. *Building Democracy in Ireland: Political Order and Cultural Integration in a Newly Independent Nation.* Cambridge: Cambridge Univ. Press, 1986.

Ranger, Terence, and Eric Hobsbawm. *The Invention of Tradition.* Cambridge: Cambridge Univ. Press, 1986.

Riain, Mícheál Ó. *Aer Lingus: 1936–1986: A Business Monograph.* Dublin: Magill Print/Aer Lingus, 1986.

Roberts, Geoffrey, and Brian Garvin, eds. *Ireland and the Second World War: Politics, Society and Remembrance.* Dublin: Four Courts Press, 2000.

Rojek, Chris, and John Urry, eds. *Touring Cultures: Transformations of Travel and Theory.* London: Routledge, 1997.

Ross, Martin, and E. Æ Somerville. *The Irish R.M.* London: Abacus, 1928, 2000.

Rothery, Sean. *Everyday Buildings of Ireland.* Dublin: Department of Architecture, College of Technology, 1975.

Schwartz, Stuart B. Introduction to *Implicit Understandings: Observing, Reporting, and Reflecting on the Encounters between Europeans and Other Peoples in the Early Modern Era,* ed. Stuart B. Schwartz, 1–22. Cambridge: Cambridge Univ. Press, 1994.

Selwyn, Tom. Introduction to *The Tourist Image: Myths and Myth Making in Tourism,* ed. Tom Selwyn, 1–32. Chichester, UK: John Wiley and Sons, 1996.

"Seven Ages: Story of the Irish State" (Program 1). *RTÉ Online* (2000), <http://www.rte.ie/tv/sevenages/prog1.html,> accessed 13 Aug. 2003.

Shaffer, Margaret S. *See America First: Tourism and National Identity, 1880–1940.* Washington: Smithsonian Institution Press, 2001.

Share, Bernard. *Bunratty: Rebirth of a Castle.* Dingle, Ireland: Brandon, 1995.

———. *The Flight of the Iolar: The Aer Lingus Experience, 1936–1986.* Dublin: Gill and Macmillan, 1986.

Shaw, Gareth, and Allan M. Williams, eds. *The Rise and Fall of British Coastal Resorts: Cultural and Economic Perspectives.* London: Mansell, 1997.

———. "Tourism and Tourist Cultures in Europe." *American Behavioral Scientist* 36, no. 2 (1992): 155–71.

Shields, Rob. *Places on the Margin: Alternative Geographies of Modernity.* London: Routledge, 1991.

Simmons, Jack. "Railways, Hotels, and Tourism in Great Britain 1839–1914." *Journal of Contemporary History* 19, no. 2 (1984): 201–22.

———. *The Victorian Railway.* London: Thames and Hudson, 1991.

Simpson, Grant G. "The Declaration of Arbroath Revitalized." *Scottish Historical Review* 1, no. 4 (1977): 11–33.

Skelly, Joseph Morrison, and Michael Kennedy, eds. *Irish Foreign Policy, 1919–66: From Independence to Internationalism.* Dublin: Four Courts Press, 2000.

Skelly, Joseph Morrison. *Irish Diplomacy at the United Nations, 1945–1965.* Dublin: Irish Academic Press, 1997.

Smith, Anthony D. *The Ethnic Origins of Nations.* Oxford: Blackwell Publishers, 1998.

———. "Gastronomy or Geology? The Role of Nationalism in the Reconstruction of Nations." *Nations and Nationalism* 1, no. 1 (1994): 3–23.

Smith, Valene L., ed. *Hosts and Guests: The Anthropology of Tourism.* Philadelphia: Univ. of Pennsylvania Press, 1989.

Smout, Christopher. "Tours in the Scottish Highlands from the Eighteenth to the Twentieth Centuries." *Northern Scotland* 5, no. 2 (1983): 99–121.

Smyth, Gerry. *Space and the Irish Cultural Imagination.* New York: Palgrave, 2001.

Stabler, Mike, and M. Thea Sinclair. *The Economics of Tourism.* London: Routledge, 1997.

Stivers, Richard. *Hair of the Dog: Irish Drinking and Its American Stereotype.* New York: Continuum, 2000.

Sweeney, Paul. *The Celtic Tiger: Ireland's Economic Miracle.* Dublin: Oak Tree Press, 1998.

Tannam, Etain. *Cross-Border Cooperation in the Republic of Ireland and Northern Ireland.* New York: St. Martin's Press, 1999.

Taras, Milton. "Nations and Language-Building: Old Theories, Contemporary Cases." *Nationalism and Ethnic Politics* 4, no. 3 (1998): 79–101.

Thaler, Peter. "National History—National Imagery: The Role of History in Postwar Austrian Nation-Building." *Central European History* 32, no. 3 (1999): 277–310.

Thomas, Alys. "Language Policy and Nationalism in Wales: A Comparative Analysis." *Nations and Nationalism* 3, no. 3 (1997): 323–44.

Tourism and Travel in Ireland. Dublin: Gill and Macmillan, 1993.

Townshend, Charles. *Ireland: The Twentieth Century.* London: Arnold, 1999.
Tuan, Yi Fu. *Space and Place: The Perspective of Experience.* London: Edward Arnold, 1979.
Turner, Louis, and John Ash. *The Golden Hordes: International Tourism and the Pleasure Periphery.* London: Constable and Company, 1975.
Urry, John. "Holiday Making in Britain since 1945." *Contemporary Record* 5, no. 1 (1991): 32–44.
———. *The Tourist Gaze: Leisure and Travel in Contemporary Societies.* London: Sage Publications, 1990.
———. "*The Tourist Gaze* 'Revisited.'" *American Behavioral Scientist* 36, no. 2 (1992): 172–86.
———. "The Tourist Gaze and the 'Environment.'" *Theory, Culture and Society* 9 (1992): 1–26.
van der Borg, Jan, Paolo Costa, and Giuseppe Gotti. "Tourism in European Heritage Cities." *Annals of Tourism Research* 23, no. 2 (1996): 306–21.
Varley, Tony, Thomas A. Boylan, and Michael P. Cuddy, eds. *Rural Crisis: Perspectives on Irish Rural Development.* Galway: Center for Development Studies, Univ. College Galway, 1991.
Vellas, François, and Lionel Bécherel. *International Tourism: An Economic Perspective.* New York: St. Martin's Press, 1995.
Vigarello, Georges. "The Tour de France." In *Realms of Memory: Rethinking the French Past,* ed. Pierre Nora, 469–500. New York: Columbia Univ. Press, 1997.
Vogel, Harold L. *Travel Industry Economics: A Guide for Financial Analysis.* Cambridge: Cambridge Univ. Press, 2001.
Wall, Geoffrey, and Timothy J. Dallen. *Tourism and Political Boundaries.* New York: Routledge, 2001.
Walton, John K. *The English Seaside Resort: A Social History, 1750–1914.* New York: St. Martin's Press, 1983.
Waters, Maureen. *The Comic Irishman.* Albany: State Univ. of New York Press, 1984.
Weber, Eugen. *Peasants into Frenchmen: The Modernization of Rural France, 1870–1914.* Palo Alto, Calif.: Stanford Univ. Press, 1976.
Weinstein, Brian. *The Civic Tongue.* New York: Longman, 1983.
Whelan, Bernadette. *Ireland and the Marshall Plan, 1947–57.* Dublin: Four Courts Press, 2000.
White, Padraic A., and Ray Mac Sharry. *The Making of the Celtic Tiger: The Inside Story of Ireland's Economic Boom.* Cork: Mercier Press, 2000.

Wilford, Rick, ed. *Aspects of the Belfast Agreement.* Oxford: Oxford Univ. Press, 2001.

Williams, Alan, ed. *Film and Nationalism.* Piscataway, N.J.: Rutgers Univ. Press, 2002.

Withers, Charles. "The Historical Creation of the Scottish Highlands." In *The Manufacture of Scottish History,* ed. Christopher Whatley and Ian Donnachie, 143–56. Edinburgh: Polygon, 1992.

Womack, Peter. *Improvement and Romance: Constructing the Myth of the Highlands.* London: Macmillan Press, 1989.

Wood, Robert E. "Tourist Ethnicity: A Brief Itinerary." *Ethnic and Racial Studies* 21, no. 2 (1998): 218–41.

Wood, Robert E., and Michael Picard, eds. *Tourism, Ethnicity, and the State in Asian and Pacific Societies.* Honolulu: Univ. of Hawai'i Press, 1997.

Wood, Roy C., and Erwin Losekoot. "Prospects for Tourism Employment in Scotland." *Scottish Affairs* 34 (2001): 91–106.

Yaeger, Patricia, ed. *The Geography of Identity.* Ann Arbor: Univ. of Michigan Press, 1996.

Zuelow, Eric G. E. "Enshrining Ireland's Nationalist History Inside Prison Walls: The Restoration of Kilmainham Jail." *Éire-Ireland* 39 (Fall/Winter 2004): 180–201.

———. "'Ingredients for Cooperation': The Role of Irish Tourism in North-South Relations, 1924–1998." *New Hibernia Review* 10, no. 1 (2006): 17–39.

———. "National Identity and Tourism in 20th Century Ireland: The Role of Collective Re-Imagining." In *Nationalism in a Global Era: The Persistence of Nations,* ed. Mitchell Young, Eric G. E. Zuelow, and Andreas Sturm, 156–75. London: Routledge, 2007.

———. "The Tourism Nexus: The Meanings of Tourism and Identity since the Irish Civil War." In *Ireland's Heritages: Critical Perspectives on Memory and Identity,* ed. Mark McCarthy, 189–213. Hampshire: Ashgate, 2005.

Index

Abram, Simon, xxiv
Aer Lingus, 28–29, 44, 53–54
Aer Rianta, 44, 53–54
Agricultural Advisory Service, 119
agritourism, 118–19
Ahearn, Bertie, 236–37
airline routes, 53–54
Almond, C. S., 108
Ancient Monuments Protection Act (1882), 140
Anderson, Benedict, xxx
Andrews, C. S. "Todd," 15–17, 45, 250n. 55
angling tourism, 201–4
Anglo-Irish Treaty (1921), xxii, 28
Arklow, County Wicklow, 195–96
Arklow Tourist Association, 195
Arts Council of Ireland, 225
Arts, Sports, and Tourism, Department of, 92, 229
Attitudes of American and English Tourists Towards Shopping in Ireland and Irish Merchandise (survey), 98
Auld Lammas Fair, 120
Austria, 2
Automobile Association, 193

Barry, David, 5, 16, 22
Barry, Naoise, 225

Bell, Archie, 104–5, 114, 138, 179
Benjamin, Walter, xxiii
Benson, S. H., 168
Bianconi, Charles, xix
Bismarck, Otto von, 139
Blair, Tony, 222–23
Blarney Castle, 186
boatmen. *See* Killarney boatmen
boglands, 213–15, 293n. 173
Boland, H. P., 24
Boland, Michael R., 79–80
Böll, Heinrich, 179
Bono (Paul Hewson), 226
Boorman, John, 225
Booth, J., 24
Bord Fáilte, An: authority for compulsory land acquisition, 188, 192; develops national tourism education program with Fógra Fáilte, 67–69; and English printers' controversy, 94; founding of, 67; and historic sites development, 143–45; merges with Fógra Fáilte, 69–70; signposting and, 193, 194–95; undertakes campaign to improve angling facilities, 202
Bord Fáilte Éireann (BFÉ): addresses perceived drop in Irish reputation for friendliness, 228; advocates government purchasing of Kenmare estate, 187; aids festivals, 133, 134;

333

Bord Fáilte Éireann (BFÉ) (*cont.*)
assesses tourism impact of September 11 attacks, 228; encourages tree planting, 196; and environmental conservation, 204, 205–6, 208–10; funds Temple Bar project, 91; and historic sites, 146, 147, 148; and Kilmainham Jail, 165; and landscape design, 207; and local interests, 79, 80; loses marketing responsibilities to Tourism Ireland Ltd., 228–29; and McDaid's calls to disband or merge with CERT, 229–30; as merger of An Bord Fáilte and Fógra Fáilte, 70; merges with Northern Irish Tourist Board to form Tourism Ireland Ltd., 223–24; and new heritage marketing, 166–67; replacement by Fáilte Ireland, 231; and RTOs, 84; and souvenirs, 116; supports agritourism, 119; and Tidy Towns and Villages Competition, 197–98, 199, 200, 201; and An Tóstal, 126–28, 132, 196; Tourism Brand Ireland and, xvi, 220–21; tourism education and, 69; tourism marketing efforts of, 96–98; and Tuosist, 75, 77, 78
Bord na Móna (Turf Development Board), 213–15
Bourne Vincent Memorial Park, 152
Braveheart (film), 225
Breen, P. J., 88
Browne, Kate, 105
Bruce, Jim, 163
Bruton, John, 222
Bunbeg, County Donegal, 109–10
Bunratty Castle, 146
Burke, Edmund, xviii
Burns, John Horne, xxviii–xxix
Byrnes, Thomas, 189–91

Cassidey, Damien, 163
Cassidey, David, 163
Céide Fields, 166
Celtic Tiger, 218–19
Childers, Erskine: cooperating with Brian Faulkner on cross-boarder tourism, 220; proposes developments at Muckross House and Glendalough, 148–49; refutes allegations about property values, 208; and folk museum at Muckross estate, 151–52; supports plan for RTOs, 83; urges Lemass and ITB to develop angling tourism, 202; works to abolish ITA, 80–82
Christenberry, Robert K., 60–62
Christenberry committee, 96
Christenberry report, 60–63, 143, 258n. 111
Clare Archaeological and Historical Society, 189
Clinton, Bill, 175
Clonakilty, County Cork, 198
coarse-fishing, 203
Cobh (heritage project), 91
Collins, Michael, xxii
Congress of Irish Trade Unions, 160
Conlon, Michael, 80
Connerton, Paul, 164
Connolly, James, 156, 161–62
conservation, 204
Construction Corps, 44
Cook, John Mason, xx
Cook, Thomas, xix, xx
Córas Iompair Éireann (Irish rail), 90, 147
Córas Trachtala (Irish Export Board), 206
Cork Chamber of Commerce, 131
Cork Choral Festival, 133
Cork County Council, 11, 13, 80
Cork Film Festival, 124, 132, 133
"Cork Makes It" (exhibition), 131

Cork Regional Group of the Federation of
    Irish Manufacturers, 131
Cork Tóstal Council, 131
Corlea Trackway, 166
Corr, J. A., 88
Cosgrave, Liam, 260n. 133
Costello, John A., 68
Council for Education, Recruitment and
    Training (CERT), 230–32
Cox, Arthur, 47
cross-border cooperation, 219–24
Crossley, Frederick W., xx–xxii, 22
Crowley, Fred, 107–8
Cultural Relations Committee, 58,
    153–54
Cumann na nGaedheal, 25–27
Cu Uladh, 108

Daiken, Leslie, 122, 123–24, 184–85,
    286n. 30
Davies, John, 172
de Bougrenet, Jacques Louis, xviii
de Fouw, Jan, 94, 117, 212, 259n. 114
Dempsey, J. F., 70
de Valera, Éamon, 109, 118, 128, 132,
    158, 160
Devlin, Liam, 84
Dillion, Owen, 97
Dingle, County Kerry: debate over name
    change of, 233–37; post–civil war
    tourism development of, 10–12, 232;
    tourism growth in, 232–33
Dingle Name Campaign, 234, 236
Dingle Peninsula, 103
Dingle Tourist Association, 11–12, 103–4
Dowling, Sean, 159, 162
Doyle, Peadar S., 147
Dublin, 91
Dublin Brigade of the Old IRA, 149, 155

Dublin Corporation, 160, 281n. 97
Dublin Evening Mail (newspaper), 163
Dublin Theatre Festival, 132, 133
Dublin Tourism (tour service), 226
Dublin Tourism RTO, 134
Dúchas, 166, 191

Easter Rising commemoration, 149
Eastern Regional Tourism Organisation, 88
Economic Cooperation Administration
    (ECA), 55–56, 58, 59, 61, 62, 64–65
Economic Regional Development Funds, 90
ecosystems, 201
Edge, The (Dave Evans), 226
Education, Department of, 157
Edward J. Burrow and Company, 94
Edwards, Hilton, 129, 274n. 121
Electricity Supply Board (ESB), 77
English Georgian Society, 141
English-Irish relations, 92–95
Ennis, County Clare, 198
Enniskillen airfield, 79, 220
European Recovery Program. *See* Marshall
    Plan
European Travel Commission, 59
European Union, 73, 89–91
External Affairs, Department of: and
    Cultural Relations Committee, 153;
    distributes promotional materials to
    consulates, 153–54; frustrations of
    with ITB, 64–65; and *Holiday* maga-
    zine controversy, xxvii–xxviii; interest
    in tourist publications' contents,
    154–55; response to Lemass's proposal
    for the ITB, 31; and tourism as foreign
    policy, 56–58
Fáilte hotel, 48–51
Fáilte Ireland (National Tourism Develop-
    ment Authority), 225, 230–32

Fáilte Téoranta, 48, 54
fairs, 119–20, 131–34. *See also* Puck Fair; An Tóstal
Fanning, Ronan, 39
Faulkner, Brian, 220
Fear Mór, An, 109
Fegan, Melissa, xix
Festival of Britain, 124–25, 126–28, 195, 273n. 101
Festival of Grand Opera (Dublin), 132
festivals. *See* fairs
Fianna Fáil, 6, 27–28, 54, 65
film, 224–25
Finance, Department of: on Gaeltacht tourism, 109, 112; historic sites and, 146; and Kilmainham Jail's restoration, 161; opposes tourism during World War II, 38–40; opposes folk museum at Muckross estate, 152; opposes Lemass's proposal for ITB, 31; opposes ITB's plans for the future, 58–59; resists ITA's request for postal advertising, 24; and tourism spending, 88
Fisheries, Department of, 201
fishing. *See* angling tourism; coarse-fishing
Fitzpatrick, J., 81
Fitzpatrick, Sean, 160
Flood tribunal, 208
Flood Report, 292–93n. 154
Fógra Fáilte (publicity board): develops national tourism education program with An Bord Fáilte, 67–69; and English printers' controversy, 94; founding of, 65–67, 260n. 133, 261n. 142; highlights musical aspects of An Tóstal, 132; merges with An Bord Fáilte, 69–70; promotes myriad sports, 130; and Puck Fair, 122–23; An Tóstal campaigns of, 127–28
Foley, J. C., 4–5, 7

Foley, Jennifer, 190–91
foot-and-mouth disease, 227
Foras Forbarthe, An (The National Planning Board), 208
Ford, John, 224–25
Foster, Roy, 113
France, 2
Freeman, Arthur C., 5
Fungie (dolphin), 233
Furlong, Irene, xxi, 246n. 22

Gaelic Athletic Association (GAA), 101, 128, 130
Gaelic-language enthusiasts, 17, 105–7, 112
Gaelic League, xxi, 101, 128
Gaelic (Irish) speakers, 101–2, 104–5
Gaelic sport, 130
Gaeltachts: efforts to improve tourist accommodations in, 110–11; and government emphasis on rural development rather than language preservation in, 111–12; and ITA promotion of tourism in, 107–8; and ITB efforts to promote tourism in, 109–10; and 1939 Tourist Traffic Act, 106–7; promoted by ITA and locals as place of Irish "purity," 103–4; as rooted in the Middle Ages, 104–5; tourism in opposed by Gaelic-language enthusiasts, 105–7
Galway Oyster Festival, 124
Garden of Remembrance, 149, 155, 162, 279n. 60
Gibson, Mel, 225
Glendalough, 147–48
Gonne, Maud, 118
Good Friday Agreement, 222
Gorman, Michael, 95, 97, 124, 153

Gort, Lord, 146
Grafton Street (Dublin), 91
Grand Tour, xvii–xviii
Gravity Bar, 174
Great Southern and Western Railway, 10, 18
Great Western Railway, 19
Greene, Roger, 64
guidebooks, 95
Guinness (Guinness Brewing Company): advertising campaigns of, 168; backs sporting events and festivals as form of marketing, 169–70; brewery museum of, 170–71; brewery tours offered by, 168–70; publishes French- and English-language guidebooks, 95; sponsors festivals, 133–34; supports ITA, 22–23; uses tourism as advertising, 167–68
Guinness, Arthur, 174, 175
Guinness Hopstore, 168, 172–73
Guinness Storehouse, 167, 173–76
Guinness stout, 224

Harbison, Peter, 189
Harrington, Howard S., 5, 7, 9, 20, 96
Harris, George, 96
Hartnett, Patrick, 144
Hawks, Tony, 114–15
Health Resorts and Watering-Places (Ireland) Act (1909), xxi, 3
Healy, Rae-Jackie, 236–37
Heaney, Seamus, 214
heritage, 167, 176
heritage centers, 166, 171–72
heritage marketing, 167
Hignett, A. H., 173
Historic Monuments Act (France), 139
historic sites: avoidance of modern history at, 150; An Bord Fáilte and, 144–45; Bord Fáilte Éireann and, 146, 148; Christenberry and Irish Home Commission reports on, 143; commemorations of modern history and, 155; development of, 148–50; Department of Finance and, 146; and Irish tourism, 137; ITA and, 142–43; ITB and, 143–44, 145–46; Office of Public Works and, 144–46; preservation of, 138–41; preservation legislation and, 141–42; private landownership and, 188, 192; property rights and, 140; trends in selection of, 146–48
Hogan, Patrick, 27, 57
Holiday (magazine), xxvi–xxix
holiday homes, 184
holiday savings-club programs, 42–43, 255n. 35
horse-drawn caravan (jaunting cars), 184
hotels, 59–60
Hugo, Victor, 139
Humphreys, Joe, 175, 176
Hunt, John, 146

Imagination Group USA, 173
Industry and Commerce, Department of, 36, 38, 40–41, 91, 94
Inland Fisheries Trust, 202, 291n. 122
International Council of Societies of Industrial Design, 206; report of, 206–7
International Festival of Music and the Arts (Dublin), 132
interparty government (first), 54–55, 64–65
Invincibles (Irish National Invincibles), 155, 158, 160, 281n. 90
IRA (Irish Republican Army), 93, 220
Ireland for Everyman (guidebook), 154

Ireland Guide, 123
Ireland: 1980 (guidebook), 123
Ireland: Official Publication (guidebook), 138
Ireland of the Welcomes (magazine), 94, 117, 132, 212, 213, 214
Irish Church Act (1869), 140
Irish Civil War, xxii–xxiii, 150
Irish Examiner (newspaper), 234
Irish Express (travel agency), 64, 65
Irish Film Board, 225
Irish Hotels Commission report, 59–60, 143
Irish Hotels Federation, 43
Irish Independent (newspaper), 20, 49
Irish Journey (Sean O'Faolain), 122
Irish Press (newspaper), 50, 64, 82, 264n. 35
Irish Republican Army. *See* IRA
Irish speakers. *See* Gealic (Irish) speakers
Irish Times, 48, 50, 182, 235
Irish Tourist (magazine), xx
Irish Tourist Association (1895), xx–xxii, 22
Irish Tourist Association (ITA): angling tourism and, 201; business support for, 22; attacked by E. T. Keane, 47; challenged by Seán Lemass, 29–31; Christenberry report's suggestions for ITB and, 61–63, 65; clashes with government, 79–82; clashes with Killarney boatmen, 18–21; continental European inspirations for, 2; Cosgrave government and board of, 17; and creation of multiboard structure, 66; demise and replacement of, 73, 85–86; efforts to promote tourism, 21–24; and English printers' controversy, 94; foundation of, 2, 4, 7–8; frustrations with interparty government, 64; funding of, 251n. 77; Gaeltacht tourism and, 103–4, 107–9; historic sites and, 137–38, 142–43; holiday savings-clubs programs and, 42–43; and Irish Hotel Commission report, 60; ITB and, 32–33; lobbies government to extend 1939 Tourist Traffic Act, 41–42; and local cooperation, 8–15, 29; markets Ireland in the United States, 96; promotion of image of Irish friendliness, 114; Puck Fair and, 122; recognizes tourist potential of Irish landscape, 179–80; reforestation efforts of, 181; relationship with Cumann na nGaedheal, 24–26; relationship with Fine Gael, 26–28; responds to dissenting voices on tourism, 17–18; RTOs and, 85; and staff's IRA ties, 16–17; statutory bodies and, 70; and threats from local interests, 80–81; ties with Ulster Tourist Development Association, 219; signposting and, 193; urban development and, 180–81; and World War II, 35–38

Irish Tourist Board (ITB): aesthetic reform and, 195–96; angling tourism and, 202; agritourism and, 119; Bord Fáilte Éireann, and, 71; Christenberry report on ITA and, 61–63, 260n. 141; development schemes of, 43–44, 47–48; disinterest in landscape development, 192; and English printers' controversy, 94; environment and, 182; environmental conservation and, 204, 205–6; Fáilte hotels development scheme and, 48–52; festivals and, 132, 133–34; under Fine Gael leadership, 54–55, 65; founding and responsibilities of, 32–33; and frustrations with interparty government, 64; Gaeltacht tourism and, 108–11; heritage marketing and, 166–67; historic sites and, 143–144, 145–46; in Irish Hotel Commission report, 60; issues report on future plans of, 58–60; Kraft durch Freude and, 52–53, 195; local interests and, 79; Marshall Plan and, 55–56, 64–65; media animosity toward, 44–47; objections to Lemass's proposal for, 31; photography and, 210; Puck Fair and, 123; signposting and, 193–94; support of by Fianna Fáil, 28; Temple Bar and, 91; threatened during World War II, 35–39; Tidy Towns and Villages Competition and, 196, 197–98, 201; Western counties, and, 77

Irish Travel (magazine), 21
Irish Travel Trade News, 87, 152
Irish Welcome Awards, 229, 232
Italy, 2
"Ivernia" (Cork-Kerry RTO), 84

Jameson's Whiskey, 224
jaunting car. *See* horse-drawn caravan
J. M. Dent and Sons, 154–55
John Hinde Studios, 210–12
Jordan, Neil, 225

Keane, E. T., 45–47
Keane, John B., 76
Kearns, Raé, 235
Kenmare, Earl of, 21
Kenmare, Lord, 9
Kenmare estate, 186–88
Kerry County Council, 11, 14–15, 236
Kerry Development Team, 76–77
Kerry Folklife Association, 152

Kerryman (newspaper), 10–11, 20, 93
Kilkenny, County, 44, 94
Kilkenny (city), 198–99
Kilkenny County Council, 14, 199
Kilkenny Design Workshop, 206
Kilkenny People (newspaper), 45–47, 48–49, 50–51, 94
Killarney, County Kerry: and arguments for premodern landscape in, 183–85; initial tourist development in, xviii; and motor launches, 19–21; resistance to Fáilte hotels in, 51; as tourist attraction, 18–19
Killarney boatmen, 18–21
Killarney Tourist Association, 9–10, 14, 19, 107, 187
Killarney Urban District Council, xxvi, 9, 51–52
Kilmainham Jail, 149, 155–56, 164–65
Kilmainham Jail restoration: early interest in, 156–58; grassroots efforts for, 162–63; and avoidance of Irish Civil War discussion, 163, 165; James Connolly memorial controversy and, 161–62; lack of government funding for, 163; workers' voluntary efforts for, 163–64, 165
Kilmainham Jail Restoration Society, 78, 149, 158–61, 162, 163
Kinsale Development Association, 12–13
kitsch, 115
Kneafsey, Moya, xxiv–xxv
Know Your Market series (tourism marketing books), 99
Koshar, Rudy, xxiii
Kraft durch Freude (KdF), 52, 257n. 78
"Kuklos," 138

Labour Party, 162

Land Commission, 31
landownership (private), 188–89, 192. *See also* Poulnabrone dolmen
dolmen landscape: depopulation and, 185–86; design and, 206–7; foreign interests and, 186–88; ITB's disinterest in, 192; and private ownership of historic sites, 188–89; tourism and development of, 180–85; travel writers and, 179; in photographic images, 210; planning and development and, 208–10
Lands, Industry and Commerce, Department of, 59, 63
Lean, David, 225, 232
Lemass, Seán: allows ITB to support angling tourism development near northern border, 202; announces plans for ITB, 32; on plan to purchase Blarney castle, 186; challenges ITA, 29–31; and development of Aer Lingus, 28–29; embraces multiboard structure, 66–67; establishes tourism publicity board (Fógra Fáilte), 65–67; on historic sites, 143–44, 149; initially opposes tourism, 26–27; on IRA and tourism, 93; on Irish friendliness image, 114; Kilmainham Jail restoration and, 162, 163; as minister of Department of Supplies, 34; and North-South tourism cooperation, 219, 222; and J. P. O'Brien, 29, 65, 66–67, 260n. 133; on tourism in Gaeltacht areas, 108
Lenihan, Brian, 186
Leonard, Lorcan C. G., 158, 159, 160, 161
Leydon, John, 29–30, 70
Linehan, Thomas, 25
literature, Irish, 131

Local Government, Department of, 194, 197
Local Government Act (1925), 8, 10, 25, 38
Local Government (Planning and Development) Act (1963), 205, 206
Local Government and Public Health, Department of, 38–39,
Loftus, Michael, 175
Lord of the Rings (J. R. R. Tolkien), 125
Lynch, Jack, 114, 186

MacAlister, R. A. S., xxi, 139, 140, 276–77n. 18
MacCannell, Dean, xxiii
MacDonagh, Martin, 7
MacEllin, Seán E., 26
MacEntee, Seán, 34, 36, 38, 105–6
MacGillycuddy, Major Ross Kinloch, 9, 14
MacLiammóir, Micheál, 129, 273–74n. 121
Magill, Joe, 164
markets. *See* fairs
Marshall Plan (European Recovery Program), 55–56, 96
McCarthy, Pete, 179, 183, 188, 207–8
McCreevy, Charlie, 220
McDaid, James, 228, 229–30
McDonnell, Canon John, 11
McElligott, J. J., 40, 66
McGilligan, Patrick, 7, 27
McGrath, Finian, 235
McMaster, Anew, 129, 273–74n. 121
McQuaid, Archbishop John Charles, 128
McShain, John, 187–88
Melai, Guus, 94, 126
Mellows, Liam, xxii
Metcalfe, Percy, 118
modernization, 18

Moore, Seamus, 16
Moran, Senator James, 3, 7, 22
Morrissey, Daniel, 6, 58
motor touring, 193
Muckross estate, 286n. 37
Muckross House, 150–51
Murphy, Con, 184
Murray, Father Laurence, 106
music, Irish, 131–32

National Gardens Competition, 199
National Graves Association, 156–57, 158, 160, 161, 162
national identity, xxvi, 101, 237–42
nationalism, xxix–xxx, 101, 268n. 5
National Monuments Act (1930), 145, 188, 192, 287n. 48
National Monuments Division of the Office of Public Works, 146
National Planning Conference, 204
National Tourism Council, 91–92
Newby, Eric, 179
Newgrange, 166
New Ross IRA Memorial Association, xxvi
New York Times, 234
Noble, David, 212
Northern Ireland, 219–24
Northern Irish Tourism Board (NITB), 220, 223–24
Norton, William, 69–70
Nugent, J. A., 69, 70

Observer (newspaper), 220
O'Brian, Conor Cruise, 154–55
O'Brien, Jim, 196
O'Brien, J. P. "Jack": attacks on, 53; becomes ITB chairman, 33; promotes tourism as national interest, 5, 38; and collapse of two-board structure, 69; death of, 261n. 151; defends ITA and ITB during World War II, 35–38; as director of Aer Rianta, 53; dismissal from ITB, 54; and founding of ITA, 5, 7; frustrations with interparty government, 64; Seán Lemass and, 29, 36, 65, 66–67, 260n. 133; local ITA branches and, 9–10; media animosity toward, 44–48; IRA connections of, 16; ITB development schemes and, 43–44; personal background of, 5; politics surrounding appointment of, 70; represents ITB at 1942 National Planning Conference, 205; staff's resistance to tourism, 15; supports summer Irish-language courses in Gaeltacht, 109
O'Brien, Tommy, 158
Ó Cathasaigh, Sean, 235
O'Connor, Barbara, 131
O'Connor, Frank, xxvi–xxviii, 247nn. 40, 46, 274n. 132
Ó Cuív, Éamon, 233–34, 235, 236
O'Doherty, Michael Kevin, 29, 59, 71, 83–84, 146, 193–94
O'Donnell, William E. P., 278n. 47
O'Donoghue, John, 231
O'Driscoll, Timothy J. "T. J.", 70–71, 80, 81, 88, 134
O'Faolain, Sean, 122
O'Farrell, "Cre," 158
Office of Public Works. *See* Dúchas
Official Guide to Ireland, 21–22
Official Guide to the Kingdom of Kerry, 122
Official Languages Act, 233
Official Placenames Act, 236
Ó Floinn, Rev. Denis, 144, 147–48
Ó hEaluighthe, Donnchadh (senator), 108

O'Higgins, Thomas F., 66, 67
O'Kelly, Michael J., 148
O'Kelly, Seán T., 34, 128
Old IRA (Old IRA Literary and Debating Society), 159, 160–61, 279n. 60, 280–81n. 83
O'Mahony, P. C., 180
O'Neill, Terence, 219
Organization for Economic Cooperation and Development (OECD), 87
Organization for European Economic Cooperation, 59
Orgy, The (Muriel Rukeyser), 271nn. 74, 78
O'Shea, Michael, 234
O'Sullivan, Eugene, 24, 252n. 90
O'Sullivan, William, 9

Palmer, Catherine A., xxiv
Pius II (pope), 139
Planning and Development Act. *See* Local Government (Planning and Development) Act (1963)
Poitín (film), 225
postcards. *See* John Hinde Studios
Posts and Telegraphs, Department of, 24
Poulnabrone dolmen, 189–92
postcolonial theory, xxv–xxvi, xxix
poverty, xviii–xix, xxvii–xxviii, 6, 74
Pozzi, T. J., 55–56, 58, 62, 64
"Pre-1960s Types" (photograph collection), 116
preservation (historic), 138–42, 144–47
Programme for Economic Expansion, 161, 164
Programme for National Recovery, 89
Public Works, Office of: and compulsory landownership in Poulnabrone dolmen case, 189–92; favors preservation of national monuments over tourism, 142; Kilmainham Jail's restoration and, 157–58, 159, 162; lacks funds for tourism development projects, 145–46, 148; opposes ITB's historic preservation activities, 144. *See also* Dúchas
Puck Fair, 120–24

Quiet Man, The (film), 225
Quinlan, W. F., 54, 56, 70
Quinn, Bob, 225
Quinn, Eamon, 85

railways, xix–xx
reforestation, 181
Regional Tourism Organisations (RTOs), 73, 82–84
remittances, 55
revenues (tourism), 50, 55, 71, 74, 86, 218, 225, 250
Ring Irish College, 109
Riordan, E. J., 7
Robertson, J. Stuart, 187
Robinson Keefe Devane, 173
rock bands, 225–26
Rogers, Will, 114
Rose of Tralee (festival), 134
Ross, Martin, 192–93
Rukeyser, Muriel, 121–22, 123, 271nn. 74, 78
rural Irish imagery, 116–19
Ryan's Daughter (film), 225, 232–33

Scanlon, Father John T., 74–78, 185–86
Scarborough, U.K., 180
Second Program on Economic Expansion, 71, 86
"See America First," 23

"See Ireland First," 23–24
September 11 attacks, 227–28
1798 Center, 166
Shannon Airport, 56
Shannon Free Airport Development Company, 78, 146
shopping, 98
signposting, 192–95
Sinn Féin, 187
Sinnott, Robert W., 5
Smyllie, R. M., 45, 48
Society of Friendly Sons of St. Patrick (Philadelphia), xxvi
Sommerville, Edith, 192
South-Eastern Regional Tourism Organisation, 88
souvenirs, 96–97, 116
Spain, 2, 73
sports, 129–30
Stephenson, Paddy, 150
stereotypes (Irish), 112–15, 176
St. James's Gate Brewery, 168, 171, 172. *See also* Guinness
St. Patrick's Day, 134
Sunday Herald News (Melbourne, Australia), 236
Sunday Press (newspaper), 76

Tailteann (ancient festival), 126
Taisce, An (National Trust for Ireland), 90, 147, 151, 205, 207
Taoiseach, Department of, 158
Tara (ancient festival), 126
Tara, Hill of, 278n. 47
Temple Bar, 90–91
Temple Bar Properties, 91
Thackeray, William, 183–84
Third Program on Economic Expansion, 87
Thomas Cook and Son, xx

Tidy Towns and Villages Competition, 77, 196–201, 290n. 106
Tolkien, J. R. R., 125
Toolan, Noel (international marketing director, BFÉ), xvi
Tóstal, An (festival): and efforts to draw tourists to fairs, 120; English printing of publicity materials for, 94; events selected for, 128–32; Festival of Britain and, 124–25, 126–27; history and, 125–26; inauguration of, 67–68; Irish–Americans as targeted audience of, 96; Irish diaspora as intended audience of, 125; lack of success of, 132–33; Tidy Towns and Villages Competition and, 196–97; Tóstal councils and, 127–28; work effort emphasized in, 131
"Tóstal Show" (pageant), 128–29
tourism: academic study of, xxiii–xxvi; and changing aesthetics in the eighteenth century, xviii; modern, xvii–xix, xxiii; as nexus of converging groups in dialogue, xxv; as nexus for national dialogue, xxx; romantic, xviii–xix
Tourism and Transport, Department of, 92
Tourism Brand Ireland, xv–xvi, 220–21, 223
Tourism Development Board, 144, 192, 193, 202
Tourism Development Plan (1994–99), 209–10
Tourism Ireland Ltd., 223–24, 228–29, 230–31
Tourism, Sport and Recreation, Department of, 92
Tourist Organisation Society of Ireland, 3–4, 6
Tourist Traffic Act (1931), 28, 29, 38, 57, 80, 83

Tourist Traffic Act (1939), 32, 35, 37–38, 39, 41, 65, 106–7, 108, 142, 192, 194, 287n. 48
Tourist Traffic Act (1952), 67, 80, 143, 145, 148, 188, 192, 287n. 48
Tourist Traffic Act (1955), 70
Tourist Traffic Act (1966), 87
tourists: American (U.S.), 60, 86, 95–96, 97–99, 103, 107, 123, 143, 181, 186, 202, 213, 218, 234, 253n. 100; British, 50, 95, 98–99, 107, 150, 163, 181, 218, 228, 253n. 100; English, 18, 50, 98–99, 136, 202; European, 50, 95, 218; French, 95, 99, 202; Gaelic-speaking, 106; Irish-American, 96, 99, 143; Irish diaspora, 125; Italian, 99; North American, 218; Northern Irish, 95; Victorian, xvi, 137, 147; youth, 226
townscapes, 199–200
Tramore, County Waterford, 44
Transport and Power, Department of, 80, 82, 86, 91
Travellers, Irish, 120, 121–22
Travel Trade Gazette Award, 229
Trimble, David, 222
Trippe, Juan, 124
Trollope, Anthony, 113
Tuosist, County Kerry, 74–78, 185–86
Turf Development Board. *See* Bord na Móna

Ulster Tourist Development Association (UTDA), 3–4, 219
Ulster Unionist Party (UUP), 222
unionists (Northern Ireland), 222, 223
U2, 225–26

Ventures Consultancy, 166
Vincent, Arthur R., 150, 151, 152

Wall, Jack, 231
West Cork Development Company, 80
West of Ireland Tourist Development Association, 3–4
Wexford Corporation, xxvi
Wexford Music Festival, 132
Wexford Opera Festival, 134
What Does Tourism Mean to You? (booklet), 68–69
Where to Eat in Ireland: Traveler's Guide to 100 Selected Restaurants (booklet), 79
Whitaker, T. K., 66
White Paper on Economic Expansion (1958), 71, 86
Wolfe, Ernest E., 13

Yeats, W. B., 118
Young, Arthur, xviii

www.ingramcontent.com/pod-product-compliance
Lightning Source LLC
LaVergne TN
LVHW041206250326
834689LV00002BA/33